The Islam/West Debate

D1564649

The Islam/West Debate

DOCUMENTS FROM A GLOBAL DEBATE ON TERRORISM, U.S. POLICY, AND THE MIDDLE EAST

EDITED BY

DAVID BLANKENHORN, ABDOU FILALI-ANSARY, HASSAN I. MNEIMNEH, AND ALEX ROBERTS

ROWMAN & LITTLEFIELD PUBLISHERS, INC.
Lanham • Boulder • New York • Toronto • Oxford

ROWMAN & LITTLEFIELD PUBLISHERS, INC.

Published in the United States of America
by Rowman & Littlefield Publishers, Inc.
A wholly owned subsidiary of The Rowman & Littlefield Publishing Group, Inc.
4501 Forbes Boulevard, Suite 200, Lanham, Maryland 20706
www.rowmanlittlefield.com

PO Box 317
Oxford
OX2 9RU, UK

Copyright © 2005 by Institute for American Values

All rights reserved. No part of this publication may be reproduced,
stored in a retrieval system, or transmitted in any form or by any
means, electronic, mechanical, photocopying, recording, or otherwise,
without the prior permission of the publisher.

British Library Cataloguing in Publication Information Available

Library of Congress Cataloging-in-Publication Data Available

ISBN 0-7425-5006-0 (cloth : alk. paper)
ISBN 0-7425-5007-9 (paper : alk. paper)

Printed in the United States of America

♾™ The paper used in this publication meets the minimum requirements of American
National Standard for Information Sciences—Permanence of Paper for Printed Library
Materials, ANSI/NISO Z39.48-1992.

Contents

The U.S.-German Dialogue

Conclusions

Editors' Notes

For consistency, we standardized the spelling of these frequently used Arabic words: Madina, Muhammad, mujahadin, Osama bin Ladin, al-Qa'ida, Qur'an, and Taliban. To the extent possible, we also standardized the transliteration of other Arabic words. In addition, we changed the British spellings of words to the American spellings.

The definite article "al" was capitalized if it appeared as part of a title, as in Al-Jazeera or *Al-Hayat*, etc.; however, when used as part of a person's name, the "al" was not capitalized, e.g., Abdulrahman al-Salimi.

References to September 11 were changed wherever possible to one of the following: September 11, 2001; September 11; or 9/11. If the text was non-American, we tended to leave the author's usage in place, such as "11th of September."

Arabic words were italicized only the first time they appeared in a particular essay. For example, words such as *jihad, umma,* and *mujahadin* were italicized only at their first appearance. The first letter of well-known Arabic words such as Allah or Qur'an were capitalized and the words were not italicized.

We went to great lengths to preserve the wording of the documents whenever possible; however, at times it was necessary to exercise our editorial right in order to render the text more legible, and therefore, obvious typographical and grammatical errors were corrected without giving note. This was especially the case with unpublished works.

≈

Acknowledgements

≈

The editors of this volume would like to thank the following for their support: Mrs. Judith Lund Biggs, Mr. Craig A. Cardon, Mr. Elijah A. Cardon, the Main Street Foundation and Mr. Chuck Stetson, the Stuart Foundation, and Mr. Robert Worsley. They would also like to acknowledge Mrs. Josephine Tramontano for her devoted and careful work in formatting the manuscript for publication. We are also grateful to Mrs. Tramontano, Dr. Bonnie Robbins, and Ms. Kate Marlborough for proofreading the manuscript, securing reprint permissions, and other efforts in helping see this book through to publication. Finally, we thank all of the authors and/or previous publishers of this volume's texts for allowing us to reprint their works.

Introduction

One

∽

Introducing the Debate

∼

Alex Roberts

In February of 2002, the international support that the United States had enjoyed immediately after 9/11 was falling victim to global discord. Anti-American sentiment was on the rise in Europe, and, in the wake of the war in Afghanistan, support for bin Ladin had reached disturbing levels in the Middle East. Early whispers of a stepped-up campaign to affect regime change in Iraq only aggravated this global polarization. Collectively, these developments threatened to convert the war against jihadism into a "clash of civilizations."

It was in this context that sixty prominent American intellectuals released an open letter, entitled "What We're Fighting For," that sought to redefine the struggle against terrorism in terms of universal human values. The authors' basic argument was that jihadist groups like al-Qa'ida pose an implacable threat to the United States and the universal values it embodies; in accordance with the stipulations of "just war" doctrine, the Unites States has a right defend itself and its values with military force when other methods will not suffice.

Upon its release, "What We're Fighting For" received little attention from American news outlets, but drew powerful responses from the Middle East and Europe. Impassioned replies to the letter and rejoinders appeared in newspapers and academic journals, and on Islamist websites; Al-Jazeera and other Arab news networks devoted significant airtime to discussion of the letter. Among those to respond to "What We're Fighting For" were such diverse and important voices as the Movement for Islamic Reform in Arabia, a leading Saudi dissident Islamist group; the prominent Saudi cleric Sheikh Safar al-Hawali; Germany's Coalition for Life and Peace; and al-Qa'ida. Throughout the remainder of 2002, these exchanges gave rise to a truly open,

substantive, and international debate on terrorism, values, and U.S. policy—
a debate unlike any other, in which Americans, jihadists, clerics, and internationalists all had the opportunity to engage one another's arguments and
views directly. The present volume chronicles that debate. It consists of the
"What We're Fighting For" letter and most of the major media, scholarly,
and Islamist responses to it.

    In this volume, one finds multiple authors using similar arguments but to
very different ends. I will therefore try in this introduction to characterize the
ideological frameworks and theses underlying this collection's major pieces,
in order that the reader might better understand what is actually being argued
in each text.

What We're Fighting For

Perhaps the most useful way to begin is with a description of "What We're
Fighting For." "What We're Fighting For" opens by arguing that there are
universal values (e.g., human equality and religious freedom) and that
America's core values and political system reflect and embody these universal values. After making this case, the authors characterize al-Qa'ida as an
implacable enemy that hates America not just for what it *does*, but also for
what it *is*—that is, for its values. It has massacred innocent American civilians, and wants nothing more than to do so again. In accordance with just
war doctrine, an established set of principles governing warfare, the U.S. has
a right to use military force against al-Qa'ida in order to defend its citizens
and values when other methods will not suffice. Ultimately, the arguments
about values, terrorism, and just war flow together in the letter because
America's right to use force is portrayed, in part, as deriving from its adherence to universal values and al-Qa'ida's violation of them.

    It could be argued that "What We're Fighting For" was an important
document for two reasons. First, it provided a moral-philosophical justification
for war against al-Qa'ida. Second, in making this case, the letter expressed
the sentiments of a large portion of the American public.

The Middle Eastern Response

This volume includes two pieces which can be categorized as conservative
Middle Eastern responses to "What We're Fighting For." They are: "How We
Can Coexist," a letter signed by 153 prominent Saudi intellectuals, and "Key
Intellectualism," an article by Heshmatollah Falahatpisheh, which appeared
in the Iranian newspaper *Resalat*. For convenience's sake I will focus on
"How We Can Coexist" because it is the more comprehensive of the two. This
letter begins by agreeing with a basic presupposition of "What We're Fighting
For": that Islam and the West share common values that are capable of sup-
porting a just and peaceful coexistence. But the Saudi authors aver that it is

not al-Qa'ida that poses the greatest threat to peace, but rather U.S. foreign policy, which is unjust and conflicts with universal values. Referring to September 11, the authors write that American foreign policy is largely to blame for "what happened." Accordingly, the U.S. should modify its aggressive policies and pursue a just world order through international institutions. These arguments about universal values and U.S. policy constitute the letter's basic thesis.

"How We Can Coexist" disagrees significantly with "What We're Fighting For" over what "freedom of religion" means. The authors of "What We're Fighting For" argue that freedom of religion is achieved through the secular state, which guarantees that all citizens can follow whatever religion they choose. For the authors of "How We Can Coexist," however, "religious freedom" means that Muslims should be allowed to fulfill their religious obligations by establishing Islamic states. They argue that the American letter's advocacy of secular government found in "What We're Fighting For" actually transforms "freedoms and rights into tools for conflict" and presents "a limited cultural vision as if it is a universal law that must be generally applied to all, forcibly if need be." In other words, "What We're Fighting For" uses "values" for narrow political ends. A sinister nexus between the rhetoric of "What We're Fighting For" and American political interests is also seen by Falahatpisheh. He writes in "Key Intellectualism" that "behind-the-scenes of the relations between America and Israel in the Islamic Middle East ... the power elite and the [signatories of 'What We're Fighting For'] have drawn up horrific plans against Islam" and are "seeking a world that would accept America's hegemony."

Despite its largely critical view of the United States, "How We Can Coexist" drew vehement opposition from some jihadis. This collection's "Please Prostrate Yourselves Privately" is a refutation of the Saudi letter written by one of these jihadis, 'Abul Bara. Bara argues that, contrary to the opinion of the Saudi intellectuals, Islam and western civilization have nothing meaningful in common. Muslims must avoid infidel ideas and culture and struggle against unbelievers until Islam triumphs: "Antagonism, fighting, and hatred between Muslims and infidels are the basics of our religion." Making frequent reference to Qur'anic passages, Bara maintains that the Saudi intellectuals have obscured the fundamental messages of Islam by taking its values— such as "justice" and "tolerance"—out of their proper context.

The underlying analytical framework of "Please Prostrate Yourselves Privately" is the ideology known as Islamism. Islamism maintains that all of society, including the Islamic religious establishment, has deviated from the "pure" Islamic community that is thought to have existed during the religion's early years. The ideology's adherents believe that two intertwined courses of action need to be taken to rectify this problem. First, Muslims must jettison accrued religious traditions and directly interpret Islam's primary texts. Second, because the goal of Islamism is a "pure" Islamic community, Muslims must engage in sociopolitical activism geared towards establishing Islamic states and encouraging individual "piety." These ideas undergird the criticisms of the Saudi letter presented in "Please Prostrate Yourselves Privately."

Two documents in this collection respond directly to "What We're Fighting For" from an Islamist perspective. They are "Options are Limited" by the Movement for Islamic Reform in Arabia (MIRA) and "Letter to the American People," which was tacitly endorsed, if not penned, by al-Qaʻida. Both letters echo arguments made in "Please Prostrate Yourselves Privately."

MIRA writes that Islam's revealed truth "really calls on its followers to overcome opponents and reach the whole world with its universal message." The "Letter to the American People" states that Muslims have the right to and will attack America if it refuses Islam. However, unlike "Please Prostrate Yourselves Privately," these two letters present a host of arguments about U.S. policies. They attack the United States for supporting Israel, stymieing Arab national liberation movements, suppressing democracy in Algeria, and even for refusing to sign the Kyoto Protocol. The two letters even conclude with conditions for a rapprochement between America and the Islamic world. The reader therefore faces some difficulty in understanding what message these letters intend to convey because they seemingly pursue two distinct lines of logic. While I do not want to suggest that there is only one sound way to interpret the letters, I do advocate the following approach: consider the totality of the arguments presented in the texts and avoid, at least initially, trying to "decode" them. This means reading the array of "secular" arguments about policies, culture, and rapprochements in light of the texts' particularistic Islamist arguments—they should be understood as complementary. Such an approach, it could be argued, brings one to the intended meaning of the texts because the authors could not have intended their arguments to be confusing or contradictory. Thus, "Options Are Limited" and "Letter to the American People" may be understood as objecting not to U.S. policy per se, but U.S. policy insofar as it is an impediment to the goals of Islamism. Indeed, in the letters, complaints about U.S. policy are woven into a larger argument for the global hegemony of Islam; the eventual "rapprochement" between the West and Islam is contingent upon the adoption of the latter by the former.

This volume's "Letter from Makkah" by Safar al-Hawali may be understood as falling somewhere between "How We Can Coexist" and the Islamist documents in terms of its ideology.

Several liberal Arab and Muslim reactions to "What We're Fighting For" are also included in this collection. The two most comprehensive are "What We're Fighting For: A Follow-up," by Saleh Bashir, Hassan I. Mneimneh, and Hazem Saghie and "The Need for a Paradigm Shift in American Thinking," which was written by Chibli Mallat and endorsed by a number of scholars in America, Europe, and the Middle East. Both articles affirm the need to defeat jihadism, but object to the vision of a "just war" against al-Qaʻida presented by "What We're Fighting For." Part of this objection is on a prima facie basis: war is evil and cannot be associated with "justice." But beyond this point, the authors contend that, between its notion of a "just war against terrorism" and its praise of American values, "What We're Fighting For" paves the way for an excessive use of military force by the United States. Woven into these criticisms is a constructive recommendation: the U.S. should pursue terrorists through international criminal courts, not through extra-legal means. Such an approach would allow the U.S. to defend itself while discouraging militarism.

The German Response

This volume includes two other pieces that advocate an internationalist approach to fighting terrorism, but do so from a somewhat different perspective than that of the liberal Arab and Muslim intellectuals. They are "A World of Peace and Justice Would Be Different" and "In the Twenty-First Century, There Is No Longer any Justification for War." Both were written by the Coalition for Life and Peace, a group of professors and NGO members based in Germany. The basic thesis of these letters is that, after the end of the Cold War, the United States "concentrated its imagination and its scientific, technical, and economic capacities on strengthening its position as the sole remaining superpower in the world, and establishing a unipolar world order." As a result, there are major imbalances in the global distribution of power. This inequity, combined with a lack of local development (e.g. political, economic, legal, infrastructural) creates "structural violence" against "have-nots," which humiliates them and hinders their "full human development." This situation engenders a "loss of inhibitions" among "have-nots" and makes them resort to terrorism in an attempt to improve their situation. September 11 is therefore construed as protest or rebellion against the powerlessness experienced by Muslims. Reflecting their etiology of terrorism, the Coalition argues that the U.S. should focus its attention on building institutions such as international criminal courts that might moderate power imbalances and therefore eradicate the roots of terrorism. Military responses to terrorism should be prohibited because war only perpetuates the conditions that create terrorism.

Other Documents

Also reprinted in this volume is a reaction to "What We're Fighting For" from leftist American professors and intellectuals. The basic point of this essay, which is entitled "Letter from U.S. Citizens to Friends in Europe," is that the United States is an arrogant and militaristic enemy of humanity.

Finally, this collection includes a number of additional pieces written by some or all of the signatories of "What We're Fighting For." These include: a response to the Saudi's "How We Can Coexist" entitled "Can We Coexist?"; a response to the Coalition for Life and Peace's "A World of Peace and Justice Would Be Different" entitled "Is the Use of Force Ever Morally Justified?"; a statement about the then-impending Iraq War, "Pre-emption, Just War and Iraq"; and, an analysis of the al-Qa'ida "Letter to the American People."

This collection also includes a number of shorter articles covering and reacting to the international debate over "What We're Fighting For." "The

New Intra-Arab Cultural Space in Form and Content" by Hassan I. Mneimneh offers a detailed discussion of the debate and how it fits into recent changes in Arab culture, media, and communications.

Conclusion

The challenges and problems at the core of the Islam-West debate were a long time in the making and they will be with us for a long time to come. Engaging one another in an open and serious dialogue will not completely solve our problems. But it will be an important tool for promoting mutual understanding, and hopefully, for finding common ground. This collection is a valuable resource for those who wish to pursue this endeavor, which must be constructive, yet rooted in critical thought.

Two

_ھ_

What We're Fighting For:
A Letter from America

_ھ_

60 U.S. Intellectuals

At times it becomes necessary for a nation to defend itself through force of arms. Because war is a grave matter, involving the sacrifice and taking of precious human life, conscience demands that those who would wage the war state clearly the moral reasoning behind their actions, in order to make plain to one another, and to the world community, the principles they are defending.

We affirm five fundamental truths that pertain to all people without distinction:

1. All human beings are born free[1] and equal in dignity and rights.

2. The basic subject of society[2] is the human person, and the legitimate role of government is to protect and help to foster the conditions for human flourishing.

3. Human beings naturally desire to seek the truth[3] about life's purpose and ultimate ends.

4. Freedom of conscience and religious freedom[4] are inviolable rights of the human person.

5. Killing in the name of God[5] is contrary to faith in God and is the greatest betrayal of the universality of religious faith.

We fight to defend ourselves and to defend these universal principles.

21

What Are American Values?

Since September 11, millions of Americans have asked themselves and one another, why? Why are we the targets of these hateful attacks? Why do those who would kill us, want to kill us?

We recognize that at times our nation has acted with arrogance and ignorance toward other societies. At times our nation has pursued misguided and unjust policies. Too often we as a nation have failed to live up to our ideals. We cannot urge other societies to abide by moral principles without simultaneously admitting our own society's failure at times to abide by those same principles. We are united in our conviction—and are confident that all people of good will in the world will agree—that no appeal to the merits or demerits of specific foreign policies can ever justify, or even purport to make sense of, the mass slaughter of innocent persons.

Moreover, in a democracy such as ours, in which government derives its power from the consent of the governed, policy stems at least partly from culture, from the values and priorities of the society as a whole. Though we do not claim to possess full knowledge of the motivations of our attackers and their sympathizers, what we do know suggests that their grievances extend far beyond any one policy, or set of policies. After all, the killers of September 11 issued no particular demands; in this sense, at least, the killing was done for its own sake. The leader of al-Qa'ida described the "blessed strikes" of September 11 as blows against America, "the head of world infidelity."[6] Clearly, then, our attackers despise not just our government, but our overall society, our entire way of living. Fundamentally, their grievance concerns not only what our leaders do, but also *who we are*.

So who are we? What do we value? For many people, including many Americans and a number of signatories to this letter, some values sometimes seen in America are unattractive and harmful. Consumerism as a way of life. The notion of freedom as no rules. The notion of the individual as self-made and utterly sovereign, owing little to others or to society. The weakening of marriage and family life. Plus an enormous entertainment and communications apparatus that relentlessly glorifies such ideas and beams them, whether they are welcome or not, into nearly every corner of the globe.

One major task facing us as Americans, important prior to September 11, is facing honestly these unattractive aspects of our society and doing all we can to change them for the better. We pledge ourselves to this effort.

At the same time, other American values—what we view as our founding ideals, and those that most define our way of life—are quite different from these, and they are much more attractive, not only to Americans, but to people everywhere in the world. Let us briefly mention four of them.[7]

The first is the conviction that all persons possess innate human dignity as a birthright, and that consequently each person must always be treated as an end rather than used as a means. The founders of the United States, drawing upon the natural law tradition as well as upon the fundamental religious claim that all persons are created in the image of God, affirmed as "self-evident" the idea that all persons possess equal dignity. The clearest political expression of a belief in transcendent human dignity is democracy. In the United States in recent generations, among the clearest cultural expressions of this idea has been the affirmation of the equal dignity of men and women, and of all persons regardless of race or color.

Second, and following closely from the first, is the conviction that universal moral truths (what our nation's founders called "laws of Nature and of Nature's God") exist and are accessible to all people. Some of the most eloquent expressions of our reliance upon these truths are found in our Declaration of Independence, George Washington's Farewell Address, Abraham Lincoln's Gettysburg Address and Second Inaugural Address, and Dr. Martin Luther King, Jr.'s Letter from the Birmingham Jail.

The third is the conviction that, because our individual and collective access to truth is imperfect, most disagreements about values call for civility, openness to other views, and reasonable argument in pursuit of truth.

The fourth is freedom of conscience and freedom of religion. These intrinsically connected freedoms are widely recognized, in our own country and elsewhere, as a reflection of basic human dignity and as a precondition for other individual freedoms.[8]

To us, what is most striking about these values is that they apply to all persons without distinction, and cannot be used to exclude anyone from recognition and respect based on the particularities of race, language, memory, or religion. That's why anyone, in principle, can become an American. And in fact, anyone does. People from everywhere in the world come to our country with what a statue in New York's harbor calls a "yearning to breathe free," and soon enough, they are Americans. Historically, no other nation has forged its core identity—its constitution and other founding documents, as well as its basic self-understanding—so directly and explicitly on the basis of universal human values. To us, no other fact about this country is more important.

Some people assert that these values are not universal at all, but instead derive particularly from western, largely Christian civilization. They argue that to conceive of these values as universal is to deny the distinctiveness of other cultures.[9] We disagree. We recognize our own civilization's achievements, but we believe that all people are created equal. We believe in the universal possibility and desirability of human freedom. We believe that certain basic moral truths are recognizable everywhere in the world. We agree with the international group of distinguished philosophers who in the late 1940s helped to shape the United Nations Universal Declaration of Human Rights, and who concluded that a few fundamental moral ideas are so widespread that they "may be viewed as implicit in man's nature as a member of society."[10] In hope, and on the evidence, we agree with Dr. Martin Luther King, Jr., that the arc of the moral universe is long, but it bends toward justice,[11] not just for the few, or the lucky, but for all people.

Looking at our own society, we acknowledge again the all too frequent gaps between our ideals and our conduct. But as Americans in a time of war and global crisis, we are also suggesting that the best of what we too casually call "American values" do not belong only to America, but are in fact the shared inheritance of humankind, and therefore a possible basis of hope for a world community based on peace and justice.

What about God?

Since September 11, millions of Americans have asked themselves and one another, what about God? Crises of this magnitude force us to think anew about first principles. When we contemplate the horror of what has occurred, and the danger of what is likely to come, many of us ask: Is religious faith part of the solution or part of the problem?

The signatories to this letter come from diverse religious and moral traditions, including secular traditions. We are united in our belief that invoking God's authority to kill or maim human beings is immoral and is contrary to faith in God. Many of us believe that we are under God's judgment. None of us believe that God ever instructs some of us to kill or conquer others of us. Indeed, such an attitude, whether it is called "holy war" or "crusade," not only violates basic principles of justice, but is in fact a negation of religious faith, since it turns God into an idol to be used for man's own purposes.[12] Our own nation was once engaged in a great civil war, in which each side presumed God's aid against the other. In his Second Inaugural Address in 1865, the sixteenth president of the United States, Abraham Lincoln, put it simply: "The Almighty has his own purposes."

Those who attacked us on September 11 openly proclaim that they are engaged in holy war. Many who support or sympathize with the attackers also invoke God's name and seem to embrace the rationale of holy war. But to recognize the disaster of this way of thinking, we as Americans need only to remember our own, and western, history. Christian religious wars and Christian sectarian violence tore apart Europe for the better part of a century. In the United States, we are no strangers to those who would murder at least in part in the name of their religious faith. When it comes to this particular evil, no civilization is spotless and no religious tradition is spotless.[13]

The human person has a basic drive to question in order to know. Evaluating, choosing, and having reasons for what we value and love are characteristically human activities.[14] Part of this intrinsic desire to know concerns why we are born and what will happen when we die, which leads us to seek the truth about ultimate ends, including, for many people, the question of God. Some of the signatories to this letter believe that human beings are by nature "religious" in the sense that everyone, including those who do not believe in God and do not participate in organized religion, makes choices about what is important and reflects on ultimate values. All of the signatories to this letter recognize that, across the world, religious faith and religious institutions are important bases of civil society, often producing results for society that are beneficial and healing, at times producing results that are divisive and violent.

So how can governments and societal leaders best respond to these fundamental human and social realities? One response is to outlaw or repress religion. Another possible response is to embrace an ideological secularism:[15] a strong societal skepticism or hostility regarding religion, based on the premise that religion itself, and especially any *public* expression of religious conviction, is inherently problematic. A third possible response is to embrace theocracy: the belief that one religion, presumably the one *true* religion, should be effectively mandatory for all members of society and therefore should receive complete or significant state sponsorship and support.

We disagree with each of these responses. Legal repression radically violates civil and religious freedom and is incompatible with democratic civil society. Although ideological secularism may have increased in our society in recent generations, we disagree with it because it would deny the public legitimacy of an important part of civil society as well as seek to suppress or deny the existence of what is at least arguably an important dimension of personhood itself.[16] Although theocracy has been present in western (though not U.S.) history, we disagree with it for both social and theological reasons. Socially, governmental establishment of a particular religion can conflict with the principle of religious freedom, a fundamental human right. In addition, government control of religion can cause or exacerbate religious conflicts and, perhaps even more importantly, can threaten the vitality and authenticity of religious institutions. Theologically, even for those who are firmly convinced of the truth of their faith, the coercion of others in matters of religious conscience is ultimately a violation of religion itself, since it robs those other persons of the right to respond freely and in dignity to the Creator's invitation.

At its best, the United States seeks to be a society in which faith and freedom can go together, each elevating the other. We have a secular state—our government officials are not simultaneously religious officials—but we are by far the western world's most religious society. We are a nation that deeply respects religious freedom and diversity, including the rights of nonbelievers, but one whose citizens recite a Pledge of Allegiance to "one nation, under God," and one that proclaims in many of its courtrooms and inscribes on each of its coins the motto, "In God We Trust." Politically, our separation of church and state seeks to keep politics within its proper sphere, in part by limiting the state's power to control religion, and in part by causing government itself to draw legitimacy from, and operate under, a larger moral canopy that is not of its own making.[17] Spiritually, our separation of church and state permits religion to be religion, by detaching it from the coercive power of government. In short, we seek to separate church and state for the protection and proper vitality of both.[18]

For Americans of religious faith, the challenge of embracing religious truth and religious freedom has often been difficult. The matter, moreover, is never settled. Ours is a social and constitutional arrangement that almost by definition requires constant deliberation, debate, adjustment, and compromise. It is also helped by, and helps to produce, a certain character or temperament, such that religious believers who strongly embrace the truth of their faith also, not as a compromise with that truth but as an aspect of it, respect those who take a different path.

What will help to reduce religiously-based mistrust, hatred, and violence in the twenty-first century? There are many important answers to this question, of course, but here, we hope, is one: deepening and renewing our appreciation of religion by recognizing religious freedom as a fundamental right of all people in every nation.

A Just War?

We recognize that all war is terrible, representative finally of human political failure. We also know that the line separating good and evil does not run between one society and another, much less between one religion and another; ultimately, that line runs through the middle of every human heart.[19] Finally, those of us—Jews, Christians, Muslims, and others—who are people of faith recognize our responsibility, stated in our holy scriptures, to love mercy and to do all in our power to prevent war and live in peace.

Yet reason and careful moral reflection also teach us that there are times when the first and most important reply to evil is to stop it. There are times when waging war is not only morally permitted, but morally necessary, as a response to calamitous acts of violence, hatred, and injustice. This is one of those times.

The idea of a "just war" is broadly based, with roots in many of the world's diverse religious and secular moral traditions.[20] Jewish, Christian, and Muslim teachings, for example, all contain serious reflections on the definition of a just war. To be sure, some people, often in the name of realism, insist that war is essentially a realm of self-interest and necessity, making most attempts at moral analysis irrelevant.[21] We disagree.[22] Moral inarticulacy in the face of war is itself a moral stance—one that rejects the possibility of reason, accepts normlessness in international affairs, and capitulates to cynicism. To seek to apply objective moral reasoning to war is to defend the possibility of civil society and a world community based on justice.

The principles of just war teach us that wars of aggression and aggrandizement are never acceptable. Wars may not legitimately be fought for national glory, to avenge past wrongs, for territorial gain, or for any other non-defensive purpose.

The primary moral justification for war is to protect the innocent from certain harm. Augustine, whose early fifth-century book, *The City of God*, is a seminal contribution to just war thinking, argues (echoing Socrates)[23] that it is better for the Christian as an individual to suffer harm rather than to commit it. But is the morally responsible person also required, or even permitted, to make for *other* innocent persons a commitment to non-self-defense? For Augustine, and for the broader just war tradition, the answer is no. If one has compelling evidence that innocent people who are in no position to protect themselves will be grievously harmed unless coercive force is used to stop an aggressor, then the moral principle of love of neighbor calls us to the use of force.

Wars may not legitimately be fought against dangers that are small, questionable, or of uncertain consequence, or against dangers that might plausibly be mitigated solely through negotiation, appeals to reason, persuasion from third parties, or other non-violent means.[24] But if the danger to innocent life is real and certain, and especially if the aggressor is motivated by implacable hostility—if the end he seeks is not your willingness to negotiate or comply, but rather your destruction—then a resort to proportionate force is morally justified.

A just war can only be fought by a legitimate authority with responsibility for public order. Violence that is free-lance, opportunistic, or individualistic is never morally acceptable.[25]

A just war can only be waged against persons who are combatants. Just war authorities from across history and around the world—whether they be Muslim, Jewish, Christian, from other faith traditions, or secular—consistently teach us that noncombatants are immune from deliberate attack. Thus, killing civilians for revenge, or even as a means of deterring aggression from people who sympathize with them, is morally wrong. Although in some circumstances, and within strict limits, it can be morally justifiable to undertake military actions that may result in the unintended but foreseeable death or injury of some noncombatants, it is not morally acceptable to make the killing of noncombatants the operational objective of a military action.

These and other just war principles[26] teach us that, whenever human beings contemplate or wage war, it is both possible and necessary to affirm the sanctity of human life and embrace the principle of equal human dignity. These principles strive to preserve and reflect, even in the tragic activity of war, the fundamental moral truth that "others"—those who are strangers to us, those who differ from us in race or language, those whose religions we may believe to be untrue—have the same right to life that we do, and the same human dignity and human rights that we do.

On September 11, 2001, a group of individuals deliberately attacked the United States, using highjacked airplanes as weapons with which to kill in less than two hours over 3,000 of our citizens[27] in New York City, southwestern Pennsylvania, and Washington, DC. Overwhelmingly, those who died on September 11 were civilians, not combatants, and were not known at all, except as Americans, by those who killed them. Those who died on the morning of September 11 were killed unlawfully, wantonly, and with premeditated malice—a kind of killing that, in the name of precision, can only be described as murder. Those murdered included people from all races, many ethnicities, most major religions. They included dishwashers and corporate executives.

The individuals who committed these acts of war did not act alone, or without support, or for unknown reasons. They were members of an international Islamicist network, active in as many as 40 countries, now known to the world as al-Qa'ida. This group, in turn, constitutes but one arm of a larger radical Islamicist movement, growing for decades and in some instances tolerated and even supported by governments, that openly professes its desire and increasingly demonstrates its ability to use murder to advance its objectives.[28]

We use the terms "Islam" and "Islamic" to refer to one of the world's great religions, with about 1.2 billion adherents, including several million U.S. citizens, some of whom were murdered on September 11. It ought to go without saying—but we say it here once, clearly—that the great majority of the world's Muslims, guided in large measure by the teachings of the Qur'an, are decent, faithful, and peaceful. We use the terms "Islamicism"[29] and "radical Islamicist" to refer to the violent, extremist, and radically intolerant religious-political movement that now threatens the world, including the Muslim world.

This radical, violent movement opposes not only certain U.S. and western policies—some signatories to this letter also oppose some of those policies—but also a foundational principle of the modern world, religious tolerance, as well as those fundamental human rights, in particular freedom of conscience and religion, that are enshrined in the United Nations Universal Declaration of Human Rights, and that must be the basis of any civilization oriented to human flourishing, justice, and peace.

This extremist movement claims to speak for Islam, but betrays fundamental Islamic principles. Islam sets its face *against* moral atrocities. For example, reflecting the teaching of the Qur'an and the example of the Prophet, Muslim scholars through the centuries have taught that struggle in the path of God (i.e., *jihad*) forbids[30] the deliberate killing of noncombatants, and requires that military action be undertaken only at the behest of legitimate public authorities. They remind us forcefully[31] that Islam, no less than Christianity, Judaism and other religions, is threatened and potentially degraded by these profaners who invoke God's name to kill indiscriminately.

We recognize that movements claiming the mantle of religion also have complex political, social, and demographic dimensions, to which due attention must be paid. At the same time, philosophy matters, and the animating philosophy of this radical Islamicist movement, in its contempt for human life, and by viewing the world as a life-and-death struggle between believers and unbelievers (whether non-radical Muslims, Jews, Christians, Hindus, or others), clearly denies the equal dignity of all persons and, in doing so, betrays religion and rejects the very foundation of civilized life and the possibility of peace among nations.

Most seriously of all, the mass murders of September 11 demonstrated, arguably for the first time, that this movement now possesses not only the openly stated desire, but also the capacity and expertise—including possible access to, and willingness to use, chemical, biological and nuclear weapons—to wreak massive, horrific devastation on its intended targets.[32]

Those who slaughtered more than 3,000 persons on September 11 and who, by their own admission, want nothing more than to do it again, constitute a clear and present danger to all people of good will everywhere in the world, not just the United States. Such acts are a pure example of naked aggression against innocent human life, a world-threatening evil that clearly requires the use of force to remove it.

Organized killers with global reach now threaten all of us. In the name of universal human morality, and fully conscious of the restrictions and requirements of a just war, we support our government's, and our society's, decision to use force of arms against them.

Conclusion

We pledge to do all we can to guard against the harmful temptations—especially those of arrogance and jingoism—to which nations at war so often seem to yield. At the same time, with one voice we say solemnly that it is crucial for our nation and its allies to win this war. We fight to defend ourselves, but we also believe that we fight to defend those universal principles of human rights and human dignity that are the best hope for humankind.

One day, this war will end. When it does—and in some respects even before it ends—the great task of conciliation awaits us. We hope that this war, by stopping an unmitigated global evil, can increase the possibility of a world community based on justice. But we know that only the peacemakers among us in every society can ensure that this war will not have been in vain.

We wish especially to reach out to our brothers and sisters in Muslim societies. We say to you forthrightly: we are not enemies, but friends.[33] We must not be enemies. We have so much in common. There is so much that we must do together. Your human dignity, no less than ours—your rights and opportunities for a good life, no less than ours—are what we believe we're fighting for. We know that, for some of you, mistrust of us is high, and we know that we Americans are partly responsible for that mistrust. But we must not be enemies. In hope, we wish to join with you and all people of good will to build a just and lasting peace.

Signatories*

Enola Aird, *Director, The Motherhood Project; Council on Civil Society*

John Atlas, *President, National Housing Institute; Executive Director, Passaic County Legal Aid Society*

Jay Belsky, *Professor and Director, Institute for the Study of Children, Families and Social Issues, Birkbeck University of London*

---

*Signatories' affiliations are listed for identification purposes only. The signatories do not, by issuing this statement, intend collectively either to endorse or condemn specific future military tactics or strategies that may be pursued during this war. The signatories wish to thank Dan Cere of McGill University in Montreal for research and editorial assistance.

David Blankenhorn, *President, Institute for American Values*
David Bosworth, *University of Washington*
R. Maurice Boyd, *Minister, The City Church, New York*
Gerard V. Bradley, *Professor of Law, University of Notre Dame*
Margaret F. Brinig, *Edward A. Howry Distinguished Professor, University of Iowa College of Law*
Allan Carlson, *President, The Howard Center for Family, Religion, and Society*
Khalid Durán, *Editor,* TransIslam Magazine
Paul Ekman, *Professor of Psychology, University of California, San Francisco*
Jean Bethke Elshtain, *Laura Spelman Rockefeller Professor of Social and Political Ethics, University of Chicago Divinity School*
Amitai Etzioni, *University Professor, The George Washington University*
Hillel Fradkin, *President, Ethics and Public Policy Center*
Samuel G. Freedman, *Professor at the Columbia University Graduate School of Journalism*
Francis Fukuyama, *Bernard Schwartz Professor of International Political Economy, Johns Hopkins University*
William A. Galston, *Professor at the School of Public Affairs, University of Maryland; Director, Institute for Philosophy and Public Policy*
Claire Gaudiani, *Senior Research Scholar, Yale Law School and former President, Connecticut College*
Robert P. George, *McCormick Professor of Jurisprudence and Professor of Politics, Princeton University*
Neil Gilbert, *Professor at the School of Social Welfare, University of California, Berkeley*
Mary Ann Glendon, *Learned Hand Professor of Law, Harvard University Law School*
Norval D. Glenn, *Ashbel Smith Professor of Sociology and Stiles Professor of American Studies, University of Texas at Austin*
Os Guinness, *Senior Fellow, Trinity Forum*
David Gutmann, *Professor Emeritus of Psychiatry and Education, Northwestern University*
Kevin J. "Seamus" Hasson, *President, Becket Fund for Religious Liberty*
Sylvia Ann Hewlett, *Chair, National Parenting Association*
James Davison Hunter, *William R. Kenan, Jr. Professor of Sociology and Religious Studies and Executive Director, Center on Religion and Democracy, University of Virginia*
Samuel Huntington, *Albert J. Weatherhead, III University Professor, Harvard University*
Byron Johnson, *Director and Distinguished Senior Fellow, Center for Research on Religion and Urban Civil Society, University of Pennsylvania*
James Turner Johnson, *Professor, Department of Religion, Rutgers University*
John Kelsay, *Richard L. Rubenstein Professor of Religion, Florida State University*
Diane Knippers, *President, Institute on Religion and Democracy*
Thomas C. Kohler, *Professor of Law, Boston College Law School*

Glenn C. Loury, *Professor of Economics and Director, Institute on Race and Social Division, Boston University*

Harvey C. Mansfield, *William R. Kenan, Jr. Professor of Government, Harvard University*

Will Marshall, *President, Progressive Policy Institute*

Richard J. Mouw, *President, Fuller Theological Seminary*

Daniel Patrick Moynihan, *University Professor, Maxwell School of Citizenship and Public Affairs, Syracuse University*

John E. Murray, Jr., *Chancellor and Professor of Law, Duquesne University*

Michael Novak, *George Frederick Jewett Chair in Religion and Public Policy, American Enterprise Institute*

Rev. Val J. Peter, *Executive Director, Boys and Girls Town*

David Popenoe, *Professor of Sociology and Co-Director of the National Marriage Project, Rutgers University*

Robert D. Putnam, *Peter and Isabel Malkin Professor of Public Policy at the Kennedy School of Government, Harvard University*

Gloria G. Rodriguez, *Founder and President, AVANCE, Inc.*

Robert Royal, *President, Faith & Reason Institute*

Nina Shea, *Director, Freedom's House's Center for Religious Freedom*

Fred Siegel, *Professor of History, The Cooper Union*

Theda Skocpol, *Victor S. Thomas Professor of Government and Sociology, Harvard University*

Katherine Shaw Spaht, *Jules and Frances Landry Professor of Law, Louisiana State University Law Center*

Max L. Stackhouse, *Professor of Christian Ethics and Director, Project on Public Theology, Princeton Theological Seminary*

William Tell, Jr., *The William and Karen Tell Foundation*

Maris A. Vinovskis, *Bentley Professor of History and Professor of Public Policy, University of Michigan*

Paul C. Vitz, *Professor of Psychology, New York University*

Michael Walzer, *Professor at the School of Social Science, Institute for Advanced Study*

George Weigel, *Senior Fellow, Ethics and Public Policy Center*

Charles Wilson, *Director, Center for the Study of Southern Culture, University of Mississippi*

James Q. Wilson, *Collins Professor of Management and Public Policy Emeritus, UCLA*

John Witte, Jr., *Jonas Robitscher Professor of Law and Ethics and Director, Law and Religion Program, Emory University Law School*

Christopher Wolfe, *Professor of Political Science, Marquette University*

Daniel Yankelovich, *President, Public Agenda*

Notes

1. From the United Nations Universal Declaration of Human Rights, Article 1.

2. *A Call to Civil Society* (New York: Institute for American Values, 1998), 16; Aristotle, *Politics VII,* 1-2.

3. Aristotle, *Metaphysics,* 1-1; John Paul II, *Fides et Ratio,* 25 (Vatican City, 1998).

4. United Nations Universal Declaration of Human Rights, Articles 18-19.

5. Bosphorus Declaration (Istanbul, Turkey, February 9, 1994); Berne Declaration (Wolfsberg/Zurich, Switzerland, November 26, 1992); and John Paul II, Papal Message for World Day of Peace, Articles 6-7 (Vatican City, January 1, 2002).

6. "Excerpt: Bin Laden Tape," *Washington Post,* December 27, 2001.

7. See *A Call to Civil Society* (New York: Institute for American Values, 1998).

8. See John Witte, Jr. and M. Christian Green, "The American Constitutional Experiment in Religious Human Rights: The Perennial Search for Principles," in Johan D. van der Vyver and John Witte, Jr. (eds.), *Religious Human Rights in Global Perspective,* vol. 2 (The Hague: Martinus Nijhoff Publishers, 1996). See also Harold J. Berman, *Law and Revolution: The Formation of the Western Legal Tradition* (Cambridge, MA: Harvard University Press, 1983); and Michael J. Perry, *The Idea of Human Rights: Four Inquiries* (New York: Oxford University Press, 1998).

9. Some people make this point as a way of condemning those "other" cultures that are presumably too inferior, or too enthralled by false beliefs, to appreciate what we in this letter are calling universal human values; others make this point as a way of endorsing (usually *one* of) those cultures that are presumably indifferent to these values. We disagree with both versions of this point.

10. Richard McKeon, "The Philosophic Bases and Material Circumstances of the Rights of Man," in *Human Rights: Comments and Interpretations* (London: Wingate, 1949), 45.

11. Martin Luther King, Jr., "Where Do We Go From Here?" in James M. Washington (ed.), *The Essential Writings and Speeches of Martin Luther King, Jr.* (New York: HarperCollins, 1986), 245.

12. John Paul II, Papal Message for World Day of Peace, Article 6 (Vatican City, January 1, 2002).

13. Intra-Christian examples of holy war or crusade emerged with particular force in Europe during the seventeenth century. According to some scholars, the principle characteristics of holy war are: that the cause for which the war is fought has a clear connection to religion (i.e., that the cause is "holy"); that the war is fought under the banner and with the presumption of divine authority and assistance (the Latin term used by eleventh century Christian crusaders was "Deus Volt," or "God wills it"); that the warriors understand themselves to be godly, or "warrior saints"; that the war is prosecuted zealously and unsparingly, since the enemy is presumed to be ungodly and therefore fundamentally "other," lacking the human dignity and rights of the godly; and finally, that warriors who die in battle are favored by God as martyrs. Eventually, in Christianity, the development of just war doctrine, with its emphasis on moral universalism, largely called for the elimination of religion as a just cause for war. As early as the sixteenth century, some natural law theorists such as Franciscus de Victoria and Francisco Suarez were explicitly condemning the use of war to spread

religion. "Difference in religion," Victoria wrote, "is not a cause of just war." See James Turner Johnson, *Ideology, Reason, and the Limitation of War: Religious and Secular Concepts 1200-1740* (Princeton: Princeton University Press, 1975), 112-123, 154. See also Roland H. Bainton, *Christian Attitudes Toward War and Peace: A Historical Survey and Critical Re-evaluation* (Nashville: Abingdon, 1960), 148.

14. *A Call to Civil Society* (New York: Institute for American Values, 1998): 16. This theme is developed in Aristotle, *Metaphysics*, 1-1; Bernard J. Lonergan, *Insight: A Study of Human Understanding* (New York: Longmans, 1958); and others.

15. We wish here to distinguish "secular" from "secularism." Secular, derived from the Latin term meaning "world" and suggesting "in the world," refers merely to functions that are separate from the church. Secularism, by contrast, is a philosophy, an "ism," a way of seeing the world based on rejection of religion or hostility to religion.

16. For this reason, advocates of secularism may underestimate the degree to which human societies, even in theory, can simply dispense with "religion." Moreover, they almost certainly miscalculate, even accepting many of their own premises, the social consequences of suppressing traditional religion. For if we understand religion to be values of ultimate concern, the twentieth century saw two world-threatening examples—Nazism in Germany, and communism in the Soviet Union—of the emergence of secular religions, or what might be called replacement religions, each violently intent on eliminating its society's traditional religious faiths (in effect, its competitor faiths), and each, when in power, ruthlessly indifferent to human dignity and basic human rights.

17. *A Call to Civil Society* (New York: Institute for American Values, 1998): 13.

18. As the leaders and scholars who produced *The Williamsburg Charter* put it in 1988, "the government acts as a safeguard, but not the source, of freedom for faiths, whereas the churches and synagogues act as a source, but not the safeguard, of faiths for freedom ... The result is neither a naked public square where all religion is excluded, nor a sacred public square with any religion established or semi-established. The result, rather, is a civil public square in which citizens of all religious faiths, or none, engage one another in the continuing democratic discourse." See James Davison Hunter and Os Guinness (eds.), *Articles of Faith, Articles of Peace: The Religious Liberty Clauses and the American Public Philosophy* (Washington, DC: The Brookings Institution, 1990), 140.

19. See Alexander Solzhenitzyn, *The Gulag Archipelago*, vol. I (New York: Harper and Row, 1974), 168.

20. See Jean Bethke Elshtain (ed.), *Just War Theory* (Oxford: Blackwell, 1992); Elshtain, Stanley Hauerwas, and James Turner Johnson, Pew Forum on Religion and Public Life Conference on "Just War Tradition and the New War on Terrorism" (http://pewforum.org/events/1005/); James Turner Johnson, *Ideology, Reason, and the Limitation of War: Religious and Secular Concepts 1200-1740* (Princeton: Princeton University Press, 1975); Johnson, *Just War Tradition and the Restraint of War: A Moral and Historical Inquiry* (Princeton: Princeton University Press, 1981); Johnson, *The Quest for Peace: Three Moral Traditions in Western Cultural History* (Princeton: Princeton University Press, 1987); Johnson, *Morality and Contemporary Warfare* (New Haven: Yale University Press, 1999); Johnson and John Kelsay (eds.), *Cross, Crescent, and Sword: The Justification and Limitation of War in Western and Islamic Tradition*

(New York: Greenwood Press, 1990); Majid Khadduri, *War and Peace in the Law of Islam* (Baltimore: Johns Hopkins University Press, 1955); John Kelsay and James Turner Johnson (eds.), *Just War and Jihad: Historical and Theoretical Perspectives on War and Peace in Western and Islamic Tradition* (New York: Greenwood Press, 1991); Terry Nardin (ed.), *The Ethics of War and Peace: Religious and Secular Perspectives* (Princeton: Princeton University Press, 1996); William V. O'Brien, *The Conduct of War and Limited War* (New York: Praeger, 1981); Rudolf Peters, *Jihad in Classical and Modern Islam* (Princeton: Markus Wiener, 1996); Paul Ramsey, *Speak Up for Just War or Pacifism* (University Park, PA: Pennsylvania State University Press, 1988); Michael Walzer, *Just and Unjust Wars* (New York: Basic Books, 1977); and Richard Wasserstrom (ed.), *War and Morality* (Belmont, CA: Wadsworth, 1970).

21. The Latin axiom is: *Inter arma silent leges* (In times of war the law is silent). Classical exemplars of this perspective include Thucydides, Niccolo Machiavelli, and Thomas Hobbes; for a more recent treatment, see Kenneth Waltz, *Man, the State and War* (Princeton: Princeton University Press, 1978). For a sensitive but critical survey of the contribution of this school of thought to international theory, see Jack Donnelly, *Realism and International Relations* (Cambridge: Cambridge University Press, 2000).

22. Intellectual and moral approaches to war as a human phenomenon can generally be divided into four schools of thought. The first can be called realism: the belief that war is basically a matter of power, self-interest, necessity, and survival, thereby rendering abstract moral analysis largely beside the point. The second can be called holy war: the belief that God can authorize the coercion and killing of nonbelievers, or that a particular secular ideology of ultimate concern can authorize the coercion and killing of nonbelievers. The third can be called pacifism: the belief that all war is intrinsically immoral. And the fourth is typically called just war: the belief that universal moral reasoning, or what some would call natural moral law, can and should be applied to the activity of war. The signatories to this letter largely disagree with the first school of thought. We unequivocally reject the second school of thought, regardless of the form it takes, or whether it springs from and purports to support our own society ("our side") or the side of those who wish us ill. Some of the signatories have much respect for the third school of thought (particularly its insistence that non-violence does not mean retreat or passivity or declining to stand for justice; quite the opposite), even as we respectfully, and with some degree of fear and trembling, differ from it. As a group we seek largely to embrace and build upon the fourth school of thought.

23. Socrates' judgment that it is better to suffer evil rather than to do it is conveyed to us by Plato in the *Apology* (32-c to 32-e) and constitutes a key moment in moral philosophy.

24. Some people suggest that the "last resort" requirement of just war theory—in essence, the requirement to explore all other reasonable and plausible alternatives to the use of force—is not satisfied until the resort to arms has been approved by a recognized international body, such as the United Nations. This proposition is problematic. First, it is novel; historically, approval by an international body has not been viewed by just war theorists as a just cause requirement. Second, it is quite debatable whether an international body such as the UN is in a position to be the best final

judge of when, and under what conditions, a particular resort to arms is justified; or whether the attempt by that body to make and enforce such judgments would inevitably compromise its primary mission of humanitarian work. According to one observer, a former UN Assistant Secretary-General, transforming the UN into "a pale imitation of a state" in order to "manage the use of force" internationally "may well be a suicidal embrace." See Giandomenico Picco, "The UN and the Use of Force," *Foreign Affairs* 73 (1994): 15. See also Thomas G. Weis, David P. Forsythe, and Roger A. Coate, *United Nations and Changing World Politics* (Boulder, CO: Westview Press, 2001), 104-106; and John Gerard Ruggie, *The United Nations and the Collective Use of Force: Whither? Or Whether?* (New York: United Nations Association of the USA, 1996).

25. In just war theory, the main goal of the legitimate authority requirement is to prevent the anarchy of private warfare and warlords—an anarchy that exists today in some parts of the world, and of which the attackers of September 11 are representative embodiments. The legitimate authority requirement does not, on the other hand, for several reasons, apply clearly or directly to wars of national independence or succession. First, these latter types of conflict occur within a state, not internationally. Moreover, in many such conflicts, the question of public legitimacy is exactly what is being contested. For example, in the war for independence that resulted in the founding of the United States, just war analysts frequently point out that the rebelling colonies themselves constituted a legitimate public authority, and further that the colonies had reasonably concluded that the British government had, in the words of our Declaration of Independence, become "destructive of these ends" of legitimate government, and therefore itself had ceased to function as a competent public authority. Indeed, even in cases in which those waging war do not in any plain sense constitute a currently functioning public authority—for example, the "Warsaw Ghetto Uprising" of Polish Jews in 1943 against the Nazi occupation—the legitimate authority requirement of just war theory does not morally invalidate the resort to arms by those resisting oppression by seeking to overthrow illegitimate authority.

26. For example, just war principles often insist that legitimate warfare must be motivated by the intention of enhancing the likelihood of peace and reducing the likelihood of violence and destruction; that it must be proportionate, such that the social goods that would result from victory in war discernably outweigh the evils that will attend the war; that it must contain the probability of success, such that lives are not taken and sacrificed in futile causes; and that it must pass the test of comparative justice, such that the human goods being defended are important enough, and gravely enough in danger, to outweigh what many just war theorists view as the standing moral presumption against war. This letter focuses largely on principles of justice in declaring war (in the terminology employed by many Christian just war thinkers, *jus ad bellum*) and in waging war (*jus in bello*). Other principles focus on justice in settling the war and restoring conditions of peace (*jus post bellum*). See Jean Bethke Elshtain (ed.), *Just War Theory* (Oxford: Blackwell, 1992); U.S. Conference of Catholic Bishops, *The Challenge of Peace: God's Promise and Our Response* (Washington, DC: United States Catholic Conference, 1983); and other sources cited above.

27. As of January 4, 2002, official estimates were that 3,119 persons had been killed by the September 11 attackers, including 2,895 in New York, 184 in Washington, and 40

in Pennsylvania. Although this letter refers to "our citizens," included among those murdered on September 11 were many citizens of other countries who were living in the U.S. at the time of the attack. "Dead and Missing," *New York Times*, January 8, 2002.

28. In addition to the murders of September 11, members of radical Islamicist organizations are apparently responsible for: the April 18, 1983 bombing of the U.S. Embassy in Beirut, killing 63 persons and injuring 120; the October 23, 1983 bombings of U.S. Marine and French paratroop barracks in Beirut, killing 300 persons; the December 21, 1988 bombing of U.S. Pan Am Flight 103, killing 259 persons; the February 26, 1993 bombing of the World Trade Center in New York City, killing six persons and injuring 1000; the June 25, 1996 bombing outside the Khobar Towers U.S. military barracks in Dhahran, Saudi Arabia, killing 19 U.S. soldiers and wounding 515; the August 7, 1998 bombing of U.S. embassies in Nairobi, Kenya, and Dar es Salaam, Tanzania, killing 224 persons and injuring more than 5,000; and the October 12, 2000 bombing of the USS Cole in Aden, Yemen, killing 17 U.S. sailors and wounding 39. This list is incomplete. (See *Significant Terrorist Incidents, 1961-2001,* Washington, DC: U.S. Department of State, Bureau of Public Affairs, October 31, 2001). In addition, members of organizations comprising this movement are also responsible for numerous failed attempts at mass murder, both in the U.S. and in other countries, including the attempt to bomb the United Nations and the Lincoln and Holland Tunnels in New York in 1993 and the attempt to bomb the Los Angeles International Airport on New Year's Eve 2000.

29. The commonly accepted term for this movement today is "Islamism." The followers of this movement are now called "Islamists." —Ed.

30. The relationship between the jihad and just war traditions is complex. Premodern jihad and just war perspectives overlapped in important ways. Both could legitimate wars aimed at advancing religion, and both sought clearly to disassociate such wars from wars involving indiscriminate or disproportionate tactics. In the modern era, jihad has largely retained its confessional component—that is, its aim of protecting and propagating Islam as a religion. The confessional dimension of jihad thinking in turn seems to be closely linked to the view of the state widely held by Muslim authorities—a view that envisions little or no separation of religion from the state. By contrast, modern Christian thinking on just war has tended to downplay its confessional elements (few Christian theologians today emphasize the value of "crusade"), replacing them with more religiously neutral arguments about human rights and shared moral norms, or what some Christian and other thinkers term "natural moral law." Some Muslim scholars today seek, in the case of jihad, more fully to recover the sense of the term as "exertion" or "striving for good" in the service of God, thereby similarly downplaying its confessional elements and emphasizing, for our increasingly plural and interdependent world, the term's more universal dimensions and applications. For example, see Sohail M. Hashmi, "Interpreting the Islamic Ethics of War and Peace," in Terry Nardin (ed.), *The Ethics of War and Peace: Religious and Secular Perspectives* (Princeton, NJ: Princeton University Press, 1996), 146-166; and Hilmi Zawati, *Is Jihad a Just War? War, Peace, and Human Rights under Islamic and Public International Law* (Lewiston, NY: Edwin Mellen, 2001).

31. For example, Muslim scholars affiliated with the Muslim World League, meeting in Mecca, recently reaffirmed that jihad strictly prohibits "the killing of

noncombatants" and attacks against "installations, sites and buildings not related to the fighting." See "Muslim scholars define 'terrorism' as opposed to legitimate jihad," *Middle East News Online* (www.middleeastwire.com), posted January 14, 2002. See also Bassam Tibi, "War and Peace in Islam," in Terry Nardin (ed.), *The Ethics of War and Peace: Religious and Secular Perspectives* (Princeton, NJ: Princeton University Press, 1996), 128-145.

32. The historian Eric Hobsbawm, in his study of the twentieth century, published in 1995, warns us in particular, as we confront the new millennium, of the emerging crisis of "non-state terrorism," made possible by the growing "privatization of the means of destruction," such that organized groups, operating at least to some degree independently of public authorities, are increasingly willing and able to perpetrate "violence and wreckage anywhere on the globe." Eric Hobsbawm, *Age of Extremes: The Short Twentieth Century 1914-1991* (London: Abacus, 1995), 560.

33. From Abraham Lincoln, First Inaugural Address, March 1861.

"What We're Fighting For: A Letter from America" was written under the aegis of the Institute for American Values and publicly released in February 2002.

The U.S.-Middle East Dialogue

Three

∾

What We're Fighting For:
A Follow-Up

≈

Saleh Bashir, Hassan I. Mneimneh,
and Hazem Saghie

The fact that American intellectuals have addressed the world on behalf of their country, through an open letter with 60 signatories,[1] is an extremely important development in the aftermath of the events of the 11th of September. These events have ushered in the beginning of a new phase in international intercourse and global history, and in the position of the United States in both. This is indeed the case whether one accepts the view that the terrorist acts were the originating cause of the new phase, as argued by many, or a mere pretext to establish a global hegemony, as argued by others.

This Letter has a twofold importance: (1) It restores, irrespective of any assessment of its contents, the validity of an intellectual dialogue that transcends local identities, countries, and cultural spheres, in its discussion of universal human values—or at least, of values which are viewed as such—as is consistent with the role of intellectuals; and (2) by resorting to the intellectual realm, it moves the American voice to a domain where a hegemony based on force is not possible. It may have been possible for the United States to impose its will on the world, single-handedly and categorically, at the military, strategic, diplomatic, and economic levels, that is, at levels where power is material and/or quantitative (a course of action often undertaken in the past decade). Such imposition remains impossible in the intellectual realm. Indeed, in the intellectual realm, where propositions are subjected to reasoned criticism, contributions from the United States are on an equal footing with contributions from all other sources.

We consider it unwarranted to accuse the signatories of the Letter of complicity with any American policy and of attempting to establish a global

41

intellectual hegemony, as do proponents of conspiracy theories, unfortunately in wide currency in the Arab world. It should be noted, however, that the weak intensity of the self-critical sections of the Letter point to a problematic approach with regard to the rest of the world community, which is best understood as a byproduct of a naïveté that generates a paternalistic attitude. Implicit in the Letter is the supposition that presenting the collective (American) cultural self is sufficient to generate the acceptance of others; this collective self is thus assumed to have an irresistible charm, and that it is ultimately superior to other collective cultural selves.

This criticism does not affect our recognition of the utmost importance of the American contribution to culture and beyond, or of the tangible benefits derived from this contribution by our societies as well as others. Nor is [it] meant as a qualification of our denunciation of all forms of anti-Americanism, from mild xenophobic rationalizations to blunt racist formulations, recognizing that anti-Americanism in our societies is assimilated into various ideological formulations, nationalistic and religious, leftist and rightist.

It is our assessment that the accord between the positions of the United States government and those espoused by the Letter is significant, far beyond any accusations of complicity or conspiracy, as indicative of the quasi-consensus that has coalesced within the United States with regard to the war on terrorism. Indeed, had the Letter been a product of the American administration or one of its agencies, as insinuated or assumed in many Arab responses, it would have been easily dismissible. As an intellectual contribution, this Letter is owed a reaction beyond the instinctive denunciation to which some of these responses have resorted.

The American intellectuals who have detailed their vision of the "War on Terrorism" in this Letter, addressing it to the world, have implicitly accepted subjecting their views to questioning and critique. Such critique should adhere to all due seriousness, by focusing on the text, its content, structure, and methodology, and should not fall back on the usual complaints against American policy, limit itself to a mere inventory of the omissions in the text (an obvious criticism that can be applied to any text), or engage in accusations against some or all of the signatories. These approaches, even if substantive, are not central to a focused critique. Instead, by developing marginal issues, they merely result in absolving the text of the criticism that it deserves.

A cursory reading of the Letter yields a preliminary conclusion, one which is indeed confirmed by further scrutiny, that it is an ideological document. It may even be the most gravely significant ideological formulation to originate from American society since the end of the Cold War. Through considerable intellectual formalism, this Letter lays the foundations for a legitimization of a global role and hegemony for the sole superpower at this moment in history. It follows what can be described as a classical approach: premises believed to be self-evident, in the form of universal principles, are stated at the beginning of the Letter, then used as a framework for the interpretation of an event that despite its gravity (or maybe because of it) remains unique and exceptional—the attacks of the 11th of September. This interpretation is used to advance a proposition, presented in ethical terms and transcending politics and history: the notion of the "just war" as a burden and a mission to be assumed by the United States, not on the basis of considerations and/or justifications stemming from it being the sole power able to assume such a role on behalf and under the supervision of the world community, but in the name of what the Letter refers to as "American values," understood as being synonymous with "universal values."

The Letter thus bases its argument on a specific American right—the right of retaliation as a result of the aggression of the 11th of September. It should be noted that, outside of limited radical circles, a quasi-consensus exists in recognizing this American right. Objections to this right, when they arise, address its application (notably in terms of its effects on Afghan civilians), and not its principle. We do, however, fear that this right, through the proposed formulation, is transformed into an absolute one, with a moral foundation, on the basis of a theoretical construct centered on the notion of the "just war." It is our contention that this construct, which is advocated forcefully in the Letter, stems from a basic fallacy that is a product not of an attempt at deception, but from a parochialism in dealing with world affairs, displayed notably through considering the September 11 aggression an event of absolute uniqueness unequaled by any other in our world.

There are indeed unique aspects for this act of aggression, from the issuing of an edict (a *fatwa*) calling on the killing of any and all Americans, to the commission of the act in a location far from where the perpetrators originate, and the absence of a traditional theater of war. This act of aggression does indeed put into application the notion of collective responsibility of all Americans towards the policy of the United States. However, stressing the uniqueness of the crime runs the risk of absolving its victim from any accountability in seeking retribution, a risk that seems materialized when the current actions of the U.S. administration are considered. It is therefore imperative to deconstruct the arguments used in advocating this construct, irrespective of the intentions of those advocating it.

The Letter starts by enunciating five principles, by "affirm[ing] five fundamental truths that pertain to all people without exception." These "truths" can be agreed upon without difficulty, if not by consensus, by a wide effective majority. There can be no hesitation in accepting the validity of the principles that state "all human beings are born free and equal in dignity and rights," and that "the basic subject of society is the human person, and the legitimate role of government is to protect and help to foster the conditions for human flourishing," and that "killing in the name of God is contrary to faith in God and is the greatest betrayal of the universality of religious faith." Some stated "truths" can even be interpreted and accepted by adherents to non-democratic thought.

The universal character of these principles is therefore not contested. In addition, the fact that American democracy derives its foundations from these principles and is indeed one of the most mature and developed systems of government in modern history is not a subject of serious dispute. The problematic aspect of the Letter is in its extension of the claim of a universal character beyond these basic principles and its application to the so-called "American values" and the American experience. In effect, while the American experience does offer a successful manifestation of democratic practice, it remains one such manifestation among many. It is part of a global phenomenon, not its totality, nor necessarily its best example. Assertions to the contrary are often beyond the realm of political thought and its methodologies, but rather belong to ideological beliefs steeped in parochialism and reductionism, and as such run the risk of contradicting the democratic framework itself, which recognizes the relativity of assessments and comparisons.

Indeed, while American democracy may be assessed as superior to many of its European counterparts in some respects, it is met or exceeded by the latter in other respects. European democracies are more concerned with the humane content of the democratic principle. This is evident in their positions towards capital punishment, their focus on human rights as a major component of their diplomatic policy and international relations, and their objections and dismay towards the treatment of the al-Qa'ida and Taliban prisoners in Guantanamo, Cuba. American democratic practice, on the other hand, appears more dogmatic and prone to revenge in many instances, and accepts violence as a tool and a component.

With regard to Arab and other Third-World societies, the American experience is unlikely to be emulated as the sole model for modernization and modernity. A more reasoned approach would strive to assimilate the sum total of the modernity effort—a global endeavor characterized by the participation of all human societies and that has witnessed its culmination in the Western European context. The acquisition of modernity in a particular society, if it were to happen, can only be through its local appropriation by the individual society, which thus imbues it with its particular character. Otherwise, even in the best-case scenario, the global community is impoverished and loses in diversity.

The American experience itself is based on this process of appropriation. It is true that the United States, as a nation and as a system of government, is the only state to be created, willingly and explicitly, with a foundation of the aforementioned universal principles. Since American independence from Britain, these principles have guided the integration of new immigrants as citizens. This is indeed an exceptional occurrence. Its exceptional character is, however, due to unique historical circumstances. Its duplication is therefore virtually impossible. It cannot be considered a model for emulation without qualification.

The United States is one of only a handful of countries founded by an act of will, with a document stating its founding principles. What is applicable to the United States is not applicable to political entities with a deep historical dimension, as is the dominant form globally. Seeking democratic forms, for the latter, has to account for the accumulated legacies that have shaped their mindset and social structures. More effort is thus needed, and progress cannot be expected to proceed linearly, as the European historical evidence of the past two centuries proves.

Even the role of religion in the "American way of life," which is almost completely different from the various secular experiences in other countries, in their different forms, does in effect derive from the same uniqueness of the historical circumstances, and therefore cannot be viewed as an ultimate model.

The Letter suggests that the United States has reached an optimal solution for the compatibility between religion and democracy, whereby religion has a recognized role within a democratic context, and is not oppressed or excluded from the public sphere. Instead, it is provided with the opportunity to express itself and prosper. This may indeed be true, recognizing that American society displays two characteristics that do not co-exist in any other Western society: a thorough integration of democratic principles, and a deep religiosity. This may be a result of the dominant Protestant faith, which favors the multiplication of denominations, and which has not experienced in its history the experience of a religion-state (along the lines of the nation-state), as witnessed by Catholicism and Islam, for example. It was therefore able to accommodate a high level of co-existence between denominations, elevating it to a guiding principle in public life, without risking the accession of any denomination to a level of hegemony over government. Protestantism, as the dominant faith of the founding era, thus left its imprint on the system of government as well as society in the United States, and allowed the accommodation of other religions along the patterns accorded for denominations. American religions have indeed evolved to acquire many of the characteristics of denominations. The reproduction of this specifically American history and experience in different locales and spaces cannot be assured, especially since neither the American experience nor American Protestantism witnessed what Europe underwent in the seventeenth and eighteenth centuries, i.e. the scientific revolution and the Enlightenment, experiences which are needed urgently in Third World societies. The American exposure to both the scientific revolution and the Enlightenment produced local forms that remained isolated from the rest of the world.

We also note that there is no simple outcome for the comparison between a democratic formulation that excludes religious expression from the public political space and one that makes room for adjacent religious absolutisms in the context of a political and societal quorum that is supposed to be based on the relativity of truth. While we do not intend to address the issue in this reply, we underline the wealth and multiplicity of the available models.

We have discussed the extension of a universal character to "American values" at relative length because of the importance assigned to it in the Letter, notably as a theoretical background to the proposition of the "Just War." Both intellectually and ethically, we have to express our reservations with regard to this proposition, even if, for the sake of argument, we were to accept the universal character of "American values." We further think that the introduction of this notion into the current international scene, with its lack of agreed upon neutral reference is outright dangerous.

It is our view that the two notions "justice" and "war" are mutually exclusive. This view stems from a philosophical position that argues for the incompatibility between violence and a number of values, notably those associated with life and humanity. It is thus not possible to combine "justice" and "war," or "justice" and "capital punishment." War is evil, and as such cannot be described as just, nor can any other positive ethical qualification be applied to it: common sense forbids the combination of evil and justice or ethics. This is particularly true in the case of the modern version of war, where the distinction between combatants and civilians is lost. It can be noted that since WWI, most of the victims of conflicts have been civilians (the most blatant example being the conflict inflicted upon Iraq for a decade, where the regime has not been affected at all).

This position does not imply an adherence to naïve pacifism. We accept the proposition that war might be a necessary choice—to fight back aggression, to protect civilians, or for other legitimate reasons. We do however disagree with the notion that such reasons create the conditions for a "just war." War, as the ultimate violence, may grant power holders the opportunity to bypass legal constraints and moral inhibitors, and as such cannot be described as ethical in an unqualified categorical way, but only in relative terms. War, at best and whatever its justifications, can be viewed as belonging to the category of "the most detestable of the permissible" that Islamic jurisprudence applies to divorce. The notion of a "just war" that endows war with ethical value is in our judgment in conflict with ethics, even in instances involving the defense of the innocent.

The danger of the notion of "just war," particularly when embraced by a power that holds a monopoly of hegemony and has the means to impose its will on the world, as is the case of the United States, risks being used as rationalization or pretext, bypassing various considerations, legal and otherwise. It furthermore transports conflicts from the context of a reality that implicitly accepts differing views, into an absolute self-legitimizing ideological framework. We fear that the treatment afforded by the American authorities to their captives in Guantanamo, Cuba is but a first example of the application of the notion of "just war" with its dehumanizing effects on the enemy. Another example is the categorization of the global community and its constituent states into "good" and "evil" camps, outside of any meaningful objective criteria. The effective result is that the party labeled "evil" is thus able to score an ideological victory against its "good" opponent, even if defeated militarily, by succeeding in dragging it to the evil exchange of warfare.

Stressing the necessary character of the war negates the fact that war is a free choice, whether against "evil" or otherwise. War is thus deprived of any potential glorification and ensuing chauvinism that might develop in the camp of those engaged in it. Furthermore, it accomplishes two goals: (1) it constrains it within the limits of established laws, and (2) it preserves its defensive character at its forefront, even if offensive action is undertaken in accordance with military or strategic considerations. This second goal helps constrain the war geographically, so that it does transform itself into a self-propelling mechanism, leading to a continuous series of battles to which succumbs one country after another (such as the Punic wars in antiquity, and the Napoleonic wars in the more recent history).

As opposed to positing it as an imperial moment, when war is understood as born out of necessity, it is subject to critique, revision, and re-definition—functions assumed nowadays by the free press, and in the ability to monitor the conditions and treatment of captives. Major differences exist between "just war" and "war of just necessity" both in terms of the centrality of violence and the effects on human victims, as a function of readiness for compromise and political engagement in general. Even in the most acute case of a war of just necessity, the conflict with fascism in WWII, it has been argued that it may have been possible, had the war been framed in terms of necessity more than justice, to spare the lives of millions of Jews. It would have been certainly possible to spare hundreds of thousands of Berlin men and women the misery and rape to which they were subjected, and it would have been possible to avoid the destruction of Dresden. The atomic bombing of the cities of Hiroshima and Nagasaki stems indeed from a presentation of the conflict as a just war, which elevated it to a level of autonomy, with successive countries succumbing to the unfolding of an imperial history.

There is no doubt that the effects of the Arab-Jewish war of 1948 would have been lessened, in both material and psychological impacts, had the focus on Jewish independence been shifted towards a stress on the necessity generated by the Nazi Holocaust and the resistance of the West to Jewish immigration.

It may be argued that such an approach is anathema to the thinking of the military and the propagandists who would assess it as defeatist. Our concern here is the role of the intellectuals who should be summoned to use all their skeptical and critical tools to resist the demons that may inhabit militarism and are summoned upon the breakout of war through the temptation of violence.

Accordingly, even the affliction of terrorism does not warrant being countered within the framework of a "just war" as suggested in the Letter, or to be dealt with outside the confines of recognized laws. Terrorism is an act of genocide, if not by the number of its victims, then by its logic and motives, since it selects its targets not as a result of political enmity or military considerations, but as a random sample that represents the ethnic, cultural, or social collective. The perpetrators of terrorism can therefore be subject to the same legal process that has prosecuted war criminals, from the Nuremberg trials to the Brussels and The Hague trials that handled war crimes and crimes against humanity committed in the Balkans and in Rwanda. The legal precedents may be applied to terrorism, avoiding the temptation to resort to extra-legal methods on the basis of the precarious notion of a "just war" that is prone to excesses.

These observations are presented for the sake of a dialogue that we consider of vital importance, with the sole aim of enhancing the critical and auto-critical approaches that are needed in our Arabic culture and life, noting that we, the signatories, do not claim any representative quality.

We do have to note the depth of the lacunae that afflict our culture in this respect, which were further exposed in the aftermath of the 11th of September, as displayed by the evident strength of a populism that was nurtured during the Cold War and of the mythological nostalgia of a bygone era, neither of which were overcome by the advent of modernity.

Addressing these issues is evidently the mission of Arab society, and Arab intellectuals in particular. It should be however noted that some American policies (which were alluded to) constitute a complicating factor. The Letter could have addressed the defects of these policies, by giving more attention to the notion of justice, especially when applied to the Palestinian people, which has suffered injustice, and still does. This injustice, and the pervasive indifference towards it are at the core of the disarray that afflicts the Middle East.

This criticism, however, should not diffuse the need for Arab efforts to engage the American other in dialogue, nor should it be construed as absolving Arab society of its primary responsibility for the lacunae that afflict it.

Notes

1. "What We're Fighting For: A Letter from America" (New York: Institute for American Values, 2002). [See chapter 2 of this volume.]

"What We're Fighting For: A Follow-Up" was originally published on April 30, 2002 in *Al-Hayat* (http://english.daralhayat.com). It was translated from the Arabic by Hassan I. Mneimneh. Reprinted with permission.

Four

❧

Key Intellectualism

❧

Heshmatollah Falahatpisheh

During the last days of their political lives, both Winston Churchill and Napoleon Bonaparte uttered the same sentence, which in essence said: "I have realized that thought alone rules in the world."

Normally one considers thought to have a positive and respectable connotation, but without a doubt, destructive ideas such as ruling over the world, especially when they find operational backers, have lacked good intentions and have been evil. Many times throughout history, intellectuals who cannot or do not want to take up arms, have turned parts of the world into ruins by resorting to the pen; the destructive force of their ink is hundreds of times greater than that of the bombs that destroyed Hiroshima and Nagasaki in 1945. The 60 American intellectuals who have supported Bush's war-against-terrorism statement are among the key intellectuals of the twentieth and twenty-first century; recently, in an action that has been rare during the lifetime of these intellectuals, they have introduced themselves as backers of war. The philosophers and intellectuals who are thinking and writing in the corners of their rooms could have planned for the happiness of the world and its people and for unity based on peace; but many of them are attached to, or partners with, the politicians and thus, with their pens, they drag humanity into conflicts and prepare the political atmosphere for crimes at the global level. Fukuyama and Huntington have already prepared themselves to write the "Mein Kampf" of Bush.

A few main points about the statement of the American intellectuals are worth pondering:

1. The necessity that America and its values be the centre of the world and the globalization trend.
2. Reliance on war being unavoidable and taking pride in a war that may have many victims.

3. Reliance on bifurcating the world between the friends of modernism and those who should not even have the right to live in their poor homes.
4. Insulting Islam and the people of over 40 Muslim countries.
5. Holding that resort to the United Nations is problematic and that it needs to be bypassed.
6. Seeking a world that would accept America's hegemony.

Some 53 years ago, in the book *The Power Elite*, C. Wright Mills spoke about what went on behind-the-scenes of democracy in America. In his opinion, the three elite groups of the wealthy, the political elite and professional politicians, and the few owners of the large companies in the military complex formed the triangle of the ruling power elite in America. But he did not point out that at the heart of this triangle are some key intellectuals like Fukuyama, Huntington, and some professional journalists, who convince and deviate the other intellectual layers and the public opinion of America regarding deals and deceitful policies of the power triangle and present plans and theories for the creation of America's hegemony.

Today, economic recession, the fall in the arms market, and the halt in the use of military products has [ef]faced the efforts of the political side of the triangle to establish an international hegemony. Thus key intellectuals have interpreted their various ideas in accordance with the military-based policy needed by Washington and are even raising the horrid plans of the past within the framework of the requirements of today.

In reality, this group has found the atmosphere suitable for imposing their twentieth century perspectives, and this situation has created the grounds for paying attention to the opinions of those who look with doubt at the principal scenario for 11 September.

Among the signatories of the letter sent to Bush, we can see the names of some who have become famous for their hegemony-seeking doctrines. Francis Fukuyama and Samuel Huntington are more famous than the others. What is interesting is that both of them, in articles following 11 September, tried to use the atmosphere for proving the theories they had presented in the previous century.

Fukuyama, the author of *The End of History and the Last Man*, one month after the events of 11 September, namely, on 11 October of last year, in an article in the *Guardian* newspaper, divided the world into the two poles of modern and backward and wrote that apart from Turkey, which has received passing grades from among the Islamic countries (based on the criteria of liberal democracy), the others resist modernism, and America can use its military might to break this resistance. He claims that Islam is the only cultural system that continually produces individuals like bin Ladin and the Taliban, those who threaten modernism.

Huntington's ideas require more pondering; in view of a number of major examples, one can consider the letter of the 60 intellectuals to have been written by the author of *The Clash of Civilizations*. On the first day of 2002, in an article entitled "The Era of the Battle of the Muslims" (*Newsweek*), he wrote: in 40 countries of the world, there are bases that threaten the West. While expressing concern about the self-awareness of Muslims, their envy regarding the West's wealth, and their anger regarding U.S.-Israeli relations, he thanked bin Ladin for causing the West to reunite. In Huntington's opinion, among the present generation in Islamic societies, there are many youths who are considered the main elements for carrying out violence against Western societies.

The group of key intellectuals has mesmerized America's society by the ugly game of power in the ruling elite triangle, to the point that, according to Noam Chomsky, today a major part of the other intellectuals and America's public opinion do not know what is transpiring behind-the-scenes of the relations between America and Israel in the Islamic Middle East.

The power elite and the key intellectuals of America have drawn up horrific plans against Islam. Maybe the name of the progressive country of Iran had been placed on the agenda of the criminals of the twenty-first century a little earlier, and this strategy is being carried out under the cover of fighting terrorism and searching for peace. Unfortunately, in these conditions, those intellectuals in the world who are concerned with humanitarian issues are on the fringes.

"Key Intellectualism" was originally published on February 2, 2002 in *Resalat* (Tehran). BBC Monitoring translated the article from the Persian, and the BBC Global News Wire-Asia Africa Intelligence Wire ran the story on February 22, 2002 with the title, "Iran Daily Denounces U.S. Intellectuals Who Support War on Terror." English © 2002, BBC Monitoring. Persian © 2002, *Resalat*. Reprinted with permission.

Five

∾

The Letter is American, the Schizophrenia Islamic

ॐ

Saad Mehio

The statement which more than 60 American intellectuals and university professors in the fields of politics, religion, and philosophy issued recently (titled: "What We're Fighting For: A Letter from America") is set to become some sort of icon that different parties will interpret the way each deems fit. This significant document which counts Samuel Huntington and Francis Fukuyama among its authors refers to such issues as American values, God, the idea of a "just war," and support for the current war on terror. The authors say they are not against the majority of Muslims, only the extremist minority that murders innocent civilians.

The U.S. administration will surely see this document as justification for its war, not only against terrorist organizations, but also against the "axis of evil" states (Iraq, Iran, and North Korea) and any other state sponsor of terrorism.

No one can blame the administration for seeing it this way, since the authors declared unequivocally that: "In the name of universal human morality...we support our government's, and our society's, decision to use force of arms against them." The authors also expressed their conviction that the war (or wars) America is engaged in at the moment are clearly "just wars" being waged against "a world-threatening evil that clearly requires the use of force to remove it."

The White House, the Pentagon, and the National Security Council (though perhaps not the State Department) will also be particularly pleased with what the document declared: "Our attackers despise not just our government, but our overall society, our entire way of life. Fundamentally, their grievances concern not only what our leaders do, but also who we are."

53

For their part, the Europeans will view the document in quite the same light as their American counterparts. But they will do so with horror rather than glee.

Judging from what French Foreign Minister Hubert Vedrine, German Foreign Minister Joschka Fischer, and European Union foreign affairs czar Javier Solana declared last week, the Europeans believe that by extending the war on terror to include countries constituting the "axis of evil," the U.S. is pursuing a "superficial policy, and treating its allies as mere satellites."

More than that, the Europeans will most likely see Washington's hand in this "Letter from America." In other words, they will suspect the authors wrote it at Washington's behest, to garner additional public support for the more difficult future phases of the war.

The Chinese and Russians, meanwhile, are probably studying the document quite closely, not to come up with definite positions regarding what it says, but to discuss its possible implications on America's global position. This is the only thing that concerns them; since the September 11 attacks, Beijing and Moscow have been biding their time and calculating how to take advantage of each new mistake the Americans make.

But what of the Muslim world, which after all, is what this document is all about? The response of the world's 1.2 billion Muslims was, in a word, schizophrenic. The Muslim majority lauded by the document's authors recognized itself in many of the points they make. For example:

- The entirely correct distinction the authors make between "Islam" and "Islamicism." The former indeed represents what the great majority of Muslims believe in—tolerance, pluralism, and justice—while the latter (as the document points out) is restricted to small groups of extreme, violent, and intolerant individuals (such as the Taliban, Osama bin Ladin, and various other fundamentalist movements).

- The distinction between positive and negative American values was also useful. Muslims discovered that the values they reject are also rejected by the majority of Americans, values such as excessive consumerism, unrestricted freedom, extreme individualism, weak familial bonds, promiscuity, and media that glorify negative values. The values cherished by Americans, meanwhile, are the stuff of dreams for most Muslims: human dignity for all, general moral values that apply to all peoples, openness and freedom of expression, and freedom of religion and worship.

Even the concept of a "just war" is applauded in the Muslim Middle East, which has historically looked down upon those who attack innocent women, children, and other non-combatants in wartime.

The behavior of Saladin, the famous Muslim leader, upon conquering Jerusalem on October 2, 1187 is well documented. Karen Armstrong (in her book *Holy War*) described this historic event as follows:

Saladin conquered the city according to the highest Islamic ideals. He did not take revenge from the 1099 massacre (when Crusaders slaughtered tens of thousands of Muslim civilians) as the Koran advised (2:193,194). Not a single Christian was killed and there was no plunder. The Christian world was impressed with his clemency to the point that (Christian) legends grew up that he had received Christian baptism.

Naturally, the 3,000 victims who were killed in New York and Washington on September 11 had nothing to do with this Muslim heritage, nor indeed with Islam itself.

But enough of the enlightened side of the schizophrenic Muslim reaction. The darker side revolves around one basic question: Why haven't these beautiful ideals once been turned into equally beautiful policies? History, both ancient and modern, supports this dark interpretation. The Western connection with the Muslim (and often Christian) East, beginning with the Crusades, through nineteenth century colonialism, and ending with the present American show of force, has been nothing more than a continuing series of invasions, aggression, and enslavement. The U.S. (and the West in general) considers the Middle East to be one vast gas station run by Arab and Muslim dictators on behalf of their Western masters.

Of course, this doesn't mean Muslims have always been angelic in their behavior. The time will come when Muslims will have to own up to their sins and errors, including occupying Spain for more than 500 years, threatening the security of Christian Europe for more than 1,000, and the intolerance they are showing to other minorities at the present time. Yet all attention is focused on Western sins. The reason for that is easy to figure out: the West won and the East was defeated. Until there is an honorable settlement or a genuine historic reconciliation, the victor shoulders an immeasurably heavier burden. The fact that the victorious side appears unjust, unfair, and not understanding only makes that burden even heavier.

Had some Arab Americans taken part in drafting the "Letter from America," they would surely have pressed for the following issues to be raised:

1. Is the war being waged by nuclear-armed Israel against the almost unarmed Palestinian people a just war? How can lofty American values be reconciled with the fact that the West Bank and Gaza are the last remaining parts of the world under foreign military occupation, where people are denied freedom, dignity, and the right to determine their own fate?

2. How much longer will the diabolical alliance between Western democracies and Eastern tyrannies last? The West might retort at this point that democracy in the Middle East is primarily the responsibility of the region's peoples. But it might be useful to listen to the Eastern point of view.

Egyptian thinker Jalal Amin (in his book, *The Arab Mashreq and the West*) says:

> It is not difficult to explain why most Western writers insist on ignoring the role played by external factors in the development of Arab countries. Doing so would put the onus squarely on the shoulders of the peoples of these countries and on their internal disputes. Yet our study of contemporary Arab history reveals that political and economic developments in the great powers have always been the decisive factors in determining the fate of the Arab East.

There are many historical events, in fact, that support Amin's point of view. Consider: the overthrow by the CIA of the Mossadegh government in Iran in the 1950s; President Dwight Eisenhower's order to "cut Gamal Abdel-Nasser down to size," which was achieved subsequently in the June 1967 war; the numerous coups d'etat Washington instigated in Syria and other Arab countries; [and] the recent U.S. decision to overthrow former ally Saddam Hussein, not because he is a dictator, but because he violated the rules laid down in Washington.

Are the Arabs allowed to achieve economic integration and independence on the EU model, or is that prohibited because of concerns over Israeli security and Western "oil security?"

Finally, will the U.S. ever decide to address the oppressed people of the Middle East using the positive American values featured in the document, instead of continuing to engage their oppressor regimes?

The "Letter from America" has indeed caused the peoples of the Middle East to suffer from an intellectual schizophrenia. This was probably not what its authors intended, especially since they concluded the document with the words: "The great task of conciliation awaits us."

And this is what the peoples of the Middle East also want: conciliation. Genuine and lasting conciliation.

But when will that happen? The signatories to the American document allude that a process of conciliation can begin soon after the current war ends.

And what are the Arabs to do in the meantime? Eat promises? Or while away their time trying to solve the riddles of the "Letter from America?" Or perhaps do both at once?

A bad case of schizophrenia indeed.

"The Letter is American, the Schizophrenia Islamic" was originally published on March 4, 2002 in *The Daily Star* (Lebanon). © 2002, *The Daily Star.* Additional Middle East articles can be found at http://www.dailystar.com.lb. Reprinted with permission.

Six

_____

Options Are Limited

_____

Movement for Islamic Reform in Arabia (MIRA)

To the signatories of "What We're Fighting For":

We read your communiqué which declares your position regarding the campaign led by your country against "terrorism." Upon considering it, reviewing American history and its relationship with the Muslim world and analyzing current events, we have arrived at the following points. We think you might benefit from considering our conclusions.*

You Have Unwittingly Put [Forth] Moral
Justification for the September Attacks

You consider the current war waged by your country a justifiable response to an attack directed against civilians. Thus, unintentionally, you legitimize strikes against America in its long history of targeting innocent civilians in many parts of the world. Your country sought and perpetrated attacks on civilians as an end in themselves, not as an unavoidable by-product of war, in many cases. If America targets civilians, according to your reasoning, then waging war against her carries moral justification. The form and intensity of such a response

_____

*Upon granting permission to reprint "Options are Limited," MIRA asked that the following two notes be included at the beginning of the text: "First: this reply was published before the war on Iraq and before moving U.S. forces outside Saudi Arabia. Second: the reader should keep in mind that honesty and sincerity in conveying the ideas might show the reply to be little bit irritant. This is the tax that has to be paid for an accurately presented (or represented) opinion." —Ed.

becomes a matter of detail. Of the scores of examples of America's targeting of civilians we choose two cases that reveal how your ethics are founded.

First: To our knowledge, America still considers dropping two nuclear bombs on Japan a morally justifiable action and refuses to apologize for it. You well know the two nuclear bombs were not aimed at military or strategic installations, but were intended to kill civilians. That act was not meant to deter an attack or to level the field in the face of Japan's advantage in battle. Japan was attacked with nuclear weapons while its armies were retreating. If America considers nuclear attacks against civilians merely to hasten an inevitable defeat of an opponent, then how could you consider the strikes against the World Trade Center and the Pentagon unjustifiable? If you claim that you do not condone America's nuclear attacks, then you should consider her act as more morally repellent than that of those who attacked New York. Accordingly, the strikes against America are as legitimate as the way her war against those who attacked her is justifiable.

Second: When Madeleine Albright was in office, expressing the views of the United States, she said that killing half a million Iraqi children through sanctions "was a price worth paying" to contain Saddam Hussein. America is aware that her policy entailed the killing of half a million children and has no problem with this, so much so that this policy is still in place. The number of children killed is now nearing a million. If you do not object to that policy, then you have forfeited your right to pass judgement on those who attacked the World Trade Center. For killing half a million Arab children is not on par with killing a few thousand as a result of targeting vital installations. Also, Iraqi civilians did not elect their government; therefore they are not responsible for the actions of their leaders, unlike Americans. If you do object to your government's policy of killing children, then you condone the waging of war against your country in the same way you bless your war against "terrorism" and the targeting of civilians.

Why Muslims?

You admit that America's foreign policy is arrogant and you speak in general terms overlooking the fact that your problem with Muslims is more specific and far deeper. You need to understand that your crimes against Muslims are particularly abhorrent. Of these we list a few:

First: The complete and unqualified support for Israel and all its crimes, defending Israel in all international forums, and adopting a policy towards our area which puts the security of Israel above any other consideration. Is it unfair for our people to view America as a partner in Israel's crimes? Is it not possible to view America's part in these crimes as more harmful since your country is the ultimate guarantor of Israel's well-being in whatever it does?

Second: America insists on maintaining its military presence in Arabia, a land sacred to Muslims and forbidden to non-Muslims. American officials persistently declare that you are there to stay indefinitely. Your decision makers claim that these forces are there by invitation of local governments. But you and your government know that those rulers do not represent their people. You know well that the peoples of the area do not want your presence and consider it both an insult and a provocation to their religious sentiment.

Third: America persists in starving Iraq although America is well aware of the plight of its civilian population. You know that sanctions are damaging the people and not the government. America insists that Iraq obey a particular UN resolution and comply with it according to America's impossible interpretation of it, while justifying Israel's defiance of scores of UN resolutions and refusing to apply any pressure to force her to comply.

Fourth: An ongoing crime committed by America against the people in our area is its continuous support of oppressive regimes and conniving with these governments to systematically ransack wealth and natural resources. These governments concede to America's theft in return for her undertaking to keep them in power against the will of their people.

It has to be said that your country's policies succeeded for a while in deterring Arabs and Muslims from fighting back. That was achieved by means of oppression and gagging, prescribed by your government and executed by the local regimes. But America's recurring crimes and persistence in disregarding religious sensibilities made hatred and desire for revenge, directed against America and the regimes sponsored by her, a most natural outcome. We think it is preposterous that you were taken by surprise at the eruption of these sentiments.

Islam and You

In your communiqué, you claim that American values and principles are a model to be followed and sought to market them to Muslims. You further claim that Islam cannot be both a religion and a basis for a state and asked Muslims to separate the state and politics from Islam. Much as you believe that your values are exemplary, Muslim belief in Islam as a religion and a basis for the state is more profound. When you promote your values and claim that they encompass freedom, justice, equality and preservation of human dignity, you know—from American experience—that this is a false presentation. On the other hand, Islam cannot be presented falsely and its values have no room for subjectivity and poetic license. Disregarding those rulers and intellectuals who try to flatter you and present you with an image of Islam which suits you, Islam's message is clear, well documented and jealously guarded, and no one can tamper with its principles. No matter how much those flatterers try to pick and choose half quotes and misrepresented dictums, the truth remains that Islam, as you may know, really calls on its followers to overcome opponents and reach the whole world with its universal message.

Muslims believe that Islam is not a list of suggestions put forward by intellectuals but a religion based on scriptures emanated from God. Muslims' belief in God means that their texts provide superior values to those you adhere to. They believe that they are your superiors in interpreting and understanding life, man, the universe and history. If you happen to be well enabled politically, militarily, economically and technically at this point in time, that does not prohibit their religion from propelling them to challenge all your abilities and overcome them. As long as you remain convinced of the superiority of your values and Muslims maintain their immovable belief that what they have is divine, you have no alternative but to admit that you and Muslims are on a collision course. No one who aims at turning this confrontation into a peaceful dialogue shall succeed.

Why Could You Not Prevent the Attack?

You spoke at length indicting the September attacks but overlooked the fact that the operation did not "come out of the blue" in a country which knew nothing of those who executed those strikes. They occurred while your security establishments were on full readiness to deal with such a threat. Did you ever ask yourselves the simple question: How could the perpetrators manage to paralyze the entire intelligence apparatus and carry out a most sophisticated operation with its enormous planning and logistics without being detected, let alone prevented, by your security forces?

No one could have been more prepared nor have committed so many resources than the U.S. Yet, here is your intelligence chief refusing to admit liability and declaring that no intelligence service could guarantee protection against such strikes in the future. It might surprise you to know that we agree with your intelligence chief in that these strikes cannot be prevented by means of security and intelligence. Politicians have to appease public opinion, but you are intellectuals and thinkers who populate think tanks and institutes and have no excuse for dodging the all-important questions about what caused that failure. To our knowledge, none of your institutes raised that question, let alone came up with an answer. Your communiqué certainly did not raise the question. This failure to raise a direct, simple and logical question means that the best of America's thinkers and opinion shapers are no different than the man in the street, offering nothing but anger and the desire for revenge. America's thinkers, it seems, are incapable of addressing an important issue such as this with deep and logical vision. This begs one question: With this apparent incapability, do you really think that you are fit to take on Islam?

How Your Opponents Changed the World

While avoiding raising the right questions, you claim that the event of the 11th of September has changed the world and that it marks a turning point in history. The event, as you see it, was not merely that of a few highjacked aircrafts colliding with buildings, but a great event from an historical perspective. Most of the signatories to your communiqué believe in the inevitability of confrontation with Islam and subscribe to the "clash of civilization" concept. You do not seem, however, to view the seriousness of the event and its historical repercussions in light of how limited the act itself was and how few were the perpetrators. Thus you fail, yet again, in raising another important question: How could a limited and besieged fringe group change the course of history? Again we do not see in the publications of American strategic studies institutes, nor in your communiqué, any mention of what the explanation might be. You chose to bypass reasoning to dwell on matters such as the enormity of the event in order to legitimize the severity of reprisals. Were you not among the adherents to the concept of confrontation, we might have excused you for failing to raise these issues. But people like you, who believe in global polarization into an U.S.-led West versus Islam, reveal their cultural and intellectual impotence when they exhibit enormous gaps in understanding so important an issue.

We Volunteer an Answer

The solution that might shed light on these contradictions, explain how the problem was never that of intelligence failure, and show how a besieged fringe group can change history, lies in understanding reality as it is. The world before and after September 11 is the same, save for one difference: the cultural confrontation between Islam and the West, America in particular, was unmasked. The group that carried out the attack might have been small and of limited resources. Yet it managed to execute the attack and amplify its repercussions by exploiting the opportunities provided by the hidden confrontation.

You might see the attack as a criminal act of "terrorist" proportion, but in its true nature, it was an act of upsetting a clumsy balance by targeting its pivotal point. This is something that you will never admit, not because you do not realize it, but because such admission acknowledges the fact that those who carried out the September missions drew strength from that reality which more than compensated for their weakness and limitations. If you allow yourselves a measure of humility, you will realize—according to this polarity—that America is the natural field for operations of this group. By "field" we do not mean place, rather we mean the cultural and intellectual environment. The way you deal with events, your manner of viewing the world, and Islam in particular, forms a fertile field for that group to attempt turning the power equation against you, and they succeeded. The manner in which your country responded to the September attacks proves this point and indicates that you will continue to provide a suitable field for those who attacked in September to strike again and again with more venom.

You Will Not Understand

Although we volunteered to address these issues and supplied an answer for them, we doubt whether you will understand or accept what we submit. That is not for want of abilities to comprehend, for you are clever people, nor it is for lack of information, for you most definitely have more information than we do. What prohibits you from understanding is your arrogance, conceit and that naïveté that comes with military, economic and political superiority. To modify your grasp of the issue according to the answers we provide means admitting cultural defeat. People like you have an automatic deterrent against admitting such defeat. But on an individual level, upon moments of solitude and absoluteness, you might begin to grasp these notions, they might find acceptance in your logical receptors, but your intellectual environment and collective reason automatically reject them. With the passage of time you are bound to suppress more and more truthful notions and find yourselves participating in founding the values of deceit and hypocrisy. It is to this state that we attribute how sixty American intellectuals who know their country's record of killing innocent civilians, ransacking other nations' wealth, sponsoring corrupt and oppressive tyrannies, and crushing human rights, can claim that American principles form the ideals for all.

The Future of Confrontation

Clearly, your ineptitude in understanding the issue is not only academic but also practical to the extent that you offer blessings to the U.S. campaign of revenge. You may believe that your government's response, aided by colossal political, media and military clamor, has brought you security, but the fact remains that this campaign raised the level of confrontation between civilizations to a critical state. Thus, it has prepared the ground for any group similar to those who carried out the September attacks to execute a bigger strike. When that happens, the American public will feel frustrated upon realizing that nothing can stop this type of opponent of America. We mean to say the "American public," for it has elected its government and blessed its actions. Thus, the repercussions of the campaign's failure will reflect upon that public as well as the government. The arrogance that barred you from putting the September events in their right pretext will prevent you from realizing that your nation is laying the ground for its self-destruction.

Options and Repercussions

Although it is now late for deciding on the right response, and although your government has opted for the choice expected of her, and despite our conviction that the chances of your understanding our vision of the September event are rather remote, it is essential that we express an opinion in the choices you face and their repercussions. Logically the options are limited to three:

First: The wide military, political, security, legal and cultural campaign already opted for by your government driven by the desire for revenge and dictated by the confrontational mentality. We think that America will see this through, especially after what appears to her as a victory in Afghanistan. Your government is perceived to have conquered the Taliban and al-Qaʻida and quenched the public thirst for revenge by displaying the captives in cages in Guantanamo.

When America first opted for this it seemed hesitant, but now it looks drunk with its perceived success to the extent that it publicly endorses Israel's bloody crimes with breathtaking brazenness. By making this choice, you have pushed yourselves towards the escalation of confrontation. It is strange that you have forgotten that the result of three years of a similar American approach after the Kenya and Tanzania bombings was the growth in your enemy's strength to the level of executing the September attacks. Your response to the September attacks does not differ in essence from your response to the bombings in Kenya and Tanzania. Your response now is merely a magnification of the previous one. Therefore, common sense tells us that the coming strike against you will be of bigger magnitude proportionately just as the September strike was a multiple of the Kenya and Tanzania bombings. In short, you don't seem to realize that this war is unique in the sense that the more you intensify the level of confrontation, the weaker and more exposed you render yourselves to be and the more daring and devastating your enemy becomes. We do not exaggerate if we assume that by this you will destroy yourselves eventually.

Second: The second option is to put security above all other considerations of life and culture. It means taking severe steps to shelter you from outside breaches. But the nature of your society means the presence of security loopholes that cannot be sealed without nullifying many of your essential civil rights and accepting living in a military-barrack society. This also means creating a monolithic existence, getting rid of any race, religion or culture that might cause a breach of social safety. It is true that such steps have already started to take shape and will continue with much more vigour after the first option fails. We anticipate that some states will opt for the secluded society solution, losing confidence in Washington, once the frustration with the first option sets in. Thus the grounds are laid for some sort of disintegration in your country.

Third: This is what we identify as the reasonable and realistic option which would guarantee that attacks, like those of September, will not happen again. An option we are confident that the American mentality and psyche will not choose. This option calls for America's men of reason and intellect to forgo arrogance and to re-examine the issues starting from scratch and contemplate why Muslims hate them and understand the nature of the confrontation with Islam. Had you opted for that, you would have decided to revise your policy towards the Muslim world and your stand on issues concerning Muslims. You would have realized that you should stop biased support for Israel immediately, withdraw your forces from Muslim land and Arabia in particular, lift sanctions against Iraq and put an end to your conniving with tyrannical regimes. In order for the reconciliation to be complete, the American government should apologize for its previous crimes against

Muslims and offer to compensate them materially and morally for those crimes. America has the means to do so if it decides to take this course.

Finally

We believe that American perception will not change, nor will its policy—certainly not until America receives the shock of another devastating event. We think that America chooses to learn the hard way. If, however there are still men of reason who have the ability of abstraction and the will to rid themselves of arrogance, they should rise today to warn their people and convince them to opt for the third option.

"Options Are Limited" originally appeared on May 15, 2002 on MIRA's website at http://www.islah.org. Reprinted with permission.

Seven

⚘

How We Can Coexist

⚘

153 Saudi Intellectuals

A little while ago, educated people had been discussing a paper prepared by the Institute for American Values entitled "What We're Fighting For" which was signed by sixty American intellectuals. It centers on a number of issues, among the most important of which is to explain the morality behind America's war on what they call "terrorism" and to call Muslims to stand with them, adopt American values, and fight against what they describe as Islamic radicalism.

We welcome dialogue and exchange. Dialogue, in principle, is a noble endeavor where we can take a good look at our moral foundations and discuss them with the intent of establishing a more just and equitable relationship between our nations and peoples. From this point of departure, we the signatories to this letter—from the land of the two mosques and the cradle of Islam, the Kingdom of Saudi Arabia—present our point of view as an informed alternative with the intent of establishing an atmosphere of mutual understanding that can be adopted by organizations and governments.

The Dialogue

We are firmly convinced that it is necessary for people of knowledge and probity to enjoy a far-reaching depth of vision. This will not permit them to pursue choices made by individuals and circles, under the pressure of circumstances, that fail to take ethics and human rights into consideration. Such are the choices that lead societies to perpetual anxiety, deprivation, and inhuman conflict.

The language of their discourse is the language of power. This is a mistake, since making power the language of dialogue tends to permit the forces of conflict to play a difficult and uncertain role in the future.

At this important juncture in history, we call upon unbiased thinkers to engage in earnest dialogue to try and bring about better understanding for both sides that will keep our peoples away from the domain of conflict and prepare the way for a better future for the generations to come who are expecting a lot from us.

We must invite everyone to the process of dialogue that we present to our world, and do so under the umbrella of justice, morality, and human rights, so we can give glad tidings to the world of a process that will bring about for it peace and tremendous good.

To the extent that dialogue is necessary and effective, it must maintain a tone of respect, clarity, and frankness. These are the prerequisites for its success. Dialogue itself can only be built upon such a foundation, and those participating in it must be willing to accept criticism and correction unflinchingly.

Therefore we say clearly and in total frankness that we are prepared to discuss any issue raised by the West, realizing that there are a number of concepts, moral values, rights, and ideas that we share with the West and that can be nurtured to bring about what is best for all of us. This means that we have common objectives. Nevertheless, we, just like you, possess our own governing principles and priorities and our own cultural assumptions.

Our Values and Guiding Principles

There are a number of basic principles and moral values that govern our dealings with other nations. These were set forth fourteen centuries ago by the messenger of Islam, Muhammad. This was before human rights organizations existed and before there was a United Nations with its international charters. Let us look at some of these:

1. The human being is inherently a sacred creation. It is forbidden to transgress against any human being, irrespective of color, ethnicity, or religion. The Qur'an says: "We have honored the descendants of Adam" (17:70).
2. It is forbidden to kill a human soul unjustly. Killing a single person is to God as heinous as killing all of humanity, just as saving a single person from death is as weighty as saving the lives of all humanity. The Qur'an says: "If anyone killed a person except as recompense for murder or spreading havoc in the land, then it would be as if he killed all of humanity. And if anyone saved a life, it would be as if he saved the lives of all humanity" (5:32).
3. It is forbidden to impose a religious faith upon a person. The Qur'an says: "There is no compulsion in religion" (2:256). A person will not even be considered a Muslim if he or she accepted Islam under duress.
4. The message of Islam asserts that human relationships must be established on the highest moral standards. Muhammad said: "I was only sent to perfect good conduct." The Qur'an says: "We sent aforetime

our messengers with clear signs and sent down with them the scripture and the balance so the people could establish justice. And We sent down iron wherein is mighty power and many benefits for mankind" (57:25). We read in another place in the Qur'an: "God does not restrain you with regard to those who do not fight you on account of your faith nor drive you out of your homes from dealing kindly and justly with them, for God loves those who are just" (60:8).

5. All the resources of the Earth were created for humanity. The Qur'an addresses this when it says: "It is He who has created for you all that is on the Earth" (2:29). These resources were only created for human beings to benefit from them within the limits of justice and for the betterment of humanity. Therefore, spoiling the environment, spreading havoc on Earth, perpetrating violence against weaker nations and fighting to wrest from them their wealth and the fruits of their prosperity, is conduct that is reviled by God. In the Qur'an we read: "When he turns his back, his aim is to spread mischief throughout the Earth and destroy crops and cattle, but Allah does not love mischief" (2:205) and: "Do not make mischief in the Earth after it has been set in order" (7:56).

6. Responsibility for a crime rests solely upon the perpetrator of that crime. No one may be punished for the crimes of another. The Qur'an says: "No bearer of burdens must bear the burdens of another" (35:18).

7. Justice for all people is their inalienable right. Oppressing them is forbidden, irrespective of their religion, color, or ethnicity. The Qur'an states: "And whenever you speak, speak justly, even if a close relative is concerned" (6:152).

8. Dialogue and invitation must be done in the best possible manner. The Qur'an says: "Invite to the way of your Lord with wisdom and good preaching and argue with them in the best manner" (16:125).

We believe in these principles, as our religion commands us to. They are the teachings of Muhammad. They agree to some extent with some of the principles that the American intellectuals put forth in their paper. We see that this agreement gives us a good platform for discussion that can bring about good for all of mankind.

The Events of September 11 and Their Implications

It is completely unreasonable to turn the tragic events of September 11 into a means of categorizing our world's ideologies, civilizations, and societies. Those attacks were unwelcome to many people in the Muslim world due to the values and moral teachings of Islam that they violated.

At the same time, we find strange the hasty conclusions made about the motivations of the attackers, restricting them to an attack on American society and its universal human values. Without going into a lengthy argument about the matter, we see it as our right and the right of all impartial thinkers, as well as the right of all Americans, to inquire as to why the attackers did not choose some other country that adheres to the same Western values. Why did they not turn their attention to other nations and societies in Asia and Africa that subscribe to idolatrous religions, for they would have been more deserving of attack if the issue with the attackers was to fight against those who disagreed with their values? Moreover, Islam teaches that the Christians are closer to the Muslims than any other people. History tells us that the prophet of Islam, Muhammad, during the early years of Islam, sent a group of his followers to one of the Christian kings of Ethiopia, because his kingdom enjoyed an unparalleled recognition of rights. It also tells us that Prophet Muhammad sent a letter to the Christian king of Rome and one to the Christian king of the Copts. Both letters were received graciously. The Qur'an speaks about the Christians as being the most morally virtuous in their dealings of all religious societies outside of Islam: "You will find that the strongest among men in enmity to the believers are the Jews and pagans, and you will find that the nearest of them in love to the believers are those who say: 'We are Christians'" (5:82).

Why must we ignore this history and permit a superficial and premature reading of events? This is not all. The laws that Islam came with are there to establish a stable life for both those who believe in it and those who do not. Furthermore, the Qur'an describes the Prophet Muhammad as "a mercy to all humanity." Yet, when one faction prefers to create a conflict with the Muslims or to ignore their rights, then Islam responds with resistance and self-defense, which are among the objectives of *jihad*. The West must realize that by blocking specific options and the moderate aspirations of the Muslim world and by creating conflicts, they will bring about perspectives in the Muslim world that will be hard to overcome in the future and will create problems for generations to come all over the world.

It is unreasonable to assume that those who attacked the United States on September 11 did not feel in some way justified for what they did because of the decisions made by the United States in numerous places throughout the world. We by no means hold the view that they were justified in striking civilian targets, but it is necessary to recognize that some sort of causative relationship exists between American policy and what happened.

From another angle, if we were to assume that the perpetrators of the September 11 attacks against the United States were the work of some special faction from within Europe, China, or Japan, or even a religious faction of the Jews, would America's decision then have been to subject them and their nations to the type of aggression that they are now confronting the Muslims with? This policy only supplies more evidence to the alleged perpetrators and their sympathizers for their claim that America is oppressing and aggressing against the Muslim world.

The events of September 11 should be an impetus for establishing a new assemblage of international institutions to establish justice and secure people's rights. They are needed to supplant institutions like the United Nations General Assembly and the UN Security Council that were established after the two World Wars to defuse the war between imperious nations. Those institutions failed to realize justice and security for the weaker peoples or protect their countries. Institutions are needed that will not act merely as a theatre for extending the reach of the great powers. How many peoples have become wretched and had their resources stripped away from them by force for the benefit of those overbearing powers?

Likewise, those events should make us turn our attention to the fact that exaggerated strength, no matter how many ways it might manifest itself, is never a sufficient guarantee of security. A small group, if they have the will, can cause massive harm and injury to their opponents, no matter how strong those opponents might be.

We have learned from history that power is not the only way to guarantee security, since the types of guarantees that come with sheer power carry with them the seeds of failure and collapse and are always accompanied by resentment and discontent from one side and arrogance from the other. But when those guarantees are built upon justice, then the possibility of their success is far greater.

If the Americans view what happened on September 11 as a turning point for them in how they define their relationship with Muslims generally, not merely with the group of people that actually carried it out, then can we be blamed when we see that the presence of the Jewish state of Israel on Palestinian land and the control they hold over it through the support of the major powers was and still is a decisive factor in defining and shaping our relationship with the West, as well as with its values and institutions?

Our Position on America

We can easily see today that the Eastern block—Japan and China—seems more alien to the understanding of the Islamic World than does the West. There are many more bridges connecting the Islamic World to the West than there are connecting it to the East. There likewise exist mutually beneficial relationships and common interests between the Muslim World and the West. It should be assumed that the West perceives it in their best interests for there to be balance and stability in the Muslim World and that it knows that the Muslim lands have provided much for them, especially economically. The West is the primary beneficiary of Muslim economic strength.

In spite of this, every individual in the Muslim World perceives that China and Japan have not caused the Muslim World any clear problem, nor have they done anything detrimental to its concerns, countries, and societies. The average Muslim perceives Easterners to be more just, balanced, and more clement than the West. This feeling has been instilled in the minds of the individual members of Muslim society by the West itself.

If the United States sought to withdraw from the world outside its borders and removed its hand from inflammatory issues, then Muslims would
not be bothered whether or not it is a progressive, democratic, or secular
nation.

The disagreement between us and American society is not about values
of justice or the choice of freedoms. Values, as we see it, are of two types.
First there are those basic human values shared by all people, values that are
in harmony with the innate nature of the human being and that our religion
calls us to. Then there are those values that are particular to a given society.
That society chooses those values and gives preference to them. We do not
wish to compel that society to abandon them since our religion teaches us
that there is no compulsion in religion.

It goes without saying that a number of those values are social preferences that are drawn from their given environment.

Likewise, we do not accept that others can force us to change our values
or deny us the right to live by them. We see it as our right—and the right of
every people—to make clear to others what we believe in order to foster better
understanding between the people of the Earth, bring about the realization
of world peace, and create opportunities for those who are searching for the
truth.

The United States, in spite of its efforts in establishing the United
Nations with its Universal Declaration of Human Rights and other similar
institutions, is among the most antagonistic nations to the objectives of these
institutions and to the values of justice and truth. This is clearly visible in
America's stance on the Palestinian issue and its unwavering support for the
Zionist occupation of Palestinian land and its justification of all the Zionist
practices that run contrary to the resolutions passed by the United Nations.
It is clearly visible in how America provides Israel with the most advanced
weapons that they turn against women, children, and old men, and with
which they topple down people's homes. At the same time, we see the Bush
administration mobilizing its military strength and preparing for war against
other countries like Iraq, justifying its actions with the claim that these countries are perpetrating human rights abuses and behaving aggressively towards
their neighbors.

This conduct of theirs creates in others a mental image of the United
States of America as a nation that respects neither international organizations nor the moral principles upon which democracy rests.

A number of the values mentioned by the American thinkers are not
exclusively American values. They come from many sources and represent the
contributions of many civilizations, among them the Islamic civilization.
Muslims and many others throughout the world do not see these values in
America because these values are effectively concealed by America's actions.
The ideal circumstances for cooperation will not be realized as long as
American civilization remains in perpetual fear of growing weak or losing its
hold on the world, and is perpetually concerned with keeping others from
developing, especially the nations of the so-called third world.

Islam and Secularism

The signatories to the American paper focused on the necessity of the separation of church and state, and they considered this to be a universal value that all the nations of the Earth should adopt. We Muslims approach the problem of the relationship between religion and the state differently. Our understanding is to protect the will of the majority and their rights while also protecting the rights of the minority. Islam is a comprehensive religion that has specific laws addressing all aspects of life. It is difficult for a nation to be respected and taken seriously by its people in an Islamic environment without adopting the laws of that religion in general. State adoption of the religion does not mean an infringement on the particular needs of the minorities who live within it or their being forced to abandon their religion and embrace Islam. The idea that there is no compulsion in religion is firmly planted in the Muslim mindset and is clearly stated in the Qur'an. The separation of church and state that the American thinkers are calling for in their letter shows a lack of understanding of how religion acts as a formative basis for culture in Islamic societies. We see secularism as inapplicable to Muslim society, because it denies the members of that society the right to apply the general laws that shape their lives and it violates their will on the pretext of protecting minorities. It does not stand to reason that protecting the rights of the minority should be accomplished by violating the rights of the majority. We see that the real concern of a religious minority is the protection of its rights and not the violation of the rights of the majority, since infringing upon the rights of the majority is not conducive to social stability and peace, whereas the rights of the minority in Muslim society are protected.

We believe that Islam is the truth, though it is not possible for the entire world to be Muslim. It is neither possible for us to force others to think the way we do, nor would Islamic Law allow us to do so if we were able to. This is a personal choice in Islamic Law. The thing that we have to do is explain the message of Islam, which is a guidance and a mercy to all humanity. However, we are not heedless of the necessities brought about by the present state of humanity and of the need to remove the obstacles that prevent people from properly understanding the message of Islam so they can, if they choose, adopt it of their own free will.

Muslims have the right to adhere to their religion, its values, and its teachings. This is an option that it will be difficult to try and withhold from them. Nevertheless, what we present is a moderate and balanced understanding and go forward to propagate it, and the West shall see that it is very different than the notions that they have about Islam. This is if the West is truly willing to afford us, our religion, and our abilities proper recognition, or at least willing to study the facts of our religion and our values in a rational and objective manner.

Islam is not an enemy of civilization; it rejects utilizing the notion of civilization for negative ends. Nor is Islam an enemy of human rights and freedoms; it rejects transforming freedoms and rights into a tool for conflict just as it rejects relying upon a limited cultural vision as if it is a universal law that must be generally applied to all, forcibly if need be. Continuing to insist upon this vision, even if it is depicted as religiously tolerant, is no less extreme than what goes on in those radical religious groups.

Oppressing others necessarily means that a choice in favor of conflict has been made. It is the catalyst that inflames the strength of resistance, which creates conditions where causing injury to others takes little instigation. The West has to realize that destruction is the least technologically dependent product in the world. It can be produced in countless ways. This will give birth to more forms of radicalism within all societies, including those that adopt separation of church and state. Those might actually turn out to be the most proficient practitioners of this type of extremism.

Just War and Terrorism

The West often speaks of the problem of terrorism and radicalism. In our view, this problem is a serious one for the world and a number of measures must be taken to deal with it. At the same time, we wish to emphasize the following points that appear to us very reasonable:

First, radicalism is not intrinsically tied to religion. Radicalism can take many forms: political, economic, or ideological. These should be given the same level of attention, because they seek to overturn the moral principles and the systems that secure human rights throughout the world.

Also, religious radicalism is not restricted to one particular religion. We admit there are radical elements among Muslims; we are also well aware that every religious persuasion in the world has its radical elements. Those who study religious thought and culture attest to this fact. Therefore, it is both unreasonable and unjust to irrationally push the issue of Islamic radicalism and then take a course of action that will further instigate it without dealing with all forms of radicalism in the world, both religious and otherwise.

Second, while we believe that the world is confronted by terrorism and radicalism in the broad sense that we have just described, we should also consider that there are a host of other problems that the world is facing with respect to rights, freedoms, and basic human needs like education, health, and nutrition. All of these need to be addressed.

We realize that many of the extremist Islamic groups—as they are called—did not want to be that way when they started, but were forced into that category by political or military forces or media machinery that blocked their access to channels of peaceful expression. Such powers were able to do away with any possible opportunity for moderation and to strike at the rights of people. This is the major cause for the extremism of Islamic movements and groups. We also realize that this same situation is right now occurring under the guise of the Western program known as the War on Terror.

Stability is the basis for rights and freedoms throughout the world. When we deny people stability and force them to live in perpetual anxiety, oppression, and misery, then they become more likely to act in an immoral and unethical manner. Bitter reality is what sets down decisions. Moreover, it is sometimes what shapes people's thoughts. When people wait a long time without their rights being addressed, it becomes highly likely that they will behave in ways that are difficult to predict and that lead to uncertain consequences.

We seriously call upon the West to become more open to Islam, look more seriously at its own programs, and behave more mildly toward the Islamic world. We also call upon them to earnestly review their position on Islam and to open channels of dialogue with prominent Islamic thinkers representing the broad current of Islamic thought and intellectuals and decision makers in the West.

It is important for the West to realize that most of the Islamic movements throughout the Muslim world and elsewhere are essentially moderate. It is necessary to maintain this situation. Moderate movements should have their rights respected. Nothing should be allowed to inflame situations for any reason. People need to be able to conduct themselves rationally and with a sense of security.

We are committed to fighting against terrorism, whether it comes from the Muslims or elsewhere. However, as long as the matter is being referred back to moral values, then why not mention other radical extremists? Why not talk about the Palestinians who are exposed, especially these days, to the most loathsome kind of terrorism possible? Their cities and refugee camps are being torn to the ground, mass murder is carried out against them, and a suffocating siege is imposed upon their innocent civilians. This is not being carried out by some individuals or secret organizations. It is being executed by the state of Israel, a member of the United Nations.

If the purpose is to pull up terrorism from its roots, then all out war is not the appropriate course of action, but peace and justice is. The world must seek this in Palestine and elsewhere.

Terrorism, according to the restricted meaning that is being used today, is but one of the forms of wrongful aggression being carried out against lives and property. It is immoral to focus on one form of aggression and turn a blind eye to all others, even though they might be more destructive and repugnant. This is a clear case of selective vision and the use of double standards.

Third, concocting conflicts does no good for either side. Those who represent conflict are not always the best representatives of this faction or that. There is nothing better than justice, consideration of people's rights and adhering to our moral values to dispel the specter of conflict. These principles must be maintained even in times of war when we are forced to go down that road.

In the West, instigating conflict stems from considering and protecting national—if not partisan—interests, even at the expense of the rights of others. The truth is that this policy is what creates a dangerous threat to national security, not only for the West, but for the entire world, not to mention the tragic and inhuman conditions that it produces.

The men throughout the world who are behind these conflicts are, by their decisions and their policies, preparing the masses to turn against them. We must intelligently monitor their behavior and protect our civil societies and the rights and security of our people. We must realize that having conflict mongers in power around the world will bring about the worst situation possible for us in the present, as well as for the future generations who will have to face the effects of our personal calculations. Yes, we should be optimistic, but we must also be clear in accounting for our actions and assessing their effects.

Civil security is in a perilous situation throughout the world in the shadow of this scramble to create conflicts and draw up programs for dealing with them. We have to move beyond slogans and realize that policies of conflict in the West are bringing about the destruction of civil security throughout the world in the name of fighting terrorism. The number of civilian casualties in Afghanistan because of American bombing increases without the American administration showing any kind of strain on its mores and values from its so-called "just war." In reality, it seems like they are merely creating circumstances in order to give a new validation for more confrontations here and there. And if the West considers September 11 as an affront to civil security in the West, then we can share with it that feeling and even the stance of rejecting attacks against civil security throughout the world. But it is important for the West to realize that civil security in the Islamic World has not seen stability for decades and a lot of the impediments to civil security have come about under the umbrella of Western policy and quite possibly due the direct actions of the West.

It is about time we realize that the use of military force or the power of the media provides no real guarantee for the future. Often matters take surprising turns, going off in directions that defy our estimation. It is as if the events of September 11 showed the uncertainty in this estimation.

Therefore, creating more avenues for dialogue and the exchange of ideas where scholars and thinkers can meet with each other is, in our opinion, the alternative to the language of violence and destruction. This is what compels us to write this letter and to participate in this discussion.

Signatories

Dr. Ibrahim b. Muhammad al-Shahwan, *Associate Professor at the School of Agriculture, King Sa'ud University*

Dr. Ibrahim b. Hamad al-Rayyis, *Member of the Teachers Board, King Sa'ud University*

Dr. Ibrahim al-Fayiz, *Associate Professor at the School of Islamic Law, Al-Imam University*

Dr. Ibrahim b. Salih al-Salamah, *School of Agriculture, King Sa'ud University*

Dr. Ibrahim Abd Allah al-Lahim, *Professor of Hadīth Studies, Al-Imam University*

Dr. Ibrahim al-Jam'an, *King Fahd Hospital*

Ibrahim b. Abd al-Rahman al-Bulayhi, *Author*

Dr. Ibrahim b. Abd Allah al-Duwayyish, *Islamic Worker and Member of the Teachers Board, Teachers' College*

Dr. Ahmed b. Said Derbas, Ph.D. Michigan State University, *Associate Professor of Education*

Dr. Ahmad al-Umayr, *Consultant at King Fahd Hospital*

Dr. Ahmad b. Uthman al-Tuwayjiri, *Member of the Consultative Council*

Dr. Ahmad b. Rashid al-Sa'id, *Member of the Teachers Board, King Sa'ud University*

Dr. Ahmad b. Ibrahim al-Turki, *Professor of Microbiology at the School of Agriculture, King Sa'ud University*

Dr. Ahmad b. Muhammad al-Shab'an, *Professor of Human Geography, Al-Imam University*

Asma al-Husayn, *Professor of Psychology, College of Education*

Dr. Afrah al-Humaydi, *Professor at the Department of Islamic Studies, Girls' College*

Dr. Umaymah bint Ahmad al-Jalahimah, *Professor of Comparative Religion, King Faysal University*

Thamer M. al-Maiman, *Author and Journalist*

Jamil Farsi, MS, *Management, San Diego, California, and Jeweler*

Dr. Jawahir bint Muhammad b. Sultan, *Lecturer and Education Director*

Jawahir bint Abd al-Rahman al-Juraysi, *Education Director*

Jawahir bint Muhammad al-Khathlan, *Directorate of Girls' Education*

Dr. Hasan al-Qahtani, *Consultant, King Fahd Hospital*

Dr. Hasan b. Salih al-Humayd, *Former Professor of Qur'anic Studies, Al-Imam University*

Dr. Hamad b. Ibrahim al-Haydari, *Professor of Islamic Law, Al-Imam University*

Hamad b. Abd al-Aziz b. Abd al-Muhsin al-Tuwayjiri, *Businessman*

Dr. al-Sharif Hamzah al-Fa'r, *Professor at the School of Islamic Law, Umm al-Qura University*

Dr. Khalid al-Qasim, *Professor at the Department of Islamic Studies, King Sa'ud University*

Dr. Khalid b. Abd al-Rahman al-Ujaymi, *Assistant Professor of Arabic Language, Al-Imam University*

Dr. Khalid b. Abd Allah al-Duwish, *Professor of Electrical Engineering, King Sa'ud University*

Dr. Khadijah Abd al-Majid, *Saudi Intellectual*

Dr. Khalid b. Muhammad al-Sulayman, *Professor of Mechanical Engineering at the King Abd al-Aziz City of Science and Technology*

Dr. Khalid b. Fahd al-Awdah, *Professor of Educational Theory, Al-Imam University*

Khalid b. Nasir al-Rudayman, *Professor at the School of Agriculture, King Sa'ud University*

Dr. Khalid b. Ali al-Mushayqih, *Professor of Islamic Law, Al-Imam University*

Dr. Riyad b. Muhammad al-Musaymiri, *Professor at the School of Theology, Al-Imam University*

Dr. Ruqayyah al-Muharib, *Professor at the Department of Islamic Studies at the Girls' College*

Dr. Rashid al-Ulaywi, *Professor at the School of Islamic Law, Al-Imam University*

Dr. Zaynab al-Dakhil, *Professor at the School of Theology, Al-Imam University*

Suhaylah Zayn al-Abidin, *Author*

Dr. Sa'd b. Abd al-Karim al-Shadukhi, *Professor of Education, Al-Imam University*

Dr. Salem Ahmad Sahab, Ph.D., Mathematics, 1981, Colorado State University, *Weekly Columnist,* Al-Madina Newspaper, *Jeddah*

Dr. Soad Jaber, *Associate Professor of Pediatrics at the School of Medicine, King Abd al-Aziz University, Jeddah*

Dr. Sa'id b. Nasir al-Ghamidi, *Professor of Theology, King Khalid University*

Dr. Sulayman b. Qasim al-Id, *Professor at the Department of Islamic Studies, King Sa'ud University*

Dr. Sami al-Suwaylim, *Member of the Islamic Law Commission, al-Rajhi Banking and Investment Corporation*

Sa'ud al-Fanaysan, *Professor of Qur'anic Studies and Former Dean of the School of Islamic Law, Al-Imam University*

Dr. Sa'ud b. Khalaf al-Dihan, *Researcher at the King Abd al-Aziz City for Science and Technology*

Sami al-Majid, *Member of the Teachers Board at the School of Islamic Law, Al-Imam University*

Salman b. Fahd al-Oadah, *Former Member of the Teachers Board at the School of Theology, Al-Imam University and General Director of the IslamToday Website*

Dr. Sultan b. Khalid b. Hithlin, *Professor of Islamic Studies, King Fahd University*

Sarah bint Muhammad al-Khathlan, *Author and Poet*

Sulayman b. Ibrahim al-Rushudi, *Attorney and Former Judge*

Dr. Sulayman b. Abd al-Aziz al-Yahya, *Dean of the School of Agriculture and Veterinary Medicine, King Sa'ud University*

Dr. Sulayman al-Rushudi, *King Abd al-Aziz City for Science and Technology*

Sulayman al-Majid, *Judge at al-Ahsa Court of Law*

Dr. Safar b. Abd al-Rahman al-Hawali, *Former Head of the Department of Theology, Umm al-Qura University*

Dr. Salih Muhammad al-Sultan, *Professor at the School of Islamic Law, Al-Imam University*

Dr. Salih b. Sulayman al-Wuhaybi, *Associate Professor at the School of Arts, King Sa'ud University and Associate General Director, World Assembly of Muslim Youth*

Dr. Salih b. Abd Allah al-Lahim, *Professor of Islamic Law, Al-Imam University*

Dr. Salih b. Abd al-Aziz al-Tuwayjiri, *Professor of Theology, Al-Imam University*

Tariq b. Abd al-Rahman al-Hawwas, *Professor of Islamic Law, Al-Imam University*

Dr. Ayid b. Abd Allah al-Qarni, *Former Professor of Hadîth Studies, Al-Imam University*

Dr. Abdul Mohsin Helal, Ph.D. International Relations, *Umm al-Qura University, Mecca*

Dr. Abdullah S. Mannaa, *Author, Publisher, and Former Editor-in-Chief,* Iqraa *and* Al-I'lam Wal-Itisal *magazines*

Dr. Omar A. Kamel, *Saudi Author and Researcher*

Omar Jastaneyeh, *Journalist*

Abd al-Aziz b. Muhammad al-Qasim, *Attorney and Former Judge*

Abd Allah b. Abd al-Aziz b. Abd al-Muhsin al-Tuwayjiri, *Businessman*

Dr. Abd al-Aziz Nasir al-Sibih, *Associate Professor of Psychology, Al-Imam University*

Dr. Abd al-Aziz b. Ibrahim al-Shahwan, *Professor and Former Dean of the School of Theology, Al-Imam University*

Dr. Abd Allah b. Wukayyil al-Shaykh, *Professor of Hadîth Studies at the Department of Prophetic Traditions, Islamic Theological College*

Dr Abd al-Wahhab b. Nasir al-Turayri, *Former Professor at the Islamic Theological College and Academic Director of the IslamToday Website*

Dr. Abd Allah al-Khalaf, *Assistant Professor at the Institute of Public Administration, Riyadh*

Dr. Awad b. Muhammad al-Qarni, *Professor at the School of Islamic Law, Al-Imam University*

Dr. Imran al-Imrani, *University Professor*

Dr. Abd al-Rahman b. Abd Allah al-Shumayri, *Professor at the School of Islamic Law, Umm al-Qura University*

Dr. Ali Ba Dahdah, *Professor at the Department of Islamic Studies, King Abd al-Aziz University*

Abd al-Karim al-Juhayman, *Author and Journalist*

Dr. Abd al-Karim b. Ibrahim al-Sallum, *Professor at the School of Islamic Law, Al-Imam University*

Dr. Abd al-Rahman al-Zunaydi, *Professor at the School of Islamic Law, Al-Imam University*

Dr. Abd Allah b. Ibrahim al-Turayqi, *Professor at the School of Islamic Law, Al-Imam University*

Dr. Umar al-Mudayfir, *Head of the Department of Psychiatry, King Fahd Hospital*

Dr. Abd al-Aziz b. Nasir al-Mani, *Professor of Arabic Literature at the Department of Arabic Language Studies, King Sa'ud University*

Dr. Abd Allah b. Nafi al-Shari, *Professor of Psychology and Former Trustee, King Sa'ud University and President of al-Nafi Office for Academic Counseling*

Dr. Abd al-Rahman b. Hadi al-Shamrani, *Assistant Professor at the School of Arts, King Sa'ud University*

Dr. Abd Allah al-Hajjaj, *Consultant, King Fahd Hospital*

Dr. Abd Allah b. Saud al-Bishr, *Member of the Teachers Board, King Sa'ud University*

Dr. Abd al-Aziz b. Ibrahim al-Amri, *Professor of History, Al-Imam University*

Abd al-Aziz al-Wushayqri, *Justice at the Supreme Court, Riyadh*

Dr. Abd al-Aziz al-Fadda, *Consultant, King Fahd Hospital*

Dr. Abd al-Rahman b. Abd al-Latif al-Usayl, *Professor of International Relations, King Fahd University*

Dr. Abd Allah b. Abd al-Aziz al-Yahya, *Assistant General Director of Islamic Propagation*

Dr. Abd Allah al-Zayidi, *Professor at the School of Islamic Law, Al-Imam University*

Abd al-Rahman b. Abd al-Aziz al-Mujaydil, *Member of the Teachers Board at the School of Theology, Al-Imam University*

Dr. Abd al-Qadir b. Abd al-Rahman al-Haydar, *School of Medicine, King Sa'ud University*

Dr. Abd Allah b. Abd al-Karim al-Uthaym, *Professor of Educational Development, Al-Imam University*

Dr. Abd Allah b. Ali al-Ju'aythin, *Former Professor of Hadîth Studies, Al-Imam University*

Dr. Umar Abd Allah al-Suwaylim, *Assistant Professor of Electrical Engineering at the School of Engineering, King Fahd University of Petroleum and Minerals*

Abd Allah b. Abd al-Rahman al-Jibrin, *Former Member of the Council for Legal Rulings*

Dr. Abd al-Rahman b. Abd Allah al-Jibrin, *Professor at the School of Islamic Law, Al-Imam University*

Dr. Abd al-Rahman b. Salih al-Khalifah, *Professor at the School of Agriculture, King Sa'ud University*

Dr. Abd Allah b. Hamad al-Sakakir, *Professor of Islamic Law, Al-Imam University*

Dr. Abd al-Aziz b. Salih al-Sam'ani, *Professor of Linguistics, Technology College*

Fayez Saleh Jamal, *Journalist,* Al-Nadwa Newspaper *and* Al-Madina Newspaper

Dr. Fahd b. Muhammad al-Rumayyan, *Professor at the School of Agriculture, King Sa'ud University*

Dr. Fahd b. Salih al-Fallaj, *Professor at the School of Technology, Indiana University of Pennsylvania*

Dr. Luluah al-Matrudi, *Professor at the School of Islamic Law, Al-Imam University*

Muhammad b. Marzuq al-Mu'aytiq, *Former Appellate Judge and Chief Justice, Al-Zulqa Court of Law*

Muhammad b. Salih al-Ali, *Member of the Teachers Board, Al-Imam University*

Muhammad b. Abd al-Aziz b. Abd al-Muhsin al-Tuwayjiri, *Businessman*

Mohammad Salahuddin Aldandarawi, *Jounalist and Publisher*

Dr. Muhammad b. Salih al-Fawzan, *Professor of Qur'anic Studies, Teachers College*

Dr. Mohammad Saeed Farsy, Ph.D., *Architectural Engineering and Former Mayor of the City of Jeddah*

Mohamed Said Tayeb, *Attorney, Publisher, and Political Activist*

Muhammad b. Abd al-Aziz al-Amir, *Justice at the Jeddah Court of Law*

Muhammad b. Sulayman al-Mas'ud, *Justice at the Jeddah Court of Law*

Dr. Muhammad b. Ahmad al-Salih, *Professor of Graduate Studies at the School of Islamic Law and Member of the Academic Board, Al-Imam University*

Muhammad b. Salih al-Duhaym, *Judge at al-Layth Court of Law*

Muhammad b. Hamad al-Mini, *Member of the Teachers Board at the School of Agriculture, King Sa'ud University*

Dr. Muhsin b. Husayn al-Awaji, *Associate Professor of Education and Founder/Director of al-Muntada al-Wasatiyyah*

Dr. Muhammad b. Sulayman al-Sudays, *Professor of Arabic Literature at the Department of Arabic language Studies, King Sa'ud University*

Dr. Muhammad b. Abd al-Rahman al-Hudayf, *Author, Scholar, and Former Member of the Teachers Board, King Sa'ud University*

Dr. Mani b. Hammad al-Juhani, *Member of the Consultative Council and General Director, World Assembly of Muslim Youth*

Dr. Marzuq b. Sunaytan b. Tinbak, *Professor of Arabic Literature, School of Arts, King Sa'ud University*

Dr. Mansur b. Ibrahim al-Hazimi, *Professor of Contemporary Arabic Literature, King Sa'ud University*

Dr. Malik b. Ibrahim al-Ahmad, *Member of the Teachers Board, King Sa'ud University*

Dr. Muhammad b. Sa'ud al-Bishr, *Member of the Teachers Board, Al-Imam University*

Dr. Muhammad b. Nasir al-Ja'wan, *Founder and Director of the Hunayn School*

Muna bint Ibrahim al-Mudayhish, *Lecturer at the School of Arabic Language, Al-Imam University*

Muhammad b. Salih b. Sultan, *Chief of Administration, al-Yamamah Institute of Journalism*

Mahdi al-Hakami, *University Professor and Regional Director of the World Assembly of Muslim Youth, Jizan*

Dr. Muhammad al-Wuhaybi, *Professor of Theology, King Sa'ud University*

Dr. Muhammad Umar Jamjum, *Professor of Civil Engineering and former General Secretary, King Abd al-Aziz University*

Dr. Muhammad Umar Zubayr, *Former General Director, King Abd al-Aziz University*

Dr. Muhammad b. Abd Allah al-Shamrani, *Professor of Islamic Law, King Sa'ud University*

Dr. Muhammad Abd al-Latif, *Consultant, King Fahd Hospital*

Dr. Muhammad al-Zuwayyid, *Consultant, King Fahd Hospital*

Dr. Muhammad b. Sulayman al-Barrak, *Al-Imam University*

Dr. Muhammad al-Urayni, *Consultant, King Fahd Hospital*

Dr. Muhammad b. Abd Allah al-Muhaymid, *Former Head of the Department of Islamic Law, Al-Imam University*

Dr. Muhammad Abd al-Aziz al-Awhali, *Associate Professor of Physics, School of Science, King Fahd University of Petroleum and Minerals*

Dr. Muhammad b. Sulayman al-Fawzan, *Professor of Hadīth Studies, Al-Imam University*

Dr. Muhammad b. Ali al-Suwid, *Chairman of the English Department, Al-Imam University*

Dr. Nora Khaled Alsaad, *Assistant Professor at the School of Arts, Department of Social Sciences, King Abd al-Aziz University*

Nurah bint Abd al-Aziz al-Khariji

Dr. Nasir b. Sa'd al-Rashid, *Professor of Arabic Literature, King Sa'ud University*

Dr. Nasir b. Masfar al-Zahrani, *Member of the Teachers Board, Umm al-Qura University*

Dr. Nasir b. Abd al-Karim al-Aql, *Professor of Theology, Al-Imam University*

Dr. Nabih b. Abd al-Rahman al-Jabr, *Professor at the Department of Accounting, Al-Imam University*

Dr. Nasir b. Sulayman al-Umar, *Former Professor of Qur'anic Studies, Al-Imam University*

Dr. Yusuf al-Ulah, *Consultant, King Fahd Hospital*

Ahmad b. Abd al-Rahman al-Suwayyan, *Editor-in-Chief,* Al-Bayan Magazine

"How We Can Coexist" originally appeared on http://www.islamtoday.net on April 29, 2002. Reprinted with permission.

Eight

∽

Please Prostrate Yourselves Privately

∾

'Abul Bara,
Center for Islamic Research and Studies

God shall be praised, Who said:

> [Muslims shall say:] "O people of the book,[1] come to a common word [of agreement], which is to not to worship any god but God and not to associate partners with God; not to make lords from some of your people." If the people of the book refuse this, then say: "Bear witness that we are Muslims."

Peace and Prayers Be Upon (PPBU) the Prophet who said: "God's curse be upon Jews and Christians who made the tombs of their prophets into mosques."[2]

At a time when Muslims' lives, honor, property, and lands are being attacked all over the world by the hands of the malevolent *nassara*,[3] headed by the protector of world infidelity, the U.S.A., we have received a statement from a group of [Saudi] intellectuals that represents the ultimate degree of subjugation, a self-defeating mindset, a defection from religious texts, and a fragmenting of the truth, i.e., focusing on some parts of the truth, while ignoring others. This statement, entitled "How We Can Coexist" was an answer to a previous statement written by the crusaders'[4] intellectuals and priests, a statement which they titled: "What We're Fighting For." After an era in which Islam was cherished and well-respected, when Islam more or less controlled the lives of infidels worldwide, we are now witnessing people who claim to follow Islam and its great ancestors[5] saying that we seriously need to coexist in peace with the West. It is only God Who can give us strength and support.

In the following lines, I will expose the errors of this statement.[6] I admit that, in doing so, I focus on some of the errors of this statement that are very minimal compared with those errors that I am not addressing. I must also admit that what is right in my criticism comes from God, and what is wrong has its source in me and evil.

The Statement's Contents

This statement came at an inappropriate time. What we expected from people like these was an appeal to the will of the men of the nation to defend their religion, their faith, and to avenge the blood that was shed by the Jews and crusaders everywhere. Instead of making a statement to bring victory to vulnerable people everywhere by all rightful means, these intellectuals produced a discourse that is no more than a way of begging and petitioning the West to start a dialogue with us. These intellectuals have taken the wrong course. Asking for a dialogue gives validity to the West's values and principles, and makes the intellectuals appear to be ashamed of stating the truth of their religion and its foundations. Such a statement is evidence of a self-defeating mindset. Indeed, this mindset was made clear by the title of the statement. The title was "How We Can Coexist"—as if it is part of our religion to coexist with the infidels!! It would have been better if this statement had clarified the stance of the Qur'an and the Sayings of the Prophet, (PPBUH), on how Muslims and infidels can coexist. However, the statement's authors have preferred to define "coexistence" from the standpoint of the West and what would make it happy.

It is even more startling to know that such a self-defeating statement came as a response to a violent statement released by a group of sixty crusaders entitled "What We're Fighting For." It is not astonishing that crusaders have the impudence to attack Islam, a religion that deserves to be followed and to be spread as a priority for the world. What is shocking is that people who follow Islam have told the infidels that they want to coexist. It is shocking particularly because it comes at a moment in which the infidels are attacking and scorning Islam and launching a crusader war against Islam. It is shocking when we know that the answer of our intellectuals is a call for coexistence, and a comprehensive and just peace. It is only God Who can give us strength and support.

The following was included in the crusaders' statement: "In the name of the general human principles and within a full consciousness of the restrictions and the requirements of a 'just war,' we support our government and community in launching this war."[7]

The crusaders' statement also mentioned: "We are united in saying that the victory of our nation and its allies will be decisive. We additionally believe that we are fighting to protect the general principles of human dignity, and human rights, such principles that form the better hope for humankind."[8] The crusaders also said that they support their government's continued war against Islamic movements in their statement. They said: "They (Islamic movements) declare explicitly their will in using intentional murder to reach their goals."[9] They are clearly referring to al-Qa'ida and other *jihadi* groups in most of their statements: "such movements possess today not just the declared will to use force, but also the capacity, the expertise—which includes the potentiality of reaching and the will to possess—to use chemical, biological and nuclear weapons to massively explode and devastate their targets."[10] After all the above, it is a shame and painful to see that our intellectuals responded by saying that we have common goals, we condemn terrorism and the September 11 attacks, and we want to combat extremism with the West to avoid wars for our people, and we want to coexist in security and comprehensive peace. This answer comes at the same time that the crusaders ask their government and allies to continue their war against Islam. Is this not a self-defeating stance? Does this not go against the true Islam of the Prophet (PPBUH)? To what extent are these intellectuals breaching God's commands? God said:

> O believers! When there is an apostate among you, God will send those whom God loves; those who are unappreciated among the believers, even though they are extremely esteemed among the infidels. Those will fight for the sake of God, as they do not fear any blame. This is God's blessing, which is given to whoever God wants to bless. God is superior and is the knower.

In spite of the way God describes the *mujahidin*,[11] the intellectuals' statement condemns their actions. The statement has included many phrases of total subjugation, begging the crusaders, rejecting *jihad*, and looking only for evidence in the religion that will satisfy the crusaders. It is only God Who can give us strength and support.

The Other Side of the Statement

This self-defeating statement, which defaces the fundamentals of our religion, is the other side of religious dialogues and interfaith conferences. In such events, Islam's representatives have not presented the fundamentals of Islam or the distinctive features of Islam, compared to other religions. They have only spoken about the secondary principles in the religion, such as condemning injustice, forbidding killing, and doing good for the people, and all other principles that do not conflict with other religions. Muslims' representatives in interfaith conferences were ashamed of declaring what is distinctive in Islam as they feared the anger of the West. The Islam of the interfaith conferences does not have *al-wala'* or *al-bara'*.[12] It is an Islam that has no jihad and has no Shari'a[13]—determined penalties. These particular principles are the ones that threaten the West and cause its fear; these constitute the source of the clash between the West and Muslims, not other principles.

Indians, for instance, immolate the wife with her husband when he dies. Buddha's followers view and buy the woman, exactly like any other commodity. Women in Buddhism must worship their husbands alongside the idol they worship. In communism women are dishonored and everybody can have sex with them. There is no property in communism as well. Regulations and principles that conflict with the human instinct exist in many nations' cultures and religions. If Americans claim that they are fighting enemies of freedom and justice, they should have fought all non-Muslim countries that have allowed injustice and lawless freedom, things that have never existed in any religion before.

However, this statement is based on the United Nations' principles and values, which are based on three principles: equality, freedom, and justice. Indeed, what the UN meant by equality, freedom, and justice is not what was explained by the message of the Prophet (PPBUH). The UN meant the strange and the corrupt concepts that exist today in the U.S.A. and Europe; things that make humans like animals. God should be believed when He said: "Those are like camels, they are even more deluded. Those are the negligent of the religion." The conclusion, then, is that the statement intended to find fault with the fundamentals of Islamic faith for the sake of creating a dialogue with the West, in line with the West's concepts and values, not from the Islamic viewpoint. This will be explained more in the following paragraphs.

No Excuse for the Signers of the Statement

It could be argued that the aim of the statement's authors was to relieve the pressures on Muslims who are suffering from the disasters caused by the Americans, even though it may be clear that the statement had a begging quality, declaring that there exist some Muslims who denounce violence, and who support the dialogue between civilizations! However, it seems that the authors themselves are not convinced of what they are doing; they primarily just want to relieve the pressures on the Muslim world. The best description for the writers is God's description, which makes them against God if they become subservient to non-believers. God said: "Believers should not choose non-believers as superiors, while ignoring believers. Those who will do this are not from God. Take a lesson of piety from such practices. God Himself warns you from this. To God is our destiny." The incident in which the Prophet (PPBUH) gives one-third of the yield of Madina to Ghotfan men so that they can stop confronting Muslims could be used in this case to justify the stance of the signers of this statement.

It is true, however, that even taking for granted the good will of the authors, the statement is still unjustifiable from the standpoint of the Qur'an and the sayings of the Prophet (PPBUH). When God says, for instance, "Take a lesson of piety from such practices" this only refers to the case when they are coerced. Coercion in Shari'a has its own particular stipulations.

Stipulations of coercion in Shari'a are not applicable to the case of the statement's authors. They were not forced to write such a statement. To accept that the authors were coerced into writing this statement, Shari'a considers that they had to do whatever the coercers wanted them to do. The proper interpretation of these stipulations means that the coerced people should do whatever the coercers want them to do, but in the most limited way, assuming that the coercion stipulations are applicable in such a case. In addition, removing the injustice against the Muslim world has its own rightful regulations and means, which does not include issuing a statement. The incident of Ghotfan is not applicable here. First, the reality and the context of the Prophet (PPBUH) are totally different from our case here. Second, the Prophet (PPBUH) is the Muslims' leader, but these signers represent only themselves. Finally, these intellectuals are not important from either their government's or the international policy makers' points of view. Nor are they important in their own country's domestic media.

We also have counter-arguments for all those who seek an excuse for the intellectuals who signed this statement—those who portray the case as if it is a case of defending Muslims. The counter-argument should be based in the answers to these questions: Who signed such a statement? Where are their statements condemning the massacres against Muslims in Palestine, in Iraq, in the Philippines, in Indonesia, in Chechnya, in Eritrea, and in Kashmir? Where are their statements denouncing the massacre in Kograt[14] in which 2,000 Muslims were burned alive over twenty days? You intellectuals, where are your statements in which you express your condolences for all the victimized nations, in which you ask God to bless them with patience? Where are your statements in which you look for solutions to the complex problems of the Muslim people? Where are your statements in which you describe the actual terrorism of these perpetrators and those who cooperate with them? Where are your statements concerning Muslim prisoners of war, who are imprisoned in the crusaders' custody? Or is it that Islamic subjugation to the West is more important that than all the above?

What Is the Purpose of the Statement?

Reading this statement, it will be clear that it contradicts many of the Shari'a regulations, particularly the basic ones. The statement also affirms the notion of a "dialogue between civilizations" rather than the "clash of civilizations" thesis. Such an affirmation is totally an infidel one that was formulated by the West. The statement includes as well what may be considered a faulty description of the religion, and it tries to convince Muslims that this incorrect version of the religion is the true Islam. The statement's authors did this only to satisfy the West. It is difficult to list all the dangerous aspects of such a statement to the Muslims' faith. One wonders, if the purpose of this statement is to send an understandable message to the West, then why was it not written directly in English!? Why was such a statement published in Arabic and published for

Muslims, which meant that it would reach the Muslim public? Or was the genuine goal of the statement to dissolve and distort the faith of Muslims, transforming it into a self-defeating faith? (Evidence of which is embedded in the statement.) We may also ask: Is the purpose of the statement to preach to the West about Islam, or to clarify its principles to the West?

All the above questions are easily answered by a knowledgeable and careful reading of this statement. Our goal is just to present a guide for answering these questions.

Ignorance or Negligence!?

Looking at the language and the content of this statement, one may find many phrases that portray the intention of its authors as an attempt to clarify some of the basic Islamic principles for the West, assuming that the West does not know these principles. Based on the assumption that the West is ignorant about Islam, it needs a "dialogue to understand the truth of our religion and its fundamentals." However, the poor writers seem to forget (or to intentionally forget) that the West has colonized Muslim countries for hundreds of years. The West has also destroyed our religious education, introducing a modern one. We still suffer from the consequences of this change today. The poor authors have overlooked the fact that the West, through this colonization, has already learned about every feature of Islam. The poor authors have ignored the fact that the West has many specialized centers to study all facets of Muslims' affairs including their intellectual life, faith, religious scholarship, and social affairs. It is since Orientalists became a presence in our countries that enormous studies about us and our religion have been produced. One of the famous distinctive works is the *al-mu'jam al-mufahras lil-fadh al-hadith*, the "Categorized Dictionary for the Sayings of the Prophet"[15] (PPBUH), a case in which a group of Orientalists collected the sayings of the Prophet (PPBUH) and categorized them. Orientalists wanted to study the nature of Islam and to find contradictions in the sayings of the Prophet so that they could use this in fighting Islam.

In spite of all these facts, the authors argue that our problem with the West is a mere misunderstanding in the West about Islam. Because of this misunderstanding, the West needs some clarification and a dialogue to comprehend our religion. What a pity that the culture and the knowledge that the authors claim to possess have not helped them to know the clearest of things.

Where Are the Religious Foundations of Their Arguments?

The statement did not reduce our problem with the crusaders to a mere problem of the West's misunderstanding of our religion, it also repeatedly attempted to find common ground between Muslims and the crusaders. The statement even has many intellectual and methodological deficiencies. The most serious problem with the statement is that it lacks a clear declaration of our religion's fundamentals which are: believing in God solely and in all His Prophets, following Muhammad (PPBUH), upholding *al-wala' wal-bara',*[16] denying all others worshiped except for God, denying all idols and idolaters, and undertaking jihad for the sake of God's path. The basis of our problem with the West is our belief in the above principles. Therefore, when the Prophet (PPBUH) invited the nassara to Islam, he did not invite them to look for a common understanding, but to worship the sole God. This is the proper interpretation of the verse the statement authors rely on. God said: "O, people of the book, come to a common word." God did not stop at that point, and did not call for finding a common ground of justice, freedom, and values. On the contrary, God continues the verse: "Not to worship but God and not to associate another god with God; not to make lords from our people or yours, while neglecting God. If they accept this, ask them to testify: 'We are Muslims.'" Based on this, why didn't the authors cite the complete verse?

The West is aggressive toward us because of al-wala' wal-bara' and jihad. Hence, how and why are the authors directing their discourse to the infidels—who attack our religion verbally and physically—while focusing on secondary issues that are not at the heart of our problem with the West? The West wants us to abandon al-wala' wal-bara' and to end jihad. This is what the West especially wants us to do. Do these intellectuals think that Muslims are permitted to relinquish al-wala' wal-bara' as well as jihad, in order to coexist with the West?

Is developing an environment of understanding between us and the West part of the Shari'a's basic requirements? It is mentioned in this statement that its writers express their views with the idea of establishing a common ground of understanding and to help governments and organizations build on such an understanding. Do not these intellectuals know that the governments of Muslims' countries and western governments are coordinating to attack the truth of Islam and the religiosity of Islamic countries, to secularize Muslim people and their realities, and to separate religion from the state? How is it that the governments that attack the truth of Islam want to construct what is beneficial to Muslims? Concerning what these intellectuals are doing, is this stupidity, or ignorance, or deception of Muslims? The reality of governments fighting today is related to religious truth, Islam, and the separation of religion from the state. This is clear and does not need more explanation. The fact is that colonial powers have withdrawn from our countries, but left behind their dependents to do whatever the colonizers want. Accordingly, how do these intellectuals think that these governments will adapt things to benefit the Muslims, while their only real agenda contains things that are opposite to Shari'a? We have been taught this by history, by experience, and by investigation.

They claim that seeking a common ground for understanding is part of Islam's religious foundations. Based on what evidence do they make this claim? Were the Prophet (PPBUH), his followers (may God's will be content with them) and all the good followers fighting infidels, invading every part of the earth to convert them to Islam, or were they sending messengers to infidels seeking a common ground of understanding? What kind of peace, security, and normalization would be achieved through this evil way? The Shari'a has arrived at a just and correct way to guarantee security for Muslims and peace for the entire world. Muslims, if they want this peace, should be committed to the Shari'a's path. The West knows the Shari'a path perfectly and fights against it.

No to Conflicts and Fights!

The intellectuals' statement declared the following:

> At this significant crossroad in history, we invite all free thinkers to initiate a serious dialogue for the well-being of both camps. A dialogue that will keep our peoples away from conflict and will pave the way for a better world for our future generations who expect a lot from us.[17]

They also said: "We should invite everyone to the dialogue we present to our world, and do so under one umbrella of justice, morals, and rights, in order to preach to the world of a project that will bring good benefits and the security for all."[18] They added: "Current occurrences make it clear that the use of force—even if there are unlimited means of force—is not a satisfactory source of security."[19] They also added:

> History taught us that guarantees of security will not be achieved exclusively through the use of force. Guarantees that have come through force have contained the seeds of their own collapse and failure because they bring anger and frustration to one party, and arrogance and overconfidence to the other party. However, when guarantees of security are built on justice, they have true opportunities for endurance.[20]

There is no power and strength save from God. We have never thought that such talk would come from those who consider themselves preachers of our religion. One would think that the cited phrases would have been written by Western thinkers, not Muslims. The previous phrases clearly assume the innocence of the infidels and denounce *jihad al-talab* [the jihad of spreading Islam[21]]. Even though the jihad al-talab is a crucial obligation for every Muslim, these intellectuals call for terminating this Islamic obligation, while they seek a dialogue and understanding with the West, under the so-called "umbrella of justice, morals, and rights." Hence, they want to replace the divine principles which are based upon detesting infidels and confronting them by words and sword—until they convert or give the tribute readily—with another set of principles, which come from the United Nation's halls. As much as we criticize the above phrases, they cannot fully describe how much these intellectuals impeach our religion.

How can the method of the Prophet (PPBUH) and his followers be described as a failed one? The Prophet's (PPBUH) fate was to use the sword to spread the worship of God. The Prophet (PPBUH) relied only upon his javelin for survival and protection. Those who would refuse the commands of God and the Prophet (PPBUH) shall have no destiny but humiliation and decline. Why, then, is the sword not the main means to compel people to worship God? Reconsidering the method of the Prophet (PPBUH) indicates to what extent their talking is outrageous. The words the intellectuals use in arguing for their case are very clear and need no clarification. We do not have to elucidate their intention. The following explains their errors:

Muslims, particularly those who know their religion, are asked to present Islam to the world, not some other "project" that is covered by an "umbrella of justice, morals and rights" concerning common understanding. Islam is the "project." The most important thing among the basics of Islam is to testify to the unity of God (God be Praised); such testimony should be included in any "project" presented to the infidels.

Moreover, on what basis do you intellectuals say that using force is not a satisfactory source of protection?! The crusader West could not protect itself except through force, after sacrificing 300 million people in its wars. It is enough for us to know that a consensus exists among Muslim scholars that protecting the heart of our religion is through jihad, not through dialogue and coexistence. You intellectuals should know that the banners of jihad will not fall down or be overcome until the Day of Judgment; jihad is the only choice for dignity as stated by religious texts.

Desertion and Prevarication

Those who signed this statement said: "The teachings of Islam describe Christians as closer to Islam than other religious groups. This was proven in history when the Prophet of Islam (PPBUH) sent a group of his followers to the king of Habasha[22] in the first years of Islam." They also mentioned the case when "Muhammad, the Prophet of Islam (PPBUH), sent messages to the King of the Romans and to the King of the Copts,[23] and these messages were very well received." The Qur'an also confirmed that Christians are the people with the highest morals and conduct among all those different religions, when the Qur'an states: "You will find that the Jews and the polytheists are the most antagonistic people to the believers, but you will find that the most cordial to believers are Christians."[24]

The fact is that all the phrases they use are correct, but these intellectuals want to use them to desecrate and prevaricate. How can they rely solely on these phrases, while ignoring all other texts that execrate Christians, in which their infidelity and their dishonesty are mentioned?

Using the foundations of Islam to seek a common ground with the West is incorrect. The West's perspective on what is good is different; it consists only of unimportant things that cannot form a common ground for coexistence, not even for a conversation or "dialogue," as they call it. In fact, the West does not believe in either Christ himself or in the Prophet (PPBUH); they do not believe in the true religion. Western people do not maintain their own religion and they do not consider the religion of Muhammad (PPBUH). So, on what basis can we appreciate them and on what basis can we communicate with them? Neither the Sheikh of Islam, Sheikh Ahmed bin Taymeya, (the author of the book *The Right Answer*), nor Ibn al-Qayem in his book (*Kitab Al-Hayara*),[25] nor other Muslim scholars, when they debated Christians in their works, told Christians that they no longer believe in their prophet 'Essa[26] and that they do not believe in Muhammad (PPBUH). They did so to clarify that Christians falsified their religion and that God will not accept from them any fair conduct, unless it is done through Islam. Hence, what is the benefit of creating a dialogue with those who are non-believers or who believe in religions that are made by popes?

So why did they mention part of the Qur'anic verse as a reference for the closeness between Christians and Muslims, but not continue the same verse? The rest of the verse is: "Because they have priests and ministers who are not arrogant."

The verse thus comes to describe Christians as closer to Muslims than Jews and polytheists. When we say, "the moon is closer to us than the sun," this does not mean that the moon is close to us. Closeness is relative. The subsequent verse explains who is closest to believers. This verse is as follows: "When they listen to the message that came from God to your Prophet, their eyes will flood with tears as they recognize the truth. They will say then, we believe in God. So, God please write our name as your witnesses." This verse explains that the closeness between Christians and Muslims exists only with those who come to Islam, because only they meet the requirements of the latter part of the verse. Some scholars—such as al-Qadi abi Ya'li and others—have even argued that the situation of Christians is worse than that of the Jews. The only way to achieve this closeness is when they believe in 'Essa and Muhammad, the Prophet (PPBUH). Christians knew the truth from him and believed him. Besides, the description of closeness does not include Americans.

When the Prophet sent his message to the kings of the nassara, it was not to beg them for something, but it was: "O, people of the book, come to a common word."

Why did these intellectuals not mention God's words, "those who said that God is one of three," which are very applicable to the West? Also, they did not mention the verse: "those who said that Christ, son of Mary, is God became infidels." They did not mention: "Battle all those who do not believe either in God or in the Day of Judgment; those who do not forbid what God forbids and do not believe in the true religion, those who are given the book. Battle them until they pay the tribute readily." Why did these intellectuals not mention the Prophet's saying: "God imprecates Jews and Christians because they made their Prophets' graves as Mosques."[27] This saying of the Prophet is agreed upon by a consensus of scholars. Perhaps it is because these texts and passages do not support the statement of the authors, which emphasizes subjugation and the willingness to be defeated. The conclusion is that what they did in their statement was look for opportunities for defection and prevarication; what they are doing is using partial understandings and references because they want the Islamic nation to neglect the principles of al-bara' regarding infidels and their idols, and to eliminate jihad from Islam.

It should be added to the above that Muslims' antagonism toward other nations does not depend on the names of these nations nor their histories, but is related to the danger that such nations pose to Islam and Muslims. Therefore, if there exists at some point a polytheist who causes less damage to Islam than a Christian, the duty at such a moment is to fight the Christian and to postpone fighting the polytheist—even when the latter is described as more antagonistic to Islam. Every rational person today would know that the Crusader America and those who follow it—Britain, Germany, France, Canada, and Australia—are more dangerous and antagonistic to Muslims than Japan, the Koreas, China and others.

Also, why are the adherents of Christ described as Christians? The word "Christian" does not appear in the Shari'a. God called them: nassara. Hence, what other reason do we have to abandon the name God and His Prophet (PPBUH) used for nassara, and to use the name Christians use for themselves (attributing themselves to 'Essa, PBUH), except to accept their wrongness, to seek closeness to them and to satisfy them! How strange, that when it comes to the nassara and idols, only nice, beautiful, and tolerant selected phrases are used, while only denigrating, intimidating, and defamatory words are used to describe the mujahidin, such as "terrorists" and "extremists" and similar words. We therefore have the right to ask a question: Who are you following, you intellectuals? And what are you discarding?

The Right Challenge!!

In their statement, the Saudi intellectuals wrote:

> Hence, we are saying clearly and explicitly that we have the capability to initiate a rational dialogue about every topic suggested by the West. We recognize that we share a set of principles of morals, rights, and knowledge that creates a common heritage between us and the West and that these can be developed, which will make the world better for all of us. This means that we share common goals. However, we—as you—have different priorities, which are the basis of our sovereignty and civilizational priorities.[28]

Wait a minute. Wait a minute! Why are you approaching the West with these intimate words indicating good will? Anyone who reads your statement would recognize that you are willing to meet this challenge—creating a dialogue with the West—because you are willing to make what's wrong right and to conceal the framework of the true religion. You are willing to do this, and you believe in it, so you do not need confirmation, clearness, and explicitness. Besides, what kind of common understanding do you seek to build with the licentious West? Since we have fundamental differences with them, there will be no gain in seeking common understanding in common areas, if they exist. All the values of the licentious West do not correspond with Shari'a. The areas of similarity between us and them like sincerity, or being committed to responsibilities, and other similar values, are secondary issues, and are not the basis of our problem with them. These intellectuals claim that every element presented by the West is a basis for dialogue, which will make things better for all of us. However, secularism, homosexuality, fornication, and polytheism are strongly promoted in the West. So, how we can find a common understanding to make things better for all of us in such a context? What kind of common religious goals can be the basis for agreement, if the basis of the differences between us and them are these religious principles?

God Describes Them as Followers, as Sheep. They Claim that Is Dignified!!

They said in their statement: "A person, in his essence, is a dignified creature. Thus, people should not be attacked, whatever their color, or race, or religion. God said: 'We dignified the descendants of Adam.'"[29]

"Whatever their color, or race, or religion"—wonderful words mentioned before in many charters, such as the United Nations charter. The use of such phrases leads us to applaud the intellectual development of the Saudi intellectuals who reiterated the same principles that are used in modern charters of nations.

How can you attribute meaning to God without knowledge!? Who said that it is forbidden to attack the polytheists? Where is the jihad al-talab? God said: "Battle them, as God will persecute them through your hands." God also said: "When the Honorific Months are gone, go and kill the polytheists wherever they are. Take them, tie them up, and lie in ambush for them. If they turn to God in repentance, and pay zakat,[30] release them. God is merciful and forgiving."

Your words are based on the principle of equality declared by the Charter of the United Nations, a principle that considers all people equal, regardless of their religion, their race or their gender. However, the principles of Islam should be superior. The Muslim slave is better than one million infidel masters. God said:

> Do not marry polytheist women until they believe. The woman who believes is better than a polytheist one, even if you like her more. The believer slave is better than the polytheist slave, even if it is he you prefer to own. Those polytheists call for hell, while God calls for paradise and forgiving. God shows people His miracles, and hopefully they will remember God.

Hence, there is no equality between those who call for hell and those who call for paradise. You did not only eliminate jihad in your statement, but you also repealed the superiority of Muslims over infidels. This claim is the most risky of all your statement's claims.

Since the statement seeks a conversation with the infidel crusader West, it is a desecration and prevarication for you to cite Qur'anic verses that speak about people in general, without citing the complete verses. The rest of the above-cited verse explains, and God says: "We dignified the descendants of Adam, and we carried them in the lands and the sea, and we gave them good produce, and we made humans superior to all our other creatures." The superiority of people in this verse refers to people when they do good deeds and when they facilitate transportation for other people through land and sea. Superiority exists also when people are given the best produce and earthly goods. This interpretation is made by Ibn Kathir. So, how can one use this verse only partially, to describe infidels as dignified people? The West understands that dignifying it means offering to it respect and upholding its man-made rights. Dignifying humans in the verse refers to the creation of humans. However, these intellectuals use it to argue for dignifying the infidel West and to maintain its man-made rights. When people are labeled as infidels, another set of verses should be used, ones more appropriate for this label; any correct scholarship would do this. Those people are described by God as followers, as sheep, and even worse. God said: "We created humans and devils for hell, those who have hearts they do not sense with, eyes they do not see with, and ears they do not hear with; these are like sheep, but they are even worse, these are the unthinking." God also said: "Do not assume that their better parts listen or rationalize. They are like sheep, but they are even worse." Moreover, God said: "Those who said that God is part of three are infidels." God further said: "Those who said that Christ, son of Mary is God, are infidels." There are many of these verses that describe this certainty about the West.

It could be argued that it is illogical to cite the above verses—ones that describe the West as infidels—in the same context of discussing the verses that speak of dignifying people in general. However, we answer that the statement's writers used the verses dignifying humans in general in a context of arguing for a common understanding between us and the West. The authors use "descendants of Adam" to denote Westerners. Why else would the authors use this verse in the part of the statement devoted to creating a common understanding between us and the West? True religion cannot ever dignify Westerners who do not believe in God; God describes them as sheep and imprecates them. God prepares a great, eternal hell for them. This is what should have been mentioned in the statement.

How You Falsified the Truth!!

They said in their statement, "no coercion in religion," as God said. Islam itself is not genuine if created through coercion.[31]

This is using right arguments for the wrong cause. The problem with the crusaders is not a matter of *'aqida al-qalb*, the depth of one's faith in one's heart; there is no dispute about this. This verse refers to forcing people to change their heart's faith, as explained by different interpreters of the Qur'an.

Why do these intellectuals quote the beginning of the verse and not continue with the rest? The complete verse reads as follows: "There shall be no coercion in religion, the right way is clearly distinguishable from evil. Those who stop believing in idols and start believing in God have an undivided, firm, reliable grip.[32] God knows all and is listener to all of us." Why did not our intellectuals explain the meaning of "stop believing in idols" to the West? Yes, our religion has no coercion. But it also says "stop believing in idols" and start believing in God, in the same way Abraham (PBUH) did. The authors inconsistently used the first part of the verse while neglecting the rest of the verse.

In addition, some groups of Qur'an interpreters have argued that the previous verse actually ends in another verse. It is the verse in which God said: "You will find some people who have a great mightiness, you should fight them until they convert to Islam." Also, God said: "O, believers, battle those infidels who turn against you. They shall find mercilessness in you. You should know that God is with believers." God further said: "O, Prophet, you should battle (*jahid*) the infidels and the hypocrites. You should be merciless with them. Their destiny is hell and what a dreadful destiny it is." Arguing that these verses conclude the previous one—"There shall be no coercion in religion"—is based on the interpretation of scholars who argue that "no coercion" does allow them to remain in their religion, even though their hearts are not with God. However, other interpreters argue that "no coercion" only refers to the heart's faith.

More importantly, what is totally disregarded by these intellectuals, is a saying by the Prophet (PPBUH); it seems that these intellectuals are ashamed of it. This saying is referenced by many credible Islamic scholars, including Ahmed and others, and it was previously cited by Ibn Omar, may God be pleased by them all. In this saying the Prophet (PPBUH) said:

> I was sent by God in this moment, and given a sword to make sure that God is worshiped solely and has no associate god. God made my life protected by my javelin. God made subordination and minimization the destiny for those who contradict my commands. Those who imitate any community, they become like part of such a community.

In another saying of the Prophet (PPBUH)—as stated in *Al-Sahihan*,[33] the Prophet (PPBUH) said:

> I was ordered to battle the people until they testify that there is no God but God and that Muhammad is the Prophet of God, and until they pray and pay the zakat (almsgiving). Only if they do this, can their blood, their property be protected by Islam. Their destiny is from God.

Another saying of the Prophet (PPBUH) refers to cases in which he sends forward one of his followers as a leader of an Islamic army. The first recommendation of the Prophet (PPBUH) was for the leader to fear God and to do all good things for his army. He advised them also to:

> Battle all infidels. Invade lands, but do not betray people, or be hardhearted. Do not kill brutally and do not kill children. If you confront the infidels, offer them three alternatives: 1) to convert to Islam; in that case stop fighting them and acknowledge their choice; 2) to not join Islam but pay tribute to be protected by Islam; in that case you should accept their choice and stop fighting them; or 3) to fight them by the might of God.

Hence, our dialogue and/or our conflict with the West—this is the cause that we should raise and promote by voice strongly—is concerning whether people are coerced to convert to Islam by force, even by threats of bodily harm, while their hearts are not with God.[34] Of course, Islam has no other alternatives: either join Islam willingly; or, pay tribute, thus joining Islam in outward actions not in one's heart and accepting Islam's protection; or, face the sword because such people deserve no life. Thus, there is no alternative for any person but to join Islam, or pay tribute, or be killed. The intellectuals who wrote this statement should have clarified this to the West, and should not have acted like those who believe in part of the Qur'an and neglect the other part. By doing this, they presented matters unrelated to the struggle between us and the West, and claimed that this presentation is Islam. The verse does not say what those intellectuals want it to say. In fact, the West has a grudge against Islam because Islam has the power to—and does—offer exclusive alternatives to infidels: follow Islam, or pay tribute, or be killed. You intellectuals should answer this question: Are these alternatives part of the religion or not? This is what should be discussed and you should stop being elusive and stop falsifying the right with the wrong.

The Exceptional Becomes the Common and the Basics Are Omitted

They said in their statement: "Hence, the basis for the relationship between Muslims and non-Muslims consists primarily of justice, good deeds, and tolerance. This is what God likes and has ordered us to do. God said: 'God ordered you to do good deeds and be tolerant of all those who did not fight you over religion and did not eject you out of your homes. God likes all tolerant and fair people.'"[35]

It seems that the principles of Islam have been changed by the authors to the extent that we are witnessing a different Islam than we know. In this new version of Islam, the secondary values become the foundation of the religion!!

The relationship between Muslims and infidels should be governed by God's saying:

> You had a good model after seeing what Abraham and his followers did, when they said to their people "We take no responsibility being with you anymore, we will not worship what you worship, willingly neglecting God. We no longer believe in you and we hate you. Between us is eternal antagonism and hatred until you believe in God solely."

There is a difference between antagonism (requiring killing), which is outward, and hatred, which is embodied in hearts. Antagonism, which can be clearly seen through behavioral signifiers, can be negated. This happens in cases in which the infidel is a Jew or Christian, or when the infidel is one of those whom God forbids killing, or because of the weakness of Muslims. This situation refers to antagonism. However, the absence of hatred from hearts does mean apostasy. God shall not accept any deeds from those who do not hate infidels. What God said to his Prophet (PPBUH) in another part of the Qur'an is the perfect prescription for the right relationship between Muslims and infidels. God said: "O, Prophet. You should fight the infidels and the hypocrites, and you should be hardhearted with them. Their destiny is hell. What a dreadful destiny!" What this verse tells us about is the basis and foundation of the relationship between Muslims and infidels. Antagonism, fighting, and hatred between Muslims and infidels are the basics of our religion. This is our way of being committed to justice, good deeds, and tolerance towards the West. However, the West considers antagonism, fighting, and hatred in the name of religion to be injustice, aggression and evil. So, what is to be believed: our conception of commitment to justice, and good deeds, or their conception?[36]

Another aspect of their statement shows that these intellectuals have relied on the West's conceptions, not Islam's, in describing the relationship between Muslims and non-Muslims. It is the way they used the previous verse, "God ordered you to do good deeds and be tolerant of all those who did not battle you in religion and did not eject you out of your homes." The verse is an exception from the natural order, which is offering justice, good deeds for siblings, relatives and Muslims and not for people who fight us. So how do these intellectuals make the exception the normal rule, while making the normal rule non-existent? Why did the statement's authors not mention that the bases of the relationship between Muslims and infidels are antagonism and hatred, and that this was God's order to Abraham, which we should follow? Assuming that this critique is not enough, some other interpreters argue that this verse ends with the verse about the sword. In fact, the statement's authors mentioned only God's command "not to fight those who did not fight us," and did not continue to the verse in which God commands us to "Fight those who fight you, and eject you from your homes, or helped those who eject you from homes. You should fight those and all those who follow them. Those are the unjust people." So, how do you intellectuals contradict the commands of God? How do you say to seek to do good deeds for those who killed us and ejected us from our homes!? How do you seek to coexist and to build a common understanding with them? Are not you afraid of being unjust?!![37]

What Principles Do You Represent?

They said in their statement: "justice between people is the people's right. Injustice is forbidden among all human beings, whatever their race, religion or nationality." God said: "If you say anything, be fair, even in the case of your relatives."[38]

The statement is full of phrases and vague conceptions that cannot be checked or verified. The idea that differences according to religion, race, and sex do not exist is frequently repeated in their statement. The reason for this was to confirm the subordination of these intellectuals to the West, and this was the main characteristic of the statement. This also includes what is mentioned in the previous paragraph about justice, injustice, and the indifference to people's race, religion or nationality. The same exact phrase was stated in the United Nations Charter, concerning the role of the Security Council in combating injustice in the world.

The word "justice" here is merely an abstraction. What does it mean? The main concern in the statement is dialogue with the West. The West understands justice as total freedom to do what it wants in the world and to promote whatever it wants to establish to be worshiped. The West thinks that justice also includes promoting unlimited homosexuality. "Justice" for the West means that the West's freedom cannot be controlled. For this reason, their devious Bush named this crusade a "war for defending freedom." These intellectuals believe that America represents freedom—licentious freedom.

The word "injustice" is understood here to mean forcing people to convert to Islam, similar to what the Prophet (PPBUH) talked about with the infidels. The West assumes that it is injustice to prevent people from committing obscene acts, infidelity, and polytheism. They think that it is injustice to initiate a jihad and invade infidels' countries to spread Islam.

Without addressing these complexities, the intellectuals make the simple claim that justice is right and injustice is forbidden. Hence, if they use the West's definitions for justice and injustice, these intellectuals become infidels, and their opinion is a significant catastrophe. However, if these intellectuals mean justice and injustice as they are conceptualized in Islam, then these definitions will be right, even though it is for these very definitions that the crusaders are initiating this war against us. For what reason do they initiate this war against Muslims but for the conflict between our definitions of "justice," and "injustice"? Genuine justice is making people worship God instead of worshiping humans; justice is to stop the injustice of other religions and to bring people to the justice of Islam. It is moving people from the narrowness of life to a broader, prosperous life and to paradise. Genuine injustice is to leave people living in infidelity and not initiate jihad against them so that they know the true religion, as the Prophet (PPBUH) did exactly with infidels.

How Strange: the Crusader War Brings Prosperity to People!!

They said in their statement: "Our statement has some commonality with the statement made by American intellectuals in their statement, and we think that such communality forms a good basis for dialogue for the good of humanity."[39]

In such a statement, the Saudi intellectuals confirm that they believe that the crusaders' statement creates a positive ground for dialogue that will benefit humanity, the same statement in which the Americans called Bush to continue his crusade-war. In the very beginning of the American intellectuals' statement it was said: "in the name of general human principles, and within a complete awareness of the restrictions and the requirement of a just war, we endorse our government's and our society's decision to use war."[40] This was the crusaders' statement. Yet, the response of our intellectuals was one of subordination. Their response argues that the Americans' statement "forms a positive ground for dialogue and the good of humankind." The only proper response to the crusaders' intellectuals is our revival as individuals and communities to support jihad, the mujahidin, and to offer more support and sustenance for the suicide bombing operations. Our intellectuals may argue that we need to transfer the battle from the military ground to the political, the economic, the cultural, the intellectual, and the social spheres and all other spheres of life. If this argument were realized, it would bring only evil to humanity because infidelity would be imposed, and Islam would be disrespected. You intellectuals should know that the prosperity of humanity comes through Islam. Islam will not be spread but through the sword. So one wonders: How is it that those who signed this statement argue that prosperity for humanity will be brought through the stance of crusaders, while those crusaders call for the eradication of Islam?! Concepts of "freedom," "justice," and "mercifulness" which were mentioned in the crusaders' statement are only defined from their infidel point of view, not from the Islamic one.

You Have the Right Only to Speak on Behalf of Yourselves

They said in their statement that "many in the Muslim world and in other parts of the world did not welcome the September attacks, because of the values, principles, and pragmatic and moral lessons that Islam has taught us."[41]

They also said: "It is irrational to suppose that those who attacked the United States on September 11 have no 'personal' motivations, motivations that were created by—and to which they were pushed—because of American decisions in different parts of the world. Though we do not think that such motivations can justify attacking civilian targets, this is an analysis to look for the causal reasons between these attacks and American policy."[42]

Such a statement is disappointing for many good people[43] in particular. Even though it was disappointing and soul-disturbing, the most serious error in releasing such a statement is its making false claims, its prevarication and its offering subordination in the name of all Muslims. It was particularly disturbing that such a statement was released from the country that has the *haraman*.[44] Those who signed this statement do not have the right to speak on behalf of Muslims in the two Holy Places as they introduced themselves in their statement. The majority of those who signed do not know the basics of the religions defined by the ancestors'[45] Muslim scholars; they are merely part of the public. Their certificates in natural sciences do not entitle them to speak about religious causes on behalf of the entire nation.

Besides, phrases in the previous two paragraphs include dreadful begging in front of the infidels; we cannot be satisfied by such statements. Those who signed this claim lied when they said that many in the Muslim world did not welcome the September invasion. This claim that many Muslims' homes had no pleasure and happiness upon seeing what happened to the crusaders contradicts the truth; this thing that had not happened for ages was such a blessed attack that we ask God to grant us similar attacks. If the media focused on a particular stratum of people who expressed anger at these attacks, we know that the media showed only what governments wanted them to show, because these governments were painfully suffering because of what happened to their masters.

Moreover, how did they conclude that it was a minority of people who were not happy with these attacks based on the "values, principles, and pragmatic and moral lessons Islam has taught us?" If this conclusion was true, we should have seen religious and legal—not political—research by one of the signers explaining to us reasons for this conclusion based on religious logic, not based on rational and intellectual logic. Only two did such religious research. However, their work included much corrupt religious evidence, for which they were repentant later.

Have You Taught Yourselves?

They said in their statement: "Why are we deciding to neglect history and be satisfied with reading about superficial occurrences? Not only does history teach us about the tolerance of Islam, the laws and systems introduced by Islam also show that they establish a stable life for believers and non-believers."[46]

Again they insist on ignoring all the differences between Muslims and non-Muslims. Why do the signers not read history carefully, both old and modern? It is known that the King of the Egyptian Christians (Copts) treated well the messenger of the Prophet (PPBUH), sending the messenger back to the Prophet with camels, cloths, and a slave. Did this prevent the Prophet's followers from invading Egypt and to compel Egyptians to enter Islam by force?

Have not the signers heard of the Crusades, launched by the European Church, against Muslims, wars in which massive numbers of people were killed and lands were destroyed? Have they not heard of the British, French, Belgian, and Italian colonization of Muslims countries? Do the signers not know that colonialism still exists—albeit indirectly—in our countries? Why did you forget history and talk to the victimizer in a self-defeating discourse? If you are not capable of telling the truth and confronting the unjust enemy alongside the mujahidin, you should be quiet. You should not disparage Islam, polluting its comprehensive message by disintegrating religious texts and transforming the struggle over totalities into one over fragments. Kindly stop trying to prevent Muslims from confronting the enemy with the mujahidin.

A Call to Bring Islam and *Nasraniya*[47] Closer!!

They said in their statement:

> It is recognized today that eastern blocks in China and Japan are more distant from the Muslim world than is the case with the West. There are more bridges, connections, mutual relations, and common interests between Muslims and the West than with those eastern communities. It is assumed that the West should understand that the more stable and more peaceful the Muslim world, the better it is for the West. The West should know that Muslim lands have provided the West with many benefits, things that have contributed to the economic growth of the West. The West is the first beneficiary of the Muslims' economic forces.[48]

They also said:

> The dispute between us and the American society does not concern values of justice, or the options of freedom. The fact is that we have two different kinds of values: general human values, which correspond to the general human instinct and our religious calls for them, and other values that are specific to particular countries, which are chosen by that country. We cannot oblige these countries to change these values, because our religion taught us that there is "no coercion in religion." In addition, when particular people prefer to adopt particular values, this occurs within a process of choosing among social options that are derived from the existing realities of this people's community. We also refuse to let outsiders impose their values or challenge our values by force. We assume that we have the right—as it is the right of any people—to clarify the truthfulness of what we believe in for other people seeking a better understanding among the people of the world. Such understanding would help to achieve international peace and to create opportunities for all those who seek the truth for the good of humanity.[49]

Such defeating phrases are not the exception in the statement, as its main goal is to get closer to the West. Also, the statement attempted to avoid any confrontation with the West, particularly concerning the West's infidelity and the evil brought by the West to the Muslim world and Islam. The previous paragraphs are just dark examples of the authors' intellectual subordination to the West, their position of degenerated begging toward the West and the Americans in particular, seeking some mercy for the signers. If not, how else can we describe the West, which colonized Muslim countries, killed and displaced millions of people, by other than by such a characteristic? Instead of emphasizing the West's crimes, and its exports of infidelity and irreligion to the Muslim world, these intellectuals greet the West and describe it as closer to us than Eastern countries, arguing that there are bridges and connections between us and the West and that the West has benefited from us economically—as if these intellectuals are submitting a request, asking the West to not stop offering its values to us, as if the West itself will be damaged if it decides to sever connections with us.

Furthermore, why the lie and the claim that our confrontation with the Americans does not concern the values of justice and freedom? On the contrary, our dispute with the American crusaders does concern the values of justice and freedom, both in terms of conceptualization and practice. Kindly know, you intellectuals, that lying to satisfy the West and neglecting our religion are things that will weaken Muslims, things that will bring no benefits to Muslims either in the current moment or in the future.

How are they claiming that we do not have the right to force particular people to change values that go against human instinct? This is a lie. Muslims ought to invade infidel countries, occupy these countries, and change their regimes into Islamic ones. Then they should ban all practices that contradict Islam, things that people do publicly, just as happened in early Islam.

If You Really Believe that Islam Is the Truth, Why Did You Not Invite the West To Join It?

They said in their statement:

> We believe that Islam is the Truth, but it is unrealistic to want the entire world to become Muslim. We are not capable of doing this, and it is not part of our religion to force others to accept our perspectives. This is our Shari'a based option: Choosing not to fight and to start a dialogue.[50]

The signers dare to say clearly to the West that Islam is the Truth. However, they did not maintain their bravery and invite the West to Islam, like the Prophet (PPBUH) did with the kings of the infidels, and with all infidel people in those kings' countries. Unfortunately, these intellectuals are offering a way out for the West by arguing that we cannot make the entire world Muslim.

They also claimed—attributing falseness to God—that our religion does not force people to adapt to our own understandings. This is fallacious. It is part of our religion to force people to adopt our religious beliefs. Doubters should refer to the history of the Prophet's followers (may God be pleased by them) when they invaded countries of the nassara. Omar (may God be pleased by him) compelled them to follow the regulations of *ahl al-zema*[51] in Islam. Such regulations include the clothing, social affairs, and the communal organization of ahl al-zema. Muslim scholars know these regulations as *al-showrat al-'umariyya* (the Stipulations of Omar). These are very well-known. The signers of this statement should refer to these regulations and incidents and know that we should force other people by the sword to adopt particular concepts, traditions, and particular postures, postures that will force them to live in humility and simplicity, as we were ordered by God to do with them, when God said: "Until they pay the tribute readily."

If you cannot launch jihad al-talab like the followers did, your weakness does not mean that jihad is no longer part of the religion or one of the religious options. You are misinterpreting the religion because you make self-defeating claims and you seek to coexist with the nassara.

We do not want your mediation, which is different from and contradicts the mediation of the Prophet (PPBUH). They said in their statement:

> It is the right of Muslims to maintain their religion, values, and instructions. This option is unchallengeable. However, we are presenting the moderate form of Islam and we want to promote such a path. Learning about this moderate conception of Islam, the Western world will discover the huge gap between this understanding and the West's previous understandings and conceptualizations of Islam. Such new learning will come to exist if the West is serious in considering us, our values, and our qualities, or at least if the West has a serious intention to read fairly the truth about our religion and to know our values.[52]

The intellectuals claim that they present a "moderate" form of Islam, which will change the West's conceptualizations and understandings of Islam. When you claim that that you are presenting "moderate Islam," and that "moderate Islam" will change the West's conceptualization about Islam, it is not the genuine Islam that you are calling for. Your version of Islam does not have any connection with the true religion of God; God is great and should be prayed to. Reviewing what is known to be the West's understanding and conceptualization of Islam proves that the West knows Islam and its basics more than many Muslims. The conceptualization of Islam that Western governments and Western intellectuals have is the precise conceptualization of Islam. This is because they have studied Islam, have done extensive research, and have devoted many resources to the study of Islam since the era of colonization. They have done this because they want to form a clear perception about Islam. The West conceptualizes our religion as a religion of jihad that abandons the religions of infidels. The new infidels know this perfectly. If Muslim intellectuals want to present a "moderate Islam" and argue that "moderate" necessitates canceling al-wala' wal-bara' and jihad and particularly the jihad al-talab, this means that these intellectuals are no longer Muslims. God is talking about their case when God says: "Jews and nassara will not be satisfied

with you until you convert to their faiths." The "moderate Islam" that will satisfy the West is falsified Islam. This "moderate Islam" you want to promote to
the West indeed contradicts the extremism and fundamentalism of Sheikh
Osama bin Ladin, the first enemy of the U.S.A. Indeed, your "moderate way"
conflicts with the moderate way of the Prophet (PPBUH) who was sent with
the sword and ordered by God to fight people until they testify that there is no
God except for God. As we have been ordered by the moderate way of the
Prophet (PPBUH), as affirmed by many scholars such as Muslim,[53] Ahmed,
and by others mentioned by Abu Horayra, "you should not start greeting Jews
and nassara. If you meet one of them in the road, force them to walk in the
narrower part of the road." This talk from the Prophet (PPBUH) refers to
civilians who had peace agreements with Muslims. But there is another talk
concerning the Militant Jews and nassara, who are like the U.S. today which
launches its war against Muslims. The Prophet (PPBUH) said about them, as
mentioned by Ahmed after Abdulah ibn Amro: "I came to you slaughtering."
This is the only acceptable model we want you to offer, and this represents the
moderate way of the Prophet (PPBUH). Your new moderate way, including
what you are doing in your statement, entails devastating the religion and
removing any differences between us and the infidels.

Calm Down; Do Not Join those Countries that Fight Islamic Terrorism

They said in their statement:

> The West frequently talks about terrorism and extremism. In our view point,
> this is a serious problem in the world. There should be many attempts and
> plans to combat and remedy such a problem. It should be known also that
> religious extremism is not associated with a particular religion. However, we
> admit that there are forms of extremism that exist among some Muslims,
> similar to the case with many other extremist religious groups.[54]

Then, these intellectuals declare that they will join the American campaign
against Islamic "terrorism," i.e., jihad. This is the last thing we expected from
these "moderates"!! They think that terrorism is a serious problem in the world,
and that it should be remedied and plans should be made to combat it. They
also stated that "Islamic extremism" is one among many forms of extremism.
But "Islamic extremism" refers primarily to Sheikh Osama bin Ladin's al-
Qa'ida, the Abu Sayaf Group, the mujahidin in Chechnya, and Hamas and
others. If such groups are not included in their opinion, then what groups do
they mean? What do they mean, particularly when they declared that they
agree with the West's point of view concerning these forms of extremism?
While the mujahidin are expecting support from these kinds of intellectuals, they receive instead an acceptance from Muslim intellectuals of the

West's definition of extremism, a broad definition that includes many. These intellectuals also argue that there should be ways for remedying extremism. Combating extremism indeed means revoking the belief in al-wala' wal-bara' and jihad, you intellectuals!!

What a shameful thing these intellectuals are doing. They have not offered victory to Islam, nor an end to infidelity. While the mujahidin are suffering, being tortured and victimized, and sacrificing their lives and the victims' for the sake of the religion, these intellectuals argue that the mujahidin are "extremists." The intellectuals also propose plans to remedy extremism. We pray for God's forgiveness for them.

The cooperation with the West to combat what is called "Islamic extremism" by any word, statement, or by any direct or indirect means is apostasy from the true religion of God. Was it not enough for you to commit the evil deed of saying that there exists "Islamic terrorism"?!! You then seek future cooperation with the West that is fighting your brothers. The extremism that needs to be fought is the one mentioned in God's saying: "Prepare as much as you can of force, and horses, to terrorize the enemy of God and your enemy, and the enemy of others whom are only known by God, and you do not know." Those who refuse the principle of terrorizing the enemy in fact are refusing God's commands and laws. The West considers relying on this verse "extremism." Are these intellectuals aware that they are denying the truth of the religion? This comes as no surprise since they promised us earlier that they are adopting a "moderate" method, and this argument is part of that method!!

The West Fights the Genuineness of Islam: Do Not Cheat Muslims, You Intellectuals!

We are calling for a serious opening of the West to Islam. We ask the West to read about Islam, its activities, and to deal quietly with Muslim realities. We ask the West to conduct a serious review of its stance concerning Islam and we also call on the West to open channels of dialogue between intellectuals and elites that represent the broad currents of thought within Islam and the intellectuals and policy makers in the West.[55]

This is what the intellectuals said in their statement.

Even though they are intellectuals, they are ignorant of, or denying, the fact that the West understands the essentials of the Islamic religion more than the Muslim public. These intellectuals think that the West's stance against Islam is due to the West's ignorance about Islam, its activities, and its principles. However, the West indeed did not treat Islam cruelly until it learned the truth about Islam and its essence. The fact is that the West has known about all religions, but never fought against any of these religions, and never persecuted any of these religions' followers. The West has mandated the debasement of Muslims after learning about their activities.

While it is true that these intellectuals do not know that the West knows the details of their religion and its essentials, they have made an even more serious mistake. This refers to their call for intellectuals and the policy makers of the West to initiate a dialogue with intellectuals who represent different schools of Islam. These intellectuals are again here deserting the religion and playing a deceptive word game. We cannot expect anyone to speak on behalf of the nations except the genuine scholars. We cannot accept that defeated elites and intellectuals speak on our behalf, converse with the West, and call for coexistence with the West. We cannot accept that such elites devastate al-bara' and the jihad against the West. These intellectuals do not call for Muslim scholars to create a dialogue with the West, but rather transfer this mission to the elites and intellectuals. This is because the signers of the statement know that Muslim scholars prohibit coexistence with the West, and they know that elites and intellectuals cannot distinguish between the religion's basic and secondary principles

What Kind of Moderation Do You Mean?

In their statement, they said:

> The West should note that the majority of Islamic movements in the Muslim and the non-Muslim world are moderate. We have to maintain this moderate mentality through recognizing the rights of these movements and groups to exist peacefully, and not create any agitation against these groups, and not allow such agitation from any party for any reason. Through the recognition of rights and the absence of agitation, we can review any action from any party rationally and honestly.[56]

These intellectuals are still playing with words and using vague terms. They describe, for instance, the majority of Islamic movements as "moderate." What is meant by "moderate?" Is it the Islamic scholars' definition or is it the West's definition? The context of the statement indicates that they mean the West's definition of a "moderate" Islamic movement. The Islamic definition of moderation is explained by God's words: "We made you a moderate nation, to be witnesses among peoples, and the Prophet (PPBUH) will testify about you." God also said: "We want from Abraham's faith descendants, but this does not include those who stultified themselves." Moderation is exemplified only by the case of the Prophet (PPBUH), who stayed in Madina for more than three months before launching military and invasive campaigns into infidel countries, targeting them in order to destroy their bulwarks, to confiscate their property, and to have them surrender their blood and their honor. The correct conception of moderation becomes very clear if we look at the path of the Prophet (PPBUH) and the tradition of his followers after him. The correct idea of moderation is illustrated in the way the Prophet (PPBUH) adopts the faith of Abraham. This is not the "Islamic moderation" you intellectuals cant about. Definitely, you do not mean the Islamic moderation, but the West's definition of moderation. The major components of the West's definition are the denial of jihad, and particularly the jihad al-talab, and the idea that Muslims should not avoid non-Muslims, their gods, their religions, and their idols. The West seeks to control the Islamic definition of jihad and al-bara' to fit within its own theoretical scope. This is the "moderation" that creates "peace"!! Our intellectuals beg the West not to become aggressors against the moderate Islamic movements, so that such movements will not be crushed. What if an act of aggression occurs against these organizations? Would they show up to defend the religion and our honor!!? By no means would they do this. They would only release a statement directed to the crusaders in which they beg the attackers for some understanding. These "moderate" groups may also deny any connection with any parties that provoke the West!! They will call for studying coexistence between Muslims and the West, paying no attention to coexistence from the perspective of Islam. Although the intellectuals and clerks of the West support their governments and the Jews in committing massacres against Muslims everywhere in the world, our intellectuals are writing statements supplicating themselves to the West in which they seek the West's satisfaction and superiority!

The statement's authors have adopted Camp David ideas. They said in the statement: "If we seek to remove the roots of terrorism, the proper means is not comprehensive war, but Just Peace; the latter is what we are looking for in Palestine and in other parts of the world."[57]

How strange are our intellectuals today? They once warned against peace and normalization with Jews in particular, with the West in general, and even with secularists who consider Islam superficially and only generally. However, now we are witnessing the appearance of Camp David ideas in our intellectuals' minds. It seems that this is the way to prove that the "cloning" experiment is succeeding. Our intellectuals have started to promote a "Just and Comprehensive Peace" in Palestine and other parts of the World. What is framed as "peace" today and what is proposed by the West and promoted by our intellectuals as common ground with the West really involves subordination and selling our land to the enemy. You intellectuals should be repentant to God and stop using such ridiculous phrases.

A Betraying Attack on the Mujahidin!

Terrorism is defined today as one form of unjust aggression against people and property. It is a morally blind understanding that focuses on one form of unjust aggression and overlooks other forms that might be more horrible and involve more killing of people, and more corruption of the earth. It is particularly unfair if overlooking some forms of aggression is done selectively, using double standards.[58]

This is what the intellectuals said in their statement.

It would have been good to see the many intellectuals who signed the statement deliver declarations and speeches supporting Islam, religious people, and the mujahidin! Instead, they released a statement that emphasizes the American and the mainstream definition of terrorism, which identifies terrorism as an attack on people and property. Such a definition indeed may include the Prophet (PPBUH) who attacked the infidels, their women, and their property, and those who were living in peaceful communities. The Prophet's (PPBUH) followers also did the same. By the mainstream and the West's definition, all the actions of the Prophet (PPBUH) and his followers are considered terrorist attacks. The attacks of the Prophet (PPBUH) and his followers violate what the West calls freedom of religion. Therefore, our Prophet (PPBUH) and his followers are considered terrorists according to these conceptualizations!! These intellectuals affirm that the term "terrorism" as it is identified today is horrific. Do they mean by using this terminology relying on the Shari'a that it is a valid conceptualization for the term? In fact, this statement is directed to the West, which does not understand any terminology but the American one.

The subordination of the intellectuals to the West here is a hard betrayal, an attack on the mujahidin—mujahidin who are waiting for support and sustenance from every Muslim. Our intellectuals maintain that what the mujahidin are doing constitutes terrorist attacks on people and property. O, mujahidin, God will support you and will not desert you, even if these intellectuals attack you.

God Said: Jihad Brings Goodness to You. Intellectuals Say No!

Creating a clash will not necessarily make things better for both parties in the struggle. Those who present each side are not necessarily the best representation of each side's community. Nothing will help us to avoid a clash but a genuine justice, sustaining rights, commitment to values and morals—even in wars if we are obliged to enter war.[59]

That is what they said in their statement.

Again here they insist that jihad—which they call a "clash"—will not be beneficial for both parties. Here they are contradicting God's saying. God said: "It is written that fighting becomes your obligation, though you hate fighting. You might like things that would be bad for you if they occurred, and you might dislike things that are good for you. God knows and you do not know." God also said: "O, believers. You should accept God and his Prophet's invitation to what will make you survive." Some of our ancestor-scholars have argued that "what makes us survive" refers to jihad. A saying for the Prophet (PPBUH) supports this interpretation. The Prophet (PPBUH) said: "Once any communities relinquish jihad, they will be subjugated." These intellectuals claim that the clash between communities; i.e., jihad, will not bring any good to the conflicting parties. However, our concern should be the Muslim world, not both parties. Based on evidence and the consensus of scholars, jihad—both the *jihad al-daf'* and jihad al-talab[60]—will not bring anything but good to Muslims.

Jihad for intellectuals has become "a clash" and malevolence. They denounce the clash of civilizations and they argue for combating this clash by promoting respect for justice, rights and values. What kind of rights and what kind of values can the West respect and can they make an agreement about?

Denying jihad al-talab is a catastrophe that does nothing except exemplify the self-defeating mentality of the statement's signers, per se. However, arguing that clash and struggle will not bring good is a grave error, an error that may squander the deeds of its doer.

We Expected that They Would Call for Jihad. But They Said...

They said in their statement:

> Thus, finding a broader space for dialogue and exchanging opinions—where intellectual, cultural and sciences figures would meet—is the alternative to the language of violence and devastation, from our point of view. Calling for dialogue is the main motivation behind us writing this statement.[61]

The previous paragraph does include their real motivation, which they describe as desiring a dialogue between intellectual, cultural and scientific figures in the Muslim world and the West. They argue that this is the alternative to the language of violence and devastation. From the Muslim side's point of view, we have jihad as the basis for invading the infidel countries. We would have expected that these intellectuals, as elites of the nation, would be in the vanguard of the mujahidin, following the good example of the Prophet (PPBUH) and his followers (may God be pleased with them) and all our good ancestors. However, these intellectuals disappoint all those who had high expectations of them, as the intellectuals call for ending violence and mutual devastation through dialogue! God is great and powerful. We have been expecting their contribution to jihad, but they are offering to end the mujahidin war though dialogue and by making accusations toward the mujahidin. It seems that their statement is the first one, but they have more severe and horrible ones. We ask God for health and strength.

Finally

It is true that this statement has greatly upset many good people who have read it. This is particularly true because it included some well-known names in science. But we think that some of these signers had an excuse because they accepted the overall content of the statement in its totality, without reading its details. Some names of some signers also have been included without them being aware of the final draft, as many of those respected people have stated. However, all those know that God cannot excuse them until they declare their condemnation of all the mistakes in this statement, particularly all the mistakes related to the essentials of the religion. Our criticism is not directed to all the respected people who were deceived in signing the statement. We assume their good will. We ask for guidance from God, for us and for those people.

As much as we were disturbed by the intellectuals' willingness to say— in the name of Islam and Muslims—that they want to coexist with the West, according to the West's values and principles, we were more disturbed by seeing ordinary people adopting the statement. After releasing the statement, people were asked to sign it in support of its content. If the releasers of the statement were honest, they would have allotted two places for signatures in the statement, one for endorsing the statement and the other for rejection. But these releasers knew that everyone would have rejected the statement. This method of voting (choosing between the right way and the wrong way) is a Western invention. In the West they vote for everything, including homosexuality; they have held votes in their parliaments approving homosexuality. The releasers of the statement should also know that introducing these complicated ideas to people will increase their rejection of these ideas. Wrong is wrong, even if a billion people have accepted it. Right is right, even if it is maintained by only one Muslim. The majority or minority opinions— all quantitative measures—do not, per se, represent either right or wrong. God said: "If you obey the majority of the people on earth, you will be misled from God's path. They are following their senses, and they are not cautious." God also said: "The majority of people, even if they are cautious, are not believers." The Prophet (PPBUH), as affirmed in *Al-Sahihan*, said: "You will find the Prophet will come to the Day of the Judgment without any followers, and you will find the Prophet that has one or two men." Does this mean that the previous Prophets were wrong because nobody followed them? Does relying on the data that shows that 85 percent of Americans support Bush's war against Islam and Muslims mean that Bush is right? If people support you in doing wrong, this does not transform wrong into right. Wrong is wrong even if it is supported by all people and they fight for it. Right is right, even if it is discarded by all people and they fight against it. Right and wrong are to be learned through the evidence in the Qur'an and the sayings of the Prophet (PPBUH) and not by their level of popular support. Would you please refer to the steady scholars to ask them whether your statement is right or wrong? Their decisive judgment would be from the Qur'an and the sayings of the Prophet (PPBUH) not one million signatures, you intellectuals.

We ask God—clear is His supremacy—to show us and the statement's authors what is right, as it is, and to bless us to follow what is right. May God show us and the statement's authors what is the wrong way, and help us to avoid it. God is superior and He is the sole entity capable of helping us with this.

Notes

1. The "people of the book" are Jews and Christians. —Trans.

2. Jews and Christians engaged in idolatry by making the shrines of the prophets places to worship God. — Trans.

3. *Nassara* is a Qur'anic name for Christians. —Trans.

4. The word "crusader(s)" as used in this essay generally refers to either intellectuals in the West or the West in general. —Trans.

5. The word "ancestors" as used here is a reference to the early leaders of Islam, particularly the companions of the Prophet and the first four Caliphs. The author is almost certainly an adherent of the "puritanical" Salafi movement, which maintains that these early leaders possessed the only correct interpretation of Islam. —Ed.

6. Here and after, any use of the word "statement" without attribution refers to the statement ("How We Can Coexist") written by the Saudi intellectuals which this text is criticizing. Also, use of the word "intellectuals" in general—without specification—refers to the Saudi intellectuals, or the authors of "How We Can Coexist." —Ed.

7. The original reads: "In the name of universal human morality, and fully conscious of the restrictions and requirements of a just war, we support our government's, and our society's, decision to use force of arms against them." See page 29 of this volume. —Ed.

8. The original reads: "At the same time, with one voice we say solemnly that it is crucial for our nation and its allies to win this war. We fight to defend ourselves, but we also believe that we fight to defend those universal principles of human rights and human dignity that are the best hope for humankind." See page 29 of this volume. —Ed.

9. The original reads: "They were members of an international Islamicist network, active in as many as 40 countries, now known to the world as al-Qa'ida. This group, in turn, constitutes but one arm of a larger radical Islamicist movement, growing for decades and in some instances tolerated and even supported by governments, that openly professes its desire and increasingly demonstrates its ability to use murder to advance its objectives." —See pages 27-28 of this volume. —Ed.

10. The original reads: "Most seriously of all, the mass murders of September 11 demonstrated, arguably for the first time, that this movement now possesses not only the openly stated desire, but also the capacity and expertise—including possible access to, and willingness to use, chemical, biological and nuclear weapons—to wreak massive, horrific devastation on its intended targets." See page 28 of this volume. —Ed.

11. *Mujahidin* means "those who strive" or, specifically in this case, "holy warriors." —Ed.

12. *Al-wala'* means "submission" (to Islam). *Al-bara'* means "avoidance" (of un-Islamic things). These concepts are taken to their extremes in some examples of old Islamic scholarship that are not part of the common consensus of Islamic scholars. These texts help al-Qa'ida's view, in which there is a clash among religions that should exist until the Day of Judgment. Based on their understanding of al-wala', Muslims should avoid non-Muslims, not love them, not be generous towards them, nor congratulate them on their special occasions, nor work with them, nor serve them. Likewise, these texts believe that to adhere to al-bara' is to hate non-Muslims and avoid socializing with them in any way. This is one of the most extremist views of al-wala' and al-bara'. This is also based on the argument that the basis of the relationship between Muslims and non-Muslims is war and fighting until the Day of Judgment. See: Hassan Abu Taleb, "What is Left from al-Qa'ida?: From Firm Organization to a non-Centralized Network and the Intellectual Umbrella," *Al-Ahram* (Cairo), October 14, 2004. —Trans.

13. Shari'a is Islamic law. It includes the Qur'an and Prophetic Sayings, as well as the major interpretation of Muslim Scholars. —Trans.

14. Kograt is a city in Kashmir on the borders of India and Pakistan that witnessed massive killing of Muslims by extremist Hindus. —Trans.

15. Here the translator offers his own English rendition of the book's title, as he was unable to locate the standard English translation. —Ed.

16. *Al-wala' wal-bara'* means al-wala' and al-bara'.

17. The version of "How We Can Coexist" used in this volume translates this particular passage in the following manner: "At this important juncture in history, we call upon unbiased thinkers to engage in earnest dialogue to try and bring about better understanding for both sides that will keep our peoples away from the domain of conflict and prepare the way for a better future for the generations to come who are expecting a lot from us." See page 66 of this volume.—Ed.

18. The version of "How We Can Coexist" used in this volume translates this particular passage in the following manner: "We must invite everyone to the process of dialogue that we present to our world, and do so under the umbrella of justice, morality, and human rights, so we can give glad tidings to the world of a process that will bring about for it peace and tremendous good." See page 66 of this volume. —Ed.

19. The version of "How We Can Coexist" used in this volume translates this particular passage in the following manner: "Likewise, those events should make us turn our attention to the fact that exaggerated strength, no matter how many ways it might manifest itself, is never a sufficient guarantee of security." See page 69 of this volume. —Ed.

20. The version of "How We Can Coexist" used in this volume translates this particular passage in the following manner: "We have learned from history that power is not the only way to guarantee security, since the type of guarantees that come with sheer power carry with them the seeds of failure and collapse and are always accompanied by resentment and discontent from one side and arrogance from the other. But when those guarantees are built upon justice, then the possibility of success is far greater." See page 69 of this volume. —Ed.

21. *Jihad al-talab* refers to the call from God to launch a holy war to spread Islam. There is a difference between this and *jihad al-daf'*, the "jihad of defense." That is why the text emphasizes many times the significance of jihad al-talab. —Trans.

22. Habasha is the name of Ethiopia in Arabic and the Qur'an. —Trans.

23. Copts are Egyptian Christians —Trans.

24. The passages of "How We Can Coexist" to which the author is referring in this paragraph can be found on page 68 of this volume. —Ed.

25. The full title for Ibn al-Qayem's book is *kitab al-hayara fi al-rad 'ala al-yahud wal-nassara*, or the "Book for the Lost in Answering the Jews and Christians." —Trans.

26. 'Essa is the Qur'anic name for Jesus. —Trans.

27. See note 2. —Ed.

28. The version of "How We Can Coexist" used in this volume translates this particular passage in the following manner: "Therefore we say clearly and in total frankness that we are prepared to discuss any issue raised by the West, realizing that there are a number of concepts, moral values, rights, and ideas that we share with the West and that can be nurtured to bring about what is best for all of us. This means that we have common objectives. Nevertheless, we, just like you, possess our own governing principles and priorities and our own cultural assumptions." See page 66 of this volume. —Ed.

29. The version of "How We Can Coexist" used in this volume translates this particular passage in the following manner: "The human being is inherently a sacred creation. It is forbidden to transgress any human being, irrespective of color, ethnicity,

or religion. The Qur'an says; 'We have honored the descendants of Adam'" (17:70). See page 66 of this volume. —Ed.

30. *Zakat* is a sum of money Muslims are obliged to pay annually as charity for the poor. It is calculated as a percentage of one's annual income. —Trans.

31. The author is referring to the following passage of "How We Can Coexist": "It is forbidden to impose a religious faith upon a person. The Qu'ran says: 'There is no compulsion in religion' (2:256). A person will not even be considered a Muslim if he or she accepted Islam under duress." See page 66 of this volume. —Ed.

32. Meaning that believers will have a firm hold on a positive destiny with God. —Trans.

33. *Al-Sahihan* are two authoritative books of sayings of the Prophet compiled by the scholars al-Bukhari and Muslem. —Trans.

34. The original is unclear and consequently a clearer translation of this passage could not be produced. —Ed.

35.The version of "How We Can Coexist" used in this volume translates this particular passage in the following manner: "The message of Islam asserts that human relationships must be established on the highest moral standards. Muhammad said: 'I was only sent to perfect good conduct.' The Qur'an says: 'We sent aforetime our messengers with clear signs and sent down with them the scripture and the balance so the people could establish justice. And We sent down iron wherein is mighty power and many benefits for mankind' (57:25). We read in another place in the Qur'an: 'God does not restrain you with regard to those who do not fight you on account of your faith nor drive you out of your homes from dealing kindly and justly with them, for God loves those who are just' (60:8)." See page 66-67 of this volume. —Ed.

36. The original is unclear and consequently a clearer translation of this paragraph could not be produced. —Ed.

37. The author argues that from God's point of view—according to this verse— all those who cooperate with the West in devastating Muslims' homes, etc., are becoming unjust. —Trans.

38. The version of "How We Can Coexist" used in this volume translates this particular passage in the following manner: "Justice for all people is their inalienable right. Oppressing them is forbidden, irrespective of their religion, color, or ethnicity. The Qur'an states: 'And whenever you speak, speak justly, even if a close relative is concerned' (6:152)." See page 67 of this volume. —Ed.

39. The version of "How We Can Coexist" used in this volume translates this particular passage in the following manner: "We believe in these principles, as our religion commands us to. They are the teachings of Muhammad. They agree to some extent with some of the principles that the American intellectuals put forth in their paper. We see that this agreement gives us a good platform for discussion that can bring about good for all of mankind." See page 67 of this volume. —Ed.

40. See note 7. —Ed.

41. The version of "How We Can Coexist" used in this volume translates this particular passage in the following manner: "Those attacks were unwelcome to many people in the Muslim world due to the values and moral teachings of Islam that they violated." See page 67 of this volume. —Ed.

42. The version of "How We Can Coexist" used in this volume translates this particular passage in the following manner: "It is unreasonable to assume that those who attacked the United States on September 11 did not feel in some way justified for what they did because of the decisions made by the United States in numerous places throughout the world. We by no means hold the view that they were justified in striking civilian targets, but it is necessary to recognize that some sort of causative

relationship exists between American policy and what happened." See page 68 of this volume. —Ed.

43. Meaning believers and religious people. —Trans.

44. *Haraman* refers to the two Holy Places of Islam, Mekka and Madina. —Trans.

45. See note 5.

46. The version of "How We Can Coexist" used in this volume translates this particular passage in the following manner: "Why must we ignore this history and permit a superficial and premature reading of events? This is not all. The laws that Islam came with are there to establish a stable life for both those who believe in it and those who do not." See page 68 of this volume. —Ed.

47. *Nasraniya* is another term for Christianity. —Trans.

48. The version of "How We Can Coexist" used in this volume translates this particular passage in the following manner: "We can easily see today that the Eastern block—Japan and China—seems more alien to the understanding of the Islamic World than does the West. There are many more bridges connecting the Islamic World to the West than there are connecting it to the East. There likewise exist mutually beneficial relationships and common interests between the Muslim world and the West. It should be assumed that the West perceives it in their best interests for there to be balance and stability in the Muslim World and that it knows that the Muslim lands have provided much for them, especially economically. The West is the primary beneficiary of Muslim economic strength." See page 69 of this volume. —Ed.

49. The version of "How We Can Coexist" used in this volume translates this particular passage in the following manner: "The disagreement between us and American society is not about values of justice or the choice of freedoms. Values, as we see it, are of two types. First there are those basic human values shared by all people, values that are in harmony with the innate nature of the human being and that our religion calls us to. Then there are those values that are particular to a given society. That society chooses those values and gives preference to them. We do not wish to compel that society to abandon them since our religion teaches us that there is no compulsion in religion. It goes without saying that a number of those values are social preferences that are drawn from their given environment. Likewise, we do not accept that others can force us to change our values or deny us the right to live by them. We see it as our right—and the right of every people—to make clear to others what we believe in order to foster better understanding between the people of the Earth, bring about the realization of world peace, and create opportunities for those who are searching for the truth." See page 70 of this volume. —Ed.

50. The version of "How We Can Coexist" used in this volume translates this particular passage in the following manner: "We believe that Islam is the truth, though it is not possible for the entire world to be Muslim. It is neither possible for us to force others to think the way we do, nor would Islamic Law allow us to do so if we were able to. This is a personal choice in Islamic Law. The thing that we have to do is explain the message of Islam, which is a guidance and a mercy to all humanity." See page 71 of this volume. —Ed.

51. *Ahl al-zema* is another name for Christians and Jews in Islam. —Trans.

52. The version of "How We Can Coexist" used in this volume translates this particular passage in the following manner: "Muslims have the right to adhere to their religion, its values, and its teachings. This is an option that it will be difficult to try and withhold from them. Nevertheless, what we present is a moderate and balanced understanding and go forward to propagate it, and the West shall see that it is very different than the notions that they have about Islam. This is if the West is truly willing to afford us, our religion, and our abilities proper recognition, or at least willing

to study the facts of our religion and our values in a rational and objective manner."
See page 71 of this volume. —Ed.

53. Muslem is the name of one Muslim scholar and one of the earlier collectors
of the Prophet's sayings. It was translated here as Muslem and not Muslim as a matter of differentiation between his name and the word Muslim. —Trans.

54. The version of "How We Can Coexist" used in this volume translates this particular passage in the following manner: "The West often speaks of the problem of terrorism and radicalism. In our view, this problem is a serious one for the world and a
number of measures must be taken to deal with it. At the same time, we wish to emphasize the following points that appear to us very reasonable: First, radicalism is not
intrinsically tied to religion. Radicalism can take many forms: political, economic, or
ideological. These should be given the same level of attention, because they seek to
overturn the moral principles and the systems that secure human rights throughout the
world. Also, religious radicalism is not restricted to one particular religion. We admit
there are radical elements among Muslims; we are also well aware that every religious
persuasion in the world has its radical elements." See page 72 of this volume. —Ed.

55. The version of "How We Can Coexist" used in this volume translates this particular passage in the following manner: "We seriously call upon the West to become
more open to Islam, look more seriously at its own programs, and behave more mildly
with the Islamic world. We also call upon them to earnestly review their position on
Islam and to open channels of dialogue with prominent Islamic thinkers representing
the broad current of Islamic thought and intellectuals and decision makers in the
West." See page 73 of this volume. —Ed.

56. The version of "How We Can Coexist" used in this volume translates this particular passage in the following manner: "It is important for the West to realize that
most of the Islamic movements throughout the Muslim world and elsewhere are
essentially moderate. It is necessary to maintain this situation. Moderate movements
should have their rights respected. Nothing should be allowed to inflame situations
for any reason. People need to be able to conduct themselves rationally and with a
sense of security." See page 73 of this volume. —Ed.

57. The version of "How We Can Coexist" used in this volume translates this particular passage in the following manner: "If the purpose is to pull up terrorism from its
roots, then all out war is not the appropriate course of action, but peace and justice is.
The world must seek this in Palestine and elsewhere." See page 73 of this volume. —Ed.

58. The version of "How We Can Coexist" used in this volume translates this particular passage in the following manner: "Terrorism, according to the restricted meaning that it is being used for today, is but one of the forms of wrongful aggression being
carried out against lives and property. It is immoral to focus on one form of aggression and turn a blind eye to all others, even though they might be more destructive
and repugnant. This is a clear case of selective vision and the use of double standards." See page 73 of this volume. —Ed.

59. The version of "How We Can Coexist" used in this volume translates this particular passage in the following manner: "Third, concocting conflicts does no good for
either side. Those who represent conflict are not always the best representatives of this
faction or that. There is nothing better than justice, consideration of the people's
rights and adhering to our moral values to dispel the specter of conflict. These principles must be maintained even in times of war when we are forced to go down that
road." See page 73 of this volume. —Ed.

60. See note 21. —Ed.

61. The version of "How We Can Coexist" used in this volume translates this particular passage in the following manner: "Therefore, creating more avenues for dialogue

and the exchange of ideas where scholars and thinkers can meet with each other is, in our opinion, the alternative to the language of violence and destruction. This is what compels us to write this letter and to participate in this discussion." See page 74 of this volume. —Ed.

"Please Prostrate Yourselves Privately" was publicly released by the Center for Islamic Research and Studies (the "media arm" of al-Qaʻida) in mid-2002. It originally appeared in Arabic on http://www.alneda.com. The English translation was commissioned by the Institute for American Values.

Nine

∝

Letter to the American People

∂

"Osama bin Ladin"

In the Name of Allah, the Most Gracious, the Most Merciful,*

> Permission to fight (against disbelievers) is given to those (believers) who are
> fought against, because they have been wronged and surely, Allah is able to
> give them (believers) victory. (Qur'an 22:39)

> Those who believe, fight in the Cause of Allah, and those who disbelieve,
> fight in the cause of Taghut (anything worshipped other than Allah e.g.
> Satan). So fight you against the friends of Satan; ever feeble is indeed the
> plot of Satan. (Qur'an 4:76)

Some American writers have published articles under the title "On what
basis are we fighting?"[1] These articles have generated a number of responses,
some of which adhered to the truth and were based on Islamic Law, and others which have not. Here we wanted to outline the truth—as an explanation
and warning—hoping for Allah's reward, seeking success and support from
Him.

---

*This letter was introduced in the British press as having been authored by Osama bin Ladin.
(See Jason Burke, "Osama issues new call to arms," *The Observer* online, November 24, 2002,
http://observer.guardian.co.uk/ worldview/story/0,11581,846511,00.html.) The version of the letter used here also appeared on the website of the *Observer* (See: http://observer.guardian.co.uk/
worldview/story/ 0,11581,845725,00.html.) While we cannot verify authorship of this letter, its
initial Arabic appearance on an al-Qa'ida-affiliated website (*al-neda*, http://www.alneda.com,
now defunct) and the lack of any subsequent disavowal of the piece by al-Qa'ida, leads us to conclude that it, at bare minimum, speaks for al-Qa'ida.

While seeking Allah's help, we form our reply based on two questions directed at the Americans: Why are we fighting and opposing you? What are we calling you to, and what do we want from you?

As for the first question: Why are we fighting and opposing you? The answer is very simple:

1. Because you attacked us and continue to attack us.
   (a) You attacked us in Palestine.
      (i) Palestine, which has sunk under military occupation for more than 80 years. The British handed over Palestine, with your help and your support, to the Jews, who have occupied it for more than 50 years; years overflowing with oppression, tyranny, crimes, killing, expulsion, destruction and devastation. The creation and continuation of Israel is one of the greatest crimes, and you are the leaders of its criminals. And of course there is no need to explain and prove the degree of American support for Israel. The creation of Israel is a crime which must be erased. Each and every person whose hands have become polluted in the contribution towards this crime must pay its price, and pay for it heavily.
      (ii) It brings us both laughter and tears to see that you have not yet tired of repeating your fabricated lies that the Jews have a historical right to Palestine, as it was promised to them in the Torah. Anyone who disputes with them on this alleged fact is accused of anti-Semitism. This is one of the most fallacious, widely-circulated fabrications in history. The people of Palestine are pure Arabs and original Semites. It is the Muslims who are the inheritors of Moses (peace be upon him) and the inheritors of the real Torah that has not been changed. Muslims believe in all of the Prophets, including Abraham, Moses, Jesus and Muhammad, peace and blessings of Allah be upon them all. If the followers of Moses have been promised a right to Palestine in the Torah, then the Muslims are the nation most worthy of this.

      When the Muslims conquered Palestine and drove out the Romans, Palestine and Jerusalem returned to Islam, the religion of all the Prophets, peace be upon them. Therefore, the call to a historical right to Palestine cannot be raised against the Islamic *umma*[2] that believes in all the Prophets of Allah (peace and blessings be upon them)—and we make no distinction between them.
      (iii) The blood pouring out of Palestine must be equally revenged. You must know that the Palestinians do not cry alone; their women are not widowed alone; their sons are not orphaned alone.
   (b) You attacked us in Somalia; you supported the Russian atrocities against us in Chechnya, the Indian oppression against us in Kashmir, and the Jewish aggression against us in Lebanon.

(c) Under your supervision, consent and orders, the governments of our countries which act as your agents, attack us on a daily basis.

  (i) These governments prevent our people from establishing the Islamic Shari'a,[3] using violence and lies to do so.

  (ii) These governments give us a taste of humiliation, and place us in a large prison of fear and subdual.

  (iii) These governments steal our umma's wealth and sell it to you at a paltry price.

  (iv) These governments have surrendered to the Jews, and handed them most of Palestine, acknowledging the existence of their state over the dismembered limbs of their own people.

  (v) The removal of these governments is an obligation upon us, and a necessary step to free the umma, to make the Shari'a the supreme law and to regain Palestine. And our fight against these governments is not separate from our fight against you.

(d) You steal our wealth and oil at paltry prices because of your international influence and military threats. This theft is indeed the biggest theft ever witnessed by mankind in the history of the world.

(e) Your forces occupy our countries; you spread your military bases throughout them; you corrupt our lands; and you besiege our sanctities, to protect the security of the Jews and to ensure the continuity of your pillage of our treasures.

(f) You have starved the Muslims of Iraq, where children die every day. It is no wonder that more than 1.5 million Iraqi children have died as a result of your sanctions, and you did not show concern. Yet when 3,000 of your people died, the entire world rises and has not yet sat down.

(g) You have supported the Jews in their idea that Jerusalem is their eternal capital, and agreed to move your embassy there. With your help and under your protection, the Israelis are planning to destroy the Al-Aqsa mosque. Under the protection of your weapons, Sharon entered the Al-Aqsa mosque, to pollute it as a preparation to capture and destroy it.

2. These tragedies and calamities are only a few examples of your oppression and aggression against us. It is commanded by our religion and intellect that the oppressed have a right to return the aggression. Do not await anything from us but *jihad*, resistance and revenge. Is it in any way rational to expect that after America has attacked us for more than half a century, that we will then leave her to live in security and peace?!!

3. You may then dispute that all the above does not justify aggression against civilians, for crimes they did not commit and offenses in which they did not partake.

(a) This argument contradicts your continuous repetition that America is the land of freedom, and its leaders in this world. Therefore, the American people are the ones who choose their government by way of their own free will; a choice which stems from their agreement to its policies. Thus the American people have chosen, consented to, and affirmed their support for the Israeli oppression of the Palestinians; the occupation and usurpation of their land; and its continuous killing, torture, punishment and expulsion of the Palestinians. The American people have the ability and choice to refuse the policies of their government and even to change it if they want.

(b) The American people are the ones who pay the taxes which fund the planes that bomb us in Afghanistan, the tanks that strike and destroy our homes in Palestine, the armies which occupy our lands in the Arabian Gulf, and the fleets which ensure the blockade of Iraq. These tax dollars are given to Israel for it to continue to attack us and penetrate our lands. So the American people are the ones who fund the attacks against us, and they are the ones who oversee the expenditure of these monies in the way they wish, through their elected candidates.

(c) Also the American army is part of the American people. It is this very same people who are shamelessly helping the Jews fight against us.

(d) The American people are the ones who employ both their men and their women in the American Forces which attack us.

(e) This is why the American people cannot be innocent of all the crimes committed by the Americans and Jews against us.

(f) Why did they attack New York and Washington? Allah, the Almighty, legislated the permission and the option to take revenge. Thus, if we are attacked, then we have the right to attack back. Whoever has destroyed our villages and towns, then we have the right to destroy their villages and towns. Whoever has stolen our wealth, then we have the right to destroy their economy. And whoever has killed our civilians, then we have the right to kill theirs.

The American government and press still refuses to answer the question: Why did they attack us in New York and Washington?

If Sharon is a man of peace in the eyes of Bush, then we are also men of peace!!! America does not understand the language of manners and principles, so we are addressing it using the language it understands.

As for the second question that we want to answer: What are we calling you to, and what do we want from you?

1. The first thing that we are calling you to is Islam.

(a) The religion of the Unification of God; of freedom from associating partners with Him, and rejection of this; of complete love of Him, the Exalted; of complete submission to His Laws; and of the discarding of all the opinions, orders, theories and religions which contradict the religion He sent down to His Prophet Muhammad (peace be upon him). Islam is the religion of all the Prophets, and makes no distinction between them—peace be upon them all.

It is to this religion that we call you; the seal of all the previous religions. It is the religion of Unification of God, sincerity, the best of manners, righteousness, mercy, honor, purity, and piety. It is the religion of showing kindness to others, establishing justice between them, granting them their rights, and defending the oppressed and the persecuted. It is the religion of enjoining the good and forbidding the evil with the hand, tongue and heart. It is the religion of jihad in the way of Allah so that Allah's Word and religion reign Supreme. And it is the religion of unity and agreement on the obedience to Allah, and total equality between all people, without regarding their colour, sex, or language.

(b) It is the religion whose book—the Qur'an—will remain preserved and unchanged, after the other Divine books and messages have been changed. The Qur'an is the miracle until the Day of Judgment. Allah has challenged anyone to bring a book like the Qur'an or even ten verses like it.

2. The second thing we call you to, is to stop your oppression, lies, immorality and debauchery that has spread among you.

(a) We call you to be a people of manners, principles, honor, and purity; to reject the immoral acts of fornication, homosexuality, intoxicants, gambling, and trading with interest. We call you to all of this that you may be freed from that which you have become caught up in; that you may be freed from the deceptive lies that you are a great nation, that your leaders spread amongst you to conceal from you the despicable state which you have reached.

(b) It is saddening to tell you that you are the worst civilization witnessed by the history of mankind:

   (i) You are the nation who, rather than ruling by the Shari'a of Allah in its Constitution and Laws, choose to invent your own laws as you will and desire. You separate religion from your policies, contradicting the pure nature which affirms Absolute Authority to the Lord and your Creator. You flee from the embarrassing question posed to you: How is it possible for Allah the Almighty to create His creation, grant them power over all the creatures and land, grant them all the amenities of life, and then deny them that which they are most in need of: knowledge of the laws which govern their lives?

   (ii) You are the nation that permits Usury, which has been forbidden by all the religions. Yet you build your economy and investments on Usury. As a result of this, in all its different forms and guises, the Jews have taken control of your economy, through which they have then taken control of your media, and now control all aspects of your life making you their servants and achieving their aims at your expense; precisely what Benjamin Franklin warned you against.

  (iii) You are a nation that permits the production, trading and use of intoxicants. You also permit drugs, and only forbid the trade of them, even though your nation is the largest consumer of them.

  (iv) You are a nation that permits acts of immorality, and you consider them to be pillars of personal freedom. You have continued to sink down this abyss from level to level until incest has spread amongst you, in the face of which neither your sense of honor nor your laws object.

Who can forget your President Clinton's immoral acts committed in the official Oval Office? After that you did not even bring him to account, other than that he "made a mistake," after which everything passed with no punishment. Is there a worse kind of event for which your name will go down in history and remembered by nations?

(v) You are a nation that permits gambling in its all forms. The companies practice this as well, resulting in the investments becoming active and the criminals becoming rich.

(vi) You are a nation that exploits women like consumer products or advertising tools calling upon customers to purchase them. You use women to serve passengers, visitors, and strangers to increase your profit margins. You then rant that you support the liberation of women.

(vii) You are a nation that practices the trade of sex in all its forms, directly and indirectly. Giant corporations and establishments are established on this, under the name of art, entertainment, tourism and freedom, and other deceptive names you attribute to it.

(viii) And because of all this, you have been described in history as a nation that spreads diseases that were unknown to man in the past. Go ahead and boast to the nations of man, that you brought them AIDS as a Satanic American Invention.

(ix) You have destroyed nature with your industrial waste and gases more than any other nation in history. Despite this, you refuse to sign the Kyoto agreement so that you can secure the profit of your greedy companies and industries.

(x) Your law is the law of the rich and wealthy people, who hold sway in their political parties, and fund their election campaigns with their gifts. Behind them stand the Jews, who control your policies, media and economy.

(xi) That which you are singled out for in the history of mankind, is that you have used your force to destroy mankind more than any other nation in history; not to defend principles and values, but to hasten to secure your interests and profits. You who dropped a nuclear bomb on Japan, even though Japan was ready to negotiate an end to the war. How many acts of oppression, tyranny and injustice have you carried out, O callers to freedom?

(xii) Let us not forget one of your major characteristics: your duality in both manners and values; your hypocrisy in manners and principles. All manners, principles and values have two scales: one for you and one for the others.

(c) The freedom and democracy that you call to is for yourselves and for the white race only; as for the rest of the world, you impose upon them your monstrous, destructive policies and governments, which you call the "American friends." Yet you prevent them from establishing democracies. When the Islamic party in Algeria wanted to practice democracy and they won the election, you unleashed your agents in the Algerian army onto them, to attack them with tanks and guns, to imprison them and torture them—a new lesson from the "American book of democracy"!!!

(d) Your policy on prohibiting and forcibly removing weapons of mass destruction to ensure world peace: it only applies to those countries which you do not permit to possess such weapons. As for the countries you consent to, such as Israel, then they are allowed to keep and use such weapons to defend their security. Anyone else who you suspect might be manufacturing or keeping these kinds of weapons, you call them criminals and you take military action against them.

(e) You are the last ones to respect the resolutions and policies of International Law, yet you claim to want to selectively punish anyone else who does the same. Israel has for more than 50 years been pushing UN resolutions and rules against the wall with the full support of America.

(f) As for the war criminals which you censure and form criminal courts for—you shamelessly ask that your own are granted immunity!! However, history will not forget the war crimes that you committed against the Muslims and the rest of the world; those you have killed in Japan, Afghanistan, Somalia, Lebanon and Iraq will remain a shame that you will never be able to escape. It will suffice to remind you of your latest war crimes in Afghanistan, in which densely populated innocent civilian villages were destroyed, and bombs were dropped on mosques causing the roof of the mosque to come crashing down on the heads of the Muslims praying inside. You are the ones who broke the agreement with the *mujahidin*[4] when they left Qunduz, bombing them in Jangi fort, and killing more than 1,000 of your prisoners through suffocation and thirst. Allah alone knows how many people have died by torture at the hands of you and your agents. Your planes remain in the Afghan skies, looking for anyone remotely suspicious.

(g) You have claimed to be the vanguards of human rights, and your Ministry of Foreign Affairs issues annual reports containing statistics of those countries that violate any human rights. However, all these things vanished when the mujahidin hit you, and you then implemented the methods of the same documented governments that you used to curse. In America, you captured thousands of Muslims and Arabs, took them into custody with neither reason, court trial, nor even disclosing their names. You issued newer, harsher laws. You hypocrites! What happens in Guatanamo is a historical embarrassment to America and its values, and it screams in your faces—you hypocrites—"What is the value of your signature on any agreement or treaty?"

3. What we call you to thirdly is to take an honest stance with yourselves—and I doubt you will do so—to discover that you are a nation without

principles or manners, and that values and principles to you are something which you merely demand from others, not that which you yourself must adhere to.

4. We also advise you to stop supporting Israel, and to end your support of the Indians in Kashmir, the Russians against the Chechens, and to also cease supporting the Manila government against the Muslims in southern Philippines.

5. We also advise you to pack your luggage and get out of our lands. We desire [this] for your [own] good, guidance and righteousness, so do not force us to send you back as cargo in coffins.

6. Sixthly, we call upon you to end your support of the corrupt leaders in our countries. Do not interfere in our politics and method of education. Leave us alone, or else expect us in New York and Washington.

7. We also call on you to deal with us and interact with us on the basis of mutual interests and benefits, rather than the policies of subdual, theft and occupation, and not to continue your policy of supporting the Jews because this will result in more disasters for you.

If you fail to respond to all these conditions, then prepare for a fight with the Islamic Nation, the Nation of Monotheism, that puts complete trust in Allah and fears none other than Him. The Nation which is addressed by its Qur'an with the words:

> Do you fear them? Allah has more right that you should fear Him if you are believers. Fight against them so that Allah will punish them by your hands and disgrace them and give you victory over them and heal the breasts of believing people. And remove the anger of their (believers') hearts. Allah accepts the repentance of whom He wills. Allah is All-Knowing, All-Wise. (Qur'an 9:13-1)

The Nation of honor and respect: "But honor, power and glory belong to Allah, and to His Messenger (Muhammad—peace be upon him) and to the believers" (Qur'an 63:8). "So do not become weak (against your enemy), nor be sad, and you will be superior (in victory) if you are indeed (true) believers" (Qur'an 3:139).

The Nation of Martyrdom; the Nation that desires death more than you desire life:

> Think not of those who are killed in the way of Allah as dead. Nay, they are alive with their Lord, and they are being provided for. They rejoice in what Allah has bestowed upon them from His bounty and rejoice for the sake of those who have not yet joined them, but are left behind (not yet martyred) that on them no fear shall come, nor shall they grieve. They rejoice in a grace and a bounty from Allah, and that Allah will not waste the reward of the believers. (Qur'an 3:169-171)

The Nation of victory and success that Allah has promised: "It is He Who has sent His Messenger (Muhammad—peace be upon him) with guidance and the religion of truth (Islam), to make it victorious over all other religions even though the Polytheists hate it" (Qur'an 61:9). "Allah has decreed that 'Verily it is I and My Messengers who shall be victorious.' Verily Allah is All-Powerful, All-Mighty" (Qur'an 58:21).

The Islamic Nation that was able to dismiss and destroy the previous evil empires like yourself; the Nation that rejects your attacks, wishes to remove your evils, and is prepared to fight you. You are well aware that the Islamic Nation, from the very core of its soul, despises your haughtiness and arrogance.

If the Americans refuse to listen to our advice and the goodness, guidance and righteousness that we call them to, then be aware that you will lose this crusade Bush began, just like the other previous Crusades in which you were humiliated by the hands of the mujahidin, fleeing to your home in great silence and disgrace. If the Americans do not respond, then their fate will be that of the Soviets who fled from Afghanistan to deal with their military defeat, political breakup, ideological downfall, and economic bankruptcy.

This is our message to the Americans, as an answer to theirs. Do they now know why we fight them and over which form of ignorance, by the permission of Allah, we shall be victorious?

Notes

1. Despite the reference to "articles," we believe the author is referring to only one document, "What We're Fighting For: A Letter from America," which is chapter 2 of this volume. —Ed.

2. *Umma* refers to the world community of Muslims. —Ed.

3. Shari'a is Islamic Law. —Ed.

4. *Mujahidin* means "those who strive" or "holy warriors." —Ed.

"Letter to the American People" was originally published on November 24, 2002 in the (London) *Observer*.

Ten

∾

Reading an Enemy:
Analyzing al-Qa'ida's "Letter to America"

∾

David Blankenhorn

The new audiotaped message purportedly from Osama bin Ladin, first broadcast on Al-Jazeera TV on February 11 [2003] is addressed to "our Muslim brothers in Iraq." It has won widespread attention, in part due to the Bush Administration's desire to link bin Ladin and al-Qa'ida to Saddam Hussein's government in Iraq. By contrast, however, much less attention was paid late last year to a much longer and more densely argued "Letter to America," also purportedly from bin Ladin.[1] First published in Arabic on an al-Qa'ida-linked website in Saudi Arabia, the letter has been widely circulated by Islamists and was first published in English by the London *Observer* on November 24 [2002]. At the time, the U.S. State Department properly told U.S. reporters that the letter's authenticity could not be verified. But many Arab journalists and experts believe that the "Letter to America" was written or authorized either by bin Ladin himself, if he is alive, or another senior al-Qa'ida leader. These facts make the letter worth reading carefully.

The "Letter to America" is al-Qa'ida's direct reply to a "Letter from America" that I helped to organize, and that was signed and publicly released by 60 U.S. intellectuals in February of last year.[2] Ultimately, however, the al-Qa'ida letter seems more concerned with Arab responses to our letter[3]—and even more with the ongoing intra-Arab debate that it has generated—than with our letter itself. The main intended audience is clearly Arab civil society, not the United States. The primary goal of the "Letter to America" is to expand the constituency for holy war in Arab and Muslim societies.

Regarding the justification for war, the "Letter to America" arguably goes even further than bin Ladin's 1998 *fatwa* (or religious ruling) ordering

Muslims to wage war against the U.S. and its allies, and to make no distinctions between military personnel and civilians. The 1998 statement can be read as justifying militant *jihad*, or holy war, as a means of reversing certain U.S. policies, in particular stationing U.S. troops in Saudi Arabia, imposing economic sanctions on Iraq, and supporting Israel. The "Letter to America" departs from this logic and makes the call to holy war against U.S. "unbelievers" total and unconditional: "Do not await anything from us but jihad, resistance, and revenge."

The letter also presents a broader justification for killing U.S. civilians. The letter argues that because the U.S. claims to be "a land of freedom," in which the people choose their leaders and participate freely in politics, "the American people cannot be innocent of the crimes" committed by their government. Of course, the idea that killing a civilian is the same as killing an enemy soldier is well outside the tradition of Islamic jurisprudence and would signal the even further radicalization of al-Qa'ida's message.

In addition, the "Letter to America" broadens and deepens al-Qa'ida's case against the United States. The letter charges that Americans reject Islam and Islamic law, and immorally "separate religion from your policies." The U.S. is dominated by Jews, who "now control all aspects of your life." Americans, including American leaders, engage in debauchery and sexual immorality. Giant American corporations "exploit women like consumer products or advertising tools, calling upon customers to purchase them." Americans encourage gambling, homosexuality, and usury. Americans claim to support democracy and human rights, but in fact prevent democracy and trample on human rights whenever doing so serves narrow U.S. interests. For these reasons, "you are the worst civilization witnessed by the history of mankind." Al-Qa'ida's call to jihad, then, is directed not merely against U.S. policies and leaders, but against U.S. society a whole. The essential aim of the "Letter to America" is to declare a war to the finish between the U.S. and Islamic civilization. The letter tells Americans bluntly: "Prepare for war with the Islamic nation."

Shrinking the Constituency for Holy War

What can those of us who oppose this message learn from it? The letter clearly aims to expand al-Qa'ida's potential base of support by defining the "us" as Islamic civilization and the "them" as the United States, the source of contemporary infidelity. Interestingly, last week's audiotaped message from bin Ladin similarly seeks to cast any forthcoming war in Iraq as between "the people of Islam" and "the infidels and unbelievers." Indeed, notwithstanding the Bush Administration's public insistence recently that the new al-Qa'ida audiotape proves that al-Qa'ida and Saddam Hussein are "partners," in fact this latest message from bin Ladin expresses nothing but contempt for Iraq's "socialist" and "infidel" government. The conflict that al-Qa'ida urgently seeks is not a clash of governments, but an armed clash of civilizations, with the Muslim world as a whole opposed to the American infidels and their allies.

For those in the U.S. and elsewhere who wish to see this way of thinking defeated, the intellectual and strategic imperatives are equally clear. As much as possible, we must seek to shrink the constituency for holy war in Muslim societies. Because al-Qa'ida and similar groups seek to portray this crisis as a war against Islam, we must deny them this definition.

We can begin by describing what we oppose more precisely. There are about 1.2 billion Muslims in the world—about one of every five inhabitants. Among all Muslims, probably a minority are Islamists, meaning that they view Islam as the defining feature of politics and want to ensure that Islam is the state religion. Among Islamists, a significant minority, who themselves are hardly unified, can be described as salafists (or revivalists), meaning that they subscribe to a past, unchanging model of Islamic law and practice, based on the experiences of the Prophet Muhammad and his immediate successors.

Among this group, only a small fraction, who typically call themselves jihadis, believe that the goal of establishing this timeless Islamic order is justifiably pursued by violence. (Their appropriation and misuse of the term jihad is tragic, since jihad is a classical Islamic term with multiple meanings.) And even among jihadis, only a handful are also takfiris, who believe that violence is justified against all persons, even Muslims, who are not jihadis. Osama bin Ladin and his comrades, at least in practice, are takfiris—one fringe of a small fraction of a minority of a sub-group called Islamists, who are probably a minority of Muslims.

The persons who have declared war against civilization itself are the self-described jihadis and those who assist them. They have not only launched an external war against the United States and its allies, but are also waging—at times with disturbing degrees of success, despite their minority status—ongoing internal campaigns to influence and intimidate a number of Muslim societies. Americans and others should specify this enemy clearly, and act upon that understanding, because unlike al-Qa'ida, we want to define this struggle accurately and in light of universal human values. "Them" is a specific network of radically intolerant murderers and their sponsors. "Us," at least potentially, is all people of good will everywhere in the world.

But some Americans speak as if they are pursuing exactly the opposite strategy. The columnist Ann Coulter wrote in the aftermath of September 11 that "we should invade their countries, kill their leaders and convert them to Christianity." Today, Coulter regularly mocks Islam in her columns. She may imagine that she is just striking a clever pose, and it may be true that few serious Americans take her seriously, but her comments are widely reported in the Islamic world as those of a prominent U.S. opinion leader.

Franklin Graham, the son and ministerial heir of the famous evangelist Billy Graham, said on national television that Islam is "a very evil and wicked religion." Jerry Vines, the former president of the Southern Baptist Convention, the nation's largest Protestant denomination, says that the Prophet Muhammad was "demon-possessed." Jerry Falwell, another evangelical leader, recently called the Prophet "a terrorist."

These and similar comments are tailor-made for al-Qa'ida's purposes, since they seem to confirm that Americans hold Islam as a religion in contempt and view it as the enemy. The Reverend Falwell even seems to endorse the view, preached fervently by bin Ladin and his associates for years, that the founder of Islam would look with favor upon today's jihadis. Could any al-Qa'ida recruitment poster have put it better?

Engaging Islam

A second way to help thwart the al-Qa'ida strategy is for intellectuals in the U.S. and in the Muslim world to engage with one another on what they have in common. One important purpose of the "Letter to America" was to chastise those Arab intellectuals who had organized formal responses to the original U.S. letter. For example, in May of 2002, 153 Saudi scholars and religious leaders, including a number of prominent Islamists, responded to the U.S. letter with their own statement, "How We Can Coexist."

The statement was highly critical but also respectful, and called for further dialogue. All summer long, the signatories to this statement were furiously and publicly denounced by Saudi militants, less for what they said than for having decided to say anything at all to their U.S. correspondents. In particular, in their Internet communications and elsewhere, al-Qa'ida insisted not merely that one or another *particular* conversation with U.S. citizens is wrong, but instead that *any* conversation—any exchange at all short of a promise of war—is against the interests of Islam. For example, one al-Qa'ida-linked statement attacking the Saudi signatories said that, instead of engaging in dialogue, "the signatories should have made clear to the West" that "a person has only three options: become a Muslim, live under the rule of Islam, or be killed."[4] The jihadis are seeking to prevent non-governmental leaders from the two civilizations even from talking to one another.

Even the Saudi government seemed upset by this citizen-to-citizen exchange. When my colleagues and I wrote back to the Saudis several months ago,[5] and our letter was published in Arabic in *Al-Hayat*, the pan-Arab newspaper based in London, the Saudi authorities censored the letter, preventing that issue of *Al-Hayat* from even entering the country. What should this tell us?

Here is what it tells me: in a time of war and discussions of war, and in a world facing the grim prospect of religious and even civilizational polarization, few tasks facing intellectuals from East and West are more important than reasoning together, in the hope of finding common ground on the dignity of the human person and the basic conditions for human flourishing. Let us begin this conversation.

Notes

1. The "Letter to America" the author is referring to is chapter 9 of this volume. —Ed.

2. The "Letter from America" the author is referring to is "What We're Fighting For: A Letter from America." See chapter 2 of this volume. —Ed.

3. The author is referring primarily to "How We Can Coexist." See chapter 7 of this volume. —Ed.

4. The author is referring to "Please Prostrate Yourselves Privately" which is chapter 8 of this volume. See page 95. —Ed.

5. The author is referring to "Can We Coexist?" which is chapter 12 of this volume. —Ed.

Edited versions of "Reading an Enemy" appeared in the *Chicago Tribune* and the *Orlando Sentinel* on February 16, 2003.

Eleven

◈

What We're Defending: A Letter from Makkah in Response to the Open Letter from Sixty American Intellectuals

◈

Dr. Safar al-Hawali

There is nothing worse than violating moral values such as freedom and peace except when an elite group chooses itself as defenders of these values, and, therefore, are willing instruments of despotism and violence. No one is worse than politicians who hurl themselves and their peoples into the flames of hostilities and wars, except for educators and academics who justify what they do. If this is the case in the land of freedom and democracy, then it is a case of inversion in the world of values, worse than the disaster of destroying a building or the killing of a few thousand people in the material world.

If sixty Soviet intellectuals in the days of Stalin gathered in support of his dictatorial methods the defect would have been obvious, but in any case it would still be less evil than the gathering of sixty intellectuals from the free world to support something of that sort.

The American president's announcement of the beginning of the second phase of the so-called "war on terrorism" coincided with the publication of the letter from sixty American academics justifying this war. Similarly, his announcement of the "axis of evil" coincided with the announcement of the intellectuals in which they identified the evil faction which—according to them—is a threat to the entire world, and in which they claimed that the events of September 11 were an attack on freedom, which corresponded to the opening of the President's address concerning the crisis. The letter was in the language of revolutionary declarations:

In the name of universal human morality, and fully conscious of the restrictions and requirements of just war, we support our government's, and our
society's decision to use force of arms...with one voice we say that the victory
of our nation and its allies in this war will be decisive. We fight to defend
ourselves, but we also believe that we fight to defend these universal principles of human rights and human dignity, which form the best hope for
humankind.[1]

If the world believed their claim to represent the American nation, then
it would dash the greatest hopes for a nation which is considered to be a
leader of the free world. However, something that provides a small glimmer
of hope in the basic good in human nature, is that these sixty do not represent the nation on whose behalf they speak. Rather, most of them are members of the well-known movement rejected by most intellectuals and people,
and even perhaps, by some members of the American administration.
Nevertheless, the sixty do not merely speak in the name of their nation, but
have delegated themselves to speak in the name of followers of the World
Religions (Muslims, Christians, Jews, and Hindus), but instead of warning
about extremism in every culture and religion, and that violence only begets
retaliatory violence, they claim that the only danger to the followers of these
faiths—and to the entire world—is the Islamic movement in all its divisions,
of which the "al-Qa'ida" organization is described as only one of its arms.
Nor were they satisfied with making misleading generalizations, but had to
plainly lie when they said that this movement "openly professes its desire
and increasingly demonstrates its ability to use murder to advance its objectives."[2] They went beyond accusing the Islamic movement to accusing
Muslim governments of "tolerating" or sometimes even supporting these
movements.

Doubtless, fair and good persons in America and throughout the world
—even those who have gone beyond accusing al-Qa'ida to convicting them—
will reject this false accusation against an international religious movement
which possesses diverse forms, locations and means, and whose general aim
is to return its community and the world to the light and justice of Islam: the
same Islam which produced the first and greatest of humane civilizations in
history—a civilization which reached from the Pacific Ocean in the East to
the Atlantic in the West, in which a level of human dignity and religious freedom was achieved whose light had not yet shined in the darkness of Europe,
which instead turned toward revolutionary violence in order to achieve slogans which in Islamic civilization were universal rights like water and air—for
all sons of man.

This is what we believed when we first saw the open letter, and now our
suspicions have been confirmed by the release of a letter from 128 American
intellectuals who oppose it, in which they accuse the war against terrorism
and its supporters of racism.[3]

For this reason, this letter of ours ought to be understood as a clarification of that of which [the] signatories [of "What We're Fighting For"] are

ignorant, or which they chose to ignore, and a reminder of that which they forgot. It is not meant to be either a refutation of the distortions against the modern Islamic movement, or a critique of American values—that would require a long and detailed presentation—it was written in the hope that they will re-examine and realize their error in the basic subject matter of the letter. That is, support for the so-called "war against terrorism" in the name of what they call "universal values"—a campaign that targets the Islamic World because of its Islamic character, without equivocation.

We are encouraged in this hope because of glimpses of truth found in the letter which our ethics require us to assume to be from the sincerity of its writers.

In actuality, the tendency to racism of the sixty signatories (which is most unfortunate) goes beyond denying the status of Islamic values to dispute the values of the West itself: "No other nation has forged its core identity—its constitution and other founding documents, as well as its basic self-under-standing—so directly and explicitly on the basis of universal human values."[4] When John Smith founded the Colony of Virginia in 1607 he said, "Heaven and Earth never agreed to better frame a place for human habitation." Thus have four centuries passed without changing this idea of superiority, as if the people of the West—at least—did not know that this nation was produced by a revolution against the most stable of Western democracies, arrogating to itself the slogans of those French intellectuals whose thought provided the foundation for the later French Revolution, so as to found the most bloody and racist society in human history.

The modern American empire is not necessarily what was intended by its Founding Fathers, just as it is not fair to claim that the American people are fully satisfied with and support the imperial military establishment in Washington. Rather, it is they who are the victims of a tremendous deception. Nevertheless, they are responsible (as is any free people) for what they believe and do. For this reason, it is their duty to judge the actions of this establishment according to ethics and values, not to believe those who would disguise them with false ethical and moral garments, and provoke their tendency toward discrimination and superiority to silence their conscience. Otherwise, they will be tricked into abandoning universal values by the claim that they are their first discoverers and their truest representatives, when the general feeling of the peoples from whom the Americans learned their values tends toward the complete opposite. Thus, the danger, which currently concerns the protectors of freedom in Britain and other nations, is that their countries will abandon some of their firm, democratic values in imitation of the American example of restricting freedoms. This reversal shows that American arrogance, which is acknowledged by the sixty intellectuals, has also cast its shadow on the world of logic, and when it is the logic of the mighty which asserts itself and there is no choice for others but to submit, that is the tragedy!

Nearly two hundred years ago Hegel claimed that the end of the dialectic of history had been achieved under the shadow of the mighty Prussian emperor. Marx stole this idea and announced that the end would only come with the establishment of the Proletarian state. When Lenin established this state he made that belief the cornerstone of revolutionary thought which overran half of this planet, and at the end of the century, Professor Fukuyama (whose fingerprints are clearly seen on this open letter) seized upon the fall of the empire of the Proletariat and made the last state to be not Prussia or Russia, but America. At this point, amazingly, he agrees with the "born-again" types, one of whom was Reagan (creator of the slogan "Evil Empire" which today has become the "Axis of Evil"), who believe in the coming Millennial Kingdom which they believe will begin around the year 2000. It is as if this were a surprising proof for Hegel's critics among the German and other philosophers who claim that he took his idea of the "end of history" from Christianity!

This intellectual detour to fabricate philosophical foundations for superiority over others demonstrates a skewed central attitude, which does not allow any consideration for others or their values, and conceals this [exclusion] by summoning others to believe in values of which they suppose themselves to be the creators or discoverers.

There is another question about the role of Professor Samuel Huntington, author of the theory of the "clash of civilizations" whose fingerprints are also clear on this letter, and who represents the other face of the crisis of American intellectuals who rejoice in the fulfillment of their prophecies, even if it comes about through the destruction of several nations of the world.

The answer in short, is that the Millennial Kingdom which the fundamentalist right[5] in America believes in, will only be achieved through blood that will be as deep as a horse's bridle for a distance of 200 miles during the slaughter of Armageddon,[6] which the fundamentalists believe will be the decisive victory of the good, Christian West over the evil, Muslim East, with the participation of 400 million men, as well-known fundamentalist Jerry Falwell claims.[7]

From this we may understand how Huntington, Fukuyama and others came to meet on the soil of the current all out war against Islam with a group of other well-known members of the American right.

From this we may also understand the lack of signatures from Americans such as Noam Chomsky, Ramsey Clark, Paul Findley and others who represent another, more just face of America to a world frightened by the somber countenance of American arrogance. Since the meeting at the "lake of blood" necessarily excludes them (and necessarily excludes most Americans, whom we believe are among the greatest lovers of truth and justice in the world, which has been proven by their great care to learn about Islam after the incidents of 11 September instead of drifting along with the media uproar created by the political administration through the means of the media deception unit exposed by Madison, as indeed these sixty intellectuals have, unfortunately, drifted.)

Not surprisingly, the events of 11 September are the last in a list of "terrorist attacks" which the sixty intellectuals cite as evidence that the just and free America (in their view) is under attack by the enemies of justice and freedom.[8] But the strange thing (in our view and the view of every seeker of truth and justice) is the absence of the other list, or what may be called the elimination from existence of the other pan[9] in the scales of justice. This was not done by the leaders of the Pentagon, but by the hands of intellectuals who want to monopolize the discussion of values, or rather, to dictate values for the world which are—in their opinion—the loftiest values and fairest scales.

The Creator of the world has revealed that He has perfected its creation in justice, and that it is the duty of man to establish human life on justice also. According to this, people who do not measure with a just measure are in collision with the laws of universe, not just with the human preachers of justice:

> The Most-Merciful, it is He Who has taught the Qur'an. He created man. He taught him eloquent speech. The sun and the moon upon their courses, and the stars and trees bow down. Heaven He has raised high, and the scales of justice He has set down: that you may not transgress the scales. So establish weight with justice, and do not fall short on the scales. (Qur'an 55:1-9)

The truth is that the other list is too heavy for any scale no matter how large, since Hiroshima alone would fill it to overflowing, so where will we place the other examples of America's pure and just war, such as Korea, Vietnam, the Gulf War...?[10]

Speaking of the Gulf, my conscience forces me to interrupt here in order to whisper to the consciences of the sympathetic mothers among the group such as Ms. Aird. While signing along with these three men and the others, how did you set aside the noblest of feminine emotions and forget the two million Iraqi children devoured by diseases caused by the vicious biological war against Iraq? Is that not enough to make you think seriously before signing onto the justification of the American bombing of the children and women of Afghanistan, which used weapons of mass destruction previously unknown to the world, putting thousands of them to death while they lie sick and starving, so isolated in their steep mountains that they never heard of the World Trade Center, the Pentagon, or al-Qa'ida?

Perhaps questions such as this are called for: Why did the atomic bomb target the general hospital of Hiroshima, from there obliterating tens of thousands of people, and deforming tens of thousands of others? Why was the 'Amariya bomb shelter in Baghdad targeted for a bombing in which 1,500 women and children were obliterated in an unprecedented hell-on-earth? Why did the bombing of Kabul target the Red Cross relief warehouse, turning their food and medicine into ash before the eyes of millions of the miserable poor? If that was an accident, then what does the repetition of the same mistake demonstrate to the world of values? If it was done on purpose, then does it have any place in the world of values?

Next, You Ask, "What Are We Fighting For?"

We accept this question as a starting point for awakening the mind and conscience, and taking account of the soul; but [if it is meant] as a prelude
intended to defend immoral behavior in opposition to the conscience of the
world, the nation, and Muslims, there is no point in theoretical discussion.

The case here is not a philosophical problem, or a theological issue; these
are moral and ethical values which we are able to test by going down to the
real world and seeing how these values take form in Kabul and Mazar-e-
Sharif after the guns go silent. Then we will know what values you were actually fighting for.

In the Gospel, Jesus said, "By their fruits you shall know them." The
American Constitution, which is the embodiment of American values,
remained preserved like a holy relic of the Middle Ages until the following two
amendments were enacted: the first prohibiting alcoholic drinks, and the second which abrogated the prohibition. Although the second is a clear example
of the defeat of values before the power of destructive lusts, that is not the
point. The point is that American values in Afghanistan have been completely
reversed. The conquering crusaders have given the Afghani people the good
news that alcohol and its accompanying vices are permitted. Despite the fact
that it is human nature to deviate, those who responded to this type of value
were a minority among the Afghani people. At the same time American values expressed themselves in tangible proof when they did everything to oppose
democracy by giving power to armed gangs from among the ethnic and religious minorities with a bloody history frequently mentioned by the Americans
themselves. They immediately set about destroying morals and behavior standards through the temptations of freedom, until it became clear that the government of the Taliban was of more advanced values then those who removed
prohibition from the American Constitution, and that the people of
Afghanistan in welcoming prohibition were of a higher standard of morality
and ethics than the American people who rejoiced at the cancellation of prohibition, and have never reconsidered it.

Three months were enough to end these vaporous (new) values, when the
Minister of Justice of the temporary government in Kabul announced under
the pressure of popular demand, that the application of the Islamic Law that
the Taliban applied is unavoidable, including the punishment for drinking
alcohol. Opium growers' and dealers' sense of the smell of American values
was truer than that of many of those who fervently support those values,
since they quickly proceeded to return to Afghanistan following the
American occupation, anticipating a new future for their humanitarian work,
and an opening of the American market which is the largest market for this
plague.

George Bernard Shaw made the sarcastic comment on the duplicity of
Western values: "I can forgive Alfred Nobel for having invented dynamite,
but only a fiend in human form could have invented the Nobel Prize."
Similarly, the Afghani people may forgive the Americans for bombing the

warehouses of food supplies, targeting orphanages, and their other actions in the name of the so-called "just war"—even the [maltreatment of the] prisoners in the Qala-e-Gangi Fortress and in Cuba—but they will never forgive their insult to the values in which they [Muslims] believe and their [the Americans'] preference for arbitrary, man-made values which are neither stable or just, and their attempt to drag them down to the lowest American values, both in war and peace.

Furthermore, the Islamic World may reluctantly come to understand the arrogance of the American administration, and its blundering and abuse, by considering it to [fall victim to] the Pharaonic tendency of all historic empires, but it absolutely will not accept American intellectuals teaching us Islamic values, and setting themselves up as preachers of these values simply because a very small number of Muslims did—or are accused of doing—an action that is minor in comparison to what the American governing institutions have done in all the inhabited continents for nearly a full century, with the very important distinction that no Muslim, whether moderate or extremist, ever thought of harming America before America's bias toward the Zionist entity and offering it every support for its terrorism and violence, and before America attacked more than one Islamic country and proceeded to classify them as "supporters of terrorism" and the "axis of evil" on the basis that the Muslims are at the head of the list and its target, which is what the open letter from the sixty intellectuals came to consecrate with a philosophical consecration.

We do not claim that what the signatories wrote was a Freudian slip. But there may have been an attempt to deceive the twinge of conscience when morality was evoked, not in the inhumanity of war, but in the military tribunals and treatment of prisoners, and the restrictions against the media and the concealing of factual information from the people, such as when the CNN news network has two separate broadcasts, one for domestic consumption, and one for overseas, reminiscent of the media in Eastern Europe during the Communist era.

However, we cannot ignore the fact that we are in a situation similar to the situation of the popes, bishops and kings of Europe during the Middle Ages who sent Crusade after Crusade against the Islamic East. The current Pope[11] has apologized to the Islamic World for those wars, but we believe these intellectuals ought to be ahead of their time and present a similar apology for what the American administration is doing to the Muslims, and therefore open the door to dialogue and understanding between the two religions and two civilizations. Unfortunately, they chose another path, and it may take centuries for us to hear this apology, if such values that call for one even exist.

The open letter contains historical and philosophical generalizations in need of a thorough examination, but we are not prepared to enter into a debate about philosophy or theology, not only because of the lack of space, but also because of our absolute conviction that we must believe in and accept as fact all that is true and just, no matter what its source, and that we must reject all that is false and unjust, no matter where it is from. The problem, which we shall consider forthwith, is that they ascribe absolute truth to the temporary historical situation of a particular nation, in a particular stage in history, calling it "universal moral principles," which is a claim any nation can make. The result will only be to transfer wars from the battlefield to the world of values, which contradicts the apparent intention of this letter as stated in its conclusion. That is, unless we believe the Zionist journalist, Thomas Friedman, who clearly states that it is the cultural war which is more important to America, and that changing the social system, regime, and school curriculum is the most important part of the battle with the Islamic world. In that case, "universal values" become a means, not a goal. The reader has a right dispute this, so we will leave off this possibility and discuss the subject based on historical facts and logic.

The logical basis of their great claim is lost for a simple reason: the principle on which these universal truths are based is the principle of "natural law." It is unacceptable to rely on invoking an obscure principle like natural law whose existence is hard to prove, let alone to accept it in [confronting] the most complicated problem to face mankind.

Rather, historical reality bears witness that the theories which have done the worst injustice to human rights were able, and are able, to base themselves on this principle.

Ricardo, in his justification of capitalist greed which was the primary motive for the colonial conquests in human history, depended on it, as did Malthus and Bentham in forbidding charity and benevolent treatment of the poor in violation of the greatest human values, more shocking than Darwin's decision that natural law is established on the principle that life is a struggle and survival is for the fittest, which became the philosophical basis for the destructive wars and totalitarian systems of Modern Europe. As for the Founding Fathers of America, they only cited it due to their belief that it was the most modern theory, just as if someone today believed in the "end of history" for example.

It is well known to researchers that Thomas Jefferson and those who worked with him borrowed the terminology of the Declaration of Independence from the ideas of English philosophy, especially John Locke, and from the founders of the ideology of the French Revolution such as Rousseau and Montesquieu. At that time, the idea of natural law and natural rights was in vogue.

The origin of the problem for them and other social philosophers was the lack of a doctrine and law on which Western thought, which aspired to freedom from "ecclesiastical theocracy," might build, and to which it might refer for judgment. This lack caused them to invent philosophical bases on which to construct. A comparison is in order at this point, between the Islamic World [which] possessed (beyond practical experience) a great legacy of revealed texts and explanatory legal codes which carefully defined universal moral truths and provided detailed laws governing human interactions six centuries before the promulgation of what the English call the "Magna Carta." Europe did not seriously attempt to emulate Islamic Law, or even borrow from it, until the Napoleonic Code of 1804, that is, a generation after the Declaration of Independence of 1776.

To clarify this we will take an example from the values that you mention, which can be summed up in two words: "freedom and equality"; two old slogans, your discussion of which contains nothing new, and which, moreover, were not the invention of the Founders. More importantly, these two values cannot possibly be derived from the vague principle of natural law in pure logic, let alone in the real world. Similarly, a little deep thought shows that they are contradictory—not complimentary—values. Here lurks the danger, as the events which transpired after the French Revolution (the revolution which clearly exalted these two slogans in the West) clearly confirm. For this reason the world historian Toynbee says: "Human history may be summed up as a struggle between these two opposing principles: the principle of freedom and principle of equality."

Since man is unable to define the limits between these two opposing principles, or rather, between the freedom of each party in the branches of human relationships (governor and governed, husband and wife, one state and another, minority and majority, etc.), and since the Universal Declaration of Human Rights has been able only to provoke a new debate of the problem (from its proclamation until now its interpretation has been disputed, and most totalitarian and violent regimes unabashedly describe themselves as democratic). Quotes such as Martin Luther King's about the "arc of justice"[12] is most like describing water as "water." Similarly, the letter's quotation of Augustine[13] is exceeded in eloquence by the quote in Gospel of one who is better than and antedates Augustine, Christ—peace be upon him—but it is only an ideal for ethical guidance. For this reason, there is no alternative but for all of humanity to return to an absolute detailed, universal source, or to borrow the phrase of Duguit, the Dean of French jurists: "It is not possible for man to legislate for man. Rather, that is possible only for an unseen absolute power beyond the power of all mankind."

This source is found in divine revelation preserved from alteration, and this is found only in Islam, and only in Islam because it is the Faith of all the prophets, and all the divine messages to humanity. In the shade of its law, freedom, justice and equality are achieved according to all their criteria and definitions, and in their most advanced forms and practices. This does not mean to equate the current state of Muslims to the ideal of Islam; we affirm the contrast between the two—not by way of the open letter, which differentiates between "Muslims" and "Islamicists,"[14] but on the basis that the human soul is bound to the earth until faith raises it to heaven. We are not speaking of nationalism here, as the signatories do, but of an international religion which is more widely spread throughout the world than any other faith. They claim that it is possible for anyone to become an American,[15] however, the reality (of that claim) does not escape anyone. In fact, however, anyone can become a Muslim, and that is the true tie that can bind all of humankind.

Islamic values are the common denominator of the positive facets of all civilizations. Not only because of the Islamic influence on most known world cultures, but because no matter how large the circle of Islam grows, it does not claim to encompass within itself all truth and justice, as many in the West may suppose (perhaps due to the errors of some Muslims in their understanding or presentation of Islam). Rather, it understands out of certitude that, as one of the principles of Islamic Law states, "Wherever justice lies, there is God's Law," and, "Wisdom is the lost property of the Believer; wherever it may be found, he may lay claim to it." The greatest truth of Islam is the exclusive devotion of worship and service to God alone, without taking any partners beside Him. Yet Islamic doctrine clearly and unequivocally states that it is the religion of all the Prophets, and specifically the religion of Abraham, and that Muhammad—blessing and peace be upon him—is only the reformer and interpreter of the Faith of Abraham.

For this reason, Islamic jurists, and even the Orthodox Caliphs, never ceased to utilize any source no matter what its origin. Moreover, the Prophet himself—blessing and peace be upon him—accepted laws derived from the practices of the Romans and Persians that conflicted with Arab custom, as did the voluminous and detailed books of the Muslim jurists concerning war and its laws based on verses of the Qur'an, hadiths of the Prophet—blessing and peace be upon him—and practical examples from the Prophetic biography and the history of the Orthodox Caliphs whose rule was the most just ever seen in history after the rule of the prophets. The great openness of Islamic civilization went beyond the barriers in whose fetters modern civilization still stumbles. There was no racial discrimination or immigration and travel restrictions to prevent a delegation of pagan Turks from Central Asia from presenting their claim to the Caliph in Damascus against the general of the Muslim army that conquered their land. Even earlier, a Coptic Christian came to Madina to complain to the second Orthodox Caliph about the deeds of the latter's son. In both cases the judgment was in favor of the plaintiff!

It is not surprising that these and many similar cases occurred. The amazing thing is that the people of that era were not surprised by them because what they saw and heard of Islamic justice caused them to be ordinary events. In contrast, we find that the American administration has given a stern warning to the American media not to publish the views of Mullah Muhammad 'Umar[16] concerning the situation. Justice demands that those who claim to uphold it allow opportunities to hear the other side. Justice is the stronger even if it is weak, and weak is the oppressor even if he is strong. That the huge American media arsenal of Voice of America radio would be restricting the half-hour broadcast of the opposing side is a decisive proof of the killer's weakness with which God strikes down tyrants no matter how mighty they may be. Otherwise, why would the mass media fear the effect on an informed public of the statement of a person frequently discredited by the same media as stupid and simple-minded?

When Islamic belief opened the gate to independent inquiry and research concerning the rules of justice in any situation within the unified framework of values disciplined by the religious texts and universal principles derived from them, it set down the firm rule upon which justice between men is established, and on which the claimant bases his claim. Therefore, the law requires hearing the claim just as it grants the opportunity to respond to it. Thus, humanity opened for the first time the gate of complementarity and mutual responsibility to protect the dignity of each human being, by granting the right to anyone—whoever he may be—to bring suit against anyone—whomever he may be—not on an abstract, literary basis as is the case with international human rights organizations, but on a compulsory, enforced basis that could not be violated even by the supreme leader of all the Muslims.

Thus, Islam made the entire Islamic society something closer to a universal organization for human rights. Because of this, Islamic society avoided—despite its vast territory—the type of factional quarreling represented by the formation of pressure groups such as unions, parties and organizations for each faction, trade, or class, let alone the war between the sexes!

It also avoided much of the tension in international relations which constantly produces wars that deplete both sides. The nation which has this for its law must be as far removed as possible from the "theocracy" which drowned Europe during the Middle Ages. Insomuch as theocracy [is defined as] as a license to kill from God—as happened with Christian sects in the Middle Ages as well as with the Muslims in the name of the Crusades[17]—it is considered apostasy in Islam in the case of those who believe in it, and an attack on the exclusive attributes of divinity for those who make such a claim. The Prophet —blessing and peace be upon him—himself only conveys a message from God, and clearly and unequivocally stated that he judged according to his opinion in a case, and that his judgment may coincide with what is actually just in the case, or it may not. He did not know the unseen, and therefore, he could not be responsible: "You come to me with your disputes, and perhaps one of you is more convincing in argument than the other so I judge in his favor according to what I hear from him. If I ever grant to someone what is rightly his brother's, I am only granting to him a piece of Hellfire."[18]

Thus, the discussion of the advantages of American secularism over theocracy becomes meaningless if it is connected with Islam, since identical or superior advantages are found in and encouraged by Islam in its universal summons to search for truth wherever it may be found, to fight superstition, blind traditionalism and bias for one's own opinion, and to discard tyranny and despotism in every form, while preserving the greatest of divine blessings upon mankind and the greatest human achievement: faith in God and obedience to his perfect and just world law.

Secularism may be the better of the two evils in the case of the West, but none of its causes exist in Islam.

Thus, Islamic civilization was the vessel for many different examples of civilization, not only during its golden age, but even in recent eras. In all due humility, nobody from this civilization claimed that it represents the end of history, or that it exemplifies universal values. Rather, these values flow within the universal entity of the Islamic community as blood flows within the body.

Let us take India and Spain as examples, since original Islamic principles were preserved in both places despite the severe decline from the peak of justice at the time of the Orthodox Caliphate. Muslims ruled India for eight centuries in which all people were equal there before Islamic Law, free in practicing their beliefs. Neither Hindus nor any others were forced to change their beliefs. Rather, there was a degree of social harmony which both the British Raj and the secular Congress party government after it were unable to achieve—a failure which led to the arrival of Hindu extremists to [power in] government, and the committing of horrible crimes against mosques and churches alike. As for Spain—which was another mode of civilization—it suffices to mention without elaboration the religious and academic freedom that flowered there in contrast to the severe fanaticism of nearby Europe. It is sufficient for us to merely recall the Catholic Inquisition that followed the fall of Islamic civilization there, and the total annihilation of its cultured people at the hands of those who learned the basics of civilization from them. Perhaps it would be appropriate to mention the example that many Muslims and non-Muslims hold to be the worst in Islamic history: the example of the Turks. This was the example that Martin Luther used to cite as the ideal of freedom of belief in contrast to the blind papist tyranny. He was amazed that a Turk could be a Jew or Christian, not only a Muslim, and that every Muslim could read the Qur'an at the time when the Pope alone reserved the right to interpret the Gospel and prohibited its translation.

This inspired his 95 Theses that he nailed to the door of the church at Wittenburg, which came to serve as the Protestant doctrine upon which the United States was founded. Istanbul was an international center of culture in which all religions and philosophies coexisted, not only in its architectural advancement that dazzled ambassadors and travelers then (and continues to do so), but also its moral and cultural advancement.

It is enough to know that the worst period of violence and violation of human rights in Turkey is associated with the removal of Islamic law, and the imitation and implementation of Western secular nationalism and legal systems from the end of the nineteenth century until the present. Yet secular Turkey is the second-place strategic ally of America after Israel.

In general, we say that Islamic justice and values are not founded on a philosophical opinion, or political theory, but that they are established on the imitation of the prophets, especially Abraham, Moses, Jesus, and Muhammad —blessing and peace be upon them all. These are sufficient in themselves to be the true universal values, and therefore, it is the duty of every person to morally be a Muslim, regardless of whether he is a Muslim, Christian, Jew, or follower of any other religion.

The difference between Islamic values and those found in the Universal Declaration of Human Rights is very great. Islam does not make dignity, freedom, justice, and legal equality rights that must be sought, but duties whose execution is incumbent on both plaintiff and defendant. Moreover, it is incumbent on others to strive to enforce them on both parties, to advise each individual of his rights should he be unaware of them, and to protest against the other party if he should reject those rights.

In contrast to the undefined terms and vague indications of values in the statements of the American Founding Fathers, the authors of the International Declaration of Human Rights, and other social philosophers since the European Enlightenment until today, and in contrast to the absence of discussion of international relations and foreign policy in the American Constitution (since it is no more than the document of a local alliance at a particular stage of an isolated people whose features had yet to be completed and, therefore, can never be universal) in contrast to all of that we say that in the divine book—the Qur'an—we find hundreds of clear and explicated verses defining accurately and in detail, the values which all humanity must apply in sincere service to God—not as lip service or pretense—since He will judge them because of it on the Day of Judgment:

> Humanity, We have created you all from a single male and female, and made you nations and tribes, that you may know each other. Truly, the most noble among you is he who is most righteous. For God is All-Knowing, All-Aware. (Qur'an 49:13)

> There is no compulsion in Religion: Truth is clearly distinguished from falsehood; so whoever rejects idols and believes in God has grasped the firmest handle, which will never break. For God is All-Hearing, All-Knowing. (Qur'an 2:256)

> Those who believe, those who are Jews, the Christians and the Sabeans, who believe in God and the Last Day, and do righteous works, shall have their reward with their Lord. They shall have no fear, nor shall they grieve. (Qur'an 2:62)

> Say: "Followers of the Bible, let us come to common terms between you and us: that we shall worship none but God; and worship none other beside Him; and that none of us shall set up lords from among ourselves other than God." If they then turn back, say: "Then bear witness that we are Muslims." (Qur'an 3:64)

> All food was lawful for the Children of Israel except that which Israel forbade for itself before the Torah was revealed. Say: "Bring the Torah and read it if you are truthful." Thereafter, whoever forges a lie about God, it is they who are wrongdoers. Say: "God speaks the truth, so follow the Faith of Abraham who departed from idolatry and worshipped none beside God." (Qur'an 2:93,94)

> Believers, fulfill your covenants. Lawful for you are the beasts of cattle other than those which are recited to you. But game animals are forbidden to you while you are within the sacred precincts or in the state of pilgrimage. For

God decrees as He will. Believers, do not violate God's sacred rites, nor the sacred month, nor the sacrificial animals, nor the garlands (which mark such animals), nor the security of those at the Holy House seeking the favor and acceptance of their Lord. But when you are outside the sacred precincts then hunt. Do not let the hatred of some people who prevented you from entering the Holy Mosque lead you to hostility. Help each other in righteousness and piety, but do not help each other in sin and hostility. Fear God: for God is severe in punishment. (Qur'an 5:1,2)

Believers, stand firmly for God, witnesses for justice. Let not the hatred of others lead you away from fair treatment. Be just: that is nearest to piety. Fear God. For God is All-Aware of what you do. (Qur'an 5:8)

Stand firmly, witnesses for God even if it may be against yourselves, or your parents, or your kin, whether rich or poor it is God who can best protect them. So do not follow your vain desires and depart from justice. If you distort justice or refuse to do it, God is All-Aware of what you do. (Qur'an 4:135)

Say: "Come, let me recite what your Lord has forbidden you": Do not worship anything beside Him, and be kind to your parents. Kill not your children from fear of want—We provide sustenance for you and for them. Do not approach indecent acts whether openly or in secret. Take not life, which God has made sacred, except by legal right. That is His commandment to you, that you may learn to reason.

Do not approach the property of the orphan unless to improve it, until he reaches maturity. Give the full and fair measure and weight. We place no burden on any soul, but that which it can bear. When you speak, be just, even if it may concern a close relative. Fulfill God's covenant. That is His commandment to you, that you may remember.

This is My straight path, so follow it. Do not follow the other paths that will cause you to scatter away from His path. That is His commandment to you, that you may be righteous. (Qur'an 6:151-153)

Your Lord has decreed that you worship none but Him, and be kind to your parents. Whether one or both of them attain old age in your lifetime say not one word of contempt, nor repel them, but speak to them in terms of honor. In mercy lower over them the wing of humility, and say: "My Lord, have mercy on them even as they cherished me in childhood."

Your Lord knows well what is within your souls: if you will be righteous, He is Most Forgiving to those who repent.

Give your kindred their rights, and the poor and the wayfarer; but do not squander away your wealth. For the wasteful are brothers of the devils, and the devil is ungrateful to His Lord. If you must turn away from them seeking the mercy you expect from your Lord, yet speak to them a word of kindness. Be neither stingy withholding your hand to your neck, nor a spendthrift stretching out his hand as far is it can go, or you will become blameworthy and destitute. Your Lord sends forth abundant or limited sustenance for whom He will. For of His servants He is All-Aware, All-Seeing.

Do not kill your children from fear of want: We shall provide sustenance for them as well as for you. Truly, killing them is a great sin.

Do not approach adultery. For it is an indecent act and an evil path. Nor take life—which God has made sacred—except by legal right. If anyone is wrongfully killed, We grant to his heir authority: but let him not be excessive in taking life; for he is assisted (by the Law).

Do not approach the property of the orphan except to improve it, until he reaches maturity; and fulfill the covenant, for covenants must be accounted for.

Give full measure when you measure, and weigh with a straight balance; that is better and more fair in the end.

Do not pursue that of which you have no knowledge. Surely, the hearing, sight, and mind, each will be questioned.

Do not walk proudly upon the earth; for you can neither rend the earth asunder, nor reach the mountains in height. All of these are evil and detested before your Lord.

These are among (the precepts) of the wisdom revealed to you from your Lord. Make no other god to be worshipped beside God, so that you will not be cast into Hell, blameworthy and rejected. (Qur'an 17:23-39)

Have you seen him who turns away, gives a little, then hardens his heart? Does he have knowledge of the unseen so that he can see? Has he not been told of that which is in the books of Moses, and of Abraham who was loyal? That none can bear the burdens of any other; that man can have nothing but what he strives for; and that he will see the fruits of his striving; then will he be reward the full reward. (Qur'an 53:33-41)

Say: "I admonish [you] with only one thing: That you would stand forth for God in pairs or singly and think. Your companion is not possessed. He is only a warner sent to you before a severe chastisement." (Qur'an 34:46)

Say: "Who grants you sustenance from the heavens and the earth?" Say: "God; and either we or you are rightly guided or in manifest error." (Qur'an 34:24)

Fight in the cause of God those who fight you, but do not initiate hostilities. For God does not love transgressors. (Qur'an 2:190)

God does not forbid you regarding those who do not fight you for your Faith, and do not drive you out of your homes, from dealing with them kindly and justly. For God loves those who are just. (Qur'an 60:8)

Among the people is one whose speech about the life of this world may dazzle you. He calls God to witness what is in his heart; but he is the most contentious of enemies. When he turns away, he strives everywhere to spread corruption in the land and to destroy crops and progeny. But God does not love corruption. When it is said to him, "Fear God," his arrogance leads him to more sin. Hell is sufficient for him, an evil resting place indeed. (Qur'an 2:204-206)

If you fear treachery from any people, pay them back in kind; for God does not love the treacherous... But if they incline towards peace, incline towards it also, and trust in God; for He is All-Hearing, All-Knowing. (Qur'an 8:58,61)

(The righteous) give food out of love of God, to the poor, the orphan, and the captive. (Qur'an 76:6)

Not all of them are alike: among the followers of the Bible are a group who are upright, reciting God's revelations throughout the night, bowing down in submission. (Qur'an 3:113)

Among the followers of the Bible are some who, if entrusted with a treasure, would readily pay it back; and among them are some who, if entrusted with a single coin, would not pay it back unless you were to stand constantly by them demanding. That is because they say: "we are not held to account for what we do to the gentiles," but they speak a lie against God when they know the truth. (Qur'an 3:76)

Among the followers of Moses is a group who guide towards truth, and by the truth do justice. (Qur'an 7:159)

Those who reject God and His messengers, and desire to separate between God and his messengers, saying, "we believe in some and reject some," desiring to take a middle course, it is they who are truly unbelievers; and We have prepared for unbelievers a humiliating chastisement. But to those who believe in God and His messengers, and make no distinction between any of the messengers, We shall soon give them their rewards. For God is Oft-Forgiving, Ever-Merciful. (Qur'an 4:150-152)

If only the followers of the Bible had believed and been righteous, We would indeed have atoned for them their evil deeds and admitted them to gardens of bliss. If only they had acted according to the Torah, the Gospel, and that which has been revealed to them from their Lord, they would surely have received provision from above them and from beneath their feet. Among them there are people who are on the right course, but evil are the deeds of many of them. (Qur'an 5:65,66)

Perhaps it is appropriate to move on to another issue in order to discover the truth about the disciplined freedom of Islam, a lighter topic which is still a sensitive issue: the issue of sex and sexuality. American values and laws restricted even the mention of unambiguous sexual terms and referral to the sexual organs until the beginning of the twentieth century. Some European novels that contained such terms were restricted from publication until the sixties. The famous Kinsey Report and other medical and sociological studies until today make clear that many Americans suffer from great ignorance about sexual subjects!

On the other hand, the Prophet—blessing and peace be upon him—who was most chaste in speech and impeccable in manners, spoke about it in clear detail. Moreover, the Qur'an itself speaks about this subject in words that are at the same time both clear and respectful, and many Muslim authors, both ancient and modern, devoted whole books, or chapters of their books to this discussion which are available to everyone. Modern medical specialists are amazed to discover how these works combined scientific biological, physiological and anatomical knowledge, as well as sound psychological and behavioral guidance in descriptive terms that are neither prudish nor trivial. Western experience is divided between total suppression with its source in monastic celibacy, and unrestricted arousal taken from the Freudians and others, while Islamic society is generally free from both.

In general, Islamic civilization did not know censorship of thought and writing in any subject, of which the rare instances of book burning only serve as evidence. If Giordano Bruno, Galileo, or others like them had been able to immigrate to the nearest Muslim country, they would not have been subjected to any persecution. As for Spinoza, his situation can be compared to his Jewish coreligionist Moses Maimonides (whose high position within the government of Islamic Egypt gave him security and freedom to express his opinions). Despite the fact that Israel is taken as an example of democracy by many Americans, let us ask the Jewish Falasha immigrants there from whom they receive better treatment, from the Muslims of their homeland and within Israel, or from the (European) members of their own religion?

In order to shed more light on the matter, there is no harm in pointing out the events that have happened in the past, and continue to happen in the states of the African lake region (Burundi and Rwanda). Islam has become a safe asylum for both sides in the repulsive racial wars there, and Western missionaries are bewildered at the nearly four million from both tribes (Hutus and Tutsis) who have embraced Islam. In his address on a national occasion in 2000, the Rwandan president expressed his great admiration for Islam, surprise at its greatness, and the speed with which it extinguished the fuse of hostility and hatred between people. The Islamic Mufti of Rwanda (who translated the address for this writer) said to me, "the President was about to publicly announce his embracing of Islam, and I am in the daily expectation that he will do so."

If we go back to the history of the Founding Fathers of the United States we discover that it was a very different matter: the United States was founded on a clear conflict between Puritan ethics (of the Calvinists) and their genocidal tendency, because of which millions of human beings among the native peoples were sacrificed, something which (along with other evidence)

provides confirmation that the [Founding] Founders were inspired to this barbaric holocaust by the law of the maculated text of the Torah, by following
the same principles [that the Torah] claimed that God commanded Joshua to
follow, in his wars against the Philistines.

When the groups of colonists were able to become a national force, the
violence was quickly directed toward the original peoples from whom the
colonists came, especially the English. The American War of Independence
was a revolution of white Protestants against a white, Protestant government.
This proves that it had no ethical meaning other than the continuation of the
principle of expansion and conquest, the principle shared by both the (British)
government and the colonists. If the matter had been one of values such as
freedom and democracy, it would have been most appropriate, out of all the
governments of the West, to obey the English government, which was indis-
putably the most democratic and open to debate of all the colonial powers.
Without praising British colonialism, we can say that the people of other
colonies rejoiced at the news of the British defeat of the Portuguese and
Spanish for this reason. Then why did the branch revolt against the root?
What lit the fuse of revolution was none other than the Sugar Law of 1764
and the (infamous) Tea Tax. Both parties fought over a land that did not
belong to either, and human rights had neither mention nor effect!

The third feature besides exterminating millions of native people, and
fighting a democratic government in a civil war, is the most repulsive of features which formed the American national existence: hunting down and
enslaving human beings simply because God created them a different color!

I do not know why the sixty intellectuals failed to praise the morality of
America's freeing the slaves, although this claim would be similar to their
claiming universal values and just war in that each is a late justification for a
long and painful situation which cannot be justified any more than you can
shield yourself from the sun with the palm of your hand. The phrase, "All
men are created equal," with which Jefferson begins the Declaration of
Independence was not used in the context of inventing or discovering universal
values, but was only an expedient argument for the equality of the white man
of the American colonies with the white man in the motherland. It never
included people of color or women. The Americans took nearly two centuries
to pass civil rights legislation and end racial discrimination during the
Johnson administration.

At the time that civil rights advocates were seeking to achieve the end of
racial discrimination through legislation (which is only theoretical, as evidenced by subsequent and continual incidents) they sought to void the racist
laws which were then fully in effect and enforced with the great popular support. As a quick example we recall that the constitution of the State of
Mississippi, section eight concerning education, paragraph 207, required separation of white children from Negro children so that each race shall have its
own schools; section ten concerning reformatories and prisons, paragraph
225, required the legislature to take appropriate measures to separate white
prisoners from black prisoners; section fourteen, general laws, paragraph 263,

declared marriage between a white person and a Negro, Mulatto, or a person of one-eighth Negro blood to be unlawful and void.

Perhaps more surprising than the laws of the State of Mississippi is the following text:

> Whoever prints, publishes, or distributes printed, typewritten, or handwritten materials inciting the population to consent to social integration and marriage between white[s] and black[s], or presenting arguments or proposals of this kind, his activity is considered an offense punishable by law by a fine not to exceed five hundred dollars, or imprisonment for a term not to exceed six months, or both.

In a document presented to the United Nations in February 1948 entitled "An Appeal to the World," the National Association for the Advancement of Colored People stated that similar laws to those of the State of Mississippi were applied in Virginia, North Carolina, South Carolina, Georgia, Alabama, Florida, Louisiana, Arkansas, Oklahoma, and Texas, and that similar but less severe laws were applied in Delaware, West Virginia, Kentucky, Tennessee, and Missouri, and that there were eight northern states that forbade intermarriage between whites and blacks: California, Colorado, Idaho, Indiana, Nebraska, Nevada, Oregon, and Utah.

The appeal then continues to detail the wrongs borne by people of color in the United States, stating that in twenty of the country's states there was (at that time) mandatory segregation of white and black pupils, while the laws of the State of Florida required school books reserved for black pupils to be stored separately from school books reserved for white pupils. In fourteen of the country's states, the law required segregation of white train passengers from black train passengers, while the laws of eight states required the establishment of separate compartments for whites and blacks. As for buses, segregation was required in eleven states. There were laws requiring the segregation of white and black patients in hospitals, and in eleven states, mental patients were also segregated according to color and race. Segregation was required between whites and blacks in prisons and reformatory institutions in eleven of the states of the Union.

There were laws mandating the segregation of whites from blacks in too many aspects to list them all. However, narrating some examples is sufficient to clarify the extent of the oppression which pursued the colored races with the force of law. In Oklahoma, the law mandated separate telephone booths for Negroes. In Texas, it was illegal for white wrestlers to fight black wrestlers, and in North Carolina, it was not permitted for Negro and White workers to work on the same floor in textile plants, nor was it permitted for Negroes to enter and exit from the same doors from which Whites entered and exited.

Before September 11, 2001, America had another September of historical events in the year 1957, when President Eisenhower ordered the unfortunate 101st Airborne Division to invade the state of Arkansas and remove the 10,000-strong Arkansas National Guard. He announced to the public that he was taking these measures to remove the disgrace which was exposed to the entire world, especially the Communist world, that human rights in America were useless when the governor of the state insisted that he would not permit black children to enter white schools, rejecting the ruling of the Federal Court with the excuse that integration would cause chaos and bloodshed in the state, and that the state would need a five-year transition period beginning with the integration of kindergartens in the year 1963.

During the senior Bush's presidency the worst race riots since the '60s in Los Angeles were sparked by police brutality in the arrest of Rodney King that shocked the President when he witnessed it on film. Similar incidents occurred during the Clinton Presidency in New York and Cincinnati.

Each incident stirs up a long history of deep-rooted racism which indicates that moral values are slogans that are quickly forgotten because the basis of those values is not true faith in God. We can compare this to the situation in Islam: at the largest gathering ever seen in ancient Arab history, the Prophet made his farewell pilgrimage in the company of the Arab rulers and the leaders of their tribes. The entire assembly was eager to see the Messenger —blessing and peace be upon him—especially the rulers of Yemen who had recently embraced Islam and come a long way. They were extremely surprised when they first glimpsed him. What they saw was the face of a prophet, not the face or appearance of a king: he was sitting on his camel along with his freed black slave Usama ibn Zayd who was sitting behind him. This is something that any Arab leader would have disdained to do—even if the man was no longer a slave. A year previous, one of the rulers, Wa'il ibn Hajr, refused to sit on the same camel with Mu'awiya ibn Abi Sufyan, who would one day become the Caliph of the Muslims.

The Prophet—blessing and peace be upon him—then delivered the greatest sermon glorifying, confirming and describing human rights known in history. He repeated a similar message on the second day (Eid al-Adhha) and the third day. In one excerpt he says: "Humanity! Do you not share one Lord and one father? Truly, there is no superiority for the Arab over the non-Arab, nor the non-Arab over the Arab, nor White over Black, nor Black over White, except by piety."[19]

One of the chiefs of the tribe of Quraysh purchased a luxurious robe owned by the famous Yemeni ruler, Dhu Yazin, before embracing Islam. He presented it as a gift to the Prophet—blessing and peace be upon him—but he refused to take it without paying its fair price. After buying it he gave it as a gift to Usama ibn Zayd. The Arabs were shocked to see the robe of Dhu Yazin worn by a freed slave. This chief of Quraysh[20] departed in awe of what he had seen. It is narrated that the rulers of Yemen freed thousands of slaves during that season out of faith in God, and in imitation of God's Messenger. In this manner, Islam transformed the values of the Arabs and other peoples, and dissolved discrimination without creating an uproar. Those who had been slaves yesterday became rulers, scholars and leaders whose high position and honor was unmatched even by the Caliphs and their sons. If the author so desired, he could fill numerous volumes with such narrations.

Before Islam the law of the jungle reigned supreme. According to it, refraining from violent revenge was a shameful weakness. One of the Arab poets mocked a certain tribe: "A tribe that does not violate its covenants/And does not a mustard seed of harm to anyone!"

But the companions of the Prophet were educated by the Qur'an, which taught them to be steadfast in the truth: "Be patient and endure as the most determined of the prophets endured."

About controlling one's temper, the Prophet—blessings and peace be upon him—counseled: "The truly strong man is not he who fights, but he that controls his anger."[21]

In this fashion, justice, kindness and helping the oppressed became the standards by which societies were judged.

A group of early Muslims fled from the persecution of the idolaters to Ethiopia. When they returned after a long absence, the Prophet—blessings and peace be upon him—asked them to speak about the wonders they had seen in that country. They said:

> While we were sitting there one day an old woman passed by carrying a water jug on her head, when a boy came by and placed his hand between her shoulder blades and pushed her onto her knees and broke her jug. When she got up she looked at him and said, "You will know, you double-crosser, when God's footstool comes down, when all mankind is gathered together, and their hands and feet are made to speak about their deeds, then you will know what is to become of me and you before Him tomorrow!"

The Prophet replied, "She spoke the truth, yes, she spoke the truth! How can Allah sanctify a nation whose weak do not take their satisfaction from their mighty ones?"[22]

Was your modern version of the Roman Empire built on the skulls of ten million Indians and slaves, or twenty million? If we add the number of slaves who died during transport or during the hunt does it reach 40 million or 100 million? Estimates vary. The number itself does not interest us. The Qur'an states an absolute law: whoever takes even one life unlawfully, it is as if he killed all humankind!

The ready-made American excuse for these atrocities is that some Americans called for freeing the slaves and that they fought the supporters of slavery and eventually won. But they purposely distort the causes of emancipation. It was not out of belief in human equality and dignity as some of them try to portray, because neither side disputed the idea that blacks were inferior to whites! The dispute was whether these inferior people had the right to freedom, and whether it would be more beneficial to the country's reputation and economy.

This detestable belief went to—and still remains at—a level that is difficult for Muslims especially to comprehend, in which even houses of worship are segregated, each race having its own churches, and a black minister in a white church is almost unheard of.

There are some facts that are very difficult for Muslims to interpret. Muslim Imams who have worked in American prisons (whose work itself bears witness to Islamic values and the necessity of them for the reform of humanity) have noted the high percentage of blacks among those sentenced for drug crimes. This seems to contradict the official statistics of the Department of Health and Human Services which indicate that there are five times as many drug addicts among whites as there are among blacks. The confusion is partially clarified when we see that police patrols in America have a dual purpose: to defend the freedom of whites, and to detect crime among blacks. But how do we interpret the statistics that show that there were twice as many blacks as whites arrested during the seventies, while in the nineties there were five times as many arrested! The answer is that since most blacks are poor, they tend to use a cheaper form of drug (crack cocaine) while whites use the more expensive form, and Congress passed legislation imposing stiffer penalties only on the cheaper form.

To this legal oppression—if that is the correct expression—I will add another cause for the increase in black prisoners and clear up the confusion.

When the novel *Roots*[23] was made into a film, statistics say it was seen by more than 130 million Americans! Why? It was not simply because it was a horrible tragedy, but because of the shock that a tragedy of that magnitude had been covered up so long by high-sounding slogans! The film irritated a deep wound in the human conscience that quickly shredded the thin layer of deception and falseness with the dawn of the truth.

According to the novel, the author discovered that he was Muslim because his ancestor, who was hunted down by the "civilized" whites, was Muslim. He was able to trace the event back so that he was able to meet his Muslim relatives seven generations removed in Gambia, who spoke to him about his kidnapped ancestor—the same story that was told to him by his grandmother!

When Columbus arrived at the "Moro"[24] Coast of Cuba and saw a minaret he exclaimed, "My God, there are mosques even in China!"

Yes, there were mosques there built in the Andalusian style, with the motto (of Muslim Granada) "There is no victor but God," written above their prayer niches. The Muslims were the first victims of ethnic cleansing on both sides of the Atlantic: on the eastern side they were hunted down and enslaved, and on the western side Muslim natives were exterminated as part of the campaign of extermination of the native people.

Today, two-billion people of different skin-colors but who share a common faith, believe that America still strives to enslave them—but with more advanced means and slogans, and that their grandchildren will someday remember that and perhaps have revenge.

There are some in Afghanistan who hope that even sooner Mullah Muhammad 'Umar will return, and that George Bush will in a few years be nothing—and the entire matter is up to God alone.

What about the Jews?

Violence against and extermination of the adversary has been a necessary token of many people since Cain killed Abel, but in all of history there has never been a less violent civilization than Islam, which, because of the Qur'an, believes that justice is an absolute value, unaffected by differences of faith, color, race, or any of the other bases which man uses to discriminate, and that God has granted every human being a safe refuge which none can deny him in this world.

The Muslim is protected by his faith, the non-Muslim is protected by his covenant with the Muslims, those under truce are protected by treaty, and those at war are protected by the conditions of legitimate war including the conditions of just cause and mercy, which caused those peoples which were conquered by the Muslims to consider the Islamic conquest to be a delivery from darkness into light, and from servitude to freedom, and they willingly and eagerly embraced the faith of the conquerors, learned their language, and merged with them as much as they could because of what they had learned of the merits of Islam.

Because of this, the Islamic countries remained a refuge for persecuted peoples throughout the world. If the scholars and thinkers, and millions who were burned at the stake by European civilization (represented both by the Church and politically motivated violence) had been able to flee to the nearest Muslim country, they would have found safety there (as thousands of Jews did).

Let us take the clearest example of this: the Jews who have the greatest hostility towards Muslims as divine revelation tells us, and as history and reality bear witness. Let us briefly examine the treatment of the Jews in Islam, and their treatment in Europe and America: in Islam they were given such care as they never experienced in any country, by reason of their being "People of the Book." The Prophet—God bless him and grant him peace—who was the most just and merciful of men, responded to their ignorant behavior with kindness, and to their intrigues with justice, as much as possible. He forgave and accepted the apologies of those who did wrong to him, despite the fact that he endured a great deal of persecution and betrayal at their hands, such as their murder plots against him in which they poisoned his food, and conspired with his enemies on several occasions. It suffices that they rejected him as they rejected Christ—peace be upon him—before, despite the clear signs and proofs concerning the truth of his message, and his overcoming the many difficult tests and trials from their Rabbis, and despite the witness of some of their scholars who embraced his faith.

Despite all of that, he never departed from fair treatment of them, and the dispute never took the form of racial discrimination. The Qur'an itself resolved this by demonstrating that good and evil are found in every nation, and that it is never right to say that one people is pure and holy and the other is unclean, as the Jews claim, which was commonly believed during the pre-Islamic age of ignorance, and was prevalent in modern Europe. Rather, mankind (or the nation) sanctifies or pollutes itself. Each individual is accountable before God at the resurrection. There are many clear and unambiguous verses about this:

> It is not according to your desires nor the desires of the followers of the Bible: Whoever does evil will be requited accordingly, nor will he find besides God any protector or helper. If any do works of righteousness as a believer, whether they be male or female, they will enter paradise, and not the least amount of injustice will be done them. Who is better in faith than one who submits his face to God and does good, and follows the faith of Abraham— turning away from idolatry? For God did take Abraham as his friend. (Qur'an 4:123-125)

> Not all of them are alike: among the followers of the Bible are a group who are upright, reciting God's revelations throughout the night, prostrating themselves. (Qur'an 3:113)

> Among the followers of the Bible are some who, if entrusted with a treasure, would readily pay it back; and among them are some who, if entrusted with a single coin, would not pay it back unless you were to stand constantly by them demanding. That is because they say: "We are not held to account for what we do to the gentiles," but they speak a lie against God when they know the truth. (Qur'an 3:76)

> Among the followers of Moses is a group who guide towards truth, and by the truth do justice. (Qur'an 7:159)

Thus, every Muslim must believe that those Jews who believed in Moses —peace be upon him—were the most favored people of their time. Later, those who believed in Jesus—peace be upon him—were the most favored people of their time. Later, those who believe in Muhammad—God's blessing and peace be upon him—are counted among his companions, who are the most favored people until the end of the world. Any Muslim who rejects the three messages, or any one of them, is not at the same level of morality. Some of them are sinners and others are virtuous. Some are disloyal and some are loyal. Some are dishonest and some are honest. Some are just and some are unjust.

Muslims do not claim to have a monopoly on justice, but acknowledge it in those non-Muslims who embrace it, as they acknowledge the injustice of those Muslims who cast it aside.

The Prophet sent some of his companions to Ethiopia during the time before the establishment of the Islamic state, because its Christian king at that time allowed no one to be treated unjustly. Similarly, 'Amr ibn al-'As bore witness that the Christians of Europe were the most resistant people to the tyranny of kings, and the most compassionate to the poor and widows.[25] As for Muslim rulers whom all Muslims agree to have been tyrants, they are too many to count.

Islam severed the subject of racism at its root when it forbade boasting of one's ancestors and descendants even if it were the truth. It forbade rivalry based on legitimate and praiseworthy titles such as whether one were from the Muhajirun (the first Muslims from Makkah who later emigrated to Madina) or the Ansar (those who later became Muslims in Madina who welcomed and assisted the Makkan immigrants), let alone aspects such as race or color.

In the Prophetic biography a well-known event occurred between the Muslims and the Jews in the Madina marketplace. A Jewish man wanted to cause chaos by igniting a rivalry with the Muslims. He loudly swore by "Him who favored Moses over all mankind." One of the Muslims answered him, "By Him who favored Muhammad over all mankind." Trouble was ready to break out when the Prophet—God's blessing and peace be on him—put an end to the problem by saying to the Muslims, "Do not make me better than Moses."

With Islam, human beings are able to give justice its due while defending themselves from the unavoidable hostilities of those who oppose them and deny them their rights: the Prophet—blessings and peace be upon him—sent one of his companions to the Jews of Khaybar to receive the money that they had agreed to pay according to their treaty with the Muslims. They attempted to bribe the companion, but he refused, saying, "By God, God's Messenger is the most beloved person to me, and by God, you are the most detested people to me, but I cannot love him and wrong you in any way!"

The long history of Islam bears witness that the Jews were not persecuted, but just the opposite, except on rare occasions. The Caliphs and Sultans usually had good relationships with the Jews and gave them preferential status above the Muslims for worldly reasons, to the extent that many Muslims complained and the scholars of Islamic Law criticized the rulers for it.

As for European history—without excusing the Jews—it is a chain of persecution of the Jews so long that it is difficult to measure. Rather, it is difficult to understand or believe some of the persecution. Besides the deep-rooted hostility and continued campaigns against them initiated by the popes, we find Luther, whose teaching was influenced by Judaism, who advised his followers at the end of his life to burn the Jewish ghettos of Germany. For this reason, some researchers consider the Nazi Holocaust to be an extension of the Protestant-inspired persecution, let alone the Catholic![26]

The ecclesiastical councils, the popes, and bishops of every sect sought to prove their faith and piety by issuing laws to punish and expel them, and to excommunicate Christians who dealt with them. In every land and church, groups were formed whose sole act of worship was to burn the Jews unless they converted to Christianity. This occurred in France, Spain, Germany and elsewhere, and when the Black Plague struck, all of Europe was overrun by violent waves of Jewish extermination, to the extent that 510 Jewish communities were destroyed in the mid-fifteenth century. Some historians estimate that not even one in five Jews escaped the destruction. All of that because of the accusation that the plague was caused by the Jews "poisoning Christian wells," despite the fact that it was a worldwide epidemic.

The atrocities committed against them (as well as against the Muslims) by the Inquisition are so well known it is not necessary to mention them. In reality, hatred of Jews was so firmly planted within the deepest recesses of the Christian soul as to be beyond the limits of logic, and totally stripped of any cause, as was also the case of Jewish hatred for Christians. Among the evidence of this is that European dictionaries used the word "Jew" not as a name for a sect of people with their own religion, but as a description for evil, malice, treachery, greed and filthiness. It is also quite apparent in literature. When the greatest English playwright, Shakespeare, wanted to choose a character to represent these attributes, he chose the Jewish "merchant of Venice," and when their great novelist, Charles Dickens wanted to show the worst type of demoralizing education he also chose a Jewish character in *Oliver Twist*. The level of hatred rose so high that Jews began to hate themselves. This happened to many intellectuals such as Marx and Freud, and before them, to Spinoza.

This is an appropriate point at which to mention the distinction of Arabic literature in this regard. Offensive attributes are not personified by race or religion in Arabic literature, they are simply used by themselves to describe whomever they describe, whether Caliphs, ministers, judges, teachers, or commoners, no matter what their religion, such as in *Kitab Al-Bukhula* (Book of Misers), *Al-Humuqa'wal-Mughafilin* (Fools and Idiots), *Al-Majanin* (The Insane), or *As-Hab Al-Hafuwat* (Committers of Gaffes).

As for America, whoever claims that it was founded on equality and freedom, its founders tried to be too clever to resort to holocausts, and too fair to kill every child like a Pharaoh. They were satisfied to try to cut off the problem at its roots by suggesting outlawing the immigration of Jews to America.

During the Constitutional Convention of 1787 Benjamin Franklin is said to have made his well-known speech:

> I fully agree with General Washington, that we must protect this young nation from an insidious influence and impenetration. The menace, gentlemen, is the Jews.
>
> In whatever country Jews have settled in any great number, they have lowered its moral tone; depreciated its commercial integrity; have segregated themselves and have not been assimilated; have sneered at and tried to undermine the Christian religion upon which that nation is founded, by objecting to its restrictions; have built up a state within the state; and when opposed have tried to strangle that country to death financially, as in the case of Spain and Portugal.
>
> For over 1,700 years, the Jews have been bewailing their sad fate in that they have been exiled from their homeland, as they call Palestine. But gentlemen, did the world give it to them in fee simple, they would at once find some reason for not returning. Why? Because they are vampires, and vampires do not live on vampires. They cannot live only among themselves. They must subsist on Christians and other people not of their race.
>
> If you do not exclude them from these United States, in their Constitution, in less than 200 years they will have swarmed here in such

great numbers that they will dominate and devour the land and change our form of government, for which we Americans have shed our blood, given our lives [and] our substance and jeopardized our liberty.

If you do not exclude them, in less than 200 years our descendants will be working in the fields to furnish them substance, while they will be in the counting houses rubbing their hands. I warn you, gentlemen, if you do not exclude Jews for all time, your children will curse you in your graves.

Jews, gentlemen, are Asiatics, let them be born where they will nor how many generations they are away from Asia, they will never be otherwise. Their ideas do not conform to an American's, and will not even thou[gh] they live among us ten generations. A leopard cannot change its spots. Jews are Asiatics, are a menace to this country if permitted entrance, and should be excluded by this Constitutional Convention.

Timurlane may have been the worst ruler in the history of Islamic civilization, but he never reached that level of racism. The Jews lived in his capital of Samarqand just as they live today in Washington.[27]

Without doubt, whoever reads modern European history must acknowledge the level of religious freedom achieved in the United States with fewer losses of life than in Europe, except that there is a terrible type of religious coercion practiced by and supported by millions of Americans under the eyes and ears of the government, intellectuals, and rights organizations, and which is, moreover, supported by most charities in American society: evangelization in which a morsel of food or a dose of medicine is placed before the mouths of those suffering from hunger or pain, and they are told, "If you express your faith in Christ and accept (original) sin, the crucifixion, and the atonement, then take this morsel or this dose, or else..."

To prove that this sort of coercion is not the exception, we should understand that 30 billion dollars a year is spent on foreign missions, and that thousands of people and dozens of supporting universities, institutes, and broadcasting organizations are all working in this area.

There is a further example difficult to interpret in light of so-called religious freedom: Did John Walker, the American youth who accepted Islam and went to Afghanistan, err in his understanding of American freedom, or does this freedom have obscure and flexible limits which can be expanded to include the Israelis who plotted terrorist activities inside America, and narrowed so as not to understand the actions of this innocent young man?

If it is his duty (according to American values) for a person to fight alongside his coreligionists and fellow citizens, then what is the problem with the Muslim volunteers who fought along with the Taliban? And why were these atrocities committed against them in Mazar-e-Sharif and Cuba?

But if what is illegal is for a person to fight people of his own nationality and religion, then what are the actions of John Walker, who may never have fired a weapon, in comparison to the butchery of the Northern Alliance who killed thousands or tens of thousands of their own people?

If only American justice had stopped at this indecent double standard, but it went beyond that to that which is not in the power of any human: seeking to change Muslims' beliefs within their own country in their school curriculum, and by forbidding the third pillar of their faith, charity, in the name of rooting out terrorism.

We ask you, does this request have even the smallest connection with justice and religious freedom? Or anything else mentioned in your letter?

What about the Events of September 11?

Readers of your letter were surprised to read that "the killers of September 11 issued no particular demands; in this sense, at least, the killing was done for its own sake."[28] This is without doubt, an insult to the intelligence of millions of people from all over the world who heard and saw the leader of the accused group speaking about the tragedy of the Palestinian people and the crimes of America in Iraq[29] and other places, connecting American security to the security of the Palestinians. This connection appears in a great number of testimonies: in the statements of world leaders, in those of the leadership of the United Nations, in reports of the international media, in American opinion polls in which 68 percent of the American public opinion wanted a solution for the Palestinian problem, even in the statements of President Bush, Secretary Powell, and Secretary Rumsfeld speaking about solving the problem and establishing a Palestinian state, and about concern to improve the political and economic situation of the Islamic world whose troubles can be attributed to American policy. Bush's repeated refusal to connect the two problems is only a response to the clear demand heard by the world, and understood by most of its leaders, the European Union being only one example of that.

So why then the recourse to this fallacy? Why this attempt to discover their motives while denying that they ever issued particular demands?

The very next paragraph gives us the answer.[30] The whole purpose of the smoke screen around their demands is only a means to say that the attackers targeted America because it is free and democratic, just as the American president stated from the beginning and has repeated many times since. This causes the reader to feel sorry for the position these intellectuals are in, and reminds one of Soviet biologists who altered the results of their research to serve Marxist ideology. But they were forced to do so, while these sixty have voluntarily presented this fallacy to support the statements of their president.

So as not to be unfair, we will ask them only one question: Why was the Palestinian problem[31] absent from the open letter when it is the fundamental current problem that preoccupies the entire world, America in particular?

Let us listen to the other side of America, the side which recognizes and faces the truth, proposing solutions that achieve America's interests—not Muslim or Palestinian interests. As long as Americans don't understand the cause of the disaster they will never arrive at a correct solution. This point of view was expressed by David Duke in a long article from which we have provided the following excerpt dealing with the issue at hand (knowing that this man cannot be accused of loving Arabs, we do not agree with his well-known opinions on other topics.)

Why was America attacked?
It is vital that we know why bin Ladin and millions of others around the world have come to hate America. Why are so many willing to risk or even sacrifice their lives to get at us? I certainly hope no one reading this is so naïve as to believe that the growing millions who hate America do so because we are "free." That canard has to be the most ridiculous notion ever sold to the American people since the pet rock. To end the threat of terrorism against the American people, we must know the true reason why we are so hated...

Perhaps we should have enough courage to consider the possible reasons why so many might hate us. Only when we have all the facts, rather than cute little clichés like "They were attacking freedom," can we decide the best way we can protect our people in the future...

Too many American politicians have treasonously betrayed the American people by blindly supporting the leading terrorist nation on earth: Israel...

I will show you documentary evidence that during the last 50 years Israel has engaged in more murderous terrorism than any other nation in the world; and that by supporting its criminal behavior, America is now reaping the fanatical hatred of hundreds of millions of people around the globe. Support for Israel's terrorism has directly led to the terrorism now going on against the United States. Most Americans don't even realize the magnitude and scope of Israeli terrorism because of the Jewish media control mentioned by General Brown. A pertinent example of their incredible media power is their ability to propagate the Big Lie that the WTC attack had nothing at all to do with Israel; that the kamikaze attackers hated and attacked Americans because we are "free"...

The Jewish-dominated American mass media and the Israeli-controlled politicians do not want the American people to fully realize the incredibly high price America pays for blindly supporting Israel. In the aftermath of the attacks on September 11, 2001, even President Bush repeated the absurd lie, alleging the attack happened because they hate the fact that we are free. If, as the media says, bin Ladin is behind the terrorism, then they know that the attack occurred not because he hates freedom. Just three years ago, ABC television and PBS *Frontline* interviewed bin Ladin during the time of the Clinton administration. Bin Ladin clearly stated why he opposed America: "They (Americans) have put themselves at the mercy of a disloyal government... it is Israel inside America. Take the sensitive ministries such as the Secretary of State and the Secretary of Defense and the CIA, you will find that the Jews have the upper hand in them. They make use of America to further their plans for the world...

"For over half a century, Muslims in Palestine have been (by the Jews) slaughtered and assaulted and robbed of their honor and of their property. Their houses have been blasted, their crops destroyed.... This is my message to the American people: to look for a serious government that looks out for their interests and does not attack other people's lands, or other people's honor..."

Duke then comments:

Notwithstanding any of his alleged crimes, bin Ladin has never in his entire life uttered a word against Democracy! The media invented the lie about attacking Democracy to hide the real truth; that America is being attacked in retaliation for the American government's support of Israel's terrorist policies in the Mideast. The unanimity of the media in propagating this huge lie without contradiction should make every thoughtful person suspect that Americans are not getting the whole truth from the media...

After going into a lengthy list of Israeli terrorism, Duke then goes on to cite evidence of Israeli complicity in the September 11 attacks:

The *Washington Times* ran a story on September 10, 2001 about a 68-page study issued by the U.S. Army School for Advanced Military Studies (SAMS). The study, issued by the elite Army officer's school, detailed the dangers of a possible U.S. Army occupational force in the Mideast. Here is the article's comment about the study's view of the Israeli Mossad: "Of the Mossad, the Israeli intelligence service, the SAMS officers say: 'Wildcard. Ruthless and cunning. Has capability to target U.S. forces and make it look like a Palestinian/Arab act.'"

Duke then comments:

Ironically, within 24 hours of the story's publication, the World Trade Center and the Pentagon were attacked. Could the "ruthless and cunning Mossad," as the U.S. Army officers describe it, covertly have been behind the attack?

Duke then presents what he calls solid evidence implicating Mossad which we will not go into here, since it is not our purpose to either prove or disprove it as much as it is our purpose to prove what is—in our opinion— the purposeful sophism of the open letter of sixty intellectuals.

Not only do we cite his evidence, but we will also cite other evidence reported in the American and Israeli press, as well as the international press:

1. The case of five Israelis who filmed the attack while it happened, as was reported in American, Israeli, and other sources.
2. The case of the arrest of six Israelis in two cars who had in their possession pictures and maps of nuclear reactors in Florida and the Alaskan pipeline, as well as "suspicious devices."
3. The suspicious trading in airline and insurance stocks at the New York Stock Exchange just prior to the events. This is a well-known occurrence which is under investigation, and it is only one piece of evidence that the Israelis at least, had prior knowledge of the events.

Let us repeat that we do not mean to exonerate the one who has been accused and convict someone else, we simply want to direct your attention to the values by which the American administration and the American media operate.

This and other evidence has been totally ignored while the media empires have rushed to accuse Muslims, and to spread anything that would cause them alone to be charged, despite the existence of wide gaps and glaring inconsistencies. We can't blame the press for its ignorance since its bias is . well-known, but we can't believe that none of our sixty intellectuals have heard any such as the following:

1. The passenger list published by the airlines contained no Arabic names, in contrast to the list published by the government.
2. Some persons whose names (of the accused) were announced have been definitively proven to be either previously deceased, or living in their home countries.
3. The dependence on evidence such as copies of the Qur'an found in their cars or homes, or the chance discovery of a letter sprinkled with Christian terms not known to or used by most Muslims.
4. The steel pillars were melted in the fire at the World Trade Center, but the passport of one of the accused was not destroyed. Why don't the Americans benefit from this discovery and create a vest for the President or a covering for the Pentagon from the same paper as the passport? And why would a suicide bomber carry his passport when he is going to his death in a few minutes?
5. The accused were young men who entered America a few months earlier, coming from the poorest country in the world, and received limited training in aviation. But the plot that was carried out was of a very high level of sophistication and required advanced technology, consideration of weather predictions, and skill in making amazingly professional maneuvers of the aircraft, in addition to the possession of detailed intelligence that caused the Secret Service to believe that the President's plane was targeted while in the air, so that reporters on board were ordered not to use their cell phones and to completely turn them off for fear of signaling the position of the plane.

Many commentators from America and other countries believe that a professional espionage organization on the level of Mossad used those young men and took advantage of their readiness for death in order to achieve its objectives. That in itself is not important to us, we only relate this to ask the sixty signatories: Is there nothing here that might cast a doubt—and we only say a doubt—and cause you to avoid rushing to judgment, while justice demands that the weakness in the evidence against one party strengthens the case against the other party?

It was expected that our American intellectuals would avoid entangling themselves in the same blunders and contradictions as the American administration which were ridiculed by many commentators throughout the world, when millions asked: "Has another suicide bomber turned up alive today like yesterday?"

"Did the President give another speech today which Powell or Rumsfeld will have to contradict tomorrow? Each denies the statements of the other, who should we believe? Why did the government cover up the incidents which occurred near the White House on the day of the attacks?"

"If the attackers' goal was to attack freedom, why didn't they attack one of the nations which is more free than America? Why did they choose the Pentagon and World Trade Center instead of the institutions of democracy and human rights in America?"

They expected intellectuals to correct the President's information; first by informing him that the Taliban is not a group of musicians, and finally, by advising him to delay pulverizing an exhausted, weak people before complete evidence is provided.

We know that the American government had prepared in advance to attack Afghanistan, and we suppose that the sixty intellectuals will not dispute that, but in any case there is no disputing that justice dictates proving the accusation, that the punishment be in proportion to the crime, and that punishment should be limited to those who committed the crime only, even if doing so takes time. Even if we assume that the need for vengeance caused the Americans to hurry the decision to fight a war, what is wrong with reconsidering it now? And why shouldn't these intellectuals be the ones to raise their voices about it?

Justice demands granting pardon and atonement for wrongdoing. If America had done so it would have been able to point to it as a witness to the world that it is brave, free, and just. Then the signatories would be able to talk!

If only America had the characteristics of the Prophet of mercy and justice, Muhammad—blessing and peace be upon him—who publicly renounced the actions of his great general, Khalid ibn al-Walid who fought a hostile tribe of idolaters, but the tribe claimed that there was a confusion of words during the battle. The Prophet gave them the benefit of the doubt because of their presumed innocence and therefore denounced the actions of Khalid and paid compensation for those of the tribe killed during the battle.

As for mercy and preferring pardon, we know of no place for these in American politics or values, since these belong to the prophets and their followers alone. The idolaters killed seventy Muslim men and the Prophet promised to kill a like number of them; when God granted him victory, he returned to Makkah and some of the Muslims said, "Now the Prophet—blessings and peace be upon him—will revenge those Muslims who were killed." But the Prophet—blessings and peace be upon him—recited to them the verse: "If you punish, then punish in proportion to the harm done you, but if you will be patient, then it is better for those who are patient." He then said, "No, we will be patient and have mercy," and pardoned all of them except for a very small number who committed particular crimes.

The conditions which you mention for just war are good, even if they don't reach the level of precision and detail defined by Islamic law, but the question is, "Does your government observe these conditions?"[32]

Who among you can say, "yes" when the entire world knows the answer is "no"?

You indicate that no war is better than war, and that war is not legitimate if it is possible to avoid it by negotiations or mediation.[33] Good words! Haven't you heard of the principle by which your government rejected the neutrality of any other party, let alone negotiations with its opponents themselves?

Did it not announce to the world that it must either be with America in all its beliefs and actions, or with the terrorists? Yet you announced, "In the name of universal human morality ... we support our government's ... decision."[34]

Let us leave aside justice and values and ask a pragmatic question: What has America gained from this arbitrary principle? [It has received only] hypocritical statements from world leaders along with an increase in resentment and hatred in all parts of the world.

Wouldn't it be better for your government to admit that rather than continuing to repeat it?

You openly accuse a group and then divide the world into those who are for and those who are against, with no possibility of neutrality, and no room for discussion. Then you dare to ascribe to [your arguments] the attributes of universal human morality and just war!

This is not the first time in the history of American wars even if it is the most arbitrary. During the Gulf War America rejected the Arab solution despite the fact that it was entirely an Arab matter.[35]

Furthermore, have you examined the statements of your own officials? Of course not, since you have added things which none of them ever said, when you said that the Islamic movement openly professes its desire and ability to use murder, and its willingness to use chemical and biological weapons...

Who made this statement? When and where?

Do you want the world to forgive your government's deeds and lies because they pale in comparison with your own deeds and lies?[36]

Who is Your Problem With?

It is most unfortunate when the view of sixty intellectuals in this age of easily accessible communications—when a researcher can access the newest publications in a matter of seconds—is nearly identical to the view of Islam of the European clergy of the Dark Ages!

Whatever the level of intolerance of the ancients, it is worse for modern people to continue the same pattern. Persisting in a sin is worse than committing it, especially when the means of ceasing are readily available.

When McVeigh blew up the federal building in Oklahoma City, the investigators possessed detailed information about his physical description as well as his political affiliation. Yet hundreds, or perhaps thousands of reporters, thousands of miles from the site, spoke about "middle-eastern features," and an Islamic connection without any official or unofficial source. Even the Pentagon announced the need for Arabic translators to work in interrogation. Finally when Clinton spoke of the total innocence of Arabs and Muslims in the matter, most of them ceased their disparagement of Islam, and harassment of Muslims. But, when Goldstein massacred people at prayer in the Mosque of Abraham (in Hebron), did the Americans speak about "Zionist terrorism"? Or did they simply talk of a crime committed by a Jewish individual? And that is only one of many examples.

On the other hand, if we supposed that all terrorist incidents in America for a century had been the work of an extremist Islamic organization, would that excuse accusing all Muslims in general or Islam itself?

America has more organizations than any other country espousing racism, extremist religions, and terrorism. [Would] it then be correct to attribute whatever actions any one of them commits to the American people, or to the religion of America itself?

Or, for example, why did the Japanese media not accuse the Chinese or the Communists of carrying out the terrorist incident in the Tokyo Metro? And that they did it because Japan is free and advanced? Was it stupidity on their part, or was it because God bestowed a different level of justice on all of them? Or is it that the American media, along with the American administration, has its own definition of justice?

Why is it that the British media do not attack Catholicism every time there is an incident in Northern Ireland? Aren't the Catholics the traditional enemies of the Protestants? Isn't the war there clearly a religious war? Hasn't the competition between them for converts in Africa led sometimes to burning missionary centers and even bloodshed?

The "al-Qa'ida" organization—if there actually is an organization— never claimed to be a part of the Islamic movement. Nor has anyone in the Islamic movement said, before or after September 11, that that organization was part of them. In fact, some of them have gone to excess in condemning them, especially in America and its allies. They have even denied that it has any connection to Islam at all!

Yet, the signatories state that this organization is but one arm of the Islamic movement! Exactly as if a Muslim writer claimed that a group such as the skinheads or the Irish Republican Army were only one arm of the International Christian movement which includes the Catholics, Protestants, Orthodox, Quakers, Mormons, Baptists, etc.

This exposes their real problem, which is in reality their problem with Islam, not with the Islamic movement. Even if we supposed that all Muslims in the world became Americans in every aspect, every incident will still be attributed to them from the first moment! What do you suppose is the cause of this? Is it reason and academic research? Or is it the residue within the unconscious that rushes out, completely bypassing the conduits of reason, which some scholars believe to be deeply-rooted violence and fabricated enemies within the European psyche mentioning this unforgettable advice: in order to make the problem clearer let us take the example of the devil. People, without excusing criminals or relieving them of any of their responsibility for their actions, attribute such actions to the devil since the origin of all sin is his temptation and enticement. Thus, he has come to be the incarnation of absolute evil. As you see, the great amount of misinformation and misconceptions about Islam has caused the people of the West (with a few exceptions) to see Islam as the incarnation of evil in their deepest feelings, even if they know intellectually that there is good and evil in every religion. Because of this the Western mind has no problem in attributing any evil deed to Islam, despite the knowledge of its actual innocence. For example, the Jim Jones (suicide) incident had no relation to Islam whatsoever, but if a book came out today or tomorrow saying that it was an Islamic act since Islam is the embodiment of evil and excuses such deeds, many people would accept it without discussion.

When (the boxer) Muhammad Ali visited the ruins of the World Trade Center a heckler said to him, "Aren't you ashamed to belong to the same religion as bin Ladin?" He replied, "Aren't you ashamed to belong to the religion that produced Adolph Hitler?" His answer was logically correct, but if the questioner believes that Hitler exchanged Christian ethics for the ethics of the devil—which he unconsciously equates with Islam—then Muhammad Ali's answer would not be unconvincing. This shows us the depth of the problem and the size of the tragedy.

The Church used to interpret the "number of the beast—666" in the Book of Revelation (the Apocalypse of John) as being Islam, and it seems that this interpretation, or a trace of it, remains within the minds of their descendants—even though they are secularists.

Thus the open letter is contradictory. It uses the voice of reason when it distinguishes between Islam and that which was done by some Muslims, and between *jihad* and terrorism; and it uses the cumulative voice of its hereditary culture within the unconscious whose errors are simply compounded by deception of the official media when it describes all Islamic movements as terroristic, or even more, when the term "international terrorism" is applied only to Muslims.

Do we believe that Islamic Civilization is absolutely perfect, or that Islamic movements are infallible? No Muslim says that. Absolute perfection belongs only to the essence of Islam—in its doctrines, values and laws. Infallibility belongs only to the Prophet himself—God's blessing and peace be upon him—in the message which he delivered from God, and then to the Muslim community as a whole, an ideal person following the Prophet. They are only infallible in that they cannot all agree on an error, despite the small number of them who are true and upright.

All Muslims know, whether they are common people, governments, movements, or nations, that the gap between the reality of the Islamic community and true Islam is the driving reason and only purpose for the existence of the Islamic reform movements. For this reason, all the Islamic movements strive—each according to its own distinct understanding and methodology—

to bring the community back to the Islamic values that are in reality, as we have seen, the universal values, not to the destroy those values as the signatories to this open letter claim.

Acknowledging this is the key to a great opportunity for dialogue between these movements and the West. That is, [dialogue depends] on Western recognition of the positive role they [Islamic reform movements] have, and their true representation of the Islamic peoples. Will the signatories to this letter or others do so? I do not believe it would be very difficult for those who love the truth and desire the welfare of humanity, as long as they are sincere.

The hostile stance towards Islam was firmly established in American policy before September 11 and afterwards. The American war against terrorism has only confirmed that fact more firmly for Muslims. The rest is yet to be seen.

If this inequity, or better yet, antagonism was limited to the Palestinian problem it could be said to be the result of the Zionist lobby in America, or if it was limited to Afghanistan it could be said to be the result of the presence there of al-Qa'ida. But when it is directed towards all Muslim countries and minorities, then how can we interpret it? To clarify this point, let us take six examples divided into two categories, from which we will deduce our results.

First, two countries: the (former) Soviet Union and China. Both are former enemies of America, and each contains minorities who demand this right [of independence]. In the first nation are the Baltic countries on one side and the Islamic nations of the Caucasus on the other. The second nation contains the Buddhists of Tibet on one side, and the Muslim (regions of China) on the other.

The opposite examples are India and the Philippines on one hand, and Indonesia and Sudan on the other. The first two have Muslim peoples who demand separation, while the last two have non-Muslim minorities who demand the very same thing.

The firm American position is:

1. Strong support of independence for the Baltic states, while ignoring the Islamic republics, even sometimes rejecting them and saying nothing about the racist extermination which the Russians carry out there.[37]
2. Strong support of the Tibetan Buddhists, while ignoring the situation of the Muslims of China, despite the fact that there are ten times as many of them.
3. Treating the separatist movements of Kashmir and the Southern Philippines as terrorists and declaring war on them.
4. Strong support for the separatist movements in Indonesia and Sudan.

If the signatories can offer any interpretation for this other than bias against Islam then please do so!

If they suppose that modification of terms such as "Islamic" and "Islamicist"[38] is sufficient to avoid the problem, than that is an even bigger problem. If they believe there is no reason to even mention the extremist fundamentalist and racist organizations in America, extremist racist organizations in Europe, Hindu fundamentalist organizations in India, and religious fundamentalist groups of Japan—in their vast number and infinite variety—then there is no benefit in dialogue with them.

If they felt that it was appropriate to mention them but simply overlooked it, then the dialogue with the Islamic movements can begin with their public apology for singling them out, or rather, for accusing them at all.

As Muslims, it does not concern us whether America was authorized to commit the atrocities that it commits against us as you claim, or not authorized as was plainly stated by officials, including the Democratic representative from Ohio, Dennis Kucinich. What you should know—if your government insists on making war on us with every means and everywhere in the world—is what we're defending.

Conclusion

We are certain that justice is an absolute value, that it is not permitted to take a life which is sacred to God, whether in the name of God or in the name of American values, that it is possible for us to [come to] a word of agreement as was revealed by God, and to reconcile [differences] based on our common welfare. On the basis of the lives of the holy prophets Noah, Abraham, Moses, Jesus and Muhammad—the blessing and peace of God be upon them all—and in application of the text of the Holy Qur'an: we express to you our readiness to debate with that which is best, and to meet with you individually or as a group, in our country or in America.

We will send our opinion to each of you, as well as to other intellectuals, and we will treat your opinions with every care.

Islam commands that all our actions be devoted as worship of God, and to endeavor to make them right as much as possible. For this reason, we would like to thank all those who have helped us to achieve this goal, and demonstrate our willingness to correct any error in our statements, to clarify any misconception, and to discuss any other subjects which we may have omitted.

I advise you—and myself—to be sincere with God, and to be certain that we will be asked concerning what we say and do, to accept that truth no matter what its source, and to interpret the statements of others according to the best possible interpretation. All of us will die, but the truth will remain forever.

Dr. Safar al-Hawali
Makkah, Saudi Arabia

Notes

1. The author is quoting from "What We're Fighting For." The original reads: "In the name of universal human morality, and fully conscious of the restrictions and requirements of a just war, we support our government's, and our society's, decision to use force of arms against them. We pledge to do all we can to guard against the harmful temptations—especially those of arrogance and jingoism—to which nations at war so often seem to yield. At the same time, with one voice we say solemnly that it is crucial for our nation and its allies to win this war. We fight to defend ourselves, but we also believe that we fight to defend those universal principles of human rights and human dignity that are the best hope for humankind. See also page 29 of this volume —Ed.

2. See "What We're Fighting For," page 28 of this volume.—Ed.

3. We believe the author is referring to "Letter from U.S. Citizens to Friends in Europe," which is chapter 21 of this volume. —Ed.

4. See "What We're Fighting For," page 23 of this volume. —Ed.

5. Only in America are there people who desire to see the planet turned into a mass of fire and ash, and openly strive with all seriousness for this horrific end, using the most modern and advanced media to bring the good news of it to all mankind. Only in America do we find fundamentalist organizations this extreme, a level of insanity which even most terrorists cannot reach. Furthermore, these fundamentalists have great political influence and tens of millions of followers, and work under the eyes and ears of the government. Not only are they hostile to everyone who disagrees with them—especially those in government, but some of them have beliefs about the federal government that [are] difficult for many rational people to fathom. All their beliefs and attitudes proceed from their belief in the final, horrible battle of Armageddon, and all [their] activities are attempts to ignite this last war. They cheer every war especially in the Mideast, in hopes that it might be the beginning of the end. If they hear of attempts to achieve peace, they use every means to convince the American government [to] avoid it and cancel it. Their desire for the end of the world is based [on] their belief that Jesus will raise them to heaven without tasting death, to witness the destruction from above the clouds. Forty percent of Americans believe the world will end in the battle of Armageddon. Twenty percent believe that it will end in their lifetimes. They seek to interpret texts of the Bible to refer to current events year by year, month by month, and day by day. Every time they err in predicting the end they simply start from scratch. There may be no stranger sites on the world wide web than theirs. Despite the dozens of incidents committed or attempted by their followers annually, such as murders, bank robberies and blowing up federal installations, they are a part of American culture and stand for conservative American values, fighting liberalism with all their might. Whenever anyone of them is arrested, he alone is accused, without assigning guilt to the movement that produced him. For the beliefs of well-known fundamentalists concerning Armageddon see: Falwell's sermons at www.trbc.org and Pat Robertson's at his CBN website.

6. See Grace Halsell's *Prophecy and Politics*.

7. *Prophecy and Politics: The End is Near.*

8. See "What We're Fighting For" note 28, page 36, this volume. —Ed.

9. In the letter only one side is given: the operations directed against Americans, but there have been only a few thousand victims of such operations. The other pan of the scale is that history proves America to be the world's most bloody, violent, and oppressive society, a record which [at] first glance makes it the farthest nation from just war. For example: (1) The killing of millions of its native peoples; (2) The killing of millions of African slaves; (3) The killing of millions of civilians during the two

world wars, including: the incineration of thousands of civilians in Germany and Japan (more than sixty cities in which more than 400 thousand people were killed, including 100 thousand in Tokyo alone), the atomic bombing of Hiroshima, [and] the atomic bombing of Nagasaki. (These last two require no comment.) In general, if the victims of these two wars were tens of millions, America is responsible for the biggest share of it.

10. After World War II America carried its wars to East and Southeast Asia (Korea, Vietnam, Laos, Cambodia, and China). Some estimates indicate that up to 22 million people were killed, most of whom were civilians, largely the elderly and children. Kissinger admits about a third of that number, but many Americans are convinced that the number is at least half.

11. Pope John Paul II.

12. The author is referring to the following quote from "What We're Fighting For": "[W]e agree with Dr. Martin Luther King, Jr., that the arc of the moral universe is long, but it bends toward justice, not just for the few, or the lucky, but for all people." See also page 23 of this volume. —Ed.

13. The author is referring to the following quote from "What We're Fighting For": "The primary moral justification for war is to protect the innocent from certain harm. Augustine, whose early fifth-century book, *The City of God*, is a seminal contribution to just war thinking, argues (echoing Socrates) that it is better for the Christian as an individual to suffer harm rather than to commit it. But is the morally responsible person also required, or even permitted, to make for *other* innocent persons a commitment to non-self-defense? For Augustine, and for the broader just war tradition, the answer is no." See page 26 of this volume. —Ed.

14. The author is referring to the following passage from "What We're Fighting For": "We use the terms "Islam" and "Islamic" to refer to one of the world's great religions, with about 1.2 billion adherents, including several million U.S. citizens, some of whom were murdered on September 11. It ought to go without saying—but we say it here once, clearly—that the great majority of the world's Muslims, guided in large measure by the teachings of the Qur'an, are decent, faithful, and peaceful. We use the terms "Islamicism" and "radical Islamicist" to refer to the violent, extremist, and radically intolerant religious-political movement that now threatens the world, including the Muslim world. See page 28 of this volume. —Ed.

15. See "What We're Fighting For," page 23 of this volume. —Ed.

16. Mullah Muhammad 'Umar was (and possibly still is) the spiritual leader of the Taliban. —Ed.

17. We believe the author means that both Christian sects and Muslims were victims during the Middle Ages at the hands of a theocracy defined as "a license to kill from God." —Ed.

18. Al-Bukhari and Muslim. [Two scholars who collected sayings of the Prophet Mohammed.]

19. Musnad of Imam Ahmad.

20. His name was Hakim ibn Hazam.

21. Al-Bukhari and Muslim.

22. Narrated by several companions including Jabir, this version of whose narration is found in Ibn Hiban.

23. By Alex Hailey.

24 "Moro" or "Moorish" is the Spanish and Portuguese term for Muslims. Similarly, Magellan called the Philippines "Moro," as well as the nation of Mauritania, and the Canary Islands. Some scholars claim that "America" itself originates from the name Marrakesh or Morocco.

25. *Sahih*, Muslim. [Sahih indicates a strong saying of the Prophet Muhammad. Muslim is a scholar who collected these sayings.]

26. *Story of Civilization* v26.

27. *Story of Civilization* v26.

28. See "What We're Fighting For," page 22 of this volume. —Ed.

29. The American government relied on the policy of annihilation by purposely killing the Iraqi people. In one instance alone (the 'Amariya bomb shelter) the number of victims (who were civilians) was almost half the number of the September 11 attacks, while the torment which they were subjected to was at least as great or greater as that which occurred in New York. I am positive that any good person [who] reads the file of this incident will be shocked, not only by its horror, but by the small amount of discussion of it in comparison to the attacks on America. However, America's just and clean war was not satisfied with that, but had to kill a million generals still in their mothers' wombs, and another million after their births. Jeff Simons says in his book about this tragedy, "I know Western observers who were stricken with depression and nervous breakdowns because of what they saw of the American torture of Iraqi children." To say nothing of the pollution of the environment whose effects may not be seen for years, and will not cease for hundreds or thousands of years as a result of the dropping of millions of tons of depleted uranium and other internationally prohibited weapons. It is an unprecedented, endless war of barbaric annihilation. All to help God's chosen people and the "men of peace" that lead them, such as General Sharon, who more closely resemble the hosts of the Assyrian spoken of in the prophecies of the Bible!

30. The author is referring to the discussion of American values in "What We're Fighting For." See pages 22-23 of this volume. —Ed.

31. Overlooking the continual support the Zionist state receives for its wars with the Arabs, we do not hesitate to say that the American government—without paying the smallest heed to justice—boastfully stands alone in support of the barbaric Israeli massacres to which the Palestinian people are subjected to, and absolutely rejects all international decisions and diplomatic norms—casting aside all values and morality: a disgraceful and outrageous situation which no conscientious person can ignore. The Zionist barbarians use advanced America military technology to strike everything: men, women, children, houses, and farms. They prevent reporters and aid workers from even entering, but American unfairness did not stop at asking the two sides to cease fire, but went beyond that and asked the nursing babies and pregnant mothers to first stop fighting.

32. The American government violated international laws and humane norms—let alone divine law—in everything having to do with this war: a war without sufficient evidence, without the United Nation's authorization, refusal of mediation or neutrality, the use of deadly and prohibited weapons previously unheard of, the targeting of mosques, and centers for humanitarian aid and the media, barbaric slaughter of civilians on the slightest pretext or without pretext, killing of surrendering troops, violating the rights of prisoners, invoking special laws in conformity with the desires of the administration, imposing a government rejected by the people, covering up information and imposing censorship of the American press itself, conflicting goals which become increasingly vague and are changed from day to day, preventing the expression of opposing opinions in the media, and finally, the issuing of a supporting letter by certain intellectuals.

The preceding are some types of American warfare. As for the other wars—it is not possible to calculate the victims or to justify it according to any concept of justice. One type is the war by proxy which has been fought in most African countries, in the states of Central and South America, and in the states of South-East Asia and other places. America makes use of local commanders who have no regard whatsoever for justice and only serve "Uncle Sam." If any of them fail, America disposes of him and his forces, and looks for a new replacement. Most of the victims of this type of warfare are hostile neighboring countries or those in which America stirs up enmity against them.

Another type is the war of intrigue which is fought in over fifty countries. Its operations include: kidnapping of leaders, revolutions, inciting riots, supporting separatists, and supporting corrupt totalitarian regimes. Many of these states are allies of America, and many of their leaders studied or resided in America for a time, or were under the patronage of its embassies. The victims of this type are the allied or neutral nations, elected governments, and nationalist leaders.

Another type is economic warfare. Many studies say that although Americans are 5 percent of the population of the world, 95% of the population is affected by American economic warfare: between those millions who die of hunger to the bankruptcy of institutions of national production, the fact is that millions of Americans are also affected by it. The only ones who profit are the monopolistic conglomerates and those nations who cooperate with them. To achieve the interests of these conglomerates—especially the arms manufacturers—America will contrive military confrontations in any part of the world. These wars are just only in proportion to the profit they produce for these corporations! Exactly as the president is electable only in proportion to the amount of campaign money he can gather. If the administration is unable to create a war for some reason, it cancels or delays some of its nuclear arms agreements, then uses the threat to national security to finance imaginary projects to be implemented by these corporations.

Another type is biological warfare. Despite the high secrecy that surrounds this evil type of warfare, the AIDS virus has exposed it to some extent. Dr. Len Horowitz, a graduate of Harvard, shook up world public opinion with evidence that AIDS and Ebola are both products of the American biological war laboratories.

Endless wars and endless justice!

33. The author is referring to the following passage from "What We're Fighting For": "Wars may not legitimately be fought against dangers that are small, questionable, or of uncertain consequence, or against dangers that might plausibly be mitigated solely through negotiation, appeals to reason, persuasion from third parties, or other non-violent means." See page 27. —Ed.

34. See note 1. —Ed.

35. The white paper published by the Jordanian government is the best source for this. The suit filed by former Attorney General Ramsey Clark also corroborates this.

36. From personal experience I can attest to this weakness in keeping to the subject of quotes. Samuel Huntington attributes a statement to me in his book, *Clash of Civilizations* (pg. 249) which was taken out of context so that the intended meaning is lost.

37. American justice in the Balkans is based on equality between the murderer and his victims. America achieved great profits in the name of this justice, the least of which was tucking Europe under its wings.

38. See note 14. —Ed.

The Institute for American Values received "What We're Defending: A Letter from Makkah in Response to the Open Letter from Sixty American Intellectuals" from Dr. Safar al-Hawali via email in mid-2002.

Twelve

❧

Can We Coexist?
A Response from Americans to Colleagues in Saudia Arabia

❧

67 U.S. Intellectuals

Dear Colleagues,

Thank you for your recent letter, "How We Can Coexist," which 153 of you publicly released in Riyadh in May of this year, in response to our letter, "What We're Fighting For," which 60 of us publicly released in Washington, DC in February of this year. We welcome your communication.

We know that your decision to write to us at all, as well as some of the comments in your letter, have caused some in your country to criticize you publicly.[1] We appreciate the spirit of civility and the desire for mutual understanding which are reflected in your letter. In that same spirit, and with that same desire, we wish to continue the conversation.

Where We Agree

Citing the words of the Qur'an and the example of the Prophet, you write that the human person is "inherently a sacred creation." Accordingly, you write that killing any human being unjustly is offensive to God and thus a betrayal of religion. You write that it is forbidden to impose a religious faith upon a person. You write that all human relationships must be based on high moral standards and good conduct. You write that justice is a universal value, and that just treatment is an inalienable right of all persons.

175

We note, and agree with, your strong emphasis on the universality of these fundamental human values. You write that these values "are shared by all people" since they are "in harmony with the innate nature of the human being." You also write that these values and guiding principles as enumerated in your letter "agree to some extent with some of the principles that the American intellectuals put forth in their paper," and that these important areas of underlying philosophical agreement provide "a good platform for discussion." Later in your letter, you write: "A number of values mentioned by those American thinkers are not exclusively American values. They come from many sources and represent the contributions of many civilizations, among them Islamic civilization."

We strongly agree. Much of our letter was an attempt to present a moral argument in universal terms. Your response, coming from the land of the two mosques and the cradle of Islam, which we respect, adds weight to that universality and gives us further reason to believe that, notwithstanding our differences, it may indeed be possible for us to reach a broadly shared understanding of the human person and civil society.

Emphasizing the importance of justice, you say that "power is not the only way to guarantee security." We agree. More specifically, in criticizing our letter you seem to call on us to avoid resorting to "the language of power." We accept the importance of your advice. But at the same time we remind you that politics, which concerns the ordering of our lives together, is in part *about* the just uses of power and can never evade the issue of power. We hope you agree that it is better to acknowledge this fact openly, rather than to presume a condition unknown to actual political and even religious life.

You insist that Islam as a religion is not "an enemy of civilization" or "an enemy of human rights." We fully agree. You write that political violence and radicalism is not "intrinsically tied to religion" or "restricted to one particular religion." We fully agree.

In this vein, we recall with regret that some Americans have made reckless and even malicious statements about Islam. Some of these statements have been widely reported. At the same time, there is much evidence that these remarks do not reflect the views of the great majority of U.S. citizens.

You call upon us as U.S. intellectuals to "earnestly review" our "position on Islam" and to "open channels of dialogue with prominent Islamic thinkers representing the broad current of Islamic thought." That is precisely our intention, as evidenced in part in our desire to respond to your letter.

Where We Misunderstand One Another

Regrettably, our frequent use of the term "American values" in our letter may have caused some confusion, for at one point in your letter you state, with disapproval, that we in the U.S. are calling upon Muslims to "adopt American values." We intended, and should have made clearer our intention, to ground our argument in universal, not national or particularistic, values. We hereby affirm that the core values upon which we take our stand are not exclusivist at all.

In discussing U.S. values in our letter, we did write that "the *best* of what we too casually call 'American values' do not belong only to America, but are in fact the shared inheritance of humankind." In addition, in part what we termed "American values" reflect the ways in which, throughout our history, we have been enriched by the traditions and understandings brought to these shores by immigrants from diverse societies across the globe. In these respects, our ultimate affirmation of the universality of core human values is quite similar to certain arguments that you make in your letter.

Another area of apparent misunderstanding concerns our use of, and your understanding of, the English terms "secular" and "secularism." Your letter says that we favor "secularism." In fact, we state specifically in our letter that we *reject* "secularism," which we define as "a way of seeing the world based on rejection of religion or hostility to religion." On the other hand, we do defend the principle of a "secular" government, by which we mean a constitutional order in which government officials do not hold office by virtue of religious standing or as a result of appointment by religious authorities. Being in favor of a "secular" state does not necessarily imply an embrace of "secularism." Indeed, for us, more the opposite is the case, which is why we wrote: "At its best, the United States seeks to be a society in which faith and freedom can go together, each elevating the other." And: "Spiritually, our separation of church and state permits religion to be religion, by detaching it from the coercive power of government."

Some of this misunderstanding may stem from problems of translation. For example, the Arabic word *'ilmani*, suggesting hostility to religion, may be the word that you would often use as a basis for translating both "secular" and "secularism," whereas the Arabic word *dunyawi*, suggesting merely the temporal, without any connotations of hostility to religion, may be a more accurate translation of what we are endorsing.

More broadly, the prevalence and consequences of ideological secularism in the U.S. and in other western societies, as well as the relationship across societies between religious faith and religious freedom, would be important subjects for further discussions between us.

Where We Disagree

Our most important disagreement with you is that nowhere in your letter do you discuss or even acknowledge the role of your society in creating, protecting, and spreading the jihadist[2] violence that today threatens the world, including the Muslim world.

For example, speaking of those who murdered 3,000 innocent persons on September 11, you do not speak in your letter of perpetrators, but instead of "alleged perpetrators." These words sadden and disappoint us. Do you expect us to believe that you are not aware that 15 of the 19 murderers of September

11 were Saudis? Or that their leader, Osama bin Ladin, was a Saudi? Or that their organization, al-Qa'ida, has for years received substantial financial support from sources in Saudi Arabia? Or that a high proportion of al-Qa'ida and Taliban fighters captured by U.S. and allied forces in Afghanistan are Saudis? Or that the spread of violence by Islamist groups across the world, from Afghanistan to Indonesia to the United States, is clearly traceable, in part, to the ongoing financial, political, and religious support for such activities in your country?

These facts are well known and are beyond empirical dispute. Yet your letter incorrectly suggests that these facts are not facts at all, but instead mere "allegations," and that this entire subject—who are these terrorists and who is supporting them?—is somehow irrelevant to the present crisis.

We are aware of some of the possible reasons for your reluctance to discuss this issue. However, if we wrote to you suggesting that slavery was merely "alleged" to have once existed in our country, or that Native Americans only "allegedly" have been the victims of injustice, we suspect that you might reply, correctly, that such fundamental denials of reality render futile any attempt at honest communication. Accordingly, to continue productively our dialogue beyond this present letter, we ask you in good faith to address specifically your perspective on the important roles played by some members of your society in the attacks of September 11 and in the worldwide spread of violence perpetrated by groups citing Islamic sources as justification.

You write that if the U.S. would "withdraw from the world outside its borders," then Muslims "would not be bothered" about the values and practices of U.S. society. This statement may be true, at least in part. At the same time, we do not think it wise or responsible for our country (or any country, for that matter) to "withdraw from the world outside its borders." We further note that many leaders and groups in your society energetically promote their own interpretations of Islam not only in the United States, but also in many countries around the world that show little intent or capacity to exercise significant influence "outside their borders."

You write that "most of the Islamic movements throughout the Muslim world and elsewhere are essentially moderate" and that it is therefore "necessary to maintain this situation." We do not claim to know with precision the current balance and direction of ideological influences in the Muslim world. We do, however, clearly recognize the current tension in the Muslim world between Islam itself, a great religion for which we have respect, and those radically intolerant religious-political groups that claim (falsely in our view) to speak for Islam. As for the merits of "maintaining" the current "situation," that situation is one in which growing numbers of innocent people around the world, including Muslims, are being murdered by radical Muslim groups, some of which are supported and encouraged by voices from your country, and some of which are currently seeking access to chemical, biological, and nuclear weapons. We have no wish, therefore, to "maintain this situation."

Opposing those in the U.S. whom you call "conflict mongers," you write that "stability is the basis for rights and freedoms throughout the world." We believe that you have largely inverted cause and effect—we believe that rights and freedoms are the basis of stability. For this reason, some of today's conditions in many Muslim societies—very little freedom of expression, an absence of democratic norms and institutions, and poor recognition by the authorities of academic freedom and other basic human rights—suggest to us that stability in your society, no less than elsewhere, will ultimately hinge in some important measure on the willingness and ability of leaders, intellectuals, and ordinary persons to demand basic rights and freedoms for everyone in society. We also hope that our own government will be more forthcoming and consistent in supporting movements toward democracy in the Muslim world.

Your major theme and ultimate conclusion, stated repeatedly in your letter, is that the attacks of September 11 in particular, and Islamist violence generally, are primarily the fault of the United States and its allies. *You brought this upon yourselves*, seems to be your basic message to us. You write, for example, that much of the instability and unrest in the Muslim world has "come about under the umbrella of Western policy and quite possibly due to the direct actions of the West."

Similarly, you write that "many of the extremist Islamic groups—as they are called—did not want to be that way when they started, but were forced into that category" by political, military, and media pressures from the U.S. and its allies. You insist that this process of social change due to outside pressure "is the major cause for the extremism of Islamic movements and groups." The U.S. resort to military force against violent Islamist groups, you tell us at several points in your letter, is only intensifying this trend. Most of all, you repeatedly insist that Israel, and U.S. support for Israel, constitute the root cause of virtually every problem discussed in your letter.

We recognize that U.S. policy, for good or for ill, is an important influence in the world, and in particular, that you strongly disagree with U.S. support for Israel. These are legitimate subjects of debate, and issues on which people of good will can, and often do, disagree. Looking to the future, many of us generally believe—as some of you may believe, and as some other Saudis may believe—that a two-state solution in the Middle East, with a viable Israel and a viable Palestine living side by side in peace and security, would be good for the Middle East and good for the world.

At the same time, we ask you sincerely to reconsider the tendency, evident in your letter, to blame everyone but your own leaders and your own society for the problems that your society faces. At times, some political leaders apparently find it useful to exploit and foment hatred of the external "other," or "the enemy," largely, it seems, in order to divert popular attention away from more immediate problems. But we urge you as intellectuals to consider whether the most urgent challenges facing your society—unemployment, the lack of democratic freedoms, the failure to build a modern, diversified economy, and the nurturing and exporting of Islamist violence—can be adequately solved through a strategy that consists largely of scapegoating other people and other nations.

The U.S. has many of its own problems, some of them quite important. Criticizing the U.S. is perfectly legitimate and, in our view, sometimes necessary. Many of us frequently do it ourselves. But the rise of Islamist violence as a threat to the world, including the Muslim world, is not a phenomenon that you in Saudi Arabia can simply blame on someone else. To do so would be irresponsibly to avoid confronting some important questions.

Here, from our perspective, are three such questions in need of clarification. First, do you believe that Islamic piety as practiced in Saudi Arabia is inconsistent with militant jihadism? Second, if you do believe that the two are inconsistent, how do you explain the prominent role of Saudis in the attacks of September 11 and, more generally, in the rise of militant jihadism as a world-threatening phenomenon? Finally, do you believe that Saudi intellectuals and religious leaders who hold that the two are inconsistent have an obligation to explain publicly and concretely why the ideas and activities of al-Qa'ida and similar groups are wrong and dangerous from an Islamic point of view? We await your response.

Can We Reason Together?

In a world threatened by violence and injustice, made anxious by war and discussions of war, and facing the grim prospect of religious and even civilizational polarization, is any task facing us as intellectuals from East and West more important than finding a time and place to reason together, in the hope of finding common ground on the dignity of the human person and the basic conditions for human flourishing?

We earnestly wish to be a part of such a dialogue, with you and with other intellectuals from the Muslim world. We recognize that the only preconditions for participating in such an initiative are good will, the recognition of our common humanity, and the willingness and freedom to engage in critical introspection as well as careful criticism of others' views.

Your decision to write to us shows that you may have a similar aspiration. We hope to find ways to continue and deepen this conversation.

Thank you again for writing to us.

Signed:*

John Atlas, *President, National Housing Institute; Executive Director, Passaic County Legal Aid Society*

Jay Belsky, *Professor and Director, Institute for the Study of Children, Families and Social Issues, Birkbeck University of London*

David Blankenhorn, *President, Institute for American Values*

David Bosworth, *University of Washington*

---

*Signatories' affiliations listed for identification purposes only.

R. Maurice Boyd, *Minister, The City Church, New York*

Gerard V. Bradley, *Professor of Law, University of Notre Dame*

Allan Carlson, *President, The Howard Center for Family, Religion, and Society*

Lawrence A. Cunningham, *Professor of Law, Boston College*

Paul Ekman, *Professor of Psychology, University of California, San Francisco*

Jean Bethke Elshtain, *Laura Spelman Rockefeller Professor of Social and Political Ethics, University of Chicago Divinity School*

Amitai Etzioni, *University Professor, The George Washington University*

Elizabeth Fox-Genovese, *Eleanore Raoul Professor of the Humanities, Emory University*

Hillel Fradkin, *President, Ethics and Public Policy Center*

Samuel G. Freedman, *Professor at the Columbia University Graduate School of Journalism*

Francis Fukuyama, *Bernard Schwartz Professor of International Political Economy, Johns Hopkins University*

Maggie Gallagher, *Institute for American Values*

William A. Galston, *Professor at the School of Public Affairs, University of Maryland; Director, Institute for Philosophy and Public Policy*

Claire Gaudiani, *Senior Research Scholar, Yale Law School, and former President, Connecticut College*

Robert P. George, *McCormick Professor of Jurisprudence and Professor of Politics, Princeton University*

Carl Gershman, *President, National Endowment for Democracy*

Neil Gilbert, *Professor at the School of Social Welfare, University of California, Berkeley*

Mary Ann Glendon, *Learned Hand Professor of Law, Harvard University Law School*

Norval D. Glenn, *Ashbel Smith Professor of Sociology and Stiles Professor of American Studies, University of Texas at Austin*

Os Guinness, *Senior Fellow, Trinity Forum*

David Gutmann, *Professor Emeritus of Psychiatry and Education, Northwestern University*

Charles Harper, *Executive Director, John Templeton Foundation*

Kevin J. "Seamus" Hasson, *President, Becket Fund for Religious Liberty*

Sylvia Ann Hewlett, *Chair, National Parenting Association*

The Right Reverend John W. Howe, *Episcopal Bishop of Central Florida*

James Davison Hunter, *William R. Kenan, Jr. Professor of Sociology and Religious Studies and Executive Director, Center on Religion and Democracy, University of Virginia*

Byron Johnson, *Director and Distinguished Senior Fellow, Center for Research on Religion and Urban Civil Society, University of Pennsylvania*

James Turner Johnson, *Professor, Department of Religion, Rutgers University*

John Kelsay, *Richard L. Rubenstein Professor of Religion, Florida State University*

Diane Knippers, *President, Institute on Religion and Democracy*

Thomas C. Kohler, *Professor of Law, Boston College Law School*

Robert C. Koons, *Professor of Philosophy, University of Texas at Austin*

Glenn C. Loury, *Professor of Economics and Director, Institute on Race and Social Division, Boston University*

Harvey C. Mansfield, *William R. Kenan, Jr. Professor of Government, Harvard University*

Will Marshall, *President, Progressive Policy Institute*

Jerry L. Martin, *President, American Council of Trustees and Alumni*

Richard J. Mouw, *President, Fuller Theological Seminary*

Daniel Patrick Moynihan, *University Professor, Maxwell School of Citizenship and Public Affairs, Syracuse University*

John E. Murray, Jr., *Chancellor and Professor of Law, Duquesne University*

Anne D. Neal, *Executive Director, American Council of Trustees and Alumni*

Virgil Nemoianu, *William J. Byron Distinguished Professor of Literature, Catholic University of America*

Michael Novak, *George Frederick Jewett Chair in Religion and Public Policy, American Enterprise Institute*

Rev. Val J. Peter, *Executive Director, Boys and Girls Town*

David Popenoe, *Professor of Sociology and Co-Director of the National Marriage Project, Rutgers University*

Gloria G. Rodriguez, *Founder and President, AVANCE, Inc.*

Robert Royal, *President, Faith & Reason Institute*

Nina Shea, *Director, Freedom's House's Center for Religious Freedom*

Fred Siegel, *Professor of History, The Cooper Union*

Theda Skocpol, *Victor S. Thomas Professor of Government and Sociology, Harvard University*

Katherine Shaw Spaht, *Jules and Frances Landry Professor of Law, Louisiana State University Law Center*

Max L. Stackhouse, *Professor of Christian Ethics and Director, Project on Public Theology, Princeton Theological Seminary*

William Tell, Jr., *The William and Karen Tell Foundation*

Maris A. Vinovskis, *Bentley Professor of History and Professor of Public Policy, University of Michigan*

Paul C. Vitz, *Professor of Psychology, New York University*

Michael Walzer, *Professor at the School of Social Science, Institute for Advanced Study*

George Weigel, *Senior Fellow, Ethics and Public Policy Center*

Roger E. Williams, *Mount Hermon Association, Inc.*

Charles Wilson, *Director, Center for the Study of Southern Culture, University of Mississippi*

James Q. Wilson, *Collins Professor of Management and Public Policy Emeritus, UCLA*

John Witte, Jr., *Jonas Robitscher Professor of Law and Ethics and Director, Law and Religion Program, Emory University Law School*

Christopher Wolfe, *Professor of Political Science, Marquette University*

George Worgul, *Executive Director, Family Institute, Duquesne University*
Daniel Yankelovich, *President, Public Agenda*

Notes

1. Some of these criticisms are reported in an article by Neil MacFarquar, "A Few Saudis Defy a Rigid Islam to Debate Their Own Intolerance," *New York Times,* July 12, 2002. [See also "Please Prostrate Yourselves Privately," which is chapter 8 of this volume.]

2. We are aware of the multiple historical meanings of the word jihad. But tragically, Muslim groups today who believe that the imperative of changing societies in order to establish an Islamic order is justifiably pursued by violence frequently describe themselves as jihadists. Some of you may believe—and many of us agree— that these groups are wrongly taking over and twisting the meaning of an important term. But this usage, however unfortunate, is currently a widespread fact.

"Can We Coexist?" was written under the aegis of the Institute for American Values and publicly released on October 23, 2002.

Thirteen

❧

Saudis Ban Paper with U.S. Scholars' Letter

☙

Alan Cooperman

Saudi Arabian censors banned yesterday's editions of the London-based newspaper *Al-Hayat* because it printed an open letter from 67 American intellectuals defending the U.S. campaign against terrorism and calling on Saudi intellectuals to denounce "militant jihadism" as un-Islamic.

U.S. experts on Saudi affairs said the censorship of the letter was the latest reflection of a debate over the morality of terrorism that has rippled through intellectual circles in many Muslim countries—and caused consternation in some Arab governments—since the September 11, 2001, attacks on the World Trade Center and Pentagon.

In an exchange of open letters that has won little attention in the United States but has been widely reported abroad, a group of American theologians, philosophers and political scientists has been arguing for eight months with counterparts in Europe and the Middle East over the moral basis for the Bush administration's "war on terrorism."

Among the figures on the U.S. side are Samuel P. Huntington of Harvard, Francis Fukuyama of Johns Hopkins and Daniel Patrick Moynihan of Syracuse University. Their first salvo, titled "What We're Fighting For," was signed by 60 scholars and appeared in February as U.S. troops entered Afghanistan.

"There are times when waging war is not only morally permitted, but morally necessary, as a response to calamitous acts of violence, hatred and injustice. This is one of those times," the Americans wrote.

A group of 103 German intellectuals responded in May. The Americans published a rebuttal in August, and the Germans wrote back in October, each time garnering heavy coverage in European newspapers.

"There are no universally valid values that allow one to justify one mass murder by another," the Germans wrote in their first missive. "The war of the 'alliance against terror' in Afghanistan is no 'just war'—an ill-starred historical concept that we do not accept—on the contrary, it flagrantly violates even the condition you cite, 'to protect the innocent from certain harm.'"

Meanwhile, 153 Saudi intellectuals also wrote a response. The American letter was heavily debated, and generally attacked, in the Egyptian and Lebanese press. It was discussed several times on the Qatar-based television station Al-Jazeera, which has a huge following in the Arab world, as well as on other radio and television stations across the Middle East.

"The depth of the reaction has been really surprising," said Hassan Mneimneh, a director of the Iraq Research and Documentation Project at Harvard. "An intellectual who is not aware of this debate is hard to find anywhere in the Arab world, from Kuwait to Morocco and Yemen to Syria."

With few exceptions, the public responses to "What We're Fighting For" have been extremely negative. But just below the surface, said Carl Gershman, president of the National Endowment for Democracy, Arab commentators have appeared "really rather flattered that here is a distinguished group of American intellectuals willing to put forward a case on level turf, to say 'This is what we believe, and we want to discuss it with you.'"

Arab governments have been another matter. "The Saudi government doesn't like this debate, particularly because the people who wrote the Saudi response are mostly Wahhabi conservatives and fundamentalists," said Ali al-Ahmed, director of the Saudi Institute, a Virginia-based nonprofit organization that promotes democracy and civil society in Saudi Arabia. "They don't want the dialogue, and I think the reason is they don't want nongovernment elements to have a voice internationally."

The response in May from 153 Saudis, "How We Can Coexist," said Islam forbids violence against innocent civilians but also suggested that injustices in U.S. foreign policy were the root cause of the September 11 attacks. The American rebuttal yesterday objected strenuously to this message. "We ask you sincerely to reconsider the tendency ... to blame everyone but your own leaders and your own society for the problems that your society faces," it said.

Mamoun Fandy, a former professor at the National Defense University who is an expert on Saudi fundamentalism, said secular Saudis had previously criticized the response from the Saudi religious conservatives.

"You have to fault the American intellectuals for cutting the Saudi liberals out of the equation and making it a conservative-to-conservative debate," he said. "It's God's boys on both sides of the Atlantic."

"Saudis Ban Paper with U.S. Scholars' Letter" was published on October 24, 2002 in *The Washington Post*. © 2002, *The Washington Post*. Reprinted with permission.

Fourteen

❧

American Values Abroad

❧

Claudia Winkler

Buried under all the coverage of the snipers' capture was a news story whose sequel makes it worth retrieving.

Last Thursday, the *Washington Post* reported that Saudi Arabia had banned editions of the Saudi-owned, London-based newspaper *Al-Hayat* containing the latest installment in an exchange of open letters between U.S. and Saudi intellectuals about September 11.[1] The new American letter apparently bothered Saudi censors. Then Al-Jazeera TV decided the banning was news.

Al-Jazeera is the independent Arabic news service funded by the Emir of Qatar and famous—or infamous—for airing on its satellite broadcasts throughout the Middle East everything from tapes of Osama bin Ladin to interviews with Israeli ministers and Saudi dissidents. On Friday, it showed an hour-long interview with the man who launched the dialogue last winter, David Blankenhorn of the Institute for American Values in New York.

Back in February, Blankenhorn's group published "What We're Fighting For," a letter signed by 60 American intellectuals including prominent neoconservatives. It made the case for military action against the Taliban and al-Qa'ida as necessary to defend "universal human morality" against "organized killers with global reach."

It drew several responses, including one signed by 153 Saudis, mostly academics, and reportedly orchestrated by Safar b. Abd al-Rahman al-Hawali, the Wahhabi former head of the department of theology at Umm al-Qura University. Their central point was that America had itself to blame.

The painstakingly courteous American reply to this missive is what the Saudi censors tried to suppress. They were foiled by Al-Jazeera's Washington bureau chief, who read long passages of the American letter on the air, then interviewed Blankenhorn at length, along with signatory Kevin Hasson, president of the Becket Fund for Religious Liberty.

Hasson calls the TV exchange "very lively" and possibly useful. He was pleased to be able to underline his satisfaction that the Saudi scholars' letter cites a basis in the Qur'an for the dignity of all human beings. This is the principle, he argues, on which Muslims can build a respect for pluralism and freedom of conscience that comports with a commitment to religious truth—just as the Catholic Church did with Vatican II. (For Hasson's discussion of freedom rooted in truth as opposed to freedom rooted in relativism, see his interesting op-ed of last December.)

Then Sunday, in a striking development, *Al-Hayat* published a piece by daily columnist Dawud al-Sharyan[2] strongly endorsing a key point made in the American letter: it is indeed indefensible for the Saudi scholars to write of the "alleged perpetrators" of September 11. We all know who the hijackers were. It's high time for Saudis to stop denying incontrovertible realities.

The column—which implicitly accepts Saudi responsibility for the spread of extremism—deserves quoting at length (in a translation by Hassan Mneimneh, co-director of the Iraq Research and Documentation Project at Harvard University):

> We seek a dialogue with the Americans, but we ignore the root of the problem, and we avoid facing the accusations directed at our religious discourse, school curricula, our attitude towards others, and our responsibility for extremist thought in many Islamic countries. This approach prevents us from engaging in an internal dialogue, as well as one with others. The objection of the American intellectuals to our approach is not surprising, since denial of truth is prevalent in both our writings and our debates. It is no longer possible to deny the truth.
>
> The denial for which the American intellectuals fault us does not serve as a means to defend our image. Maintaining it extends the life of the false information that is invented to explain events away, out of our fear of transparency and our refusal to face others and defend our position. What is hopeful is that the position of the Saudi "intellectuals" is contrasted by an openness at the official level. The speech of the Crown Prince 'Abdullah bin Abdulaziz at the Petroleum University is a clear indication of the importance of facing up to the truth, with openness and sincerity, since time no longer allows us to indulge in silence.

The patient people at the Institute for American Values could hardly have imagined a more encouraging response. For their exchange of letters to date, see americanvalues.org. Next on their wish list: a Saudi-American dialogue face to face.

Notes

1. Alan Cooperman, "Saudis Ban Paper with U.S. Scholars' Letter," October 24, 2002, the *Washington Post*. See chapter 13 of this volume. —Ed.

2. Dawud al-Sharyan, "The First Point of Disagreement," October 27, 2002, *Al-Hayat*. See chapter 15 of this volume. —Ed.

"American Values Abroad" was originally published October 29, 2002 as part of the Daily Standard at http://www.weeklystandard.com. Reprinted with the permission of *The Weekly Standard* magazine.

Fifteen

❧

The First Point of Disagreement

❧

Dawud al-Sharyan

The response sent by American intellectuals to their colleagues in Saudi Arabia[1] is worthy of lengthy discussions, and constitutes an important opportunity for a Saudi-American dialogue aiming at transcending the complications arising from the events of September 11, and affecting the relationship between the two countries. One of the most important points that is worthy of attention is "the first point of disagreement" where the American intellectuals note that when we speak of the 3,000 innocent victims who fell on September 11, we do not merely refer to "perpetrators," but to "alleged perpetrators."

These words sadden and disappoint us. Do you expect us to believe that you are not aware that 15 of the 19 murderers of September 11 were Saudis?... Or that a high proportion of al-Qaʻida and Taliban fighters captured by U.S. and allied forces in Afghanistan are Saudis?... These facts are well known and are beyond empirical dispute. Yet your letter incorrectly suggests that these facts are not facts at all, but instead mere "allegations," and that this entire subject—who are these terrorists and who is supporting them?—is somehow irrelevant to the present crisis.

Had the American intellectuals labeled this first point of disagreement "quintessential" they would not have deviated from the truth. We seek a dialogue with the Americans, but we ignore the root of the problem, and we avoid facing the accusations directed at our religious discourse, school curricula, our attitude towards others, and our responsibility for extremist thought in many Islamic countries. This approach prevents us from engaging in an internal dialogue, as well as one with others. The objection of the American intellectuals to our approach is not surprising, since denial of truth is prevalent in both our writings and our debates. It is no longer possible to deny the truth.

The denial for which the American intellectuals fault us does not serve as a means to defend our image. Maintaining it extends the life of the false information that is invented to explain events away, out of our fear of transparency and our refusal to face others and defend our position. What is hopeful is that the position of the Saudi "intellectuals" is contrasted by an openness at the official level. The speech of the Crown Prince 'Abdullah bin Abdulaziz at the Petroleum University is a clear indication of the importance of facing up to the truth with openness and sincerity, since time no longer allows us to indulge in silence.

Notes

1. The author is referring to "Can We Coexist?" See chapter 12 of this volume. — Ed.

"The First Point of Disagreement" was originally published on October 27, 2002 in *Al-Hayat* (http://english.daralhayat.com) and translated into English by Hassan I. Mneimneh. © 2002, *Al-Hayat*. Reprinted with permission.

Sixteen

৵

Learning through Letters

ৡ

Rasha Saad

The New-York-based Institute for American Values is working on a face-to-face meeting involving Saudi and other leading Arab and Muslim intellectuals early next year.

The meeting is the culmination of an ongoing debate between U.S. and Saudi intellectuals, initiated by the Institute in February, on the notion of having a just war and the means to coexist.

A few months after United States troops entered Afghanistan, an open letter entitled "What We're Fighting For," drafted by the Institute for American Values and signed by a group of 60 U.S. intellectuals, defended U.S. President George Bush's war on terrorism as a just war. The letter states that

> reason and careful moral reflection also teach us that there are times when the first and most important reply to evil is to stop it. There are times when waging war is not only morally permitted, but morally necessary, as a response to calamitous acts of violence, hatred, and injustice. This is one of those times.

The signatories also argued that the notion of a "just war" has its roots in all religions. "Jewish, Christian, and Muslim teachings, for example, all contain serious reflections on the definition of a just war," they wrote.

Among the U.S. signatories are Samuel Huntington, author of *The Clash of Civilizations* and Francis Fukuyama, author of *The End of History*.

In May, 153 Saudi intellectuals responded with a letter entitled "How We Can Coexist," which said that the September 11 attacks were unwelcome to many people in the Muslim world because they violated the values and moral teachings of Islam. The Saudis suggested, however, that injustices in U.S. foreign policy, with particular regard to the Palestinian issue and Iraq, were the root cause of the 11 September attacks.

> The United States, in spite of its efforts in establishing the United Nations with its Universal Declaration of Human Rights and other similar institutions, is among the most antagonistic nations to the objectives of these institutions and to the values of justice and truth. This is clearly visible in America's stance on the Palestinian issue and its unwavering support for the Zionist occupation of Palestinian land and its justification of all the Zionist practices that run contrary to the resolutions passed by the United Nations. It is clearly visible in how America provides Israel with the most advanced weapons that they turn against women, children, and old men, and with which they destroy people's homes. At the same time, we see the Bush administration mobilizing its military strength and preparing for war against other countries like Iraq, justifying its actions with the claim that these countries are perpetrating human rights abuses and behaving aggressively towards their neighbors.

Late in October, 67 U.S. intellectuals responded to the Saudi letter. In their correspondence entitled "Can We Coexist?" the U.S. thinkers highlighted points on which they agreed with their Saudi counterparts, points which were misunderstood, and finally, points on which they disagreed.

According to them, the most important point of disagreement with the Saudis "is that nowhere in your letter do you discuss or even acknowledge the role of your society in creating, protecting, and spreading the jihadist violence that today threatens the world, including the Muslim world."

They concluded that the problem is the Saudis' "tendency...to blame everyone but...your own society for the problems that your society faces."

While the exchange of letters seems to have highlighted more differences than understanding, the dialogue was generally welcomed as a positive step towards better understanding between the Arabs and the U.S.

While acknowledging such differences, David Blankenhorn, president of the Institute for American Values and one of the signatories of the U.S. letters, remains optimistic. "So far, the differences stand out more than the agreements, but this is only the start of dialogue. Ultimately I believe that what unites us as human beings is bigger and more important than what divides us," he told *Al-Ahram Weekly*.

Abdullah Schleifer, director of the Adham Center for Television Journalism at the American University in Cairo, believes that the general idea of exchanging letters is both valuable and thought-provoking.

> It is certainly better than what I call the knee-jerk reactions which characterize both sides of the debate, be it Saudi-American, American-Arab or American-Arab-Islamic. The Americans exhibit knee-jerk reactions by blaming everything on Arabs and Islam, and the Muslims exhibit knee-jerk reactions by blaming everything on the Americans.

The Saudi intellectuals also came under fire from Schleifer who believes that the correspondence is subject to certain limitations, one of these being that the dialogue is conducted specifically with Saudi intellectuals. "It is a pity, because in the entire realm of Islam—Arab Islam, Central Asian Islam, Indonesian Islam—the intellectual premises of Islam in Saudi Arabia are probably the narrowest and shallowest to be found anywhere," he said.

Schleifer also believes that both sides missed the real problem which, he maintains, is the point at which religion becomes an ideology. "I believe the problem is that in a world in which the spiritual dimension of religion is minimized and is increasingly politicized, people can turn their religion into an ideology like fascism or communism. And neither seems to have recognized that," he said. He also maintains that the Americans are not familiar with the notion of political Islam and the Saudi intellectuals do not even entertain it.

He believes that the American document is extremely rich and universal, and that the Saudi document tends to be shallow. "I mean, it says very nice things and it correctly quotes passages from [the] Qur'an and [the] Hadith.[1] But beyond that the document tends to be very shallow and defensive."

Jamal Khashoggi, deputy editor-in-chief of the Jeddah-based *Arab News* newspaper, maintains that the Saudi letter was not defensive but rather reflected an attempt to reach a level of mutual understanding and coexistence. He believes that the Saudis are sincere in their dialogue, going so far as to welcome meetings with the Americans despite expecting criticism.

Schleifer also points out that the U.S. letter "constantly makes note of self-criticism which basically tends to be missing on the Arab side of the debate."

But self-criticism is not a concept which is ignored by Saudi columnist Dawud al-Sharyan.[2] In his daily column in *Al-Hayat*, al-Sharyan more than once adopted a critical tone and highlighted a lot of problems within Saudi society. Referring to the fact that 15 of the 19 perpetrators of the 11 September attacks were from Saudi Arabia, al-Sharyan told the *Weekly* that "we should blame ourselves in the same way we blame the U.S. because in our Arab and Islamic rhetoric we avoid admitting what happened or at least acknowledging the gravity of what happened."

Al-Sharyan also maintains that not a single activist in any Saudi Islamic group has ever criticized Osama bin Ladin or has spoken out against acts of terrorism which use religion as a pretext for its actions. "If we do not admit that we have a problem, the problem will escalate." He also said that Islamic rhetoric at this stage must make clear statements on the crucial issues.

Al-Sharyan attributes this dilemma to the domination of certain groups within the Saudi kingdom which adopt political Islam and "refuse to admit its faults." He also added that the failure of the Arab and Islamic regimes to make decisions on crucial issues was helping these groups to remain dominant within the political arena.

But is there a real lack of understanding between the Arabs and the Americans or is there simply a conflict of interests which takes the issue beyond the cultural and ethical issues discussed in the letters?

According to Blankenhorn, part of the disagreement does indeed stem from different interests and political priorities, particularly with regard to the Israel/Palestine issue. But he also believes that the disagreements stem from divergent ideas and the way each side interprets and acts upon those ideas. "As intellectuals, we can only make limited changes to the former, but we can do a lot about the latter," he argued.

Khashoggi acknowledges that misconceptions exist and that some forces work towards deepening them. He also believes that there is generally no conflict of interest between the Arabs and the U.S., adding that the only bone of contention is the Palestinian issue. "If the Palestinian-Israeli struggle was resolved, there would be no conflict of interest."

The Saudi response to the Americans did not go unnoticed in the conservative kingdom. The letter was heavily debated and criticized by some of the Saudis as taking a mild stance on the Americans.

> The right-wing powers in Saudi Arabia criticized this dialogue initially and demanded that we take a hard-line stance with the Americans [said Kashoggi]. These powers adopt and seek to maintain the old hard-line notion of relationship between us and the Americans, one which is based on Islam versus infidelity and peace versus war. We should fight against this type of pressure.

This is easier said than done, it seems. Sources have reported that some intellectuals who were involved in the letter have yielded to pressure and withdrawn their support.

The Ministry of Information in Saudi Arabia also banned the edition of *Al-Hayat* newspaper which published the latest response of the U.S. intellectuals. The reason for this remains unknown. But Blankenhorn pointed out the positive side.

> I regret the censorship, but on the other hand, censoring the letter has probably meant that more people will read it and learn about it. Most of the letter was read live on Al-Jazeera, for example. In an age of satellite TV and widespread access to the Internet, keeping people from reading a letter or a book is no longer really possible.

While the letters were heavily debated in the Arab media, observers were surprised that the letter elicited little attention in the U.S. Blankenhorn explained that, because the U.S. is a large country and a superpower

> we often tend to be a bit insular, and not as interested as we should be in the views of others. Part of the reason for writing the letters is to show that Americans can also listen to others and communicate respectfully and honestly in the intellectual arena which, unlike military or economic affairs, is a level-playing field where all that matters is the integrity of the ideas.

But to what extent can letters change political realities?

According to al-Sharyan, political realities are complicated and it will take more than dialogue between intellectuals to affect change. He believes that Arab intellectuals have neither political nor social weight. "Only the political regimes can change political realities."

Notes

1. The Hadith is the collected sayings of the Prophet Muhammad. —Ed.
2. See chapter 14 of this volume. —Ed.

"Learning through Letters" was originally published on November 11, 2002 in *Al-Ahram Weekly* (http://weekly.ahram.org.eg). © 2002, *Al-Ahram Weekly*. Reprinted with permission.

Seventeen

❧

The New Intra-Arab
Cultural Space in Form and Content:
The Debates over an American "Letter"

❧

Hassan I. Mneimneh

Introduction

On November 24, 2002, a letter said to have been written by Osama bin Ladin, the Saudi-born leader of the al-Qa'ida terrorist network and the major figure in the global anti-American *jihad*, was published in the European press. While the London *Observer* published a full-text translation that day, the American press treated it more cautiously and did not present it as a major story. There seems to be valid doubts as to its origin. This "Letter to the American People" did circulate in Islamist circles but apparently did not appear on some of the websites usually associated with the jihadists and those sympathetic to al-Qa'ida. Most of these sites, it should be noted, were fighting what appeared to be a losing battle against law enforcement agencies, as well as freelance hackers, and were less consistently updated than in previous months. It is nonetheless noteworthy that no denial of its authenticity has appeared on these websites.

The letter is addressed to the American people, and is indeed a manifesto of grievances against U.S. policy, with American support for Israel occupying center stage. What is of particular interest is that in its preamble, this document refers to another letter, one that originates in the United States itself. This second letter, "What We're Fighting For," signed and circulated by 60 leading American intellectuals, had already generated widespread reactions and responses in Arab cultural circles. Bin Ladin's contribution, if it was really him, is only the latest installment in a debate that appears on the surface to be between the West and the Arab or Islamic worlds, but is also intensively, and perhaps more significantly, an internal Arab debate.

The original American letter, together with the responses to it—including the possible bin Ladin text—provide a case study of the new dynamics of culture in the Arab world. They also point to inter- and intracultural debates of paramount importance in the charged post-September 11 atmosphere. An analysis of the effect of the American letter allows for an understanding of these considerations and the potential, both cultural and political, of similar initiatives, whether spontaneous or planned.

The debate generated by the American letter also exposes the dynamic nature of the new intra-Arab cultural space as a platform capable of accommodating notions of communication and information sharing that transcend the nominal norms previously assumed by Arab societies, and adopted and enshrined by Arab governments, within which breaches of the sociocultural and political axiomatic consensus are relegated to the private sphere. Since its adoption of European systems of centralization and control in the nineteenth century, the state in the Arab world has indeed sought to define the shape and content of information that is made public. Building upon the accepted notion of "propriety" and extending it from a protection of religious values to include the state, both as an institution and a patriarchal authority, Arab governments largely succeeded in reducing the public space available for nonritualistic expression. This success can be further viewed as part of a totalitarizing tendency in Arab political culture expanding in the direction of the community, the family, and the individual. The decentralized nature of the new intra-Arab cultural space provides an implicit resistance to this tendency. Because it has relegated dissent and even debate to the private sphere, the Arab state order has to contend today with the evolution of a space largely outside its actual jurisdiction, in which the previous governmental gains in establishing control are undone, and within which the previously accepted notions of private and public are effectively blurred.

This paper proceeds with an exposition of the new intra-Arab cultural space, in form as well as in content. It then engages in a brief description of the "What We're Fighting For" letter and the reactions to it, and concludes with a series of observations concerning the potential for cultural debates and exchange.

A Topography of the New Intra-Arab Cultural Space

The last few decades, corresponding with the advent of new information technologies and the global revolution in communications, have witnessed the evolution of a new cultural space for the Arabic-speaking world.

Consisting of independent states and stretching from Morocco and the disputed Western Sahara by the shores of the Atlantic in the west, to Iraq and the monarchies of the Persian Gulf in the east, and from Syria in the north to Yemen in the south, the "Arab World" is a construct that often lacks a coherent definition. Its legalistic definition, based on membership in the Arab League, would thus include Somalia, Djibouti, and the Comoro Islands, all of which are non-Arabic speaking, while excluding Chad, where Arabic is indeed the lingua franca (and perhaps excluding Libya if its recent withdrawal from the Arab League is confirmed). Its nationalistic definition, through which the various nation-states are viewed as creations of a colonial past and are, as a result, of a temporary character bound to yield to the advent of a pan-Arab unity, is no longer the dominant discourse, with particularistic nationalisms confirmed in virtually every locale. Opponents of pan-Arabism have also pointed to the fact that no linguistic definition is also valid, since the spoken vernaculars of the various Arab states differ to the point of mutual unintelligibility.

This last objection notwithstanding, the formal language in all "Arab" states, used in the press as well as in public speaking, is "Modern Standard Arabic," a derivative of the classical language of Islam's holy book, the Qur'an. The use of this version of Arabic, in the context of a diglossic system allowing a sliding adjustment between two poles, a particular familial one and a common formal one, has been generally on the rise because of improved literacy and the new ubiquity of communications and media. It is this rise that is the sine qua non of the emergence of the new intra-Arab cultural space. It can be further argued that, despite the persistent claim to immutable authenticity attributed to Modern Standard Arabic—which thus shares in Arabic the same designation with the Qur'anic form of the language (*al-lugha al-'arabiyya al-fusha*), its coalescence, beginning with the nineteenth century, corresponds to a process of integration of the Middle East and North Africa into the Europe-based world-system, and the introduction of the notion of a West-centric "modernity." Linguistically, the aforementioned process of integration is mirrored through a drastic adjustment in morphological, syntactic, and lexical usages to conform to the homogenizing common European pool.

It can thus be argued that the last wave of forms to be absorbed by the Arabic-speaking world—that of the new information technologies—represents the continuation of the appropriation of Western systems of communication. This is a process that has the printing press, newspapers, radio, and television broadcasts as antecedents, and is itself part of the wider process of transformation along Western defined sociocultural, socioeconomic, and political organizational schemes. Accordingly, the global "revolution" in communications is revolutionary only in the sense of representing a relative spike in a long-term evolutionary progression.

The "spike" is evident through an examination of the evolution of the intra-Arab cultural space in just over one decade. Significant changes have occurred since 1990, with the introduction of a new media of communication and with old media acquiring new components.

Newspapers remain the main object of reading in the Arab world. In an environment where books are often viewed as luxury items, the central vehicle of cultural interchange is the newspaper. A major handicap suffered by local newspapers is their susceptibility to government control, whether direct through government ownership, or indirect through censorship and punitive measures. Prior to the Lebanese civil war in 1975, the relatively free atmosphere of Beirut offered a forum for writers from across the Arab world to express controversial views and opinions often prohibited in their respective homelands. The advent of the civil war led to the migration of many Lebanese newspaper and magazine publishing firms, as well as most Arab writers, to new venues, including Paris and London. First catering to the growing Arab expatriate community in Europe, this journalistic talent, soon coupled with capital from Saudi Arabia and other Gulf states, was poised to embrace new technologies enabling the "offshore" publication of newspapers aimed at general Arab markets. The Saudi-owned London-based *Al-Sharq Al-Awsat* thus succeeded in expanding beyond its initial target market in Saudi Arabia to become the first pan-Arab-distribution newspaper published in a foreign capital. While still constrained by its daily need to pass the scrutiny of the censors at the points of entry, its offshore publication allowed it a degree of independence and freedom of speech previously unavailable to its sister Saudi newspapers.

With the resumption of publication from London of the Lebanese newspaper *Al-Hayat* (later acquired by Saudi capital), the notion of a pan-Arab "second" newspaper, modeled after the *International Herald Tribune* and read by the business and intellectual elite in Arab cities in addition to a "first" local newspaper, was actively pursued. Simultaneously published in many Arab capitals and in major cities across the world, *Al-Hayat* has established itself as the newspaper of record of the Arab world, and succeeded in fostering a pool of diverse points of views by writers from across the Arabic-speaking world (and beyond). The offshore model has freed the paper from the crippling direct intervention of a government authority. The various local authorities are nonetheless aware of *Al-Hayat*'s vulnerability to market considerations and have repeatedly resorted to banning its distribution. Its diversified markets have nonetheless ensured that its editorial thinking remains in favor of "problematic" articles that might offend one local authority while enhancing the newspaper's overall credibility as a vehicle of free thought. Whether due to its ownership or to the disproportionate share of Saudi Arabia in its markets, the one exception that the editors of *Al-Hayat* seem to have adhered to is to avoid the publication of material patently offensive to the Saudi authorities. However, as demonstrated by an episode (described later) connected with the dialogue engendered by the "What We're Fighting For" letter, banning *Al-Hayat*, even by the Saudi authorities, is a newsworthy event that might engender counterproductive attention. This balancing element is possible through the decentralized multijurisdictional and diversified multimedia character of the new intra-Arab cultural space.

The communication technologies that made it possible for *Al-Hayat*, *Al-Sharq Al-Awsat*, and other newspapers to adopt an "out-in" distribution model, with editorial offices in a foreign venue and markets in the Arab world, also enabled major local newspapers, such as the Cairo-based *Al-Ahram*, to produce global editions. It also inaugurated the concept of syndication with the simultaneous publication of articles and opinion pieces and even prompted experimentation with global on-demand printing (the Beirut-based *Al-Nahar*, for example),

Newspapers have always been the basic component of the cultural scenes of the Arabic-speaking milieu. The advent of the new technologies has allowed a reconfiguration of the role of the newspaper, towards the confirmation of one intra-Arab cultural space, and towards a disentanglement from the means of control imposed on the newspaper sector by local government authorities.

Other periodicals and the printing industry as a whole also benefited considerably from the availability of information technologies. In particular, the proliferation and improved distribution of scholarly and intellectual journals should be noted. Often of an ephemeral duration, the lack of continuity is compensated for by the multitude of new titles. These journals provide a medium for the in-depth pursuit of subjects often addressed in newspapers, and thus assume an amplifying and confirming role for emerging issues.

Less affected by the new technologies is a medium that still retains its power as a molder of a common Arab cultural space: radio. The Egyptian leader Gamal Abdel Nasser had effectively used radio broadcasts to extend Egyptian soft power on the basis of a common Arab fate. The charged character of these broadcasts might have enhanced the attraction of the pan-Arab discourse but the repeated failure of state broadcasts to live up to expectations regarding accuracy led to the problem of credibility. Reliance on European-based authoritative radio stations date back to at least the 1970s. While both the BBC Arabic service and the Paris-based Radio Monte Carlo enjoy considerable credibility as independent and objective sources of information, Voice of America is generally perceived as a mouthpiece for the American government. The American authorities seem to realize, nonetheless, the importance of radio broadcasts as a point of entry to the Arab sociocultural scene, hence a number of new experiments, including Radio Sawa, targeted at Arab youth in select markets, and Radio Free Iraq, a limited program broadcasting from Prague. Some of these experiments seem, however, to underestimate the social skills prevalent in the Arab world at selectively consuming laced programming, skills developed over decades of virtual monopoly by the governments to cultural and intellectual output.

The most prominent component of the new intra-Arab cultural space is undoubtedly satellite television. A proliferation of stations, both government and private, has effectively compressed the Arab-speaking world into one cultural continuum. The all-news format of a number of stations, most notably Al-Jazeera, is the most obvious manifestation of this phenomenon, at least from a Western perspective. However, the new cultural space benefits from a host of stations and networks, some of which are in principle restricted in access (the ART and Orbit packages; although widespread piracy removes such restrictions), others unrestricted and cultivating aspects of Arab culture that are in stark contrast with the assumed stereotype of conservatism.

Satellite television, which is available both within and outside local regulations, is currently the main vector in the evolution of the new cultural space. Through the preponderance of talk and game shows, the interactivity of this new medium is considerable, albeit often limited by the high cost of telephone communication (thus the high percentage of callers from the Gulf states).

At the edge of the new intra-Arab cultural space lies the Internet, potentially the medium with the most room for growth. Current access is still extremely limited but significant nonetheless, with growing percentages of the population connected, both in affluent Arab states (such as the United Arab Emirates), and less affluent countries (Jordan, for example). The spread of Internet cafes compensates in the less connected areas to individual accessibility. The contribution of the Internet to the new cultural space is through not only email, listservs, websites, newsgroups, chat rooms, but also through hosted communities.

Whether in Western media and government circles or in Arab official groups, there has been an intensified focus on the use and domination of some components of the new common cultural space, notably the Internet, by Islamist groups, particularly those embracing exclusivist views. However, this focus, driven by national security considerations, is selective and not reflective of reality. Far from being an Islamist haven, the landscape of Arab cyberspace is a testimony to the permanence of the current nation-state order: ample anecdotal evidence, if not quantitative assessments, indicate that of the three levels of identity-based forums, subnational (that is, communitarian), national (that is, nation-state based), and pan-Arab, it is the middle level that seems to be the most attractive.

Beyond the Internet lies the new telephony: whether through SMS (text-based messaging), WAP (Internet access by cell phone), or the anticipated convergence with the Internet, or even through chain messages, telephony is the latest frontier in this common space.

Diversification and convergence are indeed two main features of this new space. As can be expected, the Internet is the main locale for convergence, with practically all media acquiring a virtual component. However, further synergies are also developing, as witnessed in the alliance between the Lebanese Broadcasting Corporation international satellite television channel and *Al-Hayat* newspaper in their newsgathering and dissemination operation.

The convergence in form often hides a divergence in content. The different components of the new intra-Arab cultural space point to different directions in the evolution of Arab culture(s). While the Internet seems to gravitate toward the nation-state level, satellite television programming and audiences can be better categorized as regional, or even pan-Arab. Similarly, the local (national) newspaper has not lost its potency, while the "second" newspaper is forging a permanent status for itself.

In the context of the lack of representative democracy in the Arab world, local cultural spaces assume the role of mediating between the political class and the so-called "street." The common intra-Arab cultural space acts as an amplifier. Through the interactivity of the Internet, satellite television, and the invigorated "letters to the editor" sections of newspapers, the new cultural space acquires a personalized character that allows the transferal to a shielded public space of activities usually relegated to the private space, such as political and religious opinions, and the pursuit of a sexual lifestyle in the case of homosexuals. This has the potential to affect the nature and definition of public and private in an evolving Arab society.

The Legacy of Ideologies

The complexity of the new intra-Arab cultural space in form is a reflection of the problematique of Arab culture in content, in its implicit and explicit attempts at reconciling, through ideological formulations, the advent of a Western-defined "modernity."

A brief schematic history of Arab culture in the past century can point to a succession of dominant discourses, each defining the cultural outlook of its time and generating counter discourses. At the waning of each of these dominant discourses, a trailing debate can be noted. The historical intercourse between the lands that today constitute the Arab world, and those where a belonging to the Western civilization is professed, is long and checkered. The legacies of this history, namely, colonialism, dependency, and the creation of the state of Israel, are the background against which the reception of Western "modernity" is processed. The creation of a nation-state system in the Middle East to replace the fluidity of the pre-World War I networks of cities and hinterlands preserves its potent shock quality close to a century after the fact; the adjustment to the new reality is still incomplete. The disruption of long-established, albeit already troubled, governance practices has increased the dependency of the ruling elites on outside powers, to the detriment of their supposed representation of the interests of the local constituencies. The emergence of the state of Israel, along the lines of the new nation-state parameters, at the price of the victimization of the native population of Palestine, both weakened the acceptability of the new system and diverted the resources needed for its appropriation toward a still-unresolved conflict.

Both explicitly and implicitly, the discourse of al-Qa'ida attempts to exploit the latent suspicion in Arab culture toward a world order based on the nation-state that has not well served its society in many respects: the injustice in Palestine is not resolved—it is not even properly recognized; new injustices have also emerged elsewhere, not the least of which the victimization of the people of Iraq through sanctions, then through what is perceived as an ill-conceived war of "liberation."

However, beyond its political dimension and throughout Arab culture, the advent of Western "modernity" has not been generally an unwelcome event, or even a revolutionary one. While it is possible today to contrast the holism, traditionalism, and theocracy vocally advocated by the various Islamist parties with the atomism, rationalism, and democracy that are perceived as hallmarks of Western "modernity," Islam as a cultural and religious realm had widely accommodated aspects of these values throughout its history. The success of the renewed "encounter" of the nineteenth century between the European modernizing experience and the Arab intellectuals of the Nahda (renaissance) was largely due to their conviction of the essential compatibility between the two legacies. While its European origins were recognized, "modernity" was understood as a universal value. This belief was "proven" by the Japanese model.

Clearly, the optimism of the Nahda did not come to fruition, with the whole Arab world succumbing to European designs. By focusing on its intellectual shortcomings, local assessments of the failure of Nahda syncretism largely ignored the underlying asymmetry in resources and accumulated power. The Nahda syncretism, blamed by the intellectual elites in large part for the new conditions and judged now as naïve, was replaced by their embracing a seemingly unadulterated version of European liberalism.

The advent of the age of liberalism introduced a growing disconnect in the intellectual outlook between elites and masses, as well as a divergence in their reception of Western "modernity." In the dominant intellectual discourse, religion regressed in importance. The adoption of the outward forms of Western life deceptively suggested that the retreat of religion was not limited to the intellectual discourse. While a large margin of material life, notably in urban settings, was receptive to and welcoming of the changes, the basic religiosity of individual, family, and society was not radically affected.

At the "intellectual" level, the conflict between religion and modernity was in need of resolution. This most often occurred through the subjugation of religion to the conditions of modernity. At the "mundane" level, however, the condition of potential contradiction was largely deemed viable. An implicit process of compartmentalization allowed the Muslim individual to engage in a seemingly "Western modern" way of life, with all the expected amenities (including many that are in direct conflict with the religious prescriptions, such as drinking alcohol and receiving interest on funds deposited at banks), while preserving his or her religiosity through the strict observance of prayer, fasting, alms-giving, and other religious commandments.

At all times, ideological purists of various denominations, both religious and secular, have tried to underline the alleged hypocrisy, duplicity, and fallacy of the "mundane" approach. The Arab individual was chastised either for not fully embracing "modernity" or, in reverse, for succumbing to its polluting temptation. Still, implicitly, and without any ideological enframing, Arab society resisted the purists' admonitions.

The age of liberalism came to an end with the Nakba (the "catastrophe" afflicting Palestinian society and the beginning of Palestinian exile upon the creation of the state of Israel) and the subsequent "revolutionary" coups that ushered in the advent of nationalism. Nationalism was defeated in 1967, to be replaced by an experimental leftism. While liberalism patronizingly accepted a moderately ritualistic religion, nationalism absorbed the religious experience as a historical manifestation of the cultural output of its reified "Nation," while leftism relegated it to the atavistic dimensions of a past to be overcome. Thus, the Arab intellectual scene gradually progressed in the twentieth century toward the demotion and exclusion of religion.

Neither liberalism, nationalism, nor leftism, however, was able to tackle and solve the basic political problems facing Arab society: the new nation-state system was still inefficacious in providing a representative space; dependency on outside powers was still predominant and the injustice suffered by the people of Palestine was still uncorrected. While the Arab intelligentsia had effectively failed, its abdication of its religious legacy had deepened the disconnect between it and the strata it presumably reflected. The alienation and failure of the Arab intelligentsia left many educated youth without an intellectual or ideological home.

The surrender by the intellectual elites of their customary custody of the religious legacy had left a vacuum that was filled by populist voices often dismissed as irrelevant or anachronistic. Not unexpectedly, these voices largely belonged to the minority literalist traditionalist Salafi school, whose proponents are the strictest critics of the twentieth-century demotion of religion in public life. With the dissipation of alternatives, the latent militancy of the new generations was timidly tantalized by the untested promises of return to the golden age.

The early Islamism of the last quarter of the twentieth century was mostly lower middle class urban protest militancy with little potency. The growing pains of active Islamism were exemplified by the hopeless millenarian uprising of Juhayman al-'Utaybi in Mecca in 1979, underlining the quasi-delusional quality of an intellectual effort trying to reconcile a sociopolitical critique and a literalist eschatological legacy.

A new phase was entered with the Islamic revolution in Iran and with the anti-Soviet jihad in Afghanistan. Suddenly, Islamism was no longer an atavistic fantasy, but a powerful force with real potential. A major "conversion" of Arab intellectuals—liberals, nationalists, and leftists alike—ensued. While the three effectively defunct ideologies had failed in their efforts for mass mobilization—beyond the appeal of charismatic leadership—Islamism, as a nativist force, was touted as a potential savior and as a solution for the persistent political problems.

Many Arab intellectuals perceived Islamism as a societal means to achieve the social justice and political development that the previous ideologies had failed to advance. Their utopian expectations of an evolution of Islamism toward a modernity they could recognize were both wishful thinking and a reflection of their ignorance of the growing hold of the new Salafism on Islamist formulations. In reality, Islamism in its larger part spiraled away from their understanding of modernity, as well as from their expectations of positive political outcome. Salafism, the modern out-growth of the traditionalist Salafi school, preserves this school's ideological selectiveness in referring to Islamic sources. However, it further allocates a disproportionate weight to the direct interpretation of the primary texts (Qur'an and Sunna), thus depriving itself of the extensive legacy of nuanced scholarship. Modern Salafism has engendered both jihadism and its further offshoot, Takfirism. Jihadism is the conviction that current circumstances dictate that fighting the established order is an obligation incumbent on every Muslim. Takfirism holds that failure to join the jihad is tantamount to apostasy, and is thus punishable by death. It is important to note, however, that Salafism is not all inclusive of jihadism, nor does it hold a monopoly on the innovative formulations of Islamism. Other such formulations include Sufi-based movements (whether explicitly identifying themselves as such, or using other labels, such as Ash'aris for al-Mashari'), and unbound intellectual experiments, the most notable of which might be the one undertaken by Muhammad Shahrur (1990).

A qualitative distinction exists between social Islam, as an integral component of Arab life, and Islamism, as a political expression based on Islamic principles. The two are nonetheless compatible. Islamism is viewed and understood in the Arab world as a legitimate form of political expression. Islamists and non-Islamist Muslims coexist in every Arab society. Islamism has also provided the Arab world with its first victory against Israel, the Hezbollah resistance (jihadist but not Salafist), which forced a withdrawal of the Israeli occupation forces from south Lebanon. Salafism, as a more radical program within Islamism, is less accommodating to the variably permissive social Islam; Jihadism is incompatible with it; while Talfirism calls openly for its demise. Algeria is the sad example where Takfirism was put into application.

Even prior to the September 11 attacks, a serious confrontation between two paradigms was in effect in Arab society: the implicit paradigm of symbiosis between social Islam and Western modernity, and the vocal paradigm of radical Salafism. The former has effectively accommodated the nation-state system, and accepted a de facto separation of realms of authorities—religious, political, social—while the latter posited a "return" to an integral Islam. Osama bin Ladin and his al-Qa'ida associates, as adherents of jihadism or Takfirism, were influential figures at the outskirts of this debate, but not essential to its unfurling.

However, in the aftermath of the attacks, the balance in this healthy internal confrontation between paradigms in the Arab world seemed to be in jeopardy. Rhetoric and actions on both sides have raised the specter of a "clash of civilizations." The image of the United States in the Arab world, already burdened by its seemingly unconditional support for Israel and its indifference to Arab suffering, is further damaged by the apparent American inability to properly identify "terrorism." American measures and statements have reasonably established that the target of the war is not Islam, as a religion and as a social practice. It is not clear, however, whether the elastic definition of terrorism will extend to include Islamism as a whole (a definition that would be rejected by an overwhelming majority in the Arab world), its Salafism subcurrent (a definition that would be rejected by many), or will limit itself to jihadism or Takfirism.

At the dawn of the twenty-first century, Arab society is still in the process of forging a synthesis between its Islamic heritage and Western "modernity." If not handled carefully, America's "War on Terrorism" could influence the process to the detriment or the benefit of the Arab world and beyond. The more jingoistic and disproportionate the American effort appears to be, the more likely it will be for the advocates of the "clash of civilizations" to prevail over those implicitly assuming a clash of paradigms, with all the unintended consequences to follow.

A careful reading of the post-September 11 social and intellectual debates in the Arab and Islamic worlds does indeed demonstrate that the locus of the more important component of the current conflict, the one with the longer-term ramifications, is indeed the Islamic *umma*, or global community. Whether knowingly or (more likely) not, Osama bin Ladin has compelled the Arab and Muslim worlds to confront the inherent contradictions in the difficult symbiosis between Islamic "authenticity" and Western "modernity."

While the conduct of the "War on Terrorism" could affect the evolution of Arab culture, it might be difficult to distinguish between short-term reactions and long-term trends while assessing the noticeable increase in jihadist activities, and the tangible growth in support for Salafism. It can be effectively argued that Islamism currently sets the tone of the cultural debate in the Arab world, and within it Salafism defines the terms of argumentation. Promoters of Salafism occupy a sizeable fraction of the airwaves and the bandwidth. But despite their visible success, Salafist formulations are no longer uncontested.

A nonteleological survey of the new intra-Arab cultural space does point to the implicit emergence of a more strident form of the symbiosis paradigm, rejecting Islamism, as well as leftism, and nationalism—the three grand ideologies still in debate, albeit unevenly, in Arab culture. It might be too soon to try to formally delineate the new paradigm or to enshrine its emergence as the next wave of dominant cultural discourse, especially since it seems to be lacking an explicit coherent cultural discourse. It can be tentatively referred to as Arab realism. It is globalistic, individualistic, consumeristic, nation-state anchored, with a nonideological intra-Arab or pan-Arab dimension. These various components do not amount to an ideology, and here lies the radical paradigm shift. It is more in conformity with the approach of compartmentalization that many in the Arab world have adopted with regard to the question of reconciling modernity and religion, an approach that is tolerant of contradictions.

Not unlike the new intra-Arab cultural space that succeeds in avoiding governmental controls through its decentralized diversified character, the new Arab cultural paradigm, through its diffuse nonideological aspects, is able to resist an all-out assault by its ideological opponents. It is therefore not surprising that attempts at a comprehensive formulation of the new paradigm were made by the Islamists themselves. Defined by them as "secularism" ('almaniyya), the new paradigm is presented as incompatible with Islam.

Competing definitions also take center stage in the current global conflict. In the narrowest of definitions, this conflict opposes the U.S. administration to the al-Qa'ida network. At its widest, it is the West against Islam. The active participants in this conflict have presented their own definitions: "Either you are with us, or you are with the terrorists" was the line in the sand drawn in the immediate aftermath of the September 11 attacks by the U.S. President George W. Bush. Al-Qa'ida leader Osama bin Ladin soon provided his own version of the putative dichotomy: "These events have divided the world into two camps: the camp of the faithful, and that of the unfaithful." It is a war on terrorism for the former, "an obligatory jihad against Crusaders and Jews" for the latter. Bush's definition strives to include the whole world, non-Muslim as well as Muslim, in its camp, excluding only the indeterminate minority of "terrorists," bin Ladin's seeks to establish his lines of demarcation at the limit of the "Islamic umma," the global community of Muslims. Implicitly, the battle for defining the conflict is thus taking shape within this amorphous but still real Islamic umma. Furthermore, within this same umma, the cultural civil war has not been won or settled. The interest of the opponents of the emerging paradigm is similarly to draw the demarcation lines in the cultural debate in such a way to reduce its camp while expanding their own. Al-Qa'ida espouses in effect a Takfiri approach, one that would declare most Muslims infidels; in the interest of preserving much of its support base, it has avoided presenting itself in public as such.

Debates over the American Letter

The unexpected impact of the American open letter, "What We're Fighting For," has to be understood in the context of its potential in redefining the demarcation lines in the Arab cultural debate. Soon after its publication in English in February 2002, this letter was translated and published in Arabic by the Lebanese newspaper *Al-Safir*. A flurry of reactions and responses ensued.

The American open letter is essentially a defense of the current American engagement in the war on terrorism as consistent with the notion of just war. Its assessment is based on the consideration of a number of principles or values believed to be of both American and universal validity.

We affirm five fundamental truths that pertain to all people without distinction:

1. All human beings are born free and equal in dignity and rights.
2. The basic subject of society is the human person, and the legitimate role of government is to protect and help to foster the conditions for human flourishing.
3. Human beings naturally desire to seek the truth about life's purpose and ultimate ends.
4. Freedom of conscience and religious freedom are inviolable rights of the human person.
5. Killing in the name of God is contrary to faith in God and is the greatest betrayal of the universality of religious faith. We fight to defend ourselves and to defend these universal principles.[1]

The initial reactions to the letter, not unexpectedly, came from nationalist and leftist intellectuals. Munir Shafiq, a veteran nationalist, reviewed the letter in *Al-Hayat* on February 24, providing a negative overview, underlining its failure to apply its own principles for a critique of American policies, and accusing it of ulterior motives.[2] A few days later, Waddah Shararah, a "post-leftist," countered with a nuanced critical review largely devoted to a sharp criticism of Islamist and nationalist formulations that engage in reductionist interpretations of American culture and society.[3] The letter had thus already been used in moving the demarcation lines of the presumed Western-Islamic or American-Arab cultural conflict to well inside the Arab abode, between Islamist and non-Islamist.

The debate progressed with further textual analyses of the letter, accusing it of hypocrisy in pretending to self-criticism; of hegemonistic designs for American culture; and of insulting the intelligence of the Arab readers. Edward Said, professor of comparative literature at Columbia University and a prominent figure in the Arab intellectual scene, provided his own review of the evolution of American political and intellectual discourse toward a bellicose imperial form, including a negative assessment of the letter as "a shot in a new Cold War."[4] The general critical tone persisted, still with little input from the Islamists, who otherwise dominated and set the terms of the intellectual debate. The poet Adonis, a respected figure and a postnationalist, provided a critical reading of the letter, presenting it as severely flawed in its attempt at appropriating ethical discourse to justify belligerency and comparing it to fundamentalist formulations.[5]

Other contributions in the first few weeks after the publication of the letter included a discussion of the cultural background of the letter and its dual audience (domestic and international) and a call for a re-assessment of elements in it that had generated negative interpretations in the Arabic press.[6] This contribution was later developed into a call for a reasoned Arab response on the basis of a set of dialogue principles (goodwill, respect for the intellectual formulations of others and acceptance of difference, rejection of civilizational hierarchy, recognition of the fact that the intellectual debate is both Western-Arab and intra-Arab, recognition of the need to develop the notions of freedom and individualism in Arab cultural discourse, and recognition of the need to make Western interlocutors aware of the importance of the notion of justice in Arab culture, notably with regard to Palestine).[7]

By the spring of 2002, more elaborate responses started to appear, with a critical reading of focusing on the notion of just war and its potential implications for international policy.[8] The overall tone remained distinctly negative, with Sawsan al-Abtah calling the authors of the letter delusional,[9] and virtually all commentators deploring its major lacuna: the question of Palestine. Two other main criticisms were the divergence between the principles declared in the letter and the actions of the American administration as vocalized by Ra'uf Mus'id,[10] and a complaint at the claim to the universal character of American values as stated by Salah Salim.[11]

Substantive contributions in the letter debate were also made by Ridwan al-Sayyid, who urged its authors to understand the 1948 usurpation of Palestine as comparable in its traumatic impact for Arab culture to the September 11 attack in an American context. There were also strong points made by 'Ali Harb, who highlighted what he considered the letter chose to be silent about, and by al-Fadl Shalaq, Antoine Sayf, and many others.[12]

The letter became a staple in the discussions on television talk shows, with the famous Egyptian sheikh al-Qardawi devoting an episode of his popular *al-Shari'a wa-l-Hayat* for it. Many other television programs, on Al-Jazeera and beyond, focused on the letter in detail, with the general tone evolving from outright hostility to cautious engagement.

The watershed in the response to the letter, and the Salafi entry en force in denouncing it, occurred when a group of Saudi intellectuals prepared a measured response,[13] one that accepted the goodwill of the American initiative and rejected virtually everything else in it while keeping the door open for further discussion. Salafi websites were visibly inflamed at the response letter, which they deemed was the product of "secularists," and a concerted campaign began to call on those who were redeemable among the signatories of the Saudi response to repudiate it. A few did withdraw their names.

What is significant in the flurry of Salafi activity in the following months was that virtually none of it was directed at the original American letter. It targeted the Saudi response through an extensive array of *fiqh* (Islamic jurisprudence) that placed the action of engaging the Americans in any way into a range of condemnable categories—from a blatant error to be rectified to abject treason. The Saudi response was published, among other places, on the Islamist non-Salafist website www.islamtoday.net. Another website, www.alsalafyoon.com, devoted an entire section to its systematic debunking.

With the Saudi response, which from an American perspective could be seen as failing to address the core issues, the American open letter was used to move the demarcation lines in the Arab cultural debate further toward the middle of the Islamist camp. The urgency and danger of this move was demonstrated in two ways. Regardless of its authenticity, bin Ladin's alleged letter of November 24, 2002, attempts to reverse the change in the demarcation line in restating the conflict with the Palestinian question at its core. The recent allegations that al-Qa'ida intends to sponsor anti-Israel suicide operations can also be viewed in this context. Support for the Palestinian cause cuts across ideological (nationalist, leftist, Islamist) and nonideological lines. It has not been thus far a hallmark of al-Qa'ida activism.

More significantly, the group of American intellectuals who had drafted the original letter chose to respond to their Saudi colleagues.[14] While expressing their dissatisfaction that basic elements of responsibility were lacking in the Saudi response, their new letter called for further dialogue. It was formulated in a way to neither antagonize their putative Saudi interlocutors nor to discredit them.

This dialogue seemed to carry too many unknowns, at least from the point of view of the Saudi censor who banned from distribution in Saudi

Arabia the issue of the *Al-Hayat* newspaper in which the new American letter was published. *Al-Hayat* is however available on the Internet. The ban made this dialogue newsworthy, leading to a level of exposure and coverage on Al-Jazeera and elsewhere that it would not have had otherwise received.

Conclusions

The Arab reaction to the "What We're Fighting For" open letter is significant both for its demonstration of the extension and flexibility of the new inter-Arab cultural sphere as a gauge and a generator of culture, and for revealing the need for Arab culture to define its intellectual outlook in its postnationalist, postleftist, Islamist-dominated phase.

The emergence of new media, together with the evolution of old media, has created a new inter-Arab cultural space, one that is at once unconstrained by the ideological prescriptions associated with nationalism and beyond the strict control of governments. This new space reflects the heterogeneity of the Arab reality that it serves, and the fragmentation of Arab culture. While pan-Arab discourse is receding, this new space represents, almost paradoxically, the emergence of a new commonality in form, allowing for an amplification of the diffusion and discussion of ideas and topics on a large-scale basis.

The American open letter was merely a catalyst. The story is clearly unfinished, with more episodes to come. Some preliminary conclusions can nonetheless be extracted in form as well as in content. In form, it can be noted that, owing to its diffuse character, decentralized nature, offshore components and multiple jurisdictions, the new intra-Arab cultural space provides a context where governments have less power to control the cultural debate. Within its context, censorship, and the banning of circulation of newspapers, can yield a negative effect by further exposing the subject of the ban. The established channels for the diffusion of ideas, whether in print or through the airwaves and the Internet, allow for an amplification of the effect of cultural input, in this case a letter from America. In content, it is evident that while Islamism in general, and Salafism in particular, still dominate the terms of the Arab cultural debate, its hold is not firm. A revival of a formulation based on a radical paradigm shift away from ideology is a major potential threat to its dominance. The demarcation lines in the cultural debate are within Islamic society, with a concerted effort on the part of the opponents of the new formulation to draw those lines as far away from themselves as possible.

In this Arab cultural civil conflict, both parties have recourse to external allies. Those in favor of the new formulation seek voices of diversity and dialogue in the West. "What We're Fighting For" was but one such voice. Its impact was considerable. Those opposed to the new formulation also seek American voices. Whether the call is to "kill their leaders and convert them to Christianity," proclaiming the Prophet Muhammad a "terrorist," or declaring Islam "a wicked and evil" religion, some American public figures unfortunately seem all too eager to oblige.

Notes

1. Preamble of "What We're Fighting For: A Letter from America." [See page 21 of this volume.]

2. Munir Shafiq, "sittun muthaqqafan amirikiyyan yuwajjihuna bayanan ila al-muslimin!" (Sixty American Intellectuals Issue a Statement Addressed to Muslims!), *Al-Hayat*, February 24, 2002, p.17.

3. Waddah Shararah, "maqalat muthaqqafin amirikiyyin fi al-harb al-'adila … ihtijaj li-l-usul al-khulqiyya wa-l-huquqiyya wa-imtihanuha nazaran wa-'amalan" (The Letter of American Intellectuals on Just War … Arguing its Ethical and Legal Bases and Testing it in Theory and Practice), *Al-Hayat*, February 28, 2002, p.10.

4. Edward Said, "afkar bi-sha'n Amirika" (Thoughts about America), *Al-Hayat*, March 7, 2002, p.9.

5. Adonis, "al-siyasa al-amirikiyya wa-masrah al-sharr" (American Policy and the Theater of Evil), *Al-Hayat*, March 7, 2002, p.16.

6. Hassan I. Mneimneh, "al-risala al-bayan li-l-muthaqqafin al-amirikiyyin: madkhal ila hiwar?" (The Letter-Manifesto of American Intellectuals: A Venue for Dialogue?), *Al-Hayat*, March 10, 2002, p.18.

7. Hassan I. Mneimneh, "risalat al-muthaqqafin al-amrikiyyin marratan ukhra: kay nubashir al-hiwar" (The Letter of American Intellectuals Another Time: For Dialogue to Begin), *Al-Hayat*, March 24, 2002, p.18.

8. Salih Bashir, Hassan I. Mneimneh, Hazem Saghie, "ta'qib 'ala al-risalah al-bayan li-l-muthaqqafin al-amirikiyyin" (The Manifesto-Letter of American Intellectuals, A Follow-Up), *Al-Hayat*, March 31, 2002, p.19. [See also chapter 3 of this volume.]

9. Sawsan al-Abtah, "al-muthaqqaf yahdhi aydan fi Amirika" (Intellectuals are also in Delusion in the United States), *Al-Sharq Al-Awsat*, February 28, 2002, p.12.

10. Ra'uf Mus'id, "munaqashat al-hurub al-'adila fi bayan al-muthaqqafin al-amirikiyyin" (A Discussion of Just Wars in the Manifesto of the American Intellectuals), *Al-Hayat*, April 4, 2002, p.10.

11. Salah Salim, "al-hiwar ba'idan min tashwih surat al-muslim wa-l-iktifa' bi-l-nukhab" (Dialogue beyond the Defamation of Muslims and the Focus on Elites), *Al-Hayat*, April 8, 2002, p.10.

12. Special issue of *Al-Ijtihad* (Beirut, Summer 2002), edited by Ridwan al-Sayyid and al-Fadl Shalaq.

13. "How We Can Coexist." See chapter 7 of this volume. —Ed.

14. "Can We Coexist?" See chapter 12 of this volume. —Ed.

"The New Intra-Arab Cultural Space in Form and Content" was originally published in the Fall of 2003 in *Social Research*. Reprinted with permission of the author.

Eighteen

✌

The Need for a Paradigm Shift in American Thinking: Middle Eastern Responses to "What We're Fighting For"; "Together with the Democratic Iraq Initiative and the Sharon Initiative"

➷

Chibli Mallat and Colleagues

Summary

The proposed study,* which takes the form of an answer to a debate initiated last year by U.S. colleagues in defense of the policy of their government, comprises two parts: the first addresses the fight against "terrorism," the second the problems specific to U.S. policy in the Middle East. In both cases the study proposes a fundamental shift premised on shared universal values to be applied in the protracted conflicts at hand.

In the first case, the argument is that the current planet-wide "war against terrorism" addresses the issue from the wrong angle. The precedent of two centuries of political violence, which has also been directed against civil populations in the Clausewitzian concept of all out war, reveals the legal, political and practical aporia faced by putting the issue in terms of "terrorism." This is not to say that a concerted response to the intolerable use of violence against innocents is not possible. On the contrary, such global response is made the more effective by a recourse to international law, especially to the available instruments offered by international criminal law.

The second issue, which is closely linked to the first by the specific Middle Eastern character of the massacres perpetrated on September 11, requires a paradigm shift in the appreciation of the Middle East crises in the United States. An effective response requires the adoption of a genuinely

215

universal and humanist way of thinking in response to the democratic deficit across the region, and to the bitterest regional and international conflicts, especially over Israel-Palestine and Iraq.

Definitions and Method

One can find many an area of agreement or disagreement over the logic and formulas chosen by policymakers or academics in "What We're Fighting For." The present rejoinder offers a perspective from within the Middle East, and is designed to operate as counter-narrative rather than mere rebuttal.[1] It calls for a paradigm shift in U.S. thinking about U.S. government policy in the Middle East: on the legal level, away from a war on terrorism, on the substantive level, away from the support of leaders who rely on the U.S. to pursue policies that conflict with universal (and American) human values.

The standpoint from which the answer comes is Middle Eastern. By way of contrast, responses from Indonesia or Nigeria as predominantly Muslim states are different by nature and lie outside the purview of our reflection, which is narrower geographically. The tragedy of September 11, the thousands of innocents killed in New York, the violence unleashed in the aftermath, in which many innocent people have also died, must be more precisely analyzed in terms of the "Middle Eastern character" of a conflict dominated since by the use of force.

That the message is primarily initiated by Arab Middle Easterners does not preclude other "nationals" in the region from [being] willing to share it fully or in part—and one hopes people from all hues and cries, from within America, the Middle East, or anywhere else. The present answer might be supported by Iranians, Turks, but also Kurds, Israelis, etc., because of our common geopolitical belonging, but their perspective can understandably have different concerns and nuances, although one hopes this contribution will speak also for many of them. This reflection is meant to be ambitious, and the question transatlantic colleagues should try to answer after examining it is whether they can subscribe to the reasoning and conclusions of this Response; and if not, why not? From a Mideast perspective, much of what they[2] say is acceptable wholeheartedly, though some important elements are not. Considering how grave the present situation is, this contribution chooses to concentrate on these points of contention rather than on convergence.[3]

In the letter, in addition to a section on "American" values, extensive comments were offered on religion and state, and on the conditions of a just war being fulfilled under the ongoing use of force by the U.S. government.

To start with the latter issue, any conclusions on just war will hardly be decisive, for two reasons: when the enemy is described as "terrorist," the classic pattern of war between two states is inoperative. Secondly, just wars conjure up the problem of objectives and causes, and the historical-political and legal contexts within which any war is being carried out. Nor is the concept of just war particularly enlightening insofar as conquests and aggrandizements in religiously molded contexts of centuries past offer an insufficient understanding of the qualitatively different faces of war in present times. It may be that convergence over the basic philosophical tenets of what constitutes a just war is generally acknowledged, but the response chosen here is deliberately legal-political and policy oriented. It purposefully avoids the ontological and philosophical discussion about just wars, which prevails in the U.S. letter. Much common ground is shared internationally over such philosophical, moral, or ontological tenets: aggression is unacceptable, self-defense and the right to resist are acknowledged, violence in the name of religious or any other ideological values is improper. While interminable discussions can linger on who starts a war, and when the use of violence is accepted, and by whom, the problem lies elsewhere, namely, in U.S. policy toward the peoples and individuals living in the Middle East.[4]

Far less useful in the original letter is the summary offered on "American values," which one can easily sympathize with and adopt wherever he or she might come from, by merely substituting "democratic" or "human," or indeed "religious" for "American." It is characteristically unhelpful to brandish generalities about this or that national, civilizational or religious "value": one will find in the Qur'an or in the Bible, as in any sacred text, enough verses and commentaries to defend one view and its opposite.[5] Such is the nature of scripture, which is open to radically opposed poles of exegesis over the long span of time since its canonization.[6] At the same time, the basic axiom which premises any divine message on its co-terminousness with peace and justice will never prevent those who use violence in the name of their respective creeds from being dismissive of that simple article of faith.[7]

Far more alluring is the fact that "What We're Fighting For"[8] presumes that force should be used as last resort, and that dialogue and nonviolence are the privileged means to social change and to the resolution of conflicts. One can but concur with these good intentions. The problem is that the call for dialogue by our colleagues does not prevent their unqualified endorsement of the violence waged and condoned by the U.S. government in the wake of the September 11 massacres, which is the main area of disagreement we have with them.

Our Legal Disagreement: War on Terrorism?

Months after war was massively engaged, the use of force is not about to abate, and that should raise the question of when war is supposed to end. But let us dwell first on the signatories' more positive contribution in their open letter, and indeed the most puzzling one, which is the absence of the concept of "terrorism" as a justification for their fight. While the dominant presumption is that "the Enemy is terrorism," it is remarkable that not once is the word "terror" or "terrorism" used in the colleagues' text, at a time when the U.S. government's military action abroad is based on a simple justification of its "war on terror/ism." The ambiguity is compounded by the title bestowed by the *Washington Post* in its initial coverage of the letter, and in the label thereafter adopted in the website that carries the debate.[9]

If the word "terrorism" is missing because of a conscious decision, the authors' explanation for that notable discrepancy with the U.S. government would be useful. If the absence of the words "terror" and "terrorism" in their long letter is not conscious, it would be also helpful to reflect in common on this puzzling absence, and seriously consider moving away from the allegedly consensual qualification of what happened on September 11, 2001. Shared doubts about the inchoate use of terrorism and attacks and their consequences on world policy and relations offer an important premise of a different, more constructive response to be hammered out together.

Here is our position on the issue: with regard to what happened on September 11, its depiction as a "terrorist attack" fails to convey the full horror of what happened. "Attack" is a word too general and nondescript to convey the massive loss of civilians that day. In addition, the term "terrorism" was never defined by law in any consensual manner.[10] It is a mistake to describe the tragic events on September 11 other than as "massacres," in lay parlance, and as "a crime against humanity" in international law.[11] An "attack" did take place, and "terror" ensued, but terror and attacks happen regularly on the planet without constituting the watershed that September 11 has brought onto the world stage. The signal horror of what happened that morning results from the occurrence of the large-scale and premeditated random killing of people over a short period of time, in a context which is revolting for its massiveness and the innocent people killed in it, whatever motives the killers may have been prompted by to commit the massacres.

The use of the words "massacre" (in the plural or the singular) and "crime against humanity" instead of "attack" and "terror/ism" is not merely a play on words, and the consequences are equally significant for law and policy.

As a crime against humanity, the perpetrators, facilitators, and abettors of the September 11 massacres must be sought under international law across the planet, and it is the duty of all countries and governments to help actively in their arrest, trial, and punishment after due process is served. While measured use of force should not be precluded against the rulers of a country who refuse to respond to international justice requesting the surrender of mass-scale political assassins hidden or protected on their territory, an open-ended war on any "terrorism" is ill-conceived, unjust, and interminable.

No answer is what the wrong question begets:[12] legions of scholars have failed to offer a working definition of terrorism over the two hundred years since the word appeared on the public scene in connection with state violence exercised by radicals in the French Revolution. There is no reason why the human mind should succeed presently in this impossible task. The fuzziness which is associated with "terrorism" allows any party or government on the planet to respond to a "terrorist" act, however it wishes to define it, by resorting to full-scale war on another country. Such a reaction would constitute a manifest misapplication of the search for justice to account for victims of political violence. Nor is it possible to evade the time-old problem of the terrorist and the freedom-fighter through the looking-glass of history, or the question of "state terror/ism."

In contrast, use of violence may be justified in response to the massacre carried out on September 11 because it is a crime against humanity in terms of scale, nationality of victims, and wantonness—hence the concept of crime against *humanity*. But organized, declared, and measured violence would be premised on bringing those responsible for September 11 to justice as the main objective of any coercion exercised in the course of this worldwide search. This is also why September 11 is unique in many ways, while terrorism isn't. The open-ended and over-inclusive use of military force in connection with "terrorist attacks" has already brought the planet to the brink of nuclear war by unduly stretching the justified response to a crime against humanity carried out on September 11, thus giving way to knee-jerk reactions in complex conflicts which have been plagued with violence for decades. This is most apparent in the century-long crises between India and Pakistan over Kashmir, and between Arabs and Israelis over Palestine. It also sees gruesome illustration in the case of Chechnya, amongst so many other spots of protracted political violence across the planet.

The sound appreciation of what one is fighting for is fundamental. If Americans and others agree with our concern about the incorrect and at best imprecise definition of the U.S. government's reaction to the September Massacres, as appears from their conscious (or unconscious) rejection of the use of the inchoate and inadequate words terror and terrorism in their letter, an important agreement can be reached on the universal enhancement of the rule of law. The common search for "justice infinite" can be then achieved, as was correctly described in the early action of the U.S. government and hastily abandoned soon after. The proper reaction should have obtained from the association of the retribution against the perpetrators and abettors of the massacres with *justice*. Justice translates in the need for the whole of humanity to cooperate with the U.S. authorities for the arrest and trial of all those responsible for the massacres perpetrated on September 11, in the same way as Americans and others should support and help punish any victims of massive crimes, especially those of an international nature, stretching from the Holocaust to the ongoing mass crimes in Congo.

Justice means due process, far more dedication to its projection internationally, and the identification of neutral judges and tribunals to supervise any use of violence. It cannot be a license to wage war whenever an "act of terror" is committed somewhere. The category under which the September 11 massacres should be understood is *sui generis* in criminal law. Because of its magnitude and callousness, it belongs to a specific type of crime euphemistically known as "serious violations of international humanitarian law," as these crimes are described in the Rome Convention on the ICC and derivative treaties and laws across the world. This is where the fundamental mistake of the U.S. government in its overreaching war lies, and where the support it seeks finds its blind spot among the larger Middle Eastern audience. We shall not dwell on how the U.S. has turned its back on the ICC, but call our colleagues to respond to that signal failure by living up to the principles they themselves advocate, especially in a context where the ICC is more necessary than ever to respond to mass murders such as those committed on September 11.[13]

Under this critical perspective, the problem should now appear clearly in our view of the events as they unfolded after September 11. A different approach is needed, where legal categories recognizable under international law (*jus cogens*) determine any use of violence, preferably in the shape of independent and effective national or international tribunals that the use of force would strengthen rather than undermine. International criminal tribunals in Yugoslavia and Rwanda offer a prime example, as do national tribunals such as the British House of Lords' decision in the Pinochet case and the hopes offered in Belgium, the United States, and elsewhere by so-called universal jurisdiction and the long-arm reach of justice for especially heinous crimes recognized as such by international law.

Supporting the punishment of one set of mass perpetrators of crimes by "enemies" of the United States cannot go together with supporting mass perpetration of crimes by leaders of countries which are "allies" of the U.S. From a policy perspective, the plague of double standards needs to be fought openly and consistently, and nowhere is consistency more necessary than in the Middle East, where the question "Why do they hate us?" finds its response in the dominant Mideast perception of utter injustice flowing from a decades-long practice of successive American governments in their open and unqualified support of Israeli violations of international law. Nor is the deep sense of injustice limited to the U.S. support of Israeli practices. The sense Arab Middle Easterners have of being consistently abandoned or lied to by America's policymakers also rests on the more nuanced but no less tolerant American support for long-standing autocratic governments across the region, particularly "U.S.-friendly" governments in the Arab Gulf and in the Levant.

This is also why it is preferable to base the debate on a perspective rooted in law rather than on any philosophical underpinnings described in terms of Augustinian "just wars," and American, secular, or other uncertain civilizational values (Muslim, Western, European, Judeo-Christian, Arab...). Philosophy comes after the wings of Minerva's historical owl have stopped fluttering[14]—even if it is true that the very flight of history is also informed by the strength of the moral ground, especially as it applies to the weaker side. America is on troubled terrain in recent history, and there is a groundswell of diffidence (if not hatred) of the Middle Eastern "natives" against those perceived to command the largest outside power exercised in the region, yet exercise their power *selectively*, *unjustly*, and *inconsistently*.[15]

Our Central Disagreement: U.S. Policy in the Middle East

The present message comes at a time when policy reviews are being shaped with little or no input from people from the region, and where war looms large over Iraq.[16] Trite as this proposal for a just Middle Eastern policy may sound, it is not perceived as such in the West, and this state of mind represents the most important shift advocated for the end of "Middle Eastern diffidence" and the corresponding U.S. soul-searching for "why they hate us."

Precisely because the September 11 connection is "Middle Eastern" and covers such a large area of the world stretching from Morocco to Pakistan, applications may be hard to prioritize, and history tends to confound analysts, especially in a region where tyrannical republics are turning dynastic at the very moment when the world is moving slowly, but steadily, to basic norms of democratic change. The convulsions in the Gulf around a wayward Iraq and the protractedness of the Arab-Israeli conflict—the longest now in modern world history—skew all national development, which gets over-determined by those two conflicts. Since at least the First World War, all countries and peoples of the Middle East have been closely interlocked.[17] Kuwait and Iraq are carefully watched from Tehran to Morocco. People in Beirut and Amman follow daily developments in Damascus, while Riyadh and Damascus closely observe what happens in Iraq. All closely watch and are closely watched in Israel by Jews and non-Jews under Israeli domination. Arcs of crisis are many and carry a strong regional charge. It is hard sometimes to square "global" reality with the principle, and there are legitimate questions on what should be prioritized in terms of policy.

Despite the difficulty of setting priorities, a "domino theory" of democracy should be pursued, in the belief that the exemplum of democracy in one state is closely followed across the region.[18] But the change can either come slowly, as those countries closest to basic democratic practices are encouraged, defended, or supported. Or it can come by way of a "revolution" in countries where the weight of authoritarianism compels support to those democrats who have taken on the system and are trying to change it by peaceful means.[19]

The distinction here between radical action and peaceful protest is necessary (even though not always decisive, and not necessarily absolute, as the U.S. intellectuals themselves readily accept),[20] as it is far more legitimate morally, and should be far easier practically, to talk with non-violent dissenters than with advocates of force for governmental change. By this token also, Muslim-democratic and secularly oriented dissidents rank highest in the required attention and support of Western governments and peoples, and violence-yielding actors (whether religiously animated or not) should rank lowest on the scale of "recognition." It may be appropriate to remember that Woodrow Wilson was a hero of the Middle East in the early twentieth century for his principled stand on the right of self-government against colonialism, especially in Palestine, and that, at century's end, the Iron Wall came crashing down without a single shot being fired. Middle Easterners deserve no less than a Wilsonian spirit for Israel-Palestine, and no less than the frank, open, and peaceful engagement to end the authoritarianism of U.S.-supported governments, from Tunisia to Israel to Saudi Arabia—an engagement that corresponds to the whole-hearted sympathy and support that advocates of freedom and democracy behind the Iron Curtain received during the Cold War.

True, it is often hard to think of change outside the context of regional crises, most compellingly the Iraq crisis and the fight over Palestine. The standards of "solving" these crises should not be different from those delineated above: how a crisis can be redirected, managed, or countered to help produce democrats at the helm is the key question, whether that crisis is regional or domestic, or whether it seems to move at a fast pace or looks sluggish or dormant.

Change in Iraq is on the agenda in Washington, and that may be the best news for the peoples of Iraq since the end of the Gulf War,[21] but change for the sake of change is meaningless. A serious effort must be engaged to bring democracy to Baghdad as the Allies did in Germany and Italy in World War II, in Kosovo and Serbia two years ago, and in Afghanistan now, although the Balkan and Central Asian examples show that pusillanimity remains a threat to statesmanship. Terrorism or weapons of mass destruction in the case of Iraq are *not* good reasons to go to war again. Should the use of force be pursued, only the protection of the hapless civilians of Iraq and coordination with Iraqi oppositional forces towards democracy in Baghdad can justify forms of *measured* military coercion. Here also a profound shift in the attitude of the U.S. government is required.

More practically, the large opposition to the regime can be helped to effectiveness, and its leadership encouraged amongst moderates who believe in democracy and human rights, and who have shown commitment and a track record in their years of opposition, working for the passage and implementation of the Iraq Liberation Act of 1998, an exceptional piece of legislation in U.S. and world history, the more unfortunately ignored as it remained a dead letter for four years. The ILA is however a domestic piece of legislation, and cannot run afoul of international law, so that a rising consensus in the international arena, especially in the Security Council, is also necessary. The problem is that talk of "regime change" in Iraq goes beyond what is allowed under the present state of international law regarding that country, however severe the disarmament conditions under Ceasefire Resolution 687. Nothing in contrast stands in the way of forcing the Iraqi government to comply with Resolution 688, which requires it "to cease repressing its own population."

The question of Iraq must be reformulated with two priorities in mind: How can individual Iraqis who are not responsible for their government's policy be protected in any process of change? What are the mechanisms that can be put in place to enhance the chances of an open, nonviolent successor rule?

On the first, clearly a massive bombing campaign will not be able to avoid the suffering of innocents, and the best possible scenario for Iraqis is the implementation of a "collapse" theory which can be designed with the help of Middle East and European democrats.[22] In addition to supporting the people against repression, which requires engaging seriously with the democracy-bent strands of the opposition, especially resistance within Iraq, work against dictatorship is painful and can easily lead to "excesses," and *the Iraqi opposition leaders must be held accountable* as the process of change unfolds and they get closer to power, by the proper use of *human rights monitors* to accompany the change, and the setting up of *an effective international tribunal* to try the leaders of the current government—*as well eventually as those who will use change to impose violence and misuse their victory to repeat the crimes of those whose rule they replaced.*

Iraq is a good example of the domino theory of democracy being initiated within the prism of "revolutionary" change, but the process of accountability, which must guide the determination to bring the current form of Iraqi rule to an end, cannot stop at the doorstep of Washington's nemesis in Baghdad. Accountability tolerates no exception, including the "allies," foremost amongst whom are the governors of Israel, who have expelled, dominated, subdued, or imprisoned a population as large as theirs for over fifty years. A country cannot be deemed democratic when it humiliates a population on the territory it occupies because it does not share its religion, or its particular type of nationalism. Israel is no exception to authoritarianism in the Middle East, despite the real freedom it does allow for the Jewish segment of its population. Even without dealing with the territory occupied since 1967, one must acknowledge that over a quarter of the Israeli population is not Jewish.[23] This comes in addition to the fact that the majority of the people living on the land of Palestine were expelled and prevented by sheer force from exercising a universal right to return to their homes for over a half century.[24]

Talk of Israel as "the sole democracy" in the region is both incorrect and unfair:[25] it is tantamount to justifying the ethnic cleansing of any brutal conqueror who destroys or expels the people of the territory invested, only to pretend thereafter that it is exercising freedom of choice within the exclusive segment of its conquering population, especially when it is used as bridgehead for other conquerors and colonizers. Nor can any fair observer suggest that coexistence in Israel between the two basic segments of the population or freedom of expression for non-Jews are superior to those found in other countries in the region. In Israel, state domination of non-Jews has been far more brutal and systematic than anywhere else in the Middle East, save perhaps for Iraqi Kurds at the hands of the Baath government. Until Americans acknowledge a reality which is plain to all Arab Middle Easterners, and to a significant number of people living in historic Palestine, including Jews, there will be no let up of diffidence towards U.S. policy in the region. What is required is not merely an agreement that is more comprehensive than a two-state solution and the end of occupation in the Territories, but an acknowledgment that Israel is not a democratic state and never was.[26]

This does not mean that concern with U.S. policy and attitude is limited to Israel, or that anyone can countenance the killing of innocent civilians under any justification whatsoever. The Israeli dimension is particularly sensitive because of the unabashed and self-congratulatory support of Israel by successive American governments, against the values portrayed in the U.S. intellectuals' letter, and against the law of civilized nations as can be seen from the systematic flouting of UN resolutions by Israeli governments ever since the State's inception. We shall return to it later, in the sincere belief that the seriousness with which the Iraqi dictator is dealt with must one day be applied by a just American government to those Israeli rulers who similarly advocate and practice unfettered violence.

Whether for Israel or other U.S. "allies" in the region, a common understanding with our U.S. colleagues should mean a policy where the current large number of aid "conditionalities" move away from a purely economic realm to a democratic one: the Egyptian government must be warned openly against shutting up its dissidents—most recently and cruelly Saadeddin Ibrahim—by a serious threat to diminish the large support in aid that comes annually to Cairo from Western coffers, and this would be rendered easier if a ladder of "freedom conditionalities" is adopted across the board toward the historic allies of Washington. Examples of harassed dissidents abound,[27] with nonviolent expression systematically undermined by prosecution and prison terms and a systematic use of "rule by law" instead of the rule of law.[28] Practices of authoritarianism have now extended to the whole planet, the United States included.[29]

All is not necessarily gloomy. The fight for democracy can also achieve success, and instances of success must be welcomed and rewarded. Bahrain and Morocco should be saluted for the increase in the constitutionalist dimension of their rule, and the former Moroccan Prime Minister Abd al-Rahman al-Yusufi singled out for the most remarkable shift toward democracy and concern for human rights across the Middle East in the past decade. This does not mean allowing a lapse to one-man rule in Bahrain, or giving up on the rights and pleas of the Sahrawis in Morocco, or failing to insist on the independence of Lebanon under general international principles as well as regional accords, and on the need to respect alternation at the presidential helm in accordance with the Constitution.

Morocco having offered the most remarkable embrace of democracy in the last decade, young leaders in Jordan and Syria, and the other more absolute dictators and monarchs across the region must be persuaded of the Yusufi model they need to follow to avoid the descent into repression. No tolerance should be allowed when it comes to jailing liberal dissidents. A step in support of these prisoners of conscience requires a qualitative move in Western capitals, which should embrace them openly as they do with the main dissident of Burma. This is why the precedent in Morocco is key, and the greatest success of the late King[30] was the appointment as prime minister of the leader of the opposition, whom he had jailed several times earlier.[31] Thinking of dissidents in jail or under the threat of jail for expressing their opinions, like Saadeddin Ibrahim in Egypt, Riyad Turk in Syria, Azmeh Bishara in Israel as the Yusufis—even as the Mandelas—of the Middle East is a required qualitative change in Western attitudes: in the same way our American colleagues have extended their support wholeheartedly to the dissidents under Soviet rule with little or no hesitation, a similar attitude is expected from them, and eventually from their governments, in the Middle East. This is a key objective worth fighting peacefully for.

Need for accountability for the leaders' stifling of the electoral process is true of all the privileged allies of Washington. The rule in Tunisia is as unacceptable as the one in Libya, and the lack of peaceful alternation at the top goes from the Saudi rulers to the Egyptian president who—it should be repeated, so close Egyptian rule has been to U.S. governments since it has embraced a separate peace with Israel—has renewed his term in office for a fourth time and entered his third decade as absolute ruler of Egypt;[32] or the leader of the Palestinian Authority,[33] who tried to make the world forget, on the account of the people's revolt against Israeli occupation partly for the inadequacy of his representation, that the mandate he received in the first and last elections of the Palestinian people ever is *caduque*. Decent Palestinians and other Arabs have never found a change of leadership in Palestine unhealthy. Quite the opposite: but the change should not come in the name of the "war against terrorism," but as the vindication of all those who have been stifled or jailed under his Palestinian Authority's fiat over the past years, from parliamentary leaders to civil rights advocates. The right reason is important when the U.S. challenges its Middle East "allies" as well as its "enemies."

Nor is it possible to convince anyone in the Arab world that America seeks justice so long as the current prime minister of Israel[34] is feted in Washington as a man of peace. Until he is tried for a career steeped in bloodletting and war, with massive violence directed especially against civilians, there will be no peace in the region. In the context of those serious violations of human rights, where the massacres of September 11 join a long string of mass brutality connected with the Middle East, criminal accountability for massive violations of human rights should not stop at Baghdad or Belgrade. The current ruler of Israel, who was indicted by independent Belgian prosecutors at two successive judicial levels in 2001 cannot be given any different treatment than the one offered to the Balkan indictees. Morris Draper, the foremost U.S. diplomat in charge at the time in Beirut, has affirmed that Ariel Sharon was responsible "without any doubt" for the massacres of Sabra and Shatila in 1982.[35]

International and national justice exercised internationally as in the case of Belgium under the universal jurisdiction of 1993-99 or Britain under the Torture Convention are models to be supported and developed. Activating an International Criminal Tribunal for Iraq in the very terms which presided over the ICT for Yugoslavia and the ICT for Rwanda gives far more mileage than massive bombings which essentially harm an unprotected population and forced conscripts. Western leaders should help bring the ruler of Libya to judicial account for the disappearance of Musa al-Sadr, Mansur Kekhia, and scores of Libyans, as much as he should be questioned for Lockerbie or the UTA bombing. But America will never be more cheered across the Middle East than in helping to bring the current Israeli prime minister to justice: unless our American colleagues start understanding this fair and appropriate demand to bring a criminal considered by a commission of inquiry inside his own country as "personally responsible" for a crime against humanity, the diffidence and doubt, if not open hostility, will continue. This quest for uniform justice cannot be emphasized enough, and we call on our American colleagues to open up the campaign in America to put Mr. Sharon in jail, where all mass murderers belong.[36]

The electoral process, and the change at the top is also crucial in the process of accountability. The people must be able to cast their votes freely, and the voices of the rulers when they misbehave must be equally constrained. In order to have free elections, officials and non-officials in the West must openly call for them and insist they be free, by ensuring for instance that high-level delegations of respectable people—including leaders of Nelson Mandela's persuasion in young democracies and veteran peace advocates like Jimmy Carter—attend and monitor them. They must also project their own democratic beliefs on the region, starting with their closest allies. Westerners would never accept "a Christian state," let alone a Jewish one, to rule over their own society, and the call for secularism appears loud and clear in our colleagues' letter, and should be supported insofar as it is equanimous and nuanced. "Jews" are interchangeable with other national and religious denominations, and we are concerned for the tragic loss of Arab Jewish populations across the Middle East since the establishment of the State of Israel, the subsequent impoverishment of Arab countries and increasingly monocolored and intransigent nationalisms in our own societies. Ways that would accommodate the Jewish majority's fears and concerns with the rights of non-Jews, as is tentatively done in the West by way of federalism and the courts, can be encouraged in Israel and elsewhere in the region. The disparaging way "Jews" are depicted in our countries must be fought consistently, and a serious effort for their return and compensation where appropriate must be considered as a priority for Arab governments.

In a similar vein, Islamists must be condemned whenever they take up arms and carry out violence indiscriminately, and rewarded as any other group when they operate in accordance with human rights. This is true in Algeria and elsewhere—Turkey now more than ever—and Americans should start reflecting on their unqualified support for narrow sectarian rule in the Gulf, which must also be questioned for the limitations on Christians and other minorities' peaceful practice of their religious rites. Flogging is as reprehensible in Jeddah as it is in Kabul, and torture equally unacceptable in Beirut and in Tel Aviv. Also by the same logic, the Christian dimension of Jerusalem must be rehabilitated.[37] The Judaization of the capital of the Holy Land is not acceptable and must be reversed in accordance with the concept of the *corpus separatum*, which was adopted by the United Nations half a century ago precisely for the purpose of the coexistence of communities belonging to the three world religions, in a comprehensive and balanced scheme which remains a central achievement of international law to date.

The peace process will not revive so long as the present rulers dominate Iraq, Palestine and Israel. In a new Madrid conference, if it is to reconvene, all rulers must be held at arm's length and forced to bring their opposition with them. Should they be called to the negotiating table, suspected criminals should be treated with reserve, as did U.S. diplomacy in the later stage of the Balkan negotiations, and authoritarian rulers extended a handshake only conditionally and reservedly. The more opposition figures in the halls and the less deference to the rulers, the more it is possible to exact a measure of compromise which rejects violence as the privileged means for change. In the negotiations over the Arab-Israeli conflict, as large a popular representation as possible should be sought. Palestinians in exile should be represented directly, not vicariously, and internationally run elections can be organized in the camps where they have been living in misery for sixty years. The main reason for this terrible segregation is due primarily to the fact that the governors of Israel have prevented them from coming back to their home as requested by international law, but serious efforts must also be exerted to improve their lot in the regions where they live, especially in Lebanon and the Occupied Territories, where daily life for refugees is subhuman.

The mosaic of religions, *ethnies*, and sects which has plagued the Middle East can be also the base of its renewal. For that, forms of constitutional federalism are needed across the Middle East: in Israel-Palestine, Sudan, Iraq and Turkey, Western North Africa, even Lebanon and Saudi Arabia if necessary, while all attempts at secessionism and the emergence of smaller nationalistic or sectarian entities should be categorically rejected, and actively fought. This is no less true for Palestine, where the Palestinian state risks bolstering the fearful wall which the exclusivist "national unity government" (of Israeli Jews) has conceived. Much better than an emphasis on a walled Palestinian state, a search for federal models for Israel-Palestine will allow the emergence of a community of equals in a united country rather than segregated territories built up both in concrete blocks and in Security Council resolutions. In such a profoundly different concept of coexistence in the region, the right of return can be easily acknowledged to introduce the principle of freedom of movement (and eventually establishment) for all the citizens of the Middle East, starting with the diaspora Palestinians and Jews from Arab states.

The fulfillment of this policy requires strenuous efforts in our societies, in conjunction with like-minded individuals and governments in the world, East and West. With no single country in the Arab world or the larger Middle East operating as a full-fledged democracy, a modest practical message one should ask American intellectuals to put to their leaders would sound as follows: listen to the people in the Middle East and act on principle. The rest, whether philosophies of just war, questions about the "otherness," extremists of all hues, including Christian, Jewish, and Islamic fundamentalists, and the universal affirmation of "American values" alongside "Middle Eastern values," all will fall into place much faster than one thinks. Then, with a just U.S. policy in the Middle East, both sides of the ominous East-West divide will be acting on a common platform to reverse the paradigm of hatred presently driven by extremes, including the ill-conceived "war on terrorism" carried out by the current American government with no end in sight.

Signatories

Joerg Becker, Germany, professor, Publizistik, Marburg/AUB
Randi Deguilhem, United States and France, scholar, IREMAM, Aix-en-Provence
John Donohue S.J., United States, professor, Arab and Islamic studies, Georgetown/
Université Saint-Joseph (USJ)
Wiebke Fleig, Germany, researcher
Yahya Hakim, Lebanon, consultant
Sune Haugbolle, Denmark, researcher, Oxford/AUB
Frauke Heard-Bey, scholar, history, Presidential Court, Abu Dhabi
Isam Khafaji, Iraq, economist and human rights defender, Netherlands
Elias Khouri, Lebanon, novelist and editor, *Mulhaq Al-Nahar*
Kamel Labidi, Tunisia, Tunisian journalist and human rights defender, Cairo
Chibli Mallat, Lebanon, lawyer, professor of law, USJ
Saoud al-Mawla, Lebanon, professor, Lebanese University and USJ
Katharina Noetzold, Germany, researcher, Erfurt/OIB
Soli Osel, Turkey, columnist, professor, Bilgi Un, Istanbul
Fouad Reda, Lebanon, researcher, AUB
Stefan Rosiny, Germany, professor of political science, FU Berlin
Muwaffaq Rubai'i, Iraq, Islamic oppositionist leader, human rights defender, London
Soeren Schmidt, Denmark, researcher, Roskilde University
Roland Tomb, Lebanon, professor of medicine, USJ
Leslie Tramontini, Germany, scholar of Arabic literature, Orient Institute Beirut
Stefan Weber, Germany, scholar of history, Orient Institute Beirut
Nazik Yared, Lebanon, professor, novelist, Lebanese American University

Endorsers[†] of the Democratic Iraq Initiative[‡]

Nabil Abd El Fattah, Egypt, editor-in-chief, Religious Status in Egypt, Center for
Political and Strategic Studies, al-Ahram, Cairo
Asli Bali, Turkey, attorney New York, Department of Politics, Princeton University
Melhem Chaoul, Lebanon, professor of sociology, Lebanese University
Ghassane Ghosn, Lebanon, writer and columnist
Wael Hallaq, Palestine, professor of Islamic studies, McGill University, Montreal
Mustafa Huseini, Egypt, senior columnist, *Al-Safir*
Ahmed Ibrahim, Egypt, senior researcher, Al-Ahram Center for Political and Strategic
Studies
Sadeq Jalal al-Azm, Syria, Philosophy professor, Damascus University

---

† Arab World and Turkey, excluding Iraq.
‡ See note 22 and accompanying text.

Hasan Johar, Kuwait, Member of Parliament

Kemal Kirisci, Turkey, Jean Monnet Professor, Bogazici University

Samir Khalaf, Lebanon, professor of sociology, American University of Beirut

Elias Khouri, Lebanon, novelist and editor, *Mulhaq Al-Nahar*

Kamel Labidi, Tunisia, Tunisian journalist and human rights defender

Chibli Mallat, Lebanon, lawyer, Jean Monnet Chair in European Law, USJ, Lebanon

Saoud El-Mawla, Lebanon, professor of political sociology and anthropology, Lebanese University

Jamil Mruwwe, Lebanon, editor-in-chief, *The Daily Star*

Yusri Nasrallah, Egypt, film producer

Soli Osel, Turkey, Bilgi Un, Istanbul

Abdallah Yusuf Sahar-Muhammad, Kuwait, professor of international relations, Kuwait University

Edward Said, Palestine, Columbia University, United States

Mohamed El-Sayed Said, Egypt, deputy director, Al-Ahram Center for Political and Strategic Studies, academic adviser, Cairo Institute for Human Rights Studies

Fares Sasine, Lebanon, professor of philosophy, Lebanese University

Yezid Sayegh, Palestine, professor, Cambridge University, UK

Roland Tomb, Lebanon, professor of medicine, USJ

Fawwaz Trabulsi, Lebanon, professor of politics and social studies, Lebanese American University

Fahmiyye Sharafeddin, Lebanon, professor, Lebanese University

Michael Young, Lebanon, writer and columnist

Kareem Yousef, Egypt, lawyer and law lecturer

Sharhabeel Zaeem, Palestine, lawyer, Gaza

Jihad Zein, Lebanon, op-ed and diplomatic editor, *Al-Nahar*

Notes

*This paper was originally prepared in May 2001, then expanded and edited in response to the American intellectuals' letter in support of the U.S. government's use of force in the wake of the September 11 massacres ("What We're Fighting For," February 12, 2002, posted with footnotes and commentary at www.americanvalues.org. [See also chapter 2 of this volume.]). The present text was finalized by Chibli Mallat over several collective meetings convened in 2002 to respond to the U.S. letter. Its main conclusions have been endorsed by a number of Arab and Western colleagues across the world, following a lecture organized at the German Orient Institute in Beirut in November 2002. A list of signatories follows the text [on page 228 of this volume]. The Democratic Iraq Initiative (see note 22), an offshoot of this work, has developed separately because of the urgency of the Iraq situation, and was endorsed by a different set of signatories, a list of whom also appears following the text [on pages 228-229 of this volume].

Together with the initial group of signatories, the full Arabic text and footnotes of this "blueprint for democracy in the Middle East" appeared in the op-ed page of the leading Lebanese daily, *Al-Nahar*, in two installments, on January 20 and 27, 2003, under the following titles: *"Musahama fil-jidal hawla wathiqat al-muthaqqafin al-amirkiyyin: al-haja ila tahawwul jadhri fi tariqat al-tafkir"* (Contribution to the debate over the text of the American intellectuals: The need for a paradigm shift in the way of thinking) and *"Radd 'ala risalat al-muthaqqafin al-amirkiyyin (2): 'al-'adala la tataba "ad', hakimu sharon"* (Response to the American intellectuals, "Justice is indivisible": Prosecute Sharon). "Justice is indivisible" is a citation from the thirteenth-century jurist Ibn abi al-Dam, from his book on the practice of judges (*Adab al-Qadi*, Beirut: Dar al-Kutub al-'ilmiyya, 1987, 96) and is a recurrent concept in the classical legal literature of the Islamic tradition, as natural in that context as is "equality before the law" in the American tradition. The French version appeared in *Travaux et Jours* (Beirut: USJ), Spring 2004, 73, at 115-145. To facilitate reading the document, the rest of the notes appear as endnotes.

1. We have taken note of the various reactions posted on the Institute for American Values' website and of discussions in the Arab and Western press over the past year. For purposes of simplification, it might be useful to summarize the exchanges: in the original letter, sixty U.S. intellectuals defend the vision of a military reaction to September 11 on the strength of U.S. values of democracy, values that also include their belief in a just war and in the concept of separation between state and religion. They also dwell on their puzzlement about the use of Islam as a weapon of hatred and challenge putative readers who do not share their point of view to explain why they do not agree with what the U.S. government is fighting for (["What We're Fighting For"] February 12, 2002). The answer of 153 Saudi intellectuals underlines the convergence of Islamic values with U.S./universal values. It decries the massacres of September 11 but challenges the absence of causal appreciation between September 11 and U.S. policy in the Middle East, and asks that policy either be made more balanced or that the U.S. abandon the region altogether. This in their view explains why the Far East is not perceived negatively in the region ("How We Can Coexist," www.islamtoday.net, May 7, 2002). In rebuttal, the U.S. writers challenged the application of democratic values in Saudi Arabia, asking the Saudi colleagues why they remain silent over the severe violations of human rights committed in their country and question those in application domestically and internationally by the U.S. They also challenge them over their position about *jihad* and "Islamic piety as practiced in Saudi Arabia" ("Can We Coexist?" a response from Americans to colleagues in Saudi Arabia, October 23, 2002). Two other responses also appeared in reaction to the original American text. "A Letter from United States Citizens to Friends in Europe," signed by 141 intellectuals, underlined the misuse of the concept of self-defense and the general unawareness in America "that the effect of U.S. power abroad has nothing to do with the 'values' celebrated at home" (April 14, 2002). A letter by German writers was published on May 2, 2002 in the *Frankfurter Allgemeine Zeitung* ("A World of Justice and Peace Would Be Different"), criticizing the aggressive attitudes of the U.S. government, its black-and-white view of the world, its callousness before the killing of innocent bystanders, and its impermeability to the negative effects of globalization.

2. The author is referring to the signatories of "What We're Fighting For." See pages 29-31 of this volume. —Ed.

3. In their letter, U.S. colleagues briefly mention poverty and material concerns as central problem areas in the relations between Western societies and the rest of the world. This, however, is tangential to their message, and we call on them to develop a more thorough appreciation of their leaders' lack of attention to the imbalance in world resources, compounding the risk that the ongoing tensions and crises the world overfeeds on [creates] a profound lack of equality among men and women living on the same planet. A provocative but enlightening approach ˙ᵔ the imbalance of world

resources can be found in Eduardo Galeano, *Upside Down: A Primer for the Looking-Glass World* (New York: 2000; original 1998). The need to fight poverty and its other manifestations, including pandemic illnesses like AIDS, is acknowledged by Western governments, but the acknowledgment hardly translates in any fundamental structural correction to economic policies. It is true, however, that this angle opens up a tangential avenue to the discussion at hand, and needs to be addressed in a different forum. Our colleagues who wrote the 2002 Arab UNDP Report have started the debate on that front. We shall focus here on "American values" and the policy allegedly flowing from the assertion and protection of these values by the United States after September 11, as developed in "What We're Fighting For."

4. A new definition of war is required, which is a legitimate exercise beyond the purview of the present exchange. It is discussed, for instance, in Mallat, *Democracy in America* (in Arabic, Beirut: *Dar Al-Nahar*, August 2001, chaps. 11-12, 14-16). This exercise is also under way in decision-making circles in the U.S., particularly in the context of an Iraq war; see the deserved success of Eliot A. Cohen, *Supreme Command: Soldiers, Statesmen and Leadership in Wartime* (New York 2002), with its emphasis on the need for full civilian leadership of the war. The concept of "preventive" war developed by the U.S. president in September 2002 is troubling in its present, crude form. More promising are the linkages made between moral values in foreign policy and the use of force as last resort in the works of Harold Koh (the need to pursue openly and doggedly a foreign policy that takes account of human rights), Paul Kahn (how moral can violence ever be?), and Thomas Franck (democratic governance as a basic right). Because of the unique colonial context of the nineteenth and twentieth centuries, Clausewitz, Ho Chi Minh, or Frantz Fanon have much more appropriate contributions on modern warfare than Saint Augustine, and the fourteenth-century sociologist and historian Ibn Khaldun (d. 1406) has far more illuminating insights on the dynamics of tribalism than the anachronistic literature of the Islamic canonists on jihad, a malleable concept in the classical and modern Arab texts, and one that is often misused in the West under an essentialist cultural connotation of blood-thirsty and violence-bent Islamic or Arab societies.

In any case, war in classical *fiqh* (Islamic law) is more appropriately understood as literature on *siyar*, and the traditional fiqh compendia include a book on siyar, within which the law of warfare is discussed. See, for instance, volume ten of the thirty-volume treatise of the eleventh-century Transoxanian scholar Sarakhsi, *Al-Mabsut*. The literature was known earlier as *maghazi*, literally, "conquests."

5. Examples are standard, and the Saudi colleagues [in "How We Can Coexist"] have listed the main ones on the side of tolerance, foremost the Qur'anic injunction "No compulsion in matters religious," and other sayings ascribed to Caliphs 'Umar and 'Ali supplement. There is an equally rich warmongering choice in Islamic civilization. In the Christian tradition, the episode of Jesus' anger against the merchants of the Temple is used to undermine the message of peace and nonviolence found elsewhere in the New Testament, and Jewish advocates of violence rest their references in some fiery passages of the Book of Joshua, as opposed to calls for patience, equanimity, and passive resistance as in the Book of Job or the Prophets.

6. For the concept of canonization and a better understanding of the permanence of religious history, the works of the late John Wansbrough (d. 2002) should be consulted, and the corresponding exegetical works of Muhammad Baqer al-Sadr, the leading Islamic thinker of the twentieth century, who was assassinated by the Iraqi government in April 1980. *Deuteungsbeduerftigkeit*, which is the quintessential literary character of sacred texts to allow a full range of interpretations—indeed calls for and requests interpretation—is also a Wansbroughian concept.

7. Those two axioms, *Deutungsbeduerftigkeit* and religion as a divine message of peace (note the etymological meaning of Islam, from *silm*, peace) make also the comparative study of divine messages get lost in Byzantine discussions over what is common to all worldly religions and what sets them apart from one another. Considering that Samuel Huntington is one of the signatories to the U.S. letter, it would be appropriate to reconsider the one-sided aspect (but one side is correct) of the *Clash of Civilizations* (1993 as article, 1995 as book, with civilizations defined religiously) in the light of this duality.

8. The most accurate translation of "What We're Fighting For" should be rendered as *"Ma nujahidu min ajlih"* (*nujahid* being the verb form of the substantive jihad); it offers a small example on political exoticism and its nefarious polarization, typical of which is the use of Allah for God and jihad for war or violence. María Rosa Menocal has put it well in a recent book: "One of the inappropriate and alienating ways we speak about Islam in English is to use the Arabic word Allah, God, as if it were a proper name, creating the false impression that this is some different God"; Menocal, *The Ornament of the World* (New York, 2002), 18. A good start is to stop using both words, as well as perhaps the nebulous al-Qaʻida, which fulfills an exotic scarecrow function, setting people apart by an awkward and falsely learned wording. Al-qaʻida (with the full letter *ʻayn*), means rule as well as base (as in the base of a pyramid), and it is hard to be against rules and bases. An alternative is extremist Islamists, Salafists (from *salafi*, looking to the forebears, akin to fundamentalist forms of political Christianity), or Wahhabists in reference to the Arabian peninsula origin of the violence-bent branch associated with Osama bin Ladin. Even that depiction is not quite accurate, and the name al-Qaʻida may well be a Western intelligence (unwillful) construct, [created] in or around 1997 to [refer to] an elusive phenomenon of diffuse violence and a nebulous and elusive network. The one, more sinister self-denomination of the group under the patronage of the Taliban and the "Afghan" Arabs around bin Ladin, is "the Front to Fight Jews and Crusaders."

9. The *Washington Post* article to which the author is referring is, "Academics Defend War on Terrorism" by Alan Cooperman, which appeared on February 12, 2002 (the public release date of "What We're Fighting For"). The "website that carries the debate" is the Institute for American Values' website, http://www.americanvalues.org. When the letter was posted, the webmaster used the following tagline to describe it: "Sixty scholars make the moral case for the war on terrorism." —Ed.

10. It was the U.S. government that prevented the listing of terrorism as a crime in the Rome Statutes for the International Criminal Court, because terrorism lacks a proper definition. This was and remains a correct position.

11. One should note the use of the term "mass murder" in the U.S. letter text. But again, this remains an exception in the depiction of the bloodshed on September 11, which is current both in the U.S. media and in the wording of the U.S. government as "terrorist attack." For an article covering "the rush to war and the need for a proper characterization of September 11" in an analytical spirit close to the one proposed here, see Juan E. Méndez, "Human Rights Policy in the Age of Terrorism," *Saint Louis University Law Journal* 46 (2002), 377-403.

12. For how constitutional review prevents the tyranny of majority, see John Hart Ely, *Democracy and Distrust* (Cambridge, Mass., 1980), p. 43, citing Alexander Bickel.

13. Alternatively, if the United States government is looking for a Kantian "end of history" in the sense of the suppression of political violence on earth (as the only possible workable definition of terrorism entails), then its domination of the planet *manu militari* appears as the inevitable condition to fulfill it. This belief in perpetual

peace is hardly a justification presented by the U.S. authors of the Letter, or an acceptable or realistic objective of the currently declared war on terror/ism. We trust the signatories do not think the war to end all war is at hand in what their government is fighting for. If terrorism equals the use of violence for political ends (against civilians generally, but not so necessarily, e.g., in German or British legislation in the 1970s and 1980s), where does this put Clausewitz's scientific definition of war "as the continuation of state politics by other means"?

As an important follow-up to this side discussion, it would be enticing to examine the still pertinent treatise of Emmanuel Kant on *Perpetual Peace* ("Zum ewigen Frieden," 1795) as a more ambitious horizon to a common endeavor than the parameters of "What We're Fighting For" offer or, indeed, the present Response. Kant writes prophetically in "the definitive article for a perpetual peace among states" that "one neighbor must guarantee to another his personal security, which cannot take place except in a state of legislation." This forerunner of the phrase "democracies do not enter into war against each other" is further detailed by the subjection to "a state of legislation" of the domestic scene, the international scene, and the universal scene, corresponding for Kant to "civil right, limited to a people (*jus civitatis*) ... rights of nations, regulating the relations of nations among each other (*jus gentium*), and cosmopolitan right, as far as men, or states, are considered as influencing one another, in quality of constituent parts of the great state of the human race (*jus cosmopoliticum*)" Kant, *Perpetual Peace* (New York, 1932), p. 10-11. The treatise deserves full-fledged treatment for a unique insightfulness, to be coupled with the works of the Arab poet-philosopher Abu al-'Ala' al-Ma'arri (d. 1058), author of a treaty on tolerance (*risalat al-ghufran*), a forerunner of the *Divine Comedy*. *Risalat al-ghufran* relates the redeeming features of a large number of literary and philosophical figures despite their ending up in Hell.

Ma'arri, in addition to a measured view of all religions, has also opposed killing animals to provide for people's food and even taking the bees' honeycombs away from them for man's benefit. While the issue of politics and religion is far too vast to be discussed here beyond the agreement that the use of violence in the name of religion can never be accepted, the distance between the two with regard to the state is an ever recurring question, East and West. One is greatly disturbed by the so-called Christian Zionism in the U.S., but it is also true that not enough space is allowed to a "neutral" state in the Middle East, leading to a lower threshold for tolerating religious proselytism, or criticism of any faith. A useful point of entry for dealing with "blasphemy laws" in the Middle East is the poet's advice in 1923 to his children: "*wa la tata'assabu abadan li-dinin fa kullu ta'assubin yushqi wa yurdi/likullin dinuhu wa li-kulli dinin masunu karamatin ta'ba al-tahaddi*" (Never follow religion fanatically, all fanaticism brings misery and backwardness/to each his religion, and to each religion a penumbra of dignity that will not accept a crude challenge).

14. Hegel, in the introduction to the *Philosophy of Right* (1820). A similar metaphor can be found in President Muhammad Khatami's book, *Bim-e Muj* (Fear of Waves) (Tehran, 1993), the title of which refers to a famous verse of the great Persian poet Hafez seeking in knowledge and wisdom salvation from the dark waves of history (or passion).

15. A practical and simple test consists of two guidelines which policymakers should be made to adopt by U.S. colleagues across the ocean, to start reversing the "hatred" and "diffidence" associated with the way Arab Middle Easterners perceive ... the increasing injustice of U.S. policy as carried out in the last half century.

Guideline 1. Listen to the people of the region. Regular summitry and Mideast embassies in Europe and America are insufficient and distortive. Governments overall lack legitimacy, and Middle Eastern leaders are mired in double-talk. They are concerned about the perpetuation of their personal rule before any other matter, and they react to major crises and challenges with this perpetuation as a dominant concern, whether the crisis regards Palestine, Iraq, or "Muslim fundamentalism." In such a context, the gap between peoples and governments has been increasing by the day, and the voices of the individual citizens become further distorted when it comes to their governments speaking for them abroad. As a corollary, civil society in Europe and the U.S. must force their governments to open up to civil society in the Middle East, and to narrow it down with Middle Eastern governments. This reversal of course must be done openly, determinedly, with no shame. If representatives of civil society sound political or demanding, this is no reason to shy away from them. In Middle Eastern countries, many an individual will tell the truth more readily than her head of state in policy matters. Both officials and civil society leaders in the West should not hesitate to open up to those segments in Middle Eastern civil society whose values they share. Civil society leaders in the Middle East should be encouraged in their national, regional and global networking, they must be supported financially, structurally, politically. *Mostly, support should be given openly and directly, over the head of the government and, if necessary, against it, for nonviolent political change at the top.*

Guideline 2. Western leaders should be forced to think in principled ways. America and Europe need to be attentive to the deafening call for change, and support those calls that square with Western values of freedom and progress. *Any relativity of rights is a smokescreen for repression. Any ambivalence and double standards are sharply perceived in the Middle East.*

While the expression of universal values might take a local form, such "native" expressions must be encouraged so long as they remain within the universal frame of rights shared by every person on the planet.

The checklist is simple enough. Westerners are asked to treat Middle Easterners as fellow human beings, rather than as a special category which responds to separate (read "less human") values:

(1) Have I listened to the "real voices" in the Mideast today, beyond the thousand and one official encounters? Have I given enough time and open support to the people at the receiving end of their governments' rule?

(2) Have I thought in a principled manner, have I treated the leaders and the people of the Mideast in the same way as I would treat my Canadian or French counterparts? Have I re-organized priorities in my attitude towards the Middle East without sacrificing my principles?

16. Colleagues should appreciate that the message Middle Easterners put forward as "civil society" is asymmetrical in comparison with the one advanced by American intellectuals: we have a problem of democracy in our countries far more acute than that faced by the peoples of the West, and the distance between us and our governments is far larger than the distance between Westerners and their elected representatives. This should command some appreciation of the far more difficult task one faces in articulating a full-fledged alternative policy as will be presently sketched, and the amount of metaphoric language needed to address the risks of repression. The difficulties of the Saudi colleagues after the publication of their letter ["How We Can Coexist"] are telling.

17. For a balanced and rich recent survey, see Ghassan Tuéni, Jean Lacouture and Gérard Khouri, *Un Siècle pour Rien* (Paris, 2002).

18. One advocate of the domino theory is Professor Bernard Lewis, who used it in a recent article in *The New Yorker*, and at a conference on the Future of Iraq at the American Enterprise Institute (October 5, 2002); see the full minutes on www.aei.org.

19. Jihad Zein has introduced the concept of "revolutionary American project" in his recent columns of the Lebanese daily *Al-Nahar*.

20. Reference here is to the right to resist occupation and/or dictatorship by force, which has been formally consecrated in law since the American Revolution. A similar debate has taken place in classical Islamic history over the *fitna*, or revolt/chaos. In both cases, the literature is extensive.

21. For a sense of the dislike of the Iraqi ruler, see the column of veteran Arab statesman Ghassane Tueini, *"Risala ila Saddam Hussein: al-istiqala ashraf"* (Letter to Saddam Hussein: Resignation is more honorable), *Al-Nahar*, November 11, 2002.

22. Collapse theory is discussed in Mallat, *The Middle East into the 21ˢᵗ Century* (London, 1996), 114-119, and is revived in the Democratic Iraq Initiative; for an early version, see, e.g., Nicholas Blanford, "Don't Make Saddam Mad, Make Him Lonely," September 12, 2002, and for extensive press coverage, see Reuters, NPR, CNN, *The Christian Science Monitor*, and the Arab press since January 2003. The coverage is also available on www.mallat.com. The idea of having a U.S. general rule Iraq is too ludicrously colonial to entertain seriously. For the development of the Democratic Iraq Initiative, the following petition was signed by a number of prominent Arabs: "We call upon public opinion in the Arab world to exercise pressure for the dismissal from power of Saddam Hussein and his close aides in Iraq, in order to avoid a war that threatens with catastrophe the peoples of the region, foremost amongst whom are the Iraqi people. The immediate resignation of Saddam Hussein, whose rule over three decades has been a nightmare for Iraq and the Arab world, is the only way to avoid more violence. We call likewise for the rule of democracy in Baghdad, and for the stationing across Iraq of human rights monitors from the United Nations and the Arab League, to oversee the peaceful transition of power in the country." The list of signatories as of Jan. 25, 2003 appears at the end of the present text [on pages 228-229 of this volume].

23. The French paper *Le Monde* reported in October 2002 the non-Jewish population in Israel at 27 percent of the population (not including territories occupied in 1967). The Arab-speaking non-Jewish population is estimated at 18-20 percent. The rest includes transient foreign workers, but also a large section of Russian immigrants who are not Jewish.

24. Coercive expulsion of the local Palestinian population is now acknowledged in the contributions of Israeli "revisionist" or new school history of 1948 (Tom Segev, Benny Morris, Ilan Pappe, Avi Shlaim, Nur Masalha, the last a Palestinian Israeli following the tradition of Walid Khalidi). The literature is extensive. A weak, narrow rebuttal can be read in Efraim Karsh, *Fabricating Israeli History* (London, 2000).

25. The most remarkable studies of present-day Israel are those of Baruch Kimmerling, from *Zionism and Territory* (Berkeley, 1983), to *The Invention and Decline of Israeliness* (California, 2001). A senior professor of sociology at Hebrew University, Kimmerling has this to say in his latest monograph (p.181): "Given the nature of Israeli 'reality,' as described in this book ... it is easy to conclude that only one of the five necessary conditions for considering Israel as a democracy is present.... The main reason for this is the historically inherent inability to separate religion from nationalism and nationality implicit in the 'Jewishness' of the Israeli state." The five conditions are listed as follows: "1. Periodic free elections, including the possibility of changing the ruling political elites or parties through such election; 2. Sovereignty of the people, exercised through a legislative system constructed by a parliament, according to which the judicial system operates. No independent or parallel legislative and judicial system can be created by the state; 3. Equal and inclusive citizenship and civil rights; 4. Universal suffrage where every vote is equal; 5. Protection

of the civil and human rights of minorities from the tyranny of the majority." This does not prevent "Israeli political culture and most of its academic analysts, however, [from] systematically and compulsively deny[ing] the basically undemocratic nature of the Israeli regime" (p. 182).

26. Since the long-held beliefs that "a people without land have come to a land without people" and "that Jews made the desert bloom" had stopped being bandied about in the West in the mid-1980s, there are generally three arguments made in favor of the policy of Israeli governments towards the native Palestinians since 1948. The first is that the displacement of the population that year was the same as what was done to Jewish Arabs, i.e., Jews living in Arab countries; second, that such displacement is common in war. Less often used is the example of other countries built on the displacement/massacre of the native population, probably because of the touchiness of the model in the light of the now universally "condemned" treatment of the natives throughout the European colonization of the Americas. The first argument is incorrect, the second is insufficient, and the third inadequate. All three arguments have been undermined by the continued resistance of the Palestinians to reverse a fundamental injustice. For a comparative reading of the historical treatment by the two leading historians of the Middle East, the late Albert Hourani *(A History of the Arab Peoples*, London 1992) and Bernard Lewis (*The Middle East: A Brief History of the Last 2,000 Years*, London 1995), see *"Hamesh fi ikhtilaf al-a'imma: hujrat 1948 wa uslub al-tarikh"* (A footnote in the battle of the giants: The flight of 1948 and style in history), *Al-Hayat*, March 30, 1996.

27. Taujan Faisal in Jordan, Zuhair Yahya in Tunisia, Saadeddin Ibrahim and his colleagues in Egypt, Habib Younes (and the closure of the MTV station) in Lebanon, Riad Seif and his companions in Syria, in a sad litany of Amnesty International lists over the past years. All have spent time in jail or are still imprisoned for expressing their opinions. Others, like the Egyptian Nasr Hamed Abu Zeid and the Tunisian Munsef Marzouki and most Iraqi dissidents live in exile.

28. "A closer examination of the Israeli judiciary system clarifies the fact that the judiciary not only does not extend help and protection against the arbitrariness of the government regarding its Arab subjects and does not protect civil and human rights but it also constitutes one of the most sophisticated tools of repression employed since the State of Israel was brought into being." Baruch Kimmerling, "Jurisdiction in an Immigrant-Settler Society: the 'Jewish and Democratic State,'" *Comparative Political Studies* 35 (December 2002), 1119-44.

29. In the United States, it is not just the constraints on civil liberties and due process that have elicited a battle in courts, but also the profiling of individuals with a "Middle Eastern character," let alone the inventions of legal categories like noncombatant and discovery of forlorn places like Guantanamo for prisoners of the Afghan war, just to avoid the Geneva Conventions. The major human rights organizations, and courageous circles in America, have stood up against that policy, so far with few achievements.

30. The late King to whom the author is referring is King Hassan II of Morocco. —Ed.

31. In November 2002, the U.S. government mentioned Morocco as a model to be followed elsewhere in the area. This position should be commended and amplified.

32. It was suggested already in 1993 that president Hosni Mubarak would set a remarkable precedent if he did not seek a third term, *"Al-ra'is al-sabeq jaran fil-hara"* (The former president as ordinary neighbor?), *Al-Hayat*, July 30, 1993.

33. The leader of the Palestinian Authority to whom the author is referring is Yasser Arafat. —Ed.

34. The prime minister of Israel to whom the author is referring is Ariel Sharon. —Ed.

35. It is heartening to see the introduction by former secretary of state George Shultz to the just released book by John Boykin on Ariel Sharon's brutal role in 1982, *Cursed is the Peacemaker: The American Diplomat versus the Israeli General, Beirut 1982,* (Applegate, Calif., 2002). There is mention of Sabra and Shatila in the introduction; however, far more courage is needed in the United States when it comes to Israel.

36. To give two related examples on the depth of the bias of talented and influential U.S. columnists: William Safire's unqualified support of Ariel Sharon for over two decades, to the point of salvaging him from the boycott of a large section of Israeli journalists in 1983-84 and considering him to date the ultimate "expert reference" for good and evil in and around Israel; and the case of Thomas Friedman, who made his name as a young journalist for his coverage of Sabra and Shatila, yet has not written a single line about the legal case that the victims of the massacres fought in Belgium. One still hopes for a louder and more mainstream U.S. appeal to confront a manifestly recidivist war criminal as chief ally presiding in government over the destiny of much of the Middle East. A timid—albeit encouraging, so severe has become the witch hunt against any criticism of Israel in the U.S.—call on the U.S. government "to deal with ... Sharon's Israel" appeared in a *Washington Post* column by Jim Hoagland, as well as an unprecedented description side by side of "jihadists and sharonists." The letter of a collective of nine Israeli women groups to the victims of Sabra and Shatila supporting their search for justice on the occasion of the twentieth anniversary of the impunity of Ariel Sharon offers an opportunity to break the silence and the zero-sum confrontation. See the letter Robert Fisk, "Prosecute Sharon for War Crimes, Israeli Women Say," *The Independent,* September 24, 2002; and www.indictsharon.net for the American-based section of the worldwide campaign in support of the Belgian case. More than a million people have signed an e-mail petition requesting that Sharon be brought to justice.

37. Since the occupation of East Jerusalem in 1967 by Israel, its Christian population has dwindled from 27,000 to less than 4,000, whereas West Jerusalem had been completely purged of non-Jews in 1948. For a balanced view of a long and contentious history (despite only a passing reference to the ethnic cleansing in West Jerusalem in 1948 of its non-Jewish inhabitants, on p.163), see Bernard Wasserstein, *Divided Jerusalem* (New Haven, 2001). Such forms of "ethnic cleansing" will never rest until redeemed in some effective manner. Nor should the expulsion of Jews from the Old City in 1948, or the assassination of elderly Lebanese Jews in Lebanon in the mid-1980s remain wrapped in silence. While cold-blooded mass killers must be brought to justice, as those who engineered the blowing-up of eighty-five innocent people in the Beirut suburbs on March 28, 1985, an extensive and sophisticated exercise in Truth and Justice is needed in the region. Truth and Reconciliation/Justice must include the dark role played by American and Western governments in the latter part of the twentieth century in support of authoritarian rulers in the region, from Iran's shah in the 1950s, to Saddam Hussein in the 1980s, to the present rulers of countless other countries.

"The Need for a Paradigm Shift in American Thinking" was originally published in two parts on January 20 and 27, 2003 in *Al-Nahar* (Lebanon). Reprinted with permission.

Nineteen

&

Pre-Emption, Just War and Iraq: A Statement of Principles

&

9 U.S. Intellectuals

Pacifism says that all war is morally prohibited. What is often called realism says that war is essentially about power and self-interest, rendering ethical analysis largely beside the point. In contrast to both of these perspectives, the just war tradition, developed over a period of 1500 years, says that ethical standards can and should be applied to the activity of war.

The ends of war, and the means deployed to achieve them, must be based on justice. Indeed, it is precisely because justice is so important that war is a legitimate and necessary part of political life. But just war teaching also makes clear that war is at best a necessary evil, in part because war takes human lives, and in part because war is such a blunt and uncertain instrument of policy. These twin ideas, highlighting both the centrality of justice and the problematic nature of war—von Clausewitz's famous "fog of war"— undergird the numerous requirements for declaring war justly. These include rightful cause, proper authority, the intention to pursue peace and justice, and the use of force only after other reasonable alternatives have been considered and found wanting.

These ideas also set forth the requirements for waging war justly, including proportionality of response and a clearly positive balance of benefits over costs. In addition, the just war tradition teaches that while war alters some implications of the principle of equal human dignity—the idea that even our adversaries have the same human rights that we do—war does not suspend or negate that principle. Specifically, equal human dignity requires us to observe the principle of noncombatant immunity and to do everything reasonably in our power to minimize civilian casualties.

From this just war perspective, we have supported, and continue to support, the use of military force against the murderers of September 11 and those who assist them. In February of this year, we were among those who stated: "Organized killers with global reach now threaten all of us. In the name of universal human morality, and fully conscious of the restrictions and requirements of a just war, we support our government's, and our society's, decision to use force of arms against them."[1]

Today, from this same ethical perspective, we state our views, including our critical concerns, regarding the Bush Administration's proposed strategic doctrine of pre-emption, the crisis in Iraq, and the relationship between the two.

In recent statements and documents, the Administration declares the right to initiate attacks against states deemed to be future threats to the U.S. The idea of attacking a nation that does not pose a threat today, but that may pose one in the future, is as old as war itself. But within the framework of just war theory, pre-emption can be morally justified only in rare circumstances—when the attack is likely to be imminent, the threat is grave, and preventive means other than war are unavailable.

Expanding this narrow and exceptional option into a broad doctrine at the center of U.S. foreign policy is inconsistent with the just war tradition. We are concerned that such a doctrine may well make the world a more dangerous place, especially if other nations appropriate it for their own purposes. For example, the new doctrine might appear to license India in the use of force against Pakistan, with the intention of pre-empting the possibility of Pakistani action. Particularly since both of these nations possess nuclear weapons, it should be U.S. policy to do what we can to reduce, rather than enhance, the likelihood of either of these nations pre-emptively attacking the other.

The Administration's new doctrine is also troubling to us because, at least regarding Iraq, it seems clearly to be unnecessary. Debating pre-emption in the context of Iraq obscures the fact that the U.S. has been in a low-grade military conflict with Iraq for more than a decade, stemming from our leadership of the coalition that reversed Iraq's illegal occupation of Kuwait in 1991. As long as our demand is Iraq's compliance with United Nations-approved disarmament requirements stemming from that conflict, including requirements against developing, stockpiling or using weapons of mass destruction, the U.S. doesn't need a new doctrine called pre-emption to justify an increased use of force. The relevant issue is enforcement, not pre-emption.

Would a renewed U.S.-led military assault against Iraq be just? In recent months, the Bush Administration has publicly floated numerous reasons for such a move. From the perspective of just war thinking, most of these rationales are not compelling. For example, we hear of "regime change" as a primary goal in Iraq. Regime change can be one consequence of a just war, but waging a war primarily to get rid of a foreign leader, even a dangerous one, could set a dangerous precedent and is generally inconsistent with just war principles.

We also need much more clarity on the imminence of the threat. Specifically, there seems to be little or no credible evidence indicating that

Iraq is about to launch an attack against the U.S. or any other country. Evidence of Iraq's complicity in the attacks of September 11 appears so far to be thin and inconclusive. While Iraq's government is certainly brutal and repressive, there is no evidence, so long as no-fly zones over Iraq are enforced, that Iraq's government is currently in a position to engage in widespread killings of Kurds or Shiites living in Iraq.

At the same time, one rationale for at least preparing to attack Iraq seems fully justified. The UN Security Council resolutions on disarmament and weapons inspections in Iraq, passed in 1991, have been flagrantly—and so far, with impunity—violated by the Iraqi regime. The U.S. and its allies should have been willing to fight a just war over this issue years ago, especially when Iraq effectively expelled the UN weapons inspectors in 1998. Although Iraq almost certainly does not yet possess nuclear weapons, it appears to be aggressively seeking the means to produce them. As President Bush has rightly insisted, the fact that Iraq today may be only a year away from obtaining nuclear weapons makes the regime's continued flouting of these disarmament requirements a legitimate international crisis.

For this reason, if Iraq fails to comply with demands for a renewed and unencumbered program of arms inspections by a near-term date, then the use of force to compel compliance would be both justified and necessary. Conversely, however, if Iraq does comply, the Administration should take "yes" for an answer—not because weapons inspections are a panacea, but because they worked reasonably well in Iraq in the early 1990s, and because, at least for the immediate future, they are morally preferable to full-scale U.S. military action against that country.

As President Bush recently stated, true disarmament in Iraq would constitute "regime change" in the most relevant respect—it would dramatically reduce Saddam Hussein's capacity to threaten his neighbors and the world. That should be the principal aim of U.S. policy, and we should resort to war only if we have exhausted all other reasonable means of achieving it. If we proceed in this measured, step-by-step manner, we will not only do justice, but be seen as doing justice. No other course of action could better advance the long-term prospects for a more peaceful and democratic world order.

Signatories*

David Blankenhorn, *President, Institute for American Values*
Jean Bethke Elshtain, *Laura Spelman Rockefeller Professor of Social and Political Ethics, University of Chicago Divinity School*
Francis Fukuyama, *Bernard Schwartz Professor of International Political Economy, Johns Hopkins University*
William A. Galston, *Professor at the School of Public Affairs, University of Maryland; Director, Institute for Philosophy and and Public Policy*

*Signatories' affiliations are listed for identification purposes only.

John Kelsay, *Richard L. Rubenstein Professor of Religion, Florida State University*
Robert Putnam, *Peter and Isabel Malkin Professor of Public Policy at the Kennedy School of Government, Harvard University*
Theda Skocpol, *Victor S. Thomas Professor of Government and Sociology, Harvard University*
Max L. Stackhouse, *Professor of Christian Ethics and Director, Project on Public Theology, Princeton Theological Seminary*
Paul C. Vitz, *Professor of Psychology, New York University*

Notes

1. "What We're Fighting For: A Letter from America" (Institute for American Values: February 2002). [See chapter 2 of this volume.]

"Pre-Emption, Iraq, and Just War: A Statement of Principles" was written under the aegis of the Institute for American Values and publicly released on November 14, 2002.

The U.S.-German Dialogue

Twenty

∾

A World of Justice and Peace Would Be Different

∾

103 German Intellectuals

Ladies and Gentlemen:

The mass murder [caused] by the terrorist attack on September 11 in your country, and the U.S. war in Afghanistan as a reaction to that terror also affects Europe, the Islamic world, and the future of all of us. We think it especially important that an open and critical dialogue take place throughout the world among intellectuals of civil societies about the causes and consequences of these events, to assess them and judge their significance. Please consider our response to your "What We're Fighting For" as a contribution to this.

There can be no moral justification for the horrible mass murder on September 11. We agree with you wholeheartedly about that. We also share the moral standards that you apply, namely that human dignity is inviolable, regardless of sex, color of skin, or religion, and that striving for democracy is an important foundation for the protection of human dignity, of individual freedoms, of freedom of religion, and of the human rights specified in the UN Charter.

But it is precisely these moral values, which are universally valid in our eyes, that cause us to reject the war that your government and its allies (us included) in the "alliance against terror" are waging in Afghanistan—and which has cost the lives of more than 4,000 innocent bystanders to date, including many women and children—with the same rigorousness with which we condemn the mass murder of innocent bystanders [caused] by the terrorist attack. There are no universally valid values that allow one to justify one mass murder by another. The war of the "alliance against terror" in Afghanistan is no "just war"—an ill-starred historical concept that we do not accept—on the contrary, it flagrantly violates even the condition you cite, "to protect the innocent from certain harm." Democratic states possess sufficiently developed means under the rule of law to combat crime within their sphere of influence, and to call the guilty to account. What we need to do is to extend these proven means globally, in close cooperation with other states.

We cannot understand why you do not devote a single word of your appeal to the mass murder of the Afghan civilian population resulting from the bombing campaign conducted with the most modern weapon systems. The inviolability of human dignity applies not only to people in the United States, but also to people in Afghanistan, and even to the Taliban and the al-Qa'ida prisoners at Guantanamo. In your appeal, you invoke the universality of your moral standards, while at the same time applying them only to yourselves. By this selective usage, you call precisely their universal validity into question drastically, thus evoking great doubts about the genuineness of your own avowal. How can the doubts raised about these moral standards in other cultures be dispelled, if—of all people—the elites of U.S. civilization, who see themselves as advocates and guardians of these values, bring the belief in the universality of these values into discredit? Can we expect other nations and cultures to perceive the application of dual standards as anything but the expression of continuing Western arrogance and ignorance?

And, in view of the overwhelming evidence of the historical facts, we cannot follow you when you write that your country "At times ... has pursued misguided and unjust policies." The United States made an outstanding contribution to the liberation of Europe from the yoke of Naziism. However, as a leading superpower during the period of East-West confrontation, it was also largely responsible for grave abuses in the world. By numerous covert to directly [overt] military interventions, such as in Iran, Indonesia, Chile, Guatemala, El Salvador, Nicaragua, in the Iran-Iraq war on the Iraqi side, and many others, the United States supported regimes which ruled by state terrorism and million-fold murder of opposition forces, and prevented democratization processes. Frequently enough, freely elected governments fell victim to these interventions.

Many of the undersigned hoped that, after the collapse of the Soviet Union, a new era of disarmament, international understanding, dialogue between cultures, and hope for the billions of people suffering from and humiliated by hunger and disease would begin. After four decades of hate, mutual threats, and the arms race, we expected and worked for the Western industrialized nations to put their creative potential in the service of overcoming poverty and environmental destruction, and developing democracy. But these expectations were disappointed. Instead, the United States concentrated its imagination and its scientific, technical, and economic capacities on strengthening its position as the sole remaining superpower in the world, and establishing a unipolar world order. In that order, it attempts to decide the fate of peoples largely on its own authority. Much evidence, such as the systematic establishment of U.S. military bases in the Balkans, the Middle East, and Central Asia, supports this assessment.

This makes analyses seem plausible according to which the United States, contrary to official proclamations, is not mainly pursuing humanitarian goals, combating terrorism, or seeking to prevent the spread of weapons of mass destruction in the Middle East and in Central Asia, including Afghanistan, but rather is guided by geostrategic motives. Indeed, its access to the oil wells of this region, that are essential to the world economy, and to the oil transportation routes, considerably increases the United States' geostrategic options for strengthening its hegemonic position not only vis-à-vis the weakened superpower Russia and the rising regional power China, but also vis-à-vis Europe and Japan, for the next few decades.

Despite disputes about such assessments, we all largely agree that the concentration of vast power potentials in a single country, and the military capability of imposing one's own will on others are an important source of instability in transnational and transcultural relations. It has also become a source of the feeling of impotence and of humiliation in particular for those people who feel themselves to be victims of this imbalance of power. The presence of U.S. troops within reach of Islamic holy sites in Saudi Arabia, for example, which is obviously regarded by many Muslims as a thorn in their flesh and an attack on their own culture and self-esteem, symbolizes this imbalance of power that is felt to be a threat. Their own inferiority, perceived as unjust, evokes an affective loss of inhibitions, mobilizing a huge potential for reaction, up to the willingness to sacrifice one's own life, too, in suicide assassinations. Such reactions, as a consequence of the instability of the balance of power in the present unipolar world order, are not specific to one culture. They could be triggered in any other part of the world and at any other time in new forms. A war of the winners against the suicide attacks of the losers is an anachronism. It eliminates scruples and mobilizes even greater willingness for terrorist attacks and terrorist military operations, as in the Israel-Palestine conflict. The current form of globalization, which heightens social inequalities and destroys cultural differentiation, contributes to the instabilities and tensions that erupt in violent reactions.

We are concerned to see that prominent persons in your President's entourage are demanding more and more aggressively from Europeans total obedience to America, and seeking to stifle any criticism from Europe by means of blackmail, with statements such as "Europe needs America, but America does not need Europe." The "unlimited solidarity" of our, and many another European government with the United States, and their willingness to support the war on terror uncritically, is perceived by many people here as weakness and a deprivation of the right to decide for oneself. The political class in Europe has obviously not grasped that its obsequious submission to the superior and sole superpower is not only a policy without prospects, but is also creating a favorable climate for agitation by forces of the radical Right. And, to our regret, the governments of the EU member states have until now neglected to develop an independent EU foreign, security, and peace policy for the Near and Middle East, for Central Asia, and for their relations to the Islamic world, based on cooperation, and on the indivisibility of human dignity and human rights. Indeed, we must fear that, due to their lack of any clear vision, and despite their criticism, they will in the end be willing to give moral legitimacy to an American war on Iraq, or even participate actively.

Many of us feel that the growing influence of fundamentalist forces in the United States on the political elite of your country, which clearly extends all the way to the White House, is cause for concern. The division of the world into "good" and "evil," the stigmatization of entire countries and their populations, will tend to incite racist, nationalistic, and religious fanaticism, and to deprive people of their ability to perceive living reality in a differentiated way, and of the insight that differences and cultural variety are not a misfortune, but a blessing for all, and that even the most powerful persons on earth will only prosper in the long run if the world is seen as a whole, whose richness and beauty consists in the differences. Fundamentalism begins with declaring one's own culture to be the only true, good, and beautiful one. Fundamentalist reactions to the real conflicts in our world close our eyes to civilian and nonviolent solutions for these conflicts, and only speed up the mutual escalation of terrorism and war.

With dismay, we have also heard from our American friends and professional colleagues that scholars and journalists are being put under pressure and denounced as traitors if they discuss critically or reject their government's war policy. Make sure that the pluralism of thought and liberal tradition of your country are not impaired under the pretext of combating terrorism. Help to halt the advance of the fundamentalist mentality in the United States. Those American values which you refer to with pride are being tested.

There are certainly various ways to combat terrorist suicide attacks. We have different opinions on the subject. But we are all deeply convinced that respect for human dignity is a basic precondition for all approaches to a solution. Only if the view that the West, as the most economically and militarily powerful group of cultures, is serious about the universality of human rights and dignity, that this is not merely a phrase trotted out when it is convenient, becomes accepted throughout the world, and in the economically and militarily weaker nations and cultures, only then will the likelihood increase that terrorist suicide bombings will not find the intended response, but encounter vehement rejection in all countries. Only if the weaker people of this world feel certain that no state, no matter how powerful, will injure their dignity, humiliate them, or arbitrarily harm their living conditions, only then will these people find the strength and willingness to open their eyes and hearts to the moral values of other cultures. And only then will the preconditions exist for a genuine dialogue between cultures to begin.

We need morally justified, globally acceptable, and universally respected common rules of play for the way people live together, which emphasize cooperation instead of confrontation, and undermine the anxieties created by the accelerating changes in our surroundings and the constantly growing potentials for violence, as well as the security obsessions resulting from them. This will provide opportunities to structure the mainly business-oriented globalization more justly, to tackle worldwide poverty effectively, to defuse the global environmental hazards together, to resolve conflicts by peaceful means, and to create a world culture that can speak in not just one, but many tongues.

We call on you to engage in an open dialogue with us and with intellectuals from other parts of the world about this and other perspectives for our common future.

Signatories

Prof. Hans Ackermann (Marburg)
Dr. Stephan Albrecht (Hamburg)
Dr. Franz Alt (Baden-Baden)
Prof. Elmar Altvater (Berlin)
Carl Amery (Munich)
Prof. Klaus J. Bade (Osnabrück)
Prof. Hans-Eckehard Bahr (Bochum)
Tobias Baur (Berlin)
Franz J. Bautz (Munich)
Prof. Jörg Becker (Solingen)
Dr. Peter Becker (Marburg)
Dr. Wolfgang Bender (Kronberg)
Prof. Adelheid Biesecker (Bremen)
Michael Bouteiller (Lübeck)
Prof. Elmar Brähler (Leipzig)
Dr. Dieter Bricke (Bergen)
Dr. Nikolaus and Nedialka Bubner (Berlin)
Annelie Buntenbach (Berlin)
Prof. Andreas Buro (Grävenwiesbach)
Prof. Wolfgang Däubler (Dusslingen)
Gerhard Diefenbach (Aachen)
Hermann H. Dieter (Trebbin-Blankensee)
Prof. Klaus Dörner (Hamburg)
Tankred Dorst (Munich)
Prof. Hans-Peter Dürr (Munich)
Dr. Matthias Engelke (Trier)
Prof. Andreas Flitner (Tübingen)
Helmut Frenz (Hamburg)
Prof. Georges Fülgraff (Berlin)
Prof. Bernhard Glaeser (Berlin)
Prof. Ulrich Gottstein (Frankfurt)
Dr. Franz-Theo Gottwald (Munich)
Jürgen Grässlin (Freiburg)
Bernd Hanfeld (Hamburg)

Dr. Dirk-Michael Harmsen (Karlsruhe)
Prof. Bodo Hambrecht (Berlin)
Prof. Heinz and Brigitte Häberle (Herrsching)
Irmgard Heilberger (Neuburg)
Christoph Hein (Berlin)
Prof. Peter Hennicke (Wuppertal)
Detlef Hensch (Berlin)
Prof. Wolfgang Hesse (Marburg)
Prof. Helmut Holzapfel (Kassel)
Ina Hönninger (Weßling)
Prof. Willi Hoss and Heidemarie Hoss-Rohweder (Stuttgart)
Prof. Ferdinand Hucho (Berlin)
Prof. Jörg Huffschmid (Bremen)
Otto Jaeckel (Wiesbaden)
Prof. Siegfried and Dr. Margarete Jäger (Duisburg)
Prof. Walter Jens (Tübingen)
Heiko Kauffmann (Meerbusch)
Prof. Wolfgang Klein (Berlin)
Irmgard Koll (Müllheim)
Hans Krieger (Munich)
Prof. Ekkehart Krippendorff (Berlin)
Helmar Krupp (Weingarten)
Nils Leopold (Berlin)
Herbert Leuninger (Hofheim)
Frauke Liesenborghs (Munich)
Volker Lindemann (Schleswig)
Prof. Dieter S. Lutz (Hamburg)
Prof. Birgit Mahnkopf (Berlin)
Prof. Mohssen Massarrat (Osnabrück)
Prof. Ingeborg Maus (Frankfurt)
Prof. Klaus Michael Meyer-Abich (Essen)
Prof. Klaus Meschkat (Hannover)
PD Dr. Klaus Metz (Berlin)
Prof. Dietmar Mieth (Tübingen)
Reinhard Mokros (Mönchengladbach)
Dr. Till Müller-Heidelberg (Bingen)
Prof. Norman Paech (Hamburg)
Gunda Rachert (Osnabrück)
Prof. Horst-Eberhard Richter
Dr. Fredrik Roggan (Bremen)
Prof. Rolf Rosenbrock (Berlin)
Prof. Werner Ruf (Kassel)

Peter Rühmkorf (Hamburg)
Prof. Fritz Sack (Hamburg)
Dr. Gerd Dieter Schmid (Fischbachau)
Horst Schmitthenner (Frankfurt)
Prof. Jürgen Schneider (Göttingen)
Dr. Schiltenwolf (Heidelberg)
Friedrich Schorlemmer (Wittenberg)
Prof. Herbert Schui (Buchholz)
Prof. Randeria Shalini (Berlin)
Tilman Spengler (Ambach)
Prof. Dorothee Sölle (Hamburg)
Eckart Stevens-Bartol (Munich)
Prof. Harmen Storck (Hannover)
Frank Uhe (Berlin)
Peter Vonnahme (Kaufering)
Dr. Reinhard Voß (Bad Vilbel)
Peter Wahl (Bonn)
Günter Wallraff (Cologne)
Dr. Rainer Werning (Frechen)
Christa Wichterich (Bonn)
Walter Wilken (Hannover)
Frieder-Otto Wolf (Berlin)
Dr. Herbert Wulf (Pinneberg)

"A World of Justice and Peace Would Be Different" was publicly released in May 2002 by the Koalition für Leben und Frieden (Coalition for Life and Peace). It was translated from the German by Timothy Slater. Reprinted with permission.

Twenty-One

୧

Letter from U.S. Citizens to Friends in Europe

୧

140 U.S. Intellectuals

Following the September 11, 2001 suicide attacks on the World Trade Center in New York and the Pentagon in Washington, U.S. President George W. Bush has declared an open-ended "war on terrorism." This war has no apparent limits, in place, time or the extent of destruction that may be inflicted. There is no telling which country may be suspected of hiding "terrorists" or declared to be part of an "axis of evil." The eradication of "evil" could last much longer than the world can withstand the destructive force to be employed. The Pentagon is already launching bombs described as producing the effect of earthquakes and is officially considering the use of nuclear weapons, among other horrors in its constantly improving arsenal.

The material destruction envisaged is immeasurable. So is the human damage, not only in terms of lives, but also in terms of the moral desperation and hatred that are certain to be felt by millions of people who can only watch helplessly as their world is devastated by a country, the United States, which assumes that its moral authority is as absolute and unchallengeable as its military power.

We, as United States citizens, have a special responsibility to oppose this mad rush to war. You, as Europeans, also have a special responsibility. Most of your countries are military allies of the United States within NATO. The United States claims to act in self-defense, but also to defend "the interests of its allies and friends." Your countries will inevitably be implicated in U.S. military adventures. Your future is also in jeopardy.

Many informed people both within and outside your governments are aware of the dangerous folly of the war path followed by the Bush administration. But few dare speak out honestly. They are intimidated by the various forms of retaliation that can be taken against "friends" and "allies" who fail to provide unquestioning support. They are afraid of being labeled "anti-American"—the same label absurdly applied to Americans themselves who speak out against war policies and whose protests are easily drowned out in the chorus of chauvinism dominating the U.S. media. A sane and frank European criticism of the Bush administration's war policy can help anti-war Americans make their voices heard.

Celebrating power may be the world's oldest profession among poets and men of letters. As the supreme world power, the United States naturally attracts its celebrants who urge the nation's political leaders to go ever farther in using their military might to impose virtue on a recalcitrant world. The theme is age-old and forever the same: the goodness of the powerful should be extended to the powerless by the use of force.

The central fallacy of the pro-war celebrants is the equation between "American values" as understood at home and the exercise of United States economic and especially military power abroad.

Self-celebration is a notorious feature of United States culture, perhaps as a useful means of assimilation in an immigrant society. Unfortunately, September 11 has driven this tendency to new extremes. Its effect is to reinforce a widespread illusion among U.S. citizens that the whole world is fixated, in admiration or in envy, on the United States as it sees itself: prosperous, democratic, generous, welcoming, open to all races and religions, the epitome of universal human values and the last best hope of mankind.

In this ideological context, the question raised after September 11, "Why do they hate us?" has only one answer: "Because we are so good!" Or, as is commonly claimed, they hate us because of "our values."

Most U.S. citizens are unaware that the effect of U.S. power abroad has nothing to do with the "values" celebrated at home, and indeed often serves to deprive people in other countries of the opportunity to attempt to enjoy them should they care to do so.

In Latin America, Africa, and Asia, U.S. power has more often than not been used to prop up the remnants of colonial regimes and unpopular dictators, to impose devastating commercial and financial conditions, to support repressive armed forces, to overthrow or cripple by sanctions relatively independent governments, and finally to send bombers and cruise missiles to rain down death and destruction.

The "Right of Self-Defense"

(1) Whose Right?

Since September 11, the United States feels under attack. As a result its government claims a "right to self-defense" enabling it to wage war on its own terms, as it chooses, against any country it designates as an enemy, without proof of guilt or legal procedure.

Obviously, such a "right of self-defense" never existed for countries such as Vietnam, Laos, Cambodia, Libya, Sudan or Yugoslavia when they were bombed by the United States. Nor will it be recognized for countries bombed by the United States in the future. This is simply the right of the strongest, the law of the jungle. Exercising such a "right," denied all others, cannot serve "universal values" but only undermines the very concept of a world order based on universal values with legal recourse open to all on a basis of equality.

A "right" enjoyed only by one entity—the most powerful—is not a right but a privilege exercised only to the detriment of the rights of others.

(2) How Is the United States to "Defend" Itself?

Supposedly in self-defense, the United States launched a war against Afghanistan. This was not an action specially designed to respond to the unique events of September 11. On the contrary, it was exactly what the United States was already doing, and had already planned to do, as outlined in Pentagon documents: bomb other countries, send military forces onto foreign soil and topple their governments. The United States is openly planning an all out war—not excluding use of nuclear weapons—against Iraq, a country it has been bombing for a decade, with the proclaimed aim of replacing its government with leaders selected by Washington.

(3) Precisely What Is Being "Defended"?

What is being defended is related to what was attacked. Traditionally, "defense" means defense of national territory. On September 11, an attack actually took place on and against U.S. territory. This was not a conventional attack by a major power designed to seize territory. Rather, it was an anonymous strike against particular targeted institutions. In the absence of any claim of responsibility, the symbolic nature of the targets may have been assumed to be self-explanatory. The World Trade Center clearly symbolized U.S. global economic power, while the Pentagon represented U.S. military power. Thus, it seems highly unlikely that the September 11 attacks were symbolically directed against "American values" as celebrated in the United States.

Rather, the true target seems to have been U.S. economic and military power as it is projected abroad. According to reports, 15 of the 19 identified hijackers were Saudi Arabians hostile to the presence of U.S. military bases on Saudi soil. September 11 suggests that the nation projecting its power abroad is vulnerable at home, but the real issue is U.S. intervention abroad. Indeed the Bush wars are designed precisely to defend and strengthen U.S. power abroad. It is U.S. global power projection that is being defended, not domestic freedoms and way of life.

In reality, foreign wars are more likely to undermine the domestic values cherished by civilians at home than to defend or spread them. But governments that wage aggressive wars always drum up domestic support by convincing ordinary people that war is necessary to defend or to spread noble ideas. The principal difference between the imperial wars of the past and the global thrust of the United States today is the far greater means of destruction available. The disproportion between the material power of destruction and the constructive power of human wisdom has never been more dangerously unbalanced. Intellectuals today have the choice of joining the chorus of those who celebrate brute force by rhetorically attaching it to "spiritual values," or taking up the more difficult and essential task of exposing the arrogant folly of power and working with the whole of humanity to create means of reasonable dialogue, fair economic relations and equal justice.

The right to self-defense must be a collective human right. Humanity as a whole has the right to defend its own survival against the "self-defense" of an unchecked superpower. For half a century, the United States has repeatedly demonstrated its indifference to the collateral death and destruction wrought by its self-proclaimed efforts to improve the world. Only by joining in solidarity with the victims of U.S. military power can we in the rich countries defend whatever universal values we claim to cherish.

List of Signatures*

Daphne Abeel, *Journalist (Cambridge, MA)*
Julie L. Abraham, *Professor of English (New York, NY)*
Michael Albert, *ZNet (Boston, MA)*
Janet Kestenberg Amighi, *Anthropologist, Hahneman University*
Electa Arenal, *Hispanic & Luso-Brazilian Literatures, City University of New York*
Anthony Arnove, *Editor/Publisher, South End Press (Boston, MA)*
Stanley Aronowitz, *Center for Cultural Studies, City University of New York*
Dean Baker, *Economist, Center for Economic and Policy Research (Washington, DC)*
Houston A. Baker, Jr., *Duke University*
David Barsamian, *Director, Alternative Radio (Boulder, CO)*
Rosalyn Baxandall, *Chair, American Studies at SUNY, Old Westbury*
Medea Benjamin, *Founding Director, Global Exchange (San Francisco, CA)*
Dick Bennett, *Professor Emeritus, University of Arkansas*
Larry Bensky, *KPFA/Pacifica Radio*
Norman Birnbaum, *Professor Emeritus, Georgetown University Law Center*
Joel Bleifuss, *Editor, In These Times (Chicago, IL)*
Chana Bloch, *Professor of English, Mills College*
William Blum, *Author (Washington, DC)*
Magda Bogin, *Writer, Columbia University*
Patrick Bond, *University of the Witwatersrand (Johannesburg, South Africa)*

*As of April 10, 2002.

Charles P. Boyer, *Professor of Mathematics, University of New Mexico*
Francis A. Boyle, *Professor of International Law, University of Illinois*
Gray Brechin, *Department of Geography, University of California, Berkeley*
Renate Bridenthal, *Professor Emerita of History, City University of New York*
Linda Bullard, *Environmentalist (U.S./Europe)*
Judith Butler, *University of California, Berkeley*
Bob Buzzanco, *Professor of History, University of Houston*
Helen Caldicott, *Pediatrician, Author, and Founder of Physicians for Social Responsibility*
John Cammett, *Historian (NY)*
Stephanie M.H. Camp, *Assistant Professor of History, University of Washington*
Ward Churchill, *Author (Boulder, CO)*
John P. Clark, *Professor of Philosophy, Loyola University, New Orleans*
Dan Coughlin, *Radio Executive Director (Washington, DC)*
Sandi Cooper, *Historian (New York)*
Lawrence Davidson, *Professor of Middle East History, West Chester University*
David Devine, *Professor of English (Paris, France)*
Douglas Dowd, *Economist (Bologna and San Francisco, CA)*
Madhu Dubey, *Professor, English and Africana Studies, Brown University*
Richard B. Du Boff, *Bryn Mawr College*
Peter Erlinder, *Past President, National Lawyers Guild, Law Professor (St. Paul, MN)*
Francis Feeley, *Professor of American Studies, Université Stendhal (Grenoble)*
Richard Flynn, *Professor of Literature and Philosophy, Georgia Southern University*
Michael S. Foley, *Assistant Professor of History, City University of New York*
John Bellamy Foster *(Eugene, OR)*
H. Bruce Franklin, *Professor of English and American Studies, Rutgers University*
Jane Franklin, *Author and Historian (Montclair, NJ)*
Oscar H. Gandy, Jr., *Annenberg School for Communication, University of Pennsylvania*
Jamshed Ghandhi, *Wharton School, University of Pennsylvania*
Larry Gross, *Annenberg School for Communication, University of Pennsylvania*
Beau Grosscup, *Professor of International Relations, California State University, Chico*
Zalmay Gulzad, *Professor of Asian-American Studies, Loyola University, Chicago*
Thomas J. Gumbleton, *Auxiliary Bishop, Roman Catholic Archdiocese of Detroit*
Marilyn Hacker, *Professor of English, The City College of New York*
Robin Hahnel, *Professor of Economics, American University*
Edward S. Herman, *Economist and Media Analyst (Philadelphia, PA)*
Marc W. Herold, *University of New Hampshire*
John L. Hess, *Journalist and Correspondent (New York, NY)*
David U. Himmelstein, MD, *Associate Professor of Medicine, Harvard Medical School*
W.G. Huff, *University of Glasgow*
Adrian Prentice Hull, *California State University, Monterey Bay*
Marsha Hurst, *Director, Health Advocacy Program, Sarah Lawrence College*
David Isles, *Associate Professor of Mathematics, Tufts University*

Robert Jensen, *School of Journalism, University of Texas*
Diana Johnstone, *Journalist (Paris, France)*
John Jonik, *Political Cartoonist/Activist (Philadelphia, PA)*
Louis Kampf, *Professor Emeritus of Literature, Massachusetts Institute of Technology*
Mary Kaye, *Professor of Fine Arts, Art Institute of Boston, Lesley University*
Douglas Kellner, *University of California, Los Angeles*
Michael King, *Senior News Editor,* The Austin Chronicle
Gabriel Kolko, *Author (Amsterdam, The Netherlands)*
Joyce Kolko, *Author (Amsterdam, The Netherlands)*
Claudia Koonz, *History Professor, Duke University*
Joel Kovel, *Bard College*
Marilyn Krysl, *Writer, University of Colorado*
Mark Lance, *Philosophy, Justice and Peace, Georgetown University*
Ann J. Lane, *University of Virginia*
Karen Latuchie, *Book Editor (NJ)*
Peggy Law, *Executive Director, International Media Project (Oakland, CA)*
Amy Schrager Lang, *Associate Professor of American Studies (Cambridge, MA)*
Helena Lewis, *Historian, Harvard University Humanities Center*
Dave Lindorff, *Journalist (Maple Glen, PA)*
Eric Lott, *Professor of English, University of Virginia*
Angus Love, Esq. *(Narberth, PA)*
David MacMichael, *Director, Association of National Security Alumni (Washington, DC)*
Harry Magdoff, *Co-Editor,* Monthly Review *(New York, NY)*
Sanjoy Mahajan, *Physicist, University of Cambridge (England, UK)*
Michael Marcus, *Department of Mathematics, The City College of New York*
Robert McChesney, *University of Illinois*
Jo Ann McNamara, *Historian Emerita, Hunter College*
Arthur Mitzman, *Emeritus Professor of Modern History, University of Amsterdam*
Margaret E. Montoya, *Professor, School of Law, University of New Mexico*
Robert Naiman, *Center for Economic and Policy Research (Washington, DC)*
Marilyn Nelson, *Poet/Professor, University of Connecticut*
Suzanne Oboler, *University of Illinois, Chicago*
Bertell Ollman, *Department of Politics, New York University*
Alicia Ostriker, *Professor of English, Rutgers University*
Christian Parenti, *Author, New College of California*
Michael Parenti, *Author (Berkeley, CA)*
Mark Pavlick, *Georgetown University*
Michael Perelman, *Professor of Economics, Chico State University*
Jeff Perlstein, *Executive Director, Media Alliance (San Francisco, CA)*
David Peterson, *Writer and Researcher, Chicago*
James Petras, *State University of New York, Binghamton*
Joan Pinkham, *Translator (Amherst, MA)*

Lawrence Pinkham, *Professor Emeritus of Journalism, University of Massachusetts*
Cathie Platt, *Licensed Professional Counselor (Charlottesville, VA)*
Gordon Poole, *Istituto Universitario Orientale (Naples, Italy)*
Douglas Porpora, *Professor of Sociology, Drexel University*
Larry Portis, *American Studies, Université Paul Valéry (Montpellier, France)*
Ellen Ray, *Institute for Media Analysis (New York, NY)*
Elton Rayack, *Professor of Economics Emeritus, University of Rhode Island*
Lillian S. Robinson, *Simone de Beauvoir Institute, Concordia University (Montreal)*
Rick Rozoff, *Medical Social Worker (Chicago, IL)*
Albert Ruben, *Writer*
Sten Rudstrom, *Theater Artist (Berlin, Germany)*
William H. Schaap, *Institute for Media Analysis (New York, NY)*
Ellen Schrecker, *Yeshiva University*
Gretchen Seifert, *Artist and Photographer (Chicago, IL)*
Anne Shaver, *Professor Emerita of English, Denison University*
Gerald E. Shenk, *Social & Behavioral Sciences Center, California State University, Seaside*
Mary Shepard, *Media Critic (St Paul, MN)*
Francis Shor, *Professor, Wayne State University (Michigan)*
Robert M. Smith, *Brandywine Peace Community (Swarthmore, PA)*
Alan Sokal, *Professor of Physics, New York University*
Norman Solomon, *Author and Syndicated Columnist (San Francisco, CA)*
William S. Solomon, *Rutgers University (New Brunswick, NJ)*
Sarah Standefer, *Nurse (Minneapolis, MN)*
Abraham Sussman, *Clinical Psychologist (Cambridge, MA)*
Malcolm Sylvers, *University of Venice (Italy)*
Paul M. Sweezy, *Co-Editor,* Monthly Review *(New York, NY)*
Holly Thau, *Psychotherapist (OR)*
Reetika Vazirani, *Writer (NJ)*
Gore Vidal, *Writer (Los Angeles, CA)*
Joe Volk, *Friends Committee on National Legislation (Washington, DC)*
Lynne Walker, *Historian (London, UK)*
Karin Wilkins, *University of Texas, Austin*
Howard Winant, *Temple University*
Steffie Woolhandler, MD, MPH, *Associate Professor of Medicine, Harvard Medical School*
George Wright, *Department of Political Science, California State University, Chico*
Howard Zinn, *Writer (Boston, MA)*

"Letter from U.S. Citizens to Friends in Europe" was publicly released in April 2002 by In These Times (http://www.inthesetimes.com). Reprinted with permission.

Twenty-Two

‫ؤ‬

Is the Use of Force Ever Morally Justified?

‫ؤ‬

67 U.S. Intellectuals

Dear Colleagues:

We received your recent letter, "A World of Peace and Justice Would Be Different," which 103 of you publicly released from Germany in May of this year, in response to our letter, "What We're Fighting For," which 60 of us publicly released in Washington, DC in February of this year. We are grateful to you for taking the time to write to us, and wish to continue the dialogue.

We note with appreciation and agreement your statement that "there can be no moral justification for the horrible mass murder on September 11" and your recognition that the inherent and equal dignity of human persons is a necessary foundation for serious moral reflection on this subject.

Our overall reaction to your letter is that, although you describe it as a "response," you respond only indirectly to our central argument. Above all in "What We're Fighting For," we seek to draw upon the just war tradition to argue that the use of military force against the murderers of September 11 and those who assist them is not only morally justified, but morally necessary. You apparently disagree with that conclusion, but, apart from calling the just war tradition "an ill-starred historical concept," you never coherently articulate any position on the morality of the use of force.

Let us review. Moral and intellectual approaches to war divide into four basic categories. Pacifism says that all war is morally wrong. Realism says that war is essentially about power and self-interest, and that moral analysis is therefore largely irrelevant. Holy war or crusade says that God, or some secular ideology of ultimate concern, can authorize the coercion or killing of

261

non-believers. And just war says that universal moral criteria should be applied to specific situations to determine whether the use of force is morally justified.

Which of these positions is yours? You never tell us. If you are pacifists, you should say so. It's an honorable position, although one with which we respectfully disagree. Your statements about the use of force in Afghanistan after September 11 strongly suggest an essentially pacifistic orientation. Yet you also describe U.S. participation in the Second World War as "an outstanding contribution."

If you are realists who disdain moral arguments about war, you should say so, although we doubt that you are, since your letter is full of moralistic assertions. We assume that you reject the principle of holy war. Regarding the just war tradition, the only remaining intellectual option available to you—a tradition, we remind you, that primarily seeks to *limit* rather than extol the use of force, and that has strongly influenced international law and international institutions such as the United Nations—you dismiss this entire school of thought in one contemptuous phrase, as a prelude to your harsh attack on the decision by the U.S. and its allies, including Germany, to use force against al-Qaʿida and Taliban fighters in Afghanistan.

So which is it for you? Is the use of force ever morally justified? If not, why not? If so, what are the proper moral criteria for the use of force? And how would these criteria, as you understand them, apply to the current crisis? Simply denouncing the United States for nearly everything that it has done in the world since 1945, while certainly your prerogative, does not relieve you from the responsibility of taking a clear position on these questions. We await your response.

In alarmist tones, you declare that "fundamentalist forces," which foster racism, nationalism, and religious fanaticism, are gaining ground in the U.S. and have now extended their influence "all the way to the White House." Rather than attempt to evaluate this assessment, we will simply point out that nowhere in your letter do you express alarm about "fundamentalist forces" gaining ground in the Muslim world. Quite the contrary. In your letter you suggest that the U.S. should withdraw all military personnel from Saudi Arabia, since the mere presence of these troops "is obviously regarded by many Muslims as a thorn in their flesh and an attack on their culture and self-esteem."

Why this discrepancy? Is it only "fundamentalism" in the U.S. to which you object? Is it your contention that "fundamentalist forces" in the Muslim world—groups that, in addition to disliking U.S. military personnel in their midst, prevent women from voting and even from driving cars, seek to murder novelists whose writings are perceived as critical of their religious teachings, and periodically declare war on foreigners and unbelievers—pose a lesser threat to the world today than do the "fundamentalist forces" that you fear are gaining ground in the United States?

This same indifference to the threat posed by Muslim radicals is also evident in your advice to us about how our government should have responded to the events of September 11. You recommend that criminal justice systems now operating at the national level should in the future be "extended globally," an idea that is not only vague, but also blurs the distinctions between an individual crime and an act of war. You further advise us that there are "various ways" that people who are attacked can defend themselves, but you fail to mention even one of these ways.

You describe the rise of Islamicist violence in the world as "a consequence of the instability of the balance of power in the present unipolar world order." If we understand this viewpoint correctly, you are suggesting, at least in part, that if the U.S. and its allies had *less* power and influence in the world, and if states such as Saudi Arabia, Iraq, Iran, and other states in the Middle East and in the Muslim world had *more* power and influence in the world, then the world would become a safer, less violent place. Recognizing that many (though not all) of these states whom you regard as insufficiently powerful and influential in the world are run by unelected authoritarians who oppress their own people and frequently nurture and export the terrorist violence that now threatens the world, including the Muslim world, we disagree with your prescription.

Your letter raises the subject of civilian casualties in the war in Afghanistan. The subject is a serious one, which concerns us deeply, but your treatment of it is not serious. Your factual claims are, at best, unsubstantiated. Conceptually, you conclude that civilian casualties in the war in Afghanistan constitute an example of U.S. "mass murder" that is, in moral terms, exactly the same as the murders of September 11 in New York, Washington, DC, and Pennsylvania. You tell us that no moral calculation can "justify one mass murder by another." We are saddened by these comments. For you to equate unintended civilian casualties in a theater of war, in which the cause is just, and where the goal of the combatant is to *minimize* the loss of civilian life, to the intentional killing of civilians in downtown office buildings, in which the cause is unjust, and where the goal of the combatant is to *maximize* the loss of civilian life, is an act of moral blindness.

Near the end of your letter, you write:

> Only if the view that the West, as the most economically and militarily powerful group of cultures, is serious about the universality of human rights and dignity, that this is not merely a phrase trotted out when convenient, [and it] becomes accepted throughout the world, [including] the economically and militarily weaker nations, only then will the likelihood increase that terrorist suicide bombings will not find the intended response, but encounter vehement rejection in all countries.

Notwithstanding our disagreements with you in other areas, we find important elements of insight in that statement, which may serve as one basis for future dialogue.

Thank you again for writing to us.

Signed,*

John Atlas, *President, National Housing Institute; Executive Director, Passaic County Legal Aid Society*
Jay Belsky, *Professor and Director, Institute for the Study of Children, Families and Social Issues, Birkbeck University of London*
David Blankenhorn, *President, Institute for American Values*
David Bosworth, *University of Washington*
R. Maurice Boyd, *Minister, The City Church, New York*
Gerard V. Bradley, *Professor of Law, University of Notre Dame*
Magaret F. Brinig, *Edward A. Howry Distinguished Professor, University of Iowa College of Law*
Allan Carlson, *President, The Howard Center for Family, Religion, and Society*
Lawrence A. Cunningham, *Professor of Law, Boston College*
Paul Ekman, *Professor of Psychology, University of California, San Francisco*
Jean Bethke Elshtain, *Laura Spelman Rockefeller Professor of Social and Political Ethics, University of Chicago Divinity School*
Amitai Etzioni, *University Professor, The George Washington University*
Elizabeth Fox-Genovese, *Eleanore Raoul Professor of the Humanities, Emory University*
Hillel Fradkin, *President, Ethics and Public Policy Center*
Samuel G. Freedman, *Professor at the Columbia University Graduate School of Journalism*
Francis Fukuyama, *Bernard Schwartz Professor of International Political Economy, Johns Hopkins University*
Maggie Gallagher, *Institute for American Values*
William A. Galston, *Professor at the School of Public Affairs, University of Maryland; Director, Institute for Philosophy and Public Policy*
Claire Gaudiani, *Senior Research Scholar, Yale Law School, and former President, Connecticut College*
Robert P. George, *McCormick Professor of Jurisprudence and Professor of Politics, Princeton University*
Carl Gershman, *President, National Endowment for Democracy*
Neil Gilbert, *Professor at the School of Social Welfare, University of California, Berkeley*
Mary Ann Glendon, *Learned Hand Professor of Law, Harvard University Law School*
Norval D. Glenn, *Ashbel Smith Professor of Sociology and Stiles Professor of American Studies, University of Texas at Austin*
Os Guinness, *Senior Fellow, Trinity Forum*
David Gutmann, *Professor Emeritus of Psychiatry and Education, Northwestern University*

*Signatories' affiliations listed for identification purposes only.

Charles Harper, *Executive Director, John Templeton Foundation*

Sylvia Ann Hewlett, *Chair, National Parenting Association*

The Right Reverend John W. Howe, *Episcopal Bishop of Central Florida*

James Davison Hunter, *William R. Kenan, Jr. Professor of Sociology and Religious Studies and Executive Director, Center on Religion and Democracy, University of Virginia*

Samuel Huntington, *Albert J. Weatherhead, III University Professor, Harvard University*

Byron Johnson, *Director and Distinguished Senior Fellow, Center for Research on Religion and Urban Civil Society, University of Pennsylvania*

James Turner Johnson, *Professor, Department of Religion, Rutgers University*

John Kelsay, *Richard L. Rubenstein Professor of Religion, Florida State University*

Judith Kleinfeld, *Professor of Psychology, University of Alaska, Fairbanks*

Diane Knippers, *President, Institute on Religion and Democracy*

Thomas C. Kohler, *Professor of Law, Boston College Law School*

Robert C. Koons, *Professor of Philosophy, University of Texas at Austin*

Glenn C. Loury, *Professor of Economics and Director, Institute on Race and Social Division, Boston University*

Harvey C. Mansfield, *William R. Kenan, Jr. Professor of Government, Harvard University*

Will Marshall, *President, Progressive Policy Institute*

Jerry L. Martin, *President, American Council of Trustees and Alumni*

Richard J. Mouw, *President, Fuller Theological Seminary*

Daniel Patrick Moynihan, *University Professor, Maxwell School of Citizenship and Public Affairs, Syracuse University*

John E. Murray, Jr., *Chancellor and Professor of Law, Duquesne University*

Anne D. Neal, *Executive Director, American Council of Trustees and Alumni*

Virgil Nemoianu, *William J. Byron Distinguished Professor of Literature, Catholic University of America*

Michael Novak, *George Frederick Jewett Chair in Religion and Public Policy, American Enterprise Institute*

Rev. Val J. Peter, *Executive Director, Boys and Girls Town*

David Popenoe, *Professor of Sociology and Co-Director of the National Marriage Project, Rutgers University*

Gloria G. Rodriguez, *Founder and President, AVANCE, Inc.*

Robert Royal, *President, Faith & Reason Institute*

Nina Shea, *Director, Freedom's House's Center for Religious Freedom*

Fred Siegel, *Professor of History, The Cooper Union*

Max L. Stackhouse, *Professor of Christian Ethics and Director, Project on Public Theology, Princeton Theological Seminary*

William Tell, Jr., *The William and Karen Tell Foundation*

Maris A. Vinovskis, *Bentley Professor of History and Professor of Public Policy, University of Michigan*

Paul C. Vitz, *Professor of Psychology, New York University*

Michael Walzer, *Professor at the School of Social Science, Institute for Advanced Study*
George Weigel, *Senior Fellow, Ethics and Public Policy Center*
Roger Williams, *Mount Hermon Association, Inc.*
Charles Wilson, *Director, Center for the Study of Southern Culture, University of Mississippi*
James Q. Wilson, *Collins Professor of Management and Public Policy Emeritus, UCLA*
John Witte, Jr., *Jonas Robitscher Professor of Law and Ethics and Director, Law and Religion Program, Emory University Law School*
Christopher Wolfe, *Professor of Political Science, Marquette University*
George Worgul, *Executive Director, Family Institute, Duquesne University*
Daniel Yankelovich, *President, Public Agenda*

"Is the Use of Force Ever Morally Justified?" was written under the aegis of the Institute for American Values and publicly released on August 8, 2002.

Twenty-Three

❧

The U.S.-German Conversation

❧

Claudia Winkler

For the past week, a U.S.-German debate over the war on terrorism has been raging in the German press. Here, almost no one has noticed.

Similarly, almost no one paid attention back in February when the Institute for American Values, a small New York think tank specializing in family issues, published "What We're Fighting For: A Letter from America," signed by 60 intellectuals of mostly neo-con persuasion. (Think Fukuyama, Huntington, Galston, Putnam, Weigel.)

Some Germans, however, did notice, and they responded in May with a letter of their own. Its 103 signatories are, loosely speaking, pacifist intellectuals or peace-movement activists—a more mainstream group in Germany than in the United States, given Germany's very different intellectual history. Now the Institute for American Values' comeback, published on August 8, is making front-page news and prompting comment in newspapers across Germany.

The original American letter[1] was a fairly sophisticated 20-page reflection on basic political values, separation of church and state, just war theory, and the provocation of September 11. It concluded that war is justified against the "organized killers with global reach [who] now threaten all of us."

The German reply is entitled "A World of Justice and Peace Would Be Different." It rejects the very concept of "just war" as "an ill-starred historical concept" and calls the killing of civilians in the American assault on Afghanistan "mass murder." It portrays the United States as an arrogant superpower that is planting "military bases in the Balkans, the Middle East, and Central Asia" so as to "decide the fate of peoples largely on its own authority." The source of the danger: "the growing influence of fundamentalist forces in the United States on the political elite of your country, which clearly extends all the way to the White House."

Well.

The American response—"Is the Use of Force Ever Morally Justified?"—is brief, courteous, and to the point. It nails the Germans on their incoherent sometime-pacifism: while condemning the very notion of just war, they yet praise the United States for "an outstanding contribution" in World War II. Their position, then, is not a principled opposition to all use of force. But if liberating Europeans from murderous tyranny is okay, why not Afghans?

Second, the American response notes that the Germans, while alarmed about "fundamentalist forces" that "tend to incite racist, nationalistic, and religious fanatacism," locate these forces only in the United States, never condemning the fanaticism that is causing so much trouble in the Muslim world.

Third, the Americans vigorously reject the suggestion that they would "justify one mass murder by another." "We are saddened by these comments," says the letter.

> For you to equate unintended civilian casualties in a theater of war, in which the cause is just, and where the goal of the combatant is to minimize the loss of civilian life, to the intentional killing of civilians in downtown office buildings, in which the cause is unjust, and where the goal of the combatant is to maximize the loss of civilian life, is an act of moral blindness.[2]

The person who got this interesting ball rolling in Germany is a German reporter in Washington named Malte Lehming. He was the first to report on the American reply to the Germans, and his paper, *Der Tagesspiegel*, based in Berlin but with nationwide circulation, reprinted the American letter in full. The important *Suddeutsche Zeitung* soon followed suit.

Lehming says he'd never heard of the Institute for American Values when all this began, but he's pleased with the result of their effort. "This exchange of letters has generated an instantaneous nationwide discussion in Germany," he notes. "The Iraq question speeded the process. I value this engagement between Germans and Americans."

Another German in Washington who welcomes reflection on these issues is Dieter Dettke, executive director of the Friedrich Ebert Foundation, a German-government-funded educational institute associated with the Social Democratic party. Dettke recalls Germany's long and necessary renunciation of military engagement after World War II. It left behind, he says, "a kind of escapism in Germany. We adopted a civilian power paradigm—as if simply by way of not engaging ourselves, we made a contribution to peace. We have to come to grips with a more complicated world."

"In Kosovo," he says, "the German mantra 'force will only make things worse' was turned around" when NATO bombing halted ethnic slaughter and allowed hundreds of thousands of refugees to go back home. Afghanistan was the second test case—and, Dettke notes, when the German government decided to stand with the United States, public opinion came around.

At a time when Americans' understanding of security matters seems to be diverging sharply from that of Germans and Europeans generally, the careful exchange of ideas is to be desired. Here's hoping [as] many Americans as Germans will visit the Institute for American Values website and join the dialogue.

Notes

1. The original American letter the author is referring to is "What We're Fighting For." See chapter 2 of this volume. —Ed.

2. The author is quoting from "Is the Use of Force Ever Morally Justified?" See page 263 of this volume. —Ed.

"The U.S.-German Conversation" was originally published on August 15, 2002 as part of the Daily Standard at http://www.weeklystandard.com. Reprinted with the permission of *The Weekly Standard* magazine.

Twenty-Four

֍

In the Twenty-First Century, There is No Longer Any Justification for War

෨

70 German Intellectuals

Dear Colleagues,

Your latest statement, "Is the Use of Force Ever Morally Justified?" in reply to our letter of response "A World of Justice and Peace Would Be Different" to your manifesto "What We're Fighting For," has attracted considerable attention in Germany. The attempt to make the political and military actions of the U.S.A., as the leading world power, the subject of a critical discussion, appealing to the intellectual and moral forces of the West, seems important to us, and deserves to be continued. In this respect, we thank you for your recent letter, and in our answer [we] follow up [on] your final point: the joint desire to remind the West—as the most economically and militarily powerful part of the world (society)—that it should not act egoistically in its own interests, but demonstrate credibly to all the world that it "is serious about the universality of human rights and dignity."

War and "Just War"

You express your disappointment because we only addressed your central argument of "just war" indirectly in our reply. What we find difficult is to consider the concept of "war" appropriate at all in dealing with the problems facing us (triggered by the terror attack)—and for various reasons.

Under the current law of nations, only states can wage war against one another. To term the combating of terrorists, who occur throughout the world, and some of whom come from countries such as Germany and the

U.S.A., "war" is misleading. Is the United States of America a country that is at war, a war without temporal or geographical limits, with unspecified enemies? Or are the means and laws of war to be invoked for worldwide police actions, now and in the future? As the 11th of September demonstrated in a terrifying way, every society is fundamentally open to attack and vulnerable, even without a war. The question that concerns us all is how to react appropriately to this special threat, or to such an event.

At the beginning of your letter, you raise the question, "Is the use of force ever morally justified?" Your question clearly is not about the force-counterforce equilibrium processes that are generally necessary to stabilize living systems, but the more restricted question of the moral permissibility of military violence and war, confrontation rather than constructive conflict management, and basically not between states, but between their specially equipped and trained armed forces. Due to its potential for overkill, for mass destruction, modern warfare with its mighty weaponry has become totally irrational, because it can no longer resolve the conflicts that it is supposed to resolve. And it will never be able to resolve them—given an equal respect to all mankind—but will even preserve them in aggravated form into the future, due to the hatred of many innocent persons who have come to harm. For it affects mainly those who are not participants in the conflict, and not only by direct hostile actions, but also by the destruction of their vital material and social resources, which is even more serious for the people concerned. Given the almost unlimited escalation of violence made possible by modern technology, neither an ideology of "just war" nor pacifism is ... needed to oppose all wars today, but merely pragmatic, appraising reason.

But even without this devaluation in principle, in our view, "just war" is a historical concept burdened by its past, since it invites abuse. It would require going into some detail to spell this out; we will limit ourselves to only a few remarks.

In recent centuries, there has hardly been a war that was not described as a "just" or even a "holy war" by both sides. Even the Nazi regime and the Hamas assassins declared their actions as a "just war." And the members and sympathizers of al-Qa'ida presumably see a "just" cause behind their terrorist attacks, the struggle against a predominant foreign power that threatens their own sovereignty, which finds expression in their eyes in the U.S. military-industrial complex and its symbols, the Pentagon and the World Trade Center. With the term "just war," one needs at any rate to distinguish fundamentally whether the word "just" refers to the cause (which may be justified) or to the execution, which may consist of grave crimes that are cloaked, and in the final analysis legitimized, by the term "just war."

Specifically, we ask: Can a war employing weaponry that does not combat troops, but destroys whole regions, their inhabitants, and the latter's vital resources, lay claim to the designation "just" at all? With good reason, the cynical expression "collateral damage" was chosen as "Unword of the Year," because fleeing children, women, and old men, whose death the attacker accepts and condones, are more than marginal events. It is understandable that the assessment of what can still be considered "just" will vary greatly, depending on whether one is in the shoes of the person dropping the bombs or of the person fleeing. Can one really—as you imply in your letter—give less moral weight to "unintentionally" killed civilians in Afghanistan than to intentionally killed civilians in the U.S.A.?

And who is to decide in a specific case what is just? Justice, by its nature, cannot be established by the one who was offended or harmed, but only by a higher, impartial, moral and legal authority. The power to define whether a war is just surely cannot be left to the arbitrary views of the war-making parties. In your letter, you yourselves mention the great importance and the principles of the United Nations. The United Nations and the present-day law of nations, which the United States of America played a constructive role in creating, have replaced the jungle of arbitrary decisions by self-appointed judges of war and peace. Universally valid (because created by the consensus of countries) law, which was intended to be equally applicable to all states, whether strong or weak, large or small, was one of the great cultural achievements of the twentieth century, in our opinion.

Possibilities of Defense

You ask us, "How can people who are attacked defend themselves?" That is the great question of life-and-death, since life is fundamentally vulnerable. Not only you, but we and all the six billion people on our Earth are faced with it. And the question faces the poorer people of the world, not only in developing countries, but also within our highly economically developed countries, even more urgently and threateningly. The force that they are subjected to everyday, and which hinders their full human development, is not mainly physical violence, but to a shocking extent "structural violence" that rides roughshod over their human rights and dignity. The have-nots do not themselves possess any structure that would enable them to protect and defend themselves against this "structural violence" which robs them, seemingly nonviolently, of "air to breathe" or "the right to grow their own food." Thus the question of protection must not be limited to the demand for security of the prosperous minority in the world due to the current attacks. There are basic moral requirements that are shared by all cultures. The "sufficiently developed means of democratic states under the rule of law" we mentioned, and their partial flexible extension to the international level therefore already represent a highly differentiated bundle of examples as an answer to the initial question. But such legal systems require continual development, so as to be able to deal with new forms of this question efficiently and effectively. It is apparent that extreme structural imbalances, where naked powerlessness is confronted by structural domination, make just solutions more and more difficult to mediate in practice. Such hopeless situations result more and more frequently, out of the despair they create, in acts of terrorist violence.

We would welcome it if the tradition of "primarily seeking to limit, not extol the use of force" you assert were to be made official policy as well. It is true that, officially, the U.S.A. seeks to eliminate all weapons of mass destruction from the face of the Earth—and there are many among us who have actively [been] promoting that objective for decades. But we also know that the U.S.A. does not wish to make this demand of itself, and is not even willing to abandon the option of first use. Isn't it time that the question of the legitimacy of possessing weapons of mass destruction was put not only to those who do not possess such weapons and want to have them, but also to those who already long since possess them, and in vast quantities? In our opinion, world-wide cut-backs in weapons of mass destruction, and waiving the option to use them, is the only effective way to prevent their further proliferation.

Of course, a limitation of military force has actually been practiced until now, for exploiting all the military potential to the full would amount to multiple racial suicide of humanity and destruction of the entire biosphere, which even the "victor" would not be able to survive. But this threat does loom over all of us, and is even evoked rashly. It is true that a certain degree of restraint continues to be exercised in using the worst weapons available. But this is based more on the understandable wish to prevent casualties of one's own as much as possible, and less on limiting the destructive force, whose consequences, especially for the innocent, are ignored in striking the balance (U.S. Secretary of Defense: People have to realize today that we can fight wars without casualties!), and are largely concealed from the public. Due to the inherent momentum of every war, of which victory remains the essential goal, we cannot count on rational restraint not being abandoned in the end—which is a lethal vision, in view of the present arsenals of annihilation.

You object to our statement that one must not respond to one wrong by another. Indeed, the expression "mass murder" is provocative and liable to be misunderstood, and should therefore be avoided whenever possible. However, our comparison was not meant to equate the acts of September 11 with the U.S. bombing raids, but to say that they are both wrong.

Unfortunately, since World War II—in contrast to the important Nuremberg war-crimes trials—there has been a sort of consensus among the victorious powers, but also between the former opponents, not to pursue war crimes any further. Therefore, we consider the statement in your letter "that universal moral criteria should be applied to specific situations to determine whether the use of force is morally justified" important. However, determining this is the responsibility of a higher, impartial body, which demands that these principles be observed, monitors them, and publicly condemns and convicts violations of them. This is why we support the strengthening of the United Nations and the establishment of the International Criminal Court.

There is nothing we would like more than to see the U.S.A. also strengthening international bodies and recognizing the International Criminal Court. We cannot accept legal vacuums being created so as to remove prisoners of war, war criminals, and terrorists from the internationally valid legal processes, which are a matter of course in the United States, as well.

Fundamentalisms

Our statement about the dangers of fundamentalism on the U.S. side was also provocative. Our growing concern about the ever-greater concentration of power in a few hands in the U.S.A., the only remaining superpower, seems "alarmist" to you. We all hope that you will prove to be right about this, but we have plenty of historical knowledge of how quickly, and unfortunately how easily, hard-won civil rights and the balance of powers can be sacrificed spontaneously by a large majority in a country under suitable external conditions and psychologically sophisticated pressure from above. Are you not very seriously worried by speeches about "combating evil everywhere in the world," about "rogue states" and an "axis of evil," and similar remarks by politicians, as well? We know that many U.S. citizens are just as bothered by this as we are, and by the fact that warning voices ... hardly reach the public any more since September 11, in your country of maximum freedom of the press.

But at the word "fundamentalism," some of us think not only of the intolerant and more radical religious and nationalistic tendencies, but also of the growing power of a business world that is becoming more and more a fundamentalist ersatz religion, with the motto "There is no alternative!" and employs its growing structural power to strengthen itself without any moral scruples.

We regard religious and secular fundamentalism, in their many shades, as reactions to a real or perceived attack on one's own culture, one's own identity, and on personal or national sovereignty. In the Muslim world, the opinion and feeling that Muslims are exposed to a latent threat from the West is very widespread. The al-Qa'ida terrorists derived the legitimation for their attack on September 11 against the symbols of the West from this mood; however, by their acts they injured the national pride of the people of the U.S.A., who had believed themselves invulnerable to attack, and thus triggered fundamentalist reactions in the U.S.A. in turn. One of our most urgent tasks is to break this pernicious chain reaction of fundamentalism, and to build bridges by breaking down hostile stereotypes and by a dialogue between the cultures.

Regardless of this, we do not underestimate the danger of fundamentalism and the willingness to use violence based on it in the Muslim world, despite what you think. But we are firmly convinced that warding off fundamentalist dangers can be done most effectively by strengthening the trust of the powerless of this world in universal values such as the inviolability of human dignity and rights and individual liberties, and the universal principles of law. For this, it is absolutely essential that the West, and above all the United States, give proof of its own credibility in defending universal values and legal principles. For example, it lacks moral and legal credibility to condemn Islamistic fundamentalism, and at the same time to make deals with Saudi Arabia, the most influential fundamentalist regime in the Muslim world, which is known to have supported the Taliban and the Islamists in Pakistan and to have helped create al-Qaʻida forces, and defend it by all possible means. It lacks credibility to condemn vehemently violations of human rights in Iraq, but to be silent about violations of them in Chechnya and the Israeli-Palestinian conflict. A respect for human rights and international law demands that the West should end its pernicious practice of moral and legal double standards.

Final Remarks

For the reasons given, we consider that your statements need to be challenged; and not only that: we consider them dangerous, because in a situation that is controversial in international law, you grant to a president who is ready to go to war the intellectual and moral justification to plunge the world into further military adventures with unpredictable results, instead of employing mighty America's means for a credible, globally accepted peace policy. The next escalation of military force by an assault on Iraq, with predictable destabilization and catastrophic consequences for millions of people in the countries of the Near East, and also in Europe, is being prepared under our very eyes, after all! We know that many American intellectuals agree with our assessment of the situation.

We trust that you will continue to be willing to consider our view of matters. Please consider our appeals to you as an offer of a constructive continuation of the dialogue for a more just, peaceful, and free world.

Thank you again for your reply.

Yours sincerely,

Prof. Hans Peter Dürr, Heiko Kauffmann, Prof. Mohssen Massarrat, and Frank Uhe, as representatives of the Koalition für Leben und Frieden (Coalition for Life and Peace). The Coalition is the initiator of the first statement of May 2002, signed by 103 German intellectuals, on the manifesto "What We're Fighting For," written by sixty U.S. intellectuals. This second statement by the Coalition is supported by the following persons in the Federal Republic of Germany:

Franz Alt (Baden-Baden)
Carl Amery (München)
Prof. Dr. Hans-Eckehard Bahr (Bochum)
Johann-Albrecht Bausch (Aachen)
Franz S. Bautz (München)
Prof. Dr. Jörg Becker (Solingen)
Dr. Peter Becker (Marburg)
Prof. Dr. Adelheid Biesecker (Bremen)
Michael Bouteiller (Lübeck)

Prof. Dr. Elmar Brähler (Leipzig)
Prof. Dr. Klaus Brake (Berlin)
Reiner Braun (Dortmund)
Dr. Dieter W. Bricke (Bergen)
Dr. med. Angelika Claußen (Bielefeld)
Prof. Dr. Klaus Dörner (Hamburg)
Prof. Dr. Ulrich Duchrow (Heidelberg)
Dr. Matthias Engelke (Idar-Oberstein)
Margot Esser (Uffing)
Hannah-E. and Ekke Fetköter (Uelvesbüll)
Dr. Ralph Fischer (München)
Bernd Fischerauer (München)
Prof. Dr. Andreas Flitner (Tübingen)
Prof. Dr. Ulrich Gottstein (Frankfurt)
Brigitte and Prof. Dr. Heinz Häberle (Herrsching)
Dr. Dirk-Michael Harmsen (Karlsruhe)
Irmgard Heilberger (Neuburg)
Christoph Hein (Berlin)
Prof. Dr. Peter Hennicke (Wuppertal)
Dr. Markus Hesse (Berlin)
Prof. Dr. Ing. Helmut Holzapfel (Kassel)
Dr. Margarethe und Prof. Dr. Siegfried Jäger (Duisburg)
Prof. Dr. Walter Jens (Tübingen)
Matthias Jochheim (Frankfurt/Main)
Dr. Helmut Käss (Braunschweig)
Prof. Dr. Ulrich Knauer (Berlin)
Hans Krieger (München)
Prof. Dr. Ekkehart Krippendorf (Berlin)
Prof. Dr. Ing. Helmar Krupp (Weingarten)
Prof. Dr. Ilse Lenz (Bochum)
Herbert Leuninger (Limburg)
Frauke Liesenborghs (München)
Prof. Dr. Birgit Mahnkopf (Berlin)
Prof. Dr. Klaus Meschkat (Hannover)
Franz Meyer (Leisnig)
Otto Meyer (Münster)
Prof. Dr. Klaus-Michael Meyer-Abich (Essen)
Dr. Christa Müller (München)
Michael Müller (Düsseldorf)
Dr. Till Müller-Heidelberg (Bingen)
Dr. Lars Pohlmeier (Hamburg)
Prof. Dr. Rolf Rosenbrock (Berlin)

Dr. Gerd-Dieter Schmid (Fischbachau)
Prof. Dr. Jürgen Schneider (Göttingen)
Prof. Dr. Randeria Shalini (Potsdam und Budapest)
Friedrich Schorlemmer (Wittenberg)
Dr. Henry Stahl (Berlin)
Prof. Dr. Harmen Storck (Hannover)
Uwe Timm (Minden)
Peter Vonnahme (Kaufering)
Dr. Reinhard J. Voß (Bad Vilbel)
Klaus Wagenbach (Berlin)
Konstantin Wecker (München)
Dr. Rainer Werning (Frechen)
Dr. Karin Wesner (Bielefeld)
Prof. Dr. Martin Westerhausen (Dinslaken)
Walter Wilken (Hannover)
Frieder-Otto Wolf (Berlin)

"In the Twenty-First Century, There is No Longer Any Justification for War" was publicly released in October 2002 by the Koalition für Leben und Frieden (Coalition for Life and Peace). Reprinted with permission.

Conclusions

Twenty-Five

❧

Just War and Internationalism: Oppositional or Complementary?

❧

Alex Roberts*

Among the many viewpoints offered in this collection and at a May 2004 dialogue in Malta,[1] one stands out as a potentially viable alternative to the framework presented in "What We're Fighting For." This perspective can be labeled the "internationalist approach" to terrorism and U.S. policy. It rejects the concepts of a "just war" and a "war against terrorism" and calls upon the United States to operate through international institutions—both in pursuit of terrorists and in general. The goal of this essay is to critique the internationalist approach to terrorism with the intent of bringing about some greater reconciliation of it and the just war perspective.

One qualification before I begin: there is no monolithic "internationalist perspective." Those who I am identifying as "internationalist" likely disagree with one another on any number of points. Nevertheless, there is sufficient commonality among such texts in this volume as "What We're Fighting For: A Follow-Up," "The Need for a Paradigm Shift in American Thinking," and "A World of Justice and Peace Would Be Different" to justify placing them under the rubric "internationalist perspective."

The core of the internationalist argument on terrorism and U.S policy is as follows: because the concepts of "just war" and the "war against terrorism" are vague and effectively make America the ultimate arbiter of right and wrong, using them to guide the struggle against al-Qaʻida might easily lead to an open-ended, unilateral, and excessive use of military force. According to the internationalist perspective, "What We're Fighting For" compounds this threat of excess by identifying America as an agent of universal values. The United States should therefore jettison just war doctrine and the logic of "What We're Fighting For" and accept the constraints and norms of international law. For the authors of "What We're Fighting For: A Follow-Up," this means that the doctrine of just war, "with its lack of agreed upon neutral reference" should be replaced by a concept of "necessary war" that would ensure that military action against al-Qa'ida remained defensive and within the purview of established international laws. "The Need for a Paradigm Shift in American Thinking" by Chibli Mallat suggests that the U.S. reinterpret 9/11 as a "crime against humanity" and pursue al-Qa'ida solely through international legal institutions. In short, the core argument of the internationalist position is that international law should be the framework in which power is exercised.

Three arguments often accompany this view. The first is that U.S. policy is a major cause of terrorism. Many internationalists stress, for example, that U.S. support for Israel creates an ongoing injustice that causes jihadism to thrive. The Germany-based Coalition for Life and Peace argues in this volume that U.S. domination of the world forces the weak to resort to terrorism in order to protect themselves. The second argument, often more implicit than explicit, is that the internationalist approach is inherently restrained, rational, neutral, and therefore wise, whereas just war is inherently militaristic and prone to excess. The third argument, which is suggested by the previous two, is that we can only stop jihadism by adopting the comprehensive internationalist approach: otherwise we will both fail to address the roots of jihadism and perpetuate the conditions which cause it to thrive.

The internationalist approach certainly holds a certain amount of promise. For example, many people feel deeply affected by America and globalization yet alienated from their power centers, and this has bred feelings of resentment and insecurity around the globe. Rooting U.S. political action in international institutions could help ameliorate this problem. The basic message of even-handedness enshrined in the internationalist approach is obviously a good one. Moreover, as globalization and democracy advance, so too must the place of negotiation and law in international relations.

But serious problems emerge when the internationalist paradigm is presented, as it has been in this volume and at the Malta meeting, not as a goal of politics or as a component of the struggle against jihadism, but as a total and complete framework that must be adopted in its entirety, and immediately. (While it may be that internationalists would tolerate a gradual American embrace of international institutions, their discourses as presented do not make any room for other substantive political formulations; we are therefore forced to consider the internationalist approach as a totalizing one). In making such a strong argument, internationalists overestimate the plausibility and utility of their approach.

In order to demonstrate this point, I will offer a brief analysis of Islamism and jihadism, because I believe internationalism inadequately addresses these phenomena. Islamism is an ideology, formulated in response to colonialism and rapid modernization during the early twentieth century, that maintains that all aspects of society and the individual must be made to conform with Islam. Its adherents engage in sociopolitical activism geared towards establishing Islamic states and encouraging individual "piety." In the 1960s an Egyptian

Islamist ideologue named Sayyid Qutb realized that his compatriots were too "impious" (Westernized) to be capable of voluntarily establishing an Islamic state. He realized, in other words, that noncompulsory Islamism was not going to work. In light of his revelation, Qutb developed the idea that a small group of "elect" Muslims would have to establish the Islamic state by waging a war against the existing state and society. Following the 1967 loss to Israel and a population boom for which Egypt was unprepared, Qutb's militant brand of Islamism was put into practice by a number of disenfranchised, frustrated young Muslims who established guerrilla groups. They attacked government assets, battled troops, and even assassinated President Anwar Sadat in 1981. But by the mid-1990s these groups and similar ones elsewhere in the Middle East had suffered numerous defeats and a loss of public support. Some of these jihadis, including Osama bin Ladin and others left over from the Afghan War, reassembled in the Sudan and decided (for various reasons) that their inability to establish Islamic states could be overcome by globalizing *jihad* and attacking America. United in this belief and espousing an apocalyptic, millenarian version of Islamism, they formed "al-Qa'ida" and migrated to Afghanistan to prepare for global jihad. The rest of the story, from bin Ladin's 1998 declaration of war against America to 9/11, is well known.

Three points about al-Qa'ida are important to note. First, al-Qa'ida and its affiliates have successfully recruited members in large part by targeting uprooted Muslims living away from home. These individuals are generally not particularly religious, but their desire for an identity and a sense of community makes them susceptible to indoctrination by jihadists.[2] Al-Qa'ida is not disproportionately composed of the poor, Palestinians, or other marginalized people. Second, the group's success in drumming up support in the Arab world has much to do with its propaganda. This propaganda emphasizes goals that are marginal (we are fighting for the Palestinians, to change U.S. policy, etc.) to the organization and obscures al-Qa'ida's true raison d'etre: to establish a global Salafi[3] state. Third, to the extent that al-Qa'ida's complaints about U.S. policy are not propaganda, they must still be read within the totality of the group's proclamations. If one closely reads "Letter to the American People," which was endorsed if not written by al-Qa'ida, it becomes clear that the author does not object to U.S. policy per se, but U.S. policy insofar as it is an impediment to the goals of Islamism: complaints about U.S. policy are woven into a larger argument advocating the global hegemony of Islam.

The point to take from all of this discussion is that the al-Qa'ida brand of jihadism is a narrow, obscure offshoot of the greater Islamist movement and has relatively little to do with Islam, U.S. policy, or the sentiments of average Arab Muslims. More than anything, it is a consequence of a string of failures within Islamism itself; it is a desperate marriage of violence, propaganda, and cultic practices formulated by a small group of individuals who wish to revive a failing jihad.

One can therefore reject outright the specific internationalist argument presented by the Coalition for Life and Peace. Al-Qa'ida's terrorism is not, as the Coalition claims, any sort of rational response to American power or policies. The organization is driven by other motives. One must also reject the Coalition's insinuation that a U.S. adoption of an internationalist approach to world affairs would ipso facto eradicate the "roots" of terrorism.

There are also many reasons to believe that the internationalist approach in general cannot serve as a viable platform from which to combat jihadism (and other injustices). The most important of these is that the preconditions for effective political action on an international scale do not currently exist.

International law is an aggregate of treaties and resolutions affirmed by sovereign nations, containing rules and principles that are open to interpretation. As such, it, like other modern systems of law, must derive its operative norms and efficacy from the assent and will of the community to which it applies. International law also relies upon political institutions for its implementation. Given this reality, international law can only produce an effective, proactive response to terrorism if there exists a genuine "world community," beyond the sovereign states, that will interpret the law in a common way and back that interpretation with political will.

But there is no such community today. Anti-Americanism is rife, and the rhetoric of international law is often used as an instrument to counter American power. Both Europe and the U.S. use international institutions to advance their own interests. China often ignores international law outright.

Illegitimate governments, through alternating between aggressive and conciliatory postures, are able to use the UN's preference for diplomacy to avoid punishment and gain de facto legitimacy. These are just a few examples of the Hobbesian realities—natural and ineradicable aspects of international affairs—that render the "international community" a non-reality. The international accord and collective will assumed by internationalism simply does not exist, at least yet.

The lack of a true international community is often evident in internationalist arguments themselves. "The Need for a Paradigm Shift in American Thinking," for example, states that 9/11 should be construed as "a crime against humanity" and that the "perpetrators, facilitators, and abettors of the September 11 massacres must be sought under international law across the planet ... it is the duty of all countries and governments to help actively in their arrest, trial, and punishment after due process is served." But if the "world community" were real and the phrase "crime against humanity" really meant something, then the internationalist approach to fighting terrorism would have been implemented spontaneously and naturally long ago by nations other than the United States. There would be an extant internationalist movement compelling the United States to join it. "Paradigm Shift" even seems to acknowledge the lack of an operative international community by making the United States almost the sole agent responsible for establishing the internationalist regime.

Casting American power as the guarantor of internationalism causes "Paradigm Shift" to vacillate between internationalism and unilateralism (even neoconservatism). At times it is argued that the U.S. must intervene in

Middle Eastern affairs to encourage democracy and justice: the U.S. should "bring democracy to Baghdad," pursue regime change in Israel, ensure free elections and the success of democratic movements in the Middle East, help bring Muammar Khaddafi to justice, and so on. But the essay also argues for a complete American adherence to internationalism, stating, for example, that any U.S. action in Iraq needs a "rising consensus in the international arena" and should adhere to a "'collapse' theory which can be designed with the help of Middle East and European democrats." The program for change offered by "Paradigm Shift" will likely fail to work for the same reason it would be poorly received in the U.S.: it acknowledges that American power is an independent reality and calls for its exercise, yet seeks to place it solely in service of "internationalist" norms and goals. Moreover, it overestimates the actual extent of American power.

"Paradigm Shift" and the internationalist argument in general simply rest on too many contradictions and reifications to be accepted by the U.S. as the sole framework for conducting international affairs.

Whether it is described as ensuring "constraint" or "due process,"[4] the internationalist approach clearly intends to limit, if not end, unilateral political-military action by the United States (against terrorism and in general). Such strict multilateralism has two potential problems from an American perspective. First, al-Qa'ida is an implacable enemy, driven by a fanatical commitment to irrational goals, that possesses a strong desire to massacre large numbers of Americans in particular. It will have to be militarily, structurally, and ideologically broken—not simply prosecuted. As such, saving innocent Americans from mass slaughter may at some point require rapid, aggressive, or preemptive action without due process and a global consensus. Second, there is a lack of consensus among internationalist advocates on what constitutes legitimate self-defense. Several advocates of internationalism who attended the Malta meeting expressed support for the war against the Taliban and al-Qa'ida in Afghanistan, but this often seemed to stem from personal opinion rather than a clearly stated definition of "actionable threat." The Coalition for Life and Peace meanwhile congratulates the U.S. in this volume for helping liberate Europe in World War II, but then states that war cannot be used today. It bases this proclamation on the odd and incorrect assertion that contemporary weaponry "does not combat troops, but destroys whole regions [and] their inhabitants." We may presume that this disagreement and ambiguity would persist if internationalism were instituted. While there is no reason that the U.S. cannot accept the authority of international institutions to a degree, the aforementioned problems make it impossible for us to subjugate ourselves to them. It must be remembered that the attacks of September 11 bred a deep sense of insecurity in the United States. Americans need to feel that the political frameworks under which they live address the threat of asymmetric warfare.

In addition, internationalism, like other "ism's" tends to convert opinions into truths. This problem can be observed at several points in "What We're Fighting For: A Follow-Up." The letter objects to American exceptionalism but then proceeds to list the ways in which Europe is superior to the United States. It also asserts that the role, or a role, of the intellectual is to resist "militarism." Such ideals and distinctions are culturally-based, and need to be presented as arguments rather than self-evident truths.

What internationalists need to do in general, I argue, is accept or better acknowledge the limits of their paradigm and adopt a more realistic approach to global affairs.

This means accepting other political frameworks, including just war doctrine, at least to some degree. Americans need a way, an authentic way, to think about their own power. Just war doctrine can fulfill that role for the many Americans who do not accept the internationalist paradigm. Adherence to just war doctrine does not preclude adherence to international law: just war stipulates that only "legitimate authorities" may wage war, and many Americans have begun to develop the idea that the world's most "legitimate authority" is the *United Nations*. Just war doctrine is therefore a potential bridge to internationalism; it is not a zero-sum relationship. Indeed, since international law amounts to little unless it is organically integrated into the society to which it applies, one could even argue that international law depends upon "just war" doctrine in the American context. Therefore, it would seem more productive to encourage the nexus of local traditions and international institutions than to propose a cosmopolitan ethos.

Internationalists' apprehensions about just war doctrine appear to derive in part from a misinterpretation of it. Just war is a conceptual framework for weighing the morality of military action in specific cases and for limiting war once it has begun. It is not a part of a specific political vision and it does not produce a definitive picture of "right" and "wrong." "What We're Fighting For" applied just war doctrine to an *existing* policy (the decision to use force against al-Qaʿida) in order to make an argument about the morality of that policy. In presenting a positive comprehensive argument, it actually paved the way for greater debate about the war against al-Qaʿida, as this volume demonstrates.

Two additional points related to the letter must be mentioned. First, the authors of "What We're Fighting For" argued that America embodies universal values *specifically* in order to argue that America is a legitimate authority capable of waging a "just" war. Second, America is a democratic, diverse, contentious place in which many people care little for or downright object both to the concept of just war and to "What We're Fighting For."

However, the internationalist contributions to this volume incorrectly conflate "just war" with the "war against terrorism" and interpret "What We're Fighting For" as a *positive political formulation*. They also ignore the debate and openness that surround discussion of just war in the United States. The result is that the writing of "What We're Fighting For" is portrayed as the beginning of a new epoch in which an American monolith will identify itself as the chosen agent of universal values and then engage in unrestrained warfare. To be sure, just war can be abused: it can lead to or legitimize an excessive use of force, and it is important to be aware of that possibility. But in a world where international institutions often remain inactive during genocides, potential excess is not a compelling reason to abandon just war. It is reasonable to ask internationalists to engage just war doctrine in a more serious fashion by seeking to understand it on its own terms.

A realistic approach to international affairs would also seek to break down problems into manageable parts. One should be able to combat jihadism by attacking its immediate sources without necessarily having to alter global trends and regional conditions. Furthermore, reflexively linking jihadism to Islam-West and Middle Eastern affairs only helps jihadis to legitimize their cause.

The pragmatic approach would also focus more on local contexts. There is perhaps no better way to reconcile American unilateralism and internationalism than by engaging in a serious study of how both approaches would likely affect a given country. Such an approach would temper extremes and emphasize issues on which most people agree, such as democratization and economic diversification. It would also help us arrive at some reasonable assessment of how U.S. policy is actually damaging the Middle East and how we might rectify the problem. As it is, this subject is too often dominated by exaggeration, unfounded assertions supposedly derived from analyses of the "Arab street," and American avoidance of culpability. We need to move away from both denial and the rhetoric of pathology, and towards a concept of "dysfunction" in describing U.S.-Islam problems. Significantly, a realistic approach would also allow us to target and coordinate policies in a much more nuanced and productive fashion. This is most important to defeating jihadism: jihadism will ultimately be defeated in local contexts by local actors, and any major external intrusion, be it "liberal" or "conservative," can easily disturb this process.

A realistic approach could have resulted in a much better collective handling of the Iraq War. For all the talk about multilateralism and humanitarianism, it was a war "cooked up by neoconservatives in Washington" that liberated the Iraqi people and removed Saddam Hussein. This war constituted the only serious attempt by a world power to assist the Iraqi people over the last decade. Unfortunately, the response of many nations and international organizations to the Iraq effort has been to present a dazzling array of arguments geared towards constraining America and securing the predominance of international institutions at all costs, arguments in which the Iraqi people have become something of an afterthought. We have heard that sanctions were "working" and that political "pressure" and diplomacy should have been used.

How much better it would have been if the international community had simply acknowledged that a war was needed to remove Saddam Hussein (a good thing) and then had proactively developed a plan or resolution that *conditionalized* and controlled this war. If internationalists had offered reasonable, moral recommendations—not a labyrinth of arguments designed to safeguard an inadequate international system—an effective, mutually-beneficial symbiosis of American power and internationalism could have been accomplished. Instead the international community has chosen a non-constructive path that puts wind in the sails of the current insurgency. The realistic standard must be applied to America as well: the failure to gauge the currents present in Iraqi society clearly resulted in insufficient reconstruction plans, which helped ensure the insurgency's flourishing.

Today, as the world struggles to find equilibrium, Americans and Arab Muslims alike find themselves vulnerable and disoriented. Dialogue will remain a vital tool in the quest to establish solid common ground. An adoption of a pragmatic approach to international affairs—even if it involves little more than changing the discursive context in which arguments are presented—may help make this dialogue a more productive one.

Notes

*I am grateful to Louisa Roberts for her invaluable input on this paper's contents and her editorial assistance.

1. A conference of 24 Arab and American scholars held in Malta during May 18-20, 2004 which was sponsored by the Institute for American Values and at which "What We're Fighting For" and the notion of a "just war against terrorism" were discussed. From henceforth in the present text I will refer to it as the "Malta meeting."

2. Marc Sageman, "Understanding Terror Networks," Research note. http://www.fpri.org/enotes/20041101.middleeast.sageman.understandingterrornetworks.html

3. Salafists believe that Muslims should reject the interpretations of Islam that have evolved over time and directly interpret the basic texts of Islam.

4. "What We're Fighting For: A Follow-Up" (see chapter 18 of this volume) and "The Need for a Paradigm Shift in American Thinking" (see chapter 3 of this volume), respectively.

Twenty-Six

≈

The Arab World and the United States: A Just War?

෨

Abdulrahman al-Salimi

To provide a better understanding of the background of our main topic, I would like to review three key historical events, each separated by nearly a century, that have influenced Arab-Western relations:

1. Napoleon's Campaign in Egypt in 1798
2. The Sykes-Picot Agreement of 1916
3. The First Persian Gulf War, 1990-1991

The first event engendered a concept within the Islamic world that imperialism comes from the West under the guise of liberating Muslims from their oppressive rulers. This marks the beginning of the era of imperialism in the Middle East. The second event demonstrated that the West could directly intervene in the political affairs of the Arab world, and in doing so, it created the contemporary Middle East with the demarcation of modern-day Arab states. The third event coincides with the fall of the Soviet Union, the advent of economic globalization, and the information technology revolution. The Gulf War gave the West, in particular the U.S., the occasion to directly intervene to settle intra-Arab disputes. This is further evidenced by the Oslo Agreement and the end of the Lebanese war.

It is against this backdrop that two influential American theses have developed: the "clash of civilizations" and "the end of history." This hypothesizing triggered a widespread reaction across the world and has exacerbated the American-Arab conflict to its core. For many, these theories reinforced the conflict by linking it inextricably to religious and cultural disagreement. This has manifested itself in a wave of radical thinking in segments of the

Islamic world as seen in the civil war in Algeria, the Islamic government in Sudan, the radical movement in Afghanistan and Central Asia, and extending to assassination attempts and suicide bombings in Egypt, Yemen, Saudi Arabia, and Jordan. These movements have mainly targeted American interests in the region. In Europe, a concurrent wave is seen through emerging anti-Muslim attitudes and actions in society.

It is within this historical context that the article "What We're Fighting For: A Letter from America" was published by *Al-Hayat* in February of 2002. For the many who read it, the letter shed light on the Institute for American Values and the principles of "just war;" and it highlighted the rationale of American and European parties who are striving to eliminate the radical Islamists responsible for the attacks on September 11, 2001. A substantial volume of reviews and opinions on this article followed, and in this presentation, I would like to comment on the ensuing dialogue, building upon our three-day meeting with our American counterparts in Malta.[1]

In this commentary, I want to draw attention to four key issues: 1) the meaning of subscribing to American values and the proclaimed new American message; 2) the milieu of the Muslim world that led to radical Islamists; 3) the principles of just war; and lastly 4) the future of Arab-American relations.

On the first issue, I have not seen a great deal of disagreement between us as Muslims or Arabs and the Americans we met [in Malta] regarding the belief in "greater human values." This should come as no surprise since Muslims are instructed to acknowledge the diversity of humankind: "O mankind we created you male and female and have formed you into nations and tribes that you may know one another" (Sura 49:13). Getting to know each other, I believe, is more than acknowledging the existence of diversity; it is co-existing in harmony with each other. This is part of having shared values, and throughout history, Islam is known to have been a leader in recognizing this and enacting legislation so that other beliefs could co-exist with Islam.

On the global scene, it was not until the end of the Second World War, with the suffering of many African and Asian nations, that the United Nations established guidelines on human rights and actively promoted respect for our common humanity. This was an important development for the advancement of shared values, and it raises an important question: Does any one segment of humankind have the right to impose values on the world as the arbitrator of these shared values? This is what we felt from our American counterparts and from the Bush administration through their proclamation of a new and special message related to human rights and freedoms. If such assertions were restricted to internal discourse within America and its relevance to democracy, no one would object. However, equating shared human values with American values that are then forced on other parts of the world by coercive means will not be accepted by the majority of people around the world. Otherwise, each of us would have the right to impose his or her values on others without accountability and the input of others as to what are truly shared values. This then becomes an intrusion on freedom rather than a harbinger of it.

It is now imperative that the promotion of shared values have a shared administration under the auspices of an institution like the United Nations. For example, the U.S. war on Afghanistan had support from the broader world community, but unfortunately, the U.S. war on Iraq did not, which has created divisions among the world community. This was further complicated by the fact that the reasons for war were far from convincing for many of us. Initially it was claimed that the purpose of the war on Iraq was to eliminate weapons of mass destruction that were alleged to be held by the Saddam regime. Later a link between Saddam and al-Qa'ida was announced by the Bush administration with no clear evidence to support this claim. Then it was asserted that the purpose of the war was to spread democratic values in Iraq. I do not want to debate these intentions here, but I would like to say that shared values must be considered as shared responsibilities. Because of shared values, we cannot be selective in the responsibilities this implies, such as the 800,000 Rwandan casualties or the thousands of Palestinians killed under Israeli occupation. This is the basis upon which we implore the Israeli prime minister to end the occupation of Palestine.

The second issue has to do with Islamic radicals. The "Letter from America" highlighted the atrocities committed in the name of Islam. This is readily admitted, and there is no need to debate this. The attack on the World Trade Center is a terrorist act and the perpetrators should be punished. Moreover, the radical ideology behind the attack must be eliminated. Following the attack, Bush told the world that Islam had been hijacked and that moderate and irenic Muslims must act to reclaim it. This statement deserves considerable attention by Muslims. The reality is that the moderate parties within Islam are weaker following considerable tension and divergence in the Muslim world during the '80s and '90s. Two factors must be considered here: 1) the United States, along with some Arab countries, took advantage of the radicalism of certain Muslim groups to confront the communists in Afghanistan and other places and 2) following this, the attempts in Arab states toward reform and democratization only further stimulated radical thinking. Thus, the radical trend of some Muslims within the Arab world was incited by these two factors. Having said this, a proper perspective of the scope of radicalism must be maintained. One must remember that though bin Ladin is of Arab origin, not many Arabs are following his path. There is now increased appreciation of this by the West so that radicalism within Islam is understood as localized and not endemic within the Muslim world. This is a positive step, yet in addressing the radical and militant expressions of Islam, the letter from the Americans focused on the elimination of radical Muslims rather than their radical ideology in general, which is misguided and rather alarming.

The third issue is that of just war. It is expounded on by American scholars based on three suppositions: 1) Americans are messengers of freedom and human rights; 2) unjustified force was used against them; and 3) they have the right to defend themselves. We have no objection to self-defense, including attacking al-Qa'ida in Afghanistan. It gave rise to a new government; however, the country is now divided on the basis of ethnic and religious minorities. After this, the U.S. invaded Iraq and spread its forces across the Muslim world. The critical component of this is that the U.S. administration believes in preemptive strikes, hence justifying the use of force against those who are deemed threatening. According to the American scholars we met in Malta, this is declared as a principle of a just war.

We may find that at times there may be consensus for such action, but this leads to the fourth and [most] critical issue. We urge that all such situations must have the collective agreement of world states to gain peace for all nations. It seems that current U.S. policy ignores the need for sufficient multilateralism on security issues, as well as the need to take into account other nations' concerns in general. This undermines the efficacy of world organizations. Otherwise, why have them!

To understand the Arab perspective you must remember that we are nations that were colonized, and we freed our lands. We believe that the struggle to free ourselves from occupation, as in Palestine, is justified. Nevertheless, this must always be done with great care so that it does not descend into wars where many innocent people suffer. Therefore as one invokes the principles of just war after the 11th of September, one must remember that the surge in *jihad* is a direct result of fighting the occupation, in particular, the occupation of Palestine. We firmly believe that the world community could have intervened and solved this disagreement. If the leading countries of the world, including the U.S., had pushed for international law to be applied, then the will of the world community and its international security laws would have prevailed over war.

In conclusion, a good relationship between the Arab world and the U.S. cannot be built on war, even if deemed a just war. The 11th of September was a tragic anomaly, which made it all the more shocking, and we should all work diligently to prevent its repetition on the world stage. World peace is not being served if Iraq is a point of revenge. The future of positive relationships between the Arab world and America must be grounded on shared values and shared interests. America, along with others, must use its influence to stimulate dialogue and consensus on these values. Peace will only be found when there is mutual respect and harmony on both sides.

This book is a serious effort to support the concept of dialogue and better understanding, which is greatly appreciated from our side.

Notes

1. The author is referring to a meeting organized by the Institute for American Values held in Malta, May 18-20, 2004. The meeting brought together authors of "What We're Fighting For: A Letter from America" and Muslim intellectuals from the Arab world. Abdulrahman al-Salimi was present at this meeting.

꒰

Selected Bibliography

꒱

Works Reprinted in this Volume

9 U.S. intellectuals under the aegis of the Institute for American Values. "Pre-Emption, Iraq, and Just War: A Statement of Principles." Public letter released on November 14, 2002.

60 U.S. intellectuals under the aegis of the Institute for American Values. "What We're Fighting For: A Letter from America." Public letter released in February 2002.

67 U.S. intellectuals under the aegis of the Institute for American Values. "Is the Use of Force Ever Morally Justified?" Public letter released on August 8, 2002.

67 U.S. intellectuals under the aegis of the Institute for American Values. "Can We Coexist? A Response from Americans to Colleagues in Saudia Arabia." Public letter released on October 23, 2002.

70 German intellectuals under the aegis of the Coalition for Life and Peace. "In the Twenty-First Century, There Is No Longer Any Justification for War." Public letter released in 2002.

103 German intellectuals under the aegis of the Coalition for Life and Peace. Translated from the German by Timothy Slater. "A World of Justice and Peace Would Be Different." *Frankfurter Allgemeine*, May 2, 2002.

140 U.S. intellectuals. "Letter from U.S. Citizens to Friends in Europe." Public letter released by In These Times in May 2002. http://www.inthesetimes.com.

294 Selected Bibliography

153 Saudi intellectuals. "How We Can Coexist." Public letter released in May 2002. http://www.islamtoday.com/showme2.cfm?cat_id=29&sub_cat_id=471.

Bara, 'Abul. "Please Prostrate Yourselves Privately." Public letter released by the Center for Islamic Studies and Research, May 2002. http://alneda.com.

Bashir, Saleh, Hassan I. Mneimneh, and Hazem Saghie. "What We're Fighting For: A Follow-Up." Translated from the Arabic by Hassan I. Mneimneh. *Al-Hayat* (London), April 30, 2002.

Blankenhorn, David. "Reading an Enemy: Analyzing al-Qa'ida's 'Letter to America'." February 18, 2003, http://www.americanvalues.org/html/reading_an_enemy.html.

Cooperman, Alan. "Saudis Ban Paper with U.S. Scholars' Letter." *Washington Post*, October 24, 2002.

Falahatpisheh, Heshmatollah. "Key Intellectualism." *Resalat* (Tehran), February 21, 2002. Translated and reprinted by BBC. Global News Wire-Asia Africa Intelligence Wire, February 22, 2002. http://www.lexisnexis.com.

al-Hawali, Safar. "What We're Defending: A Letter from Makkah in Response to the Open Letter from Sixty American Intellectuals." Public letter released in May 2002.

Mallat, Chibli and Colleagues. "The Need for a Paradigm Shift in American Thinking: Middle Eastern Responses to 'What We're Fighting For'; 'Together with the Democratic Iraq Initiative and the Sharon Initiative'." Public letter released in 2002. http://www.mallat.com/englishversion.htm.

Mehio, Saad. "The Letter is American, the Schizophrenia Islamic." *Daily Star* (Lebanon), March 4, 2002. http://www.dailystar.com.lb.

Mneimneh, Hassan I. "The New Intra-Arab Cultural Space in Form and Content: The Debates Over an American 'Letter'." *Social Research* 70 (2003): 907-932.

Movement for Islamic Reform in Arabia. "Options Are Limited." Public letter released on May 15, 2002. http://www.islah.org.

al-Qa'ida. "Letter to the American People." Translated and reprinted by *Observer* (London), November 24, 2002. http://observer. guardian.co.uk/worldview/story/0,11581,845725,00.html.

Saad, Rasha. "Learning through Letters." *Al-Ahram Weekly Online* 611 (Cairo), November 2002. http://weekly.ahram.org.eg/2002/611/re6.htm.

al-Sharyan, Dawud. "The First Point of Disagreement." *Al-Hayat* (London), October 27, 2002. (Translated from the Arabic by Hassan Mneimneh).

Winkler, Claudia. "American Values Abroad." *Weekly Standard*, October 29, 2002. http://www.weeklystandard.com/Content/Public/Articles/000/000/001/826ekedk.asp.

———. "The U.S.-German Conversation." *Weekly Standard*, August 15, 2002. http://www.weeklystandard.com/Content/Public/Articles/000/000/001/548rpsjb.asp.

Additional Sources

Arabic

al-Abtah, Susan. "Intellectuals are also in Delusion in the United States." *Al-Sharq Al-Awsat* (London), February 28, 2002.

Adonis. "American Policy and the Theater of Evil." *Al-Hayat* (London), March 7, 2002.

Mneimneh, Hassan I. "The Letter of American Intellectuals Another Time: For Dialogue to Begin." *Al-Hayat* (London), March 24, 2002.

———. "The Letter-Manifesto of American Intellectuals: A Venue for Dialogue?" *Al-Hayat* (London), March 10, 2002.

Mus'id, Ra'uf. "A Discussion of Just Wars in the Manifesto of the American Intellectuals." *Al-Hayat* (London), April 4, 2002.

Salim, Salah. "Dialogue beyond the Defamation of Muslims and the Focus on Elites." *Al-Hayat* (London), April 8, 2002.

"Saudi Intellectuals React to the Statement about Just War." *Al-Jazeera*, May 13, 2002. http://www.aljazeera.net/Channel/archive/archive?ArchiveId=90653.

al-Sayyid, Ridwan and al-Fadl Shalaq. *Al-Ijtihad,* special issue, (Beirut), Summer 2002.

Shafiq, Muneer. "Another Time with the Letter of the American Intellectuals." *Al-Hayat* (London), March 3, 2002.

————. "Sixty American Intellectuals Issue a Statement Addressed to Muslims!" *Al-Hayat* (London), February 24, 2002.

Shararah, Waddah. "The Letter of American Intellectuals on Just War … Arguing its Ethical and Legal Bases and Testing it in Theory and Practice." *Al-Hayat* (London), February 28, 2002.

"Statement Banned from Appearing in 'Al-Hayat' in Saudi Arabia," IslamOnline.net, October 23, 2002. http://www.islamonline.net/Arabic/news/2002-10/24/article16.shtml.

"The American Intellectuals and the Saudi Intellectuals." Al-Jazeera, October 29, 2002. http://www.aljazeera.net/programs/washington/articles/2002/10/10-29-1.htm.

English

Ahmad, Ayesha. "American Intellectuals Ask Europeans to Condemn Bush's War on Terrorism." IslamOnline.net, April 19, 2002. http://www.islamonline.net/English/News/2002-04/19/article65.shtml.

American Institute for Contemporary German Studies. "The Just War Debate: Transatlantic Values in Transition?" Summary of seminar held on May 1, 2002. http://www.aicgs.org/events/2002/fukuyama_summary.shtml.

Burke, Jason. "Osama Issues New Call to Arms." *Observer* (London), November 24, 2002. http://observer.guardian.co.uk/worldview/story/0,11581,846511,00.html.

Cooperman, Alan. "Academics Defend U.S. War on Terrorism." *Washington Post,* February 12, 2002.

Elshtain, Jean Bethke. "The Groves of Academe." *Books and Culture*, July/August, 2003. http://www.ctlibrary.com.

————. "A Just War?" *Boston Globe*, October 6, 2002.

Green, Jody et al. "Response to German Intellectuals by Average American Citizens." Public letter released on December 5, 2002. http://www.americanvalues.org/html/response_from_average_american.html.

Said, Edward. "Thoughts about America." *Al-Ahram Weekly Online* 575 (Cairo), February 28–March 6, 2002. http://weekly.ahram.org.eg/2002/575/op2.htm.

Schroeder, Steven. "'We' is as Problematic as 'What': A War of Words." Paper, Conference on War and Virtual War at Mansfield College, Oxford, UK, July 2002. http://www.inter-disciplinary.net/Schroeder.pdf.

French

60 U.S. intellectuals under the aegis of the Institute for American Values. "Lettre d'Amérique, les raisons d'un combat." Translation of "What We're Fighting For" by Jean-François Kleiner. *Le Monde*, February 15, 2002.

Broché, Jean-Claude. "60 intellectuels américains pour la guerre." *Le Soir*, February 16-17, 2002.

"Guerre morale." *Les Echos*, March 1, 2002.

"Soixante intellectuels américains expliquent 'Pourquoi nous nous battons'." Agence France Press, February 14, 2002.

"Soixante intellectuels américains pour la guerre," *Le Monde*, February 15, 2002.

Vernet, Daniel. "Les intellectuals, la guerre et Mr. Bush." *Le Monde*, February 21, 2002.

German

60 U.S. intellectuals under the aegis of the Institute for American Values. "Wofur wir kampfen." Translation of "What We're Fighting For" by Michael Walzer. *Frankfurter Rundschau Online*, February 19, 2002. http://www.fr-aktuell.de.

60 U.S. intellectuals under the aegis of the Institute for American Values. "Wofur wir kampfen," Translation of "What We're Fighting For." *Neue Zurcher Zeitung,* February 23-24, 2002.

"Amerikanische Intellektuelle fuer 'grechten Krieg' gegen Terrorismus Berlin." Deutsche Presse-Agentur, February 12, 2002.

"Antikriegsaufruf deutscher Intellektueller." *Die Tageszeitung*, September 26, 2002.

Blankenhorn, David. "... was wir für Wahrheit halten." Interview by Bernd Pickert. *Die Tageszeitung* (Berlin), September 10, 2002.

Bolling, Klaus. "Was heißt 'gerechter Krieg'?" *Die Meinung*, February 17, 2002.

"Deutsche Intellektuelle kritisieren US-Anti-Terrorpolitik." Deutsche Presse-Agentur, *Europadienst*, May 2, 2002.

"Gelehrte in den USA rufen zum gerechten Krieg" *Berliner Zeitung*, February 13, 2002.

Herzinger, Richard. "Kann der Krieg moralisch erklart werden?" *Die Zeit*, February 20, 2002.

Jeismann, Michael. "Aus Amerika: Ein Aufruf an Die Kulturwelt." *Frankfurter Allgemeine Zeitung*, February 14, 2002.

Köhler, Andrea. "Wo also stehen Sie?" *Neue Zürcher Zeitung*, August 13, 2002.

Landwehr, Arthur. "Intellektuelle zum Kreig." *Dienstag*, February 12, 2002.

Lau, Jörg. "Welche Freiheit? Welche Werte?" *Die Zeit*, February 21, 2002.

Lehming, Malte. "Der Feind schreibt." *Der Tagesspiegel*, November 27, 2002.

———. "Kampf um Gerechtigkeit." *Der Tagesspiegel*, February 17, 2002.

Misik, Robert. "Collateral Damage." *Die Tageszeitung*, February 28, 2002.

von Rimscha, Robert. "Tugend und Terror." *Der Tagesspiegel,* November 27, 2002.

Rorty, Richard. "Ich kann Bush nicht vertrauen." Interview by Peter Körte. *Frankfurter Allgemeine Sonntagszeitung*, February 24, 2002.

Schandl, Franz and Norbert Trenkle. "Editorial." *Krisis* 25 (2002).

Schneider, Peter. "Die aufgeklarte Variante des Dschichad." *Der Tagesspiegel*, February 14, 2002.

———. "Die falsche Gewissheit." *Der Spiegel*, August 26, 2002.

Schloemann, Johan. "Immer feste druff!" *Frankfurter Allgemeine Zeitung*, March 13, 2002.

"US-Brandbrief gegen deutsche Intellektuelle." *Spiegel Online*, August 9, 2002. http://www.spiegel.de.

"US-Intellektuell fur einen 'gerechten Krieg'." *Neue Zurcher Zeitung*, March 8, 2002.

"Verrat an 'den Idealen der Wissenschaft'." *Der Tagesspiegel*, February 17, 2002.

Wenzel, Uwe Justus. "Die Gestalt des Intellektuellen." *Neue Zürcher Zeitung*, March 9, 2002.

Wittstock, Uwe. "Gegen den Terror." *Die Welt,* February 13, 2002.

Zielcke, Andreas. "Ein Aufruf-Zeichen." *Suddeutsche Zeitung*, Febrary 14, 2002.

Polish

"Sprawiedliwa wojna z terroyamen." *Rzeczpospolita*, March 5, 2002.

Portuguese

60 U.S. intellectuals under the aegis of the Institute for American Values, "Carta da America: as razoes de uma Guerra," Translation by Paolo Sotero of "What We're Fighting For." *O Estado de S. Paulo*, February 17, 2002.

Spanish

60 U.S. intellectuals under the aegis of the Institute for American Values "Por qué luchamos: Una Carta desde América." Translation of "What We're Fighting For." http://www.filosofos.org.

"Intelectuales a favor de la Guerra." *La Vanguardia*, February 15, 2002.

Vidal-Beneyto, José. "La guerra ideological." *El Pais,* February 16, 2002. http://www.elpais.es.